THE NATURE of PERSONAL REALITY:
A Seth Book

THE NATURE of PERSONAL REALITY: A Seth Book

by
Jane Roberts

Notes by Robert F. Butts

PRENTICE-HALL, INC., Englewood Cliffs, N.J.

Printed in the United States of America

Prentice-Hall International, Inc., London
Prentice-Hall of Australia, Pty. Ltd., Sydney
Prentice-Hall of Canada, Ltd., Toronto
Prentice-Hall of India Private Ltd., New Delhi
Prentice-Hall of Japan, Inc., Tokyo

10 9 8 7

Library of Congress Cataloging in Publication Data

Roberts, Jane
    The nature of personal reality.

    1. Spirit writings. I. Seth. II. Title
BF1301.R593   133.9'3   74-7356
ISBN 0-13-610576-9

This book is dedicated
to
Robert Butts
"Joseph"

Without whose dedication
and work it could not
appear in its present form

Introduction by Jane Roberts

I'm proud to publish this book under my own name, though I don't fully understand the mechanics of its production or the nature of the personality I assume in delivering it. I had no conscious work to do on the book at all. I simply went into trance twice a week, spoke in a "mediumistic" capacity for Seth, or as Seth, and dictated the words to my husband, Robert Butts, who wrote them down.

I consider the book "mine" in that I don't believe it could have been written without me and my particular abilities. On the other hand, I realize that far more is involved. I had to read the manuscript to find out what was in it, for example; and to that extent the book doesn't seem mine. But what does that mean?

My idea briefly is this: Our usual orientation is focused pretty exclusively in what we think of as the "real" world, but there are many realities. By shifting our consciousness, we can glimpse these alternate realities, and all of them are the appearance that Reality takes under certain conditions. I don't believe that we can necessarily describe one in terms of another.

For years I've been confused, trying to define Seth in the usual true-and-false world of facts. There he's accepted as an independent spirit—a spirit guide by those with spiritualistic beliefs—or as some displaced portion of my own personality by the scientific community. I couldn't accept either idea, at least not in undiluted form.

If I said, "Look, people, I don't think Seth is a spirit *in the way you mean*," then this was interpreted as an acknowledgement that Seth was *only* a portion of my personality. Some people thought that I was trying to put Seth down, or deny them the aid of a super-being when at last they thought they'd found one.

Actually, I think that the selves we know in normal life are only the three-dimensional actualizations of other source-selves from which we receive our energy and life. Their reality can't be contained in the framework of our creaturehood, though it is being constantly translated through our present individuality.

The "spirit guide" designation may be a handy symbolic representation of this idea, and I'm not saying that spirit guides do not exist. I *am* saying that the idea deserves greater examination, for the spirit guide may represent something far different than we think. The idea can also be limiting if it always places revelatory knowledge outside of us, and tries to make literal some extraordinary phenomena that may be beyond such interpretation.

While I was trying to define Seth that way and questioning whether or not he was a spirit guide, I was closed off to some extent from his greater reality, which exists in terms of vast imaginative and creative power that is bigger than the world of facts and can't be contained in it. Seth's personality is quite observable in our sessions, for example, but the source of that personality isn't. For that matter, the origin of *any* personality is mysterious and not apparent in the objective world. My job is to enlarge the dimensions of that world and people's concepts of it.

Seth's books may be the product of another dimensional

aspect of my own consciousness not focused in this reality, plus something else that is untranslatable in our terms, with Seth a great psychic creation more real than any "fact." His existence may simply lie in a different order of events than the one we're used to.

I'm not saying that we shouldn't apply what we learn to the ordinary world. Certainly I'm trying to do that, and Seth wrote this book to help people deal more effectively with their daily lives. I am insisting that we must be very careful about making literal interpretations, lest we limit a multidimensional phenomenon by tying it down to a three-dimensional fact system.

Intuitively and emotionally we often understand more than we intellectually realize. Trying to define revelatory knowledge, or a Seth, in terms of our limited ideas about human personality is like trying to translate, say, a rose to the number 3, or trying to explain one in terms of the other.

The funny thing is that a personality *not* focused in our reality can help people live in that world more effectively and joyfully by showing them that other realities also exist. In this book Seth is saying that you can change your experience by altering your beliefs about yourself and physical existence.

To me, the Seth Material is no longer a continuing manuscript of fascinating theories to be carefully judged against reality. In a strange way it has come alive. The concepts within it live. I experience them and because of this my personal reality has expanded. I've begun to glimpse the greater inner dimensions from which our usual lives emerge, and to familiarize myself with other alternate methods of perception that can be used not only to see other "worlds," but help us deal more effectively with this one.

While Seth was producing this book, my own life was immeasurably enriched in unforeseen ways. Frequent psychedelic-type experiences paralleled Seth's dictated material, and my own creative and psychic abilities developed into some entirely new areas.

Just before Seth began *The Nature of Personal Reality: A*

Seth Book, for instance, I found myself embarked on a new venture I call the Sumari development. Sumari refers to a "family" of consciousnesses who share certain overall characteristics. There is a language involved that isn't a language in usual terms. I think that it operates as a psychological and psychic framework that frees me from normal verbal reference, letting me express and communicate inner feelings and data that lie just beneath formalized word patterns.

The Sumari development constantly expanded as Seth produced this book. Now various altered states of consciousness are involved. In one I write Sumari poetry and in another I translate what I've written. At a different level I sing Sumari songs, showing musical knowledge and accomplishment far beyond my normal talents or background. The songs can also be translated, but they communicate emotionally whether or not the words are understood. In yet another state of consciousness, material is received that is supposed to represent remnants of ancient Speaker manuscripts. (These are also translated later.) Seth defines the Speakers as teachers, both physical and non-physical, who constantly interpret and communicate inner knowledge through the ages. My husband has also written Sumari, but I have to translate it for him.

As Seth continued dictating *The Nature of Personal Reality,* I wrote a complete poetry manuscript, *Dialogues of the Soul and Mortal Self in Time,* in which I worked out many of my own beliefs as per suggestions Seth was giving in his book. This led to another group of poems, *The Speakers.* To me this all means that there is a rich vein of creativity and knowledge available to each according to his abilities, just beneath the surface of usual consciousness. I believe that it is a part of our human heritage, accessible to some extent to any person who explores the inner dimensions of the mind.

Dialogues of the Soul and Mortal Self in Time, The Speakers, and some Sumari poetry are being combined into a book that will be published soon by Prentice-Hall. I consider it a companion book to this one. It shows what was happening in my personal reality while Seth was writing his book on the subject, and reveals how the creative impetus splashes out into all areas of the personality. Seth often refers to the poems and to the experiences that initiated them. Many of those events occurred as I tried to understand the relationship between his world and mine, and the connection between inner and outer experience.

But beside this, as Seth was dictating this present book, I also found myself suddenly writing a novel, *The Education of Oversoul 7,* which was produced more or less automatically. Oversoul Seven, the main character, achieved his own kind of reality. I'd say mentally, "Okay, Seven, let's have the next chapter," and there it was as quickly as I could write it down. Portions of the book also came in the dream state.

I know that Seven and his teacher, Cyprus, exist in certain terms, yet their reality can't be explained either in the usual fact world. For example, the novel included many Sumari poems and portions of Speaker manuscripts; and when I sing Sumari I identify with Cyprus, who is supposed to be a fictional character. I could also tune into Seven for help with personal challenges, I discovered.

I love to go full-blast ahead, using my abilities as freely as possible. Yet quite as strongly I'm often scandalized intellectually by the same events that intuitively intrigue me, or by the interpretations placed upon them. It does no good to pretend otherwise, and I think there's a good reason for this sometimes uneasy blend of intuition and intellect.

I'm learning that both elements are important in my work and in Seth's. And perhaps my own refusal to accept pat answers leads me to search so intensely, and is responsible to some degree for my "bringing in" a Seth instead of a Mad Hatter.

The Sumari development, along with the experiences connected with *The Education of Oversoul 7* and *The Nature of Personal Reality,* brought up so many questions that I was forced to seek a larger framework in which to understand what was happening. As a result I'm working on a book called *Aspect*

Psychology, which I hope will present a theory of personality large enough to contain man's psychic nature and activities. Seth refers to *Aspects,* as we call it, in this present book, and it should be published sometime in 1975.

In the meantime all I can say is this: We live in a world of physical facts but these spring from a deeper realm of creativity, and in a real sense facts are fictions that spring alive in our experience. All facts. Seth, then, is as much a fact as I am or you are, and in a strange way he straddles both worlds. I hope that *Aspects* will also span the world of facts and the rich inner realities from which they come, for our experience includes each.

The Nature of Personal Reality not only enriched my creative life but challenged my ideas and beliefs. I agree wholeheartedly with the concepts Seth presents here, while realizing that they run counter to many accepted religious, social, and scientific dogmas. Certainly this book is an answer to all those who have written for help in applying Seth's ideas to ordinary living, and I am certain that it will assist many people in dealing with the varied events and problems of daily life.

Seth's main idea is that we create our personal reality through our conscious beliefs about ourselves, others, and the world. Following this is the concept that the "point of power" is in the present, not in the past of this life or any other. He stresses the individual's capacity for conscious action, and provides excellent exercises designed to show each person how to apply these theories to any life situation.

The message is plain: We are not at the mercy of the subconscious, or helpless before forces that we cannot understand. The conscious mind directs unconscious activity and has at its command all of the powers of the inner self. These are activated according to our ideas about reality. "We are gods couched in creaturehood," Seth says, given the ability to form our experience as our thoughts and feelings become actualized.

Seth first mentioned *The Nature of Personal Reality* in Session 608, April 5, 1972, only shortly after Rob and I had finished reading proofs for his previous book, *Seth Speaks: The Eternal Validity of the Soul*. He actually began dictation on April 10, 1972, but our personal reality was suddenly disturbed when we were caught in the flood caused by Tropical Storm Agnes. As a result, as you'll see in Rob's notes, further work on the book was delayed for some time.

Seth often uses episodes from our lives as specific examples of larger issues, and our experiences with the flood served as a starting point for his discussion of personal beliefs and disasters. In several other instances he also used our life situation as his source material—an intriguing turnabout.

Since the early days of our sessions, which began in late 1963, Seth has consistently called me Ruburt, and Rob, Joseph, saying that these names refer to the greater selves from which our present identities spring. He continues that practice in this book.

As usual, Rob methodically records each session in his own version of shorthand and then types it. This is much easier and faster than taping each session, replaying it, and then typing. Periodically Rob notes the passage of time, to show how long it takes Seth to get through a particular passage. Seth himself dictates the words to be underlined or put in quotes or parentheses. Often he indicates the placement of colons and other punctuation as well.

This book should help each reader understand the nature of private experience and use that knowledge to make daily living more creative and enjoyable.

Jane Roberts
Elmira, New York
November 6, 1973

Contents

Preface by Seth:
The Manufacture of Personal Reality

SESSION 609, APRIL 10, 1972,
9:29 P.M. MONDAY

(Jane first mentioned a couple of weeks ago that Seth, her trance personality, would start another book of his own soon. The idea had just "come" to her after supper one night. We hadn't taken it very seriously, since we'd finished proofreading Seth's first book, Seth Speaks: The Eternal Validity of the Soul,* *only last month; certainly we weren't prepared for the fact that he was quite capable of launching another such project so quickly. Nor did Jane have any conscious thoughts about subject matter, or a title, for any projected Seth book.*

(However, in last Wednesday's regularly scheduled session Seth had confirmed her anticipations in so many words—but without setting a date:

("Now: Ruburt [as Seth calls Jane] is quite correct. We <u>are</u> preparing for another one, and giving you a rest in between.

("The volumes automatically unite the material and present

Seth Speaks, 1972, and Jane's *The Seth Material,* 1970, were published by Prentice-Hall, Inc. Both will be referred to throughout this book.

xvii

it within certain frameworks of discipline . . . As you now know, some considerable time is taken with your preparation of notes, and so I have been waiting a while.

("Ruburt sensed this quite clearly, and as usual feels twinges, wondering what I am going to write about and what kind of a book it will be. Such a book can be given quite normally and quietly along with your regular routine of sessions, adding to your own knowledge and ultimately helping others also. I suggest the simplest of formats; always the least complicated as far as any mechanics are concerned. Do you follow me?

("Yes," I'd answered, whereupon Seth had discussed other matters for the rest of the evening.

(As we sat for tonight's session, Jane said, "Well, Seth's all ready and I've got the urge to get going. Maybe he'll start his book . . ." She hasn't been dwelling upon the subject particularly—or at least I don't remember her saying much about it.

(The energy at Jane's command still impresses me, especially when I consider that she weighs less than ninety-five pounds. Given her permission, Seth can come through very powerfully indeed. Her delivery now though was average. By this I mean that when she speaks for Seth her voice drops in register, becomes somewhat stronger, and acquires Seth's own deliberate but unique accent and rhythm. Jane took off her glasses and placed them on the coffee table between us. The next moment, her eyes much darker, she was in full trance.)

Now: Good evening.

("Good evening, Seth.")

We will call this evening's essay "The Manufacture of Personal Reality."

Experience is the product of the mind, the spirit, conscious thoughts and feelings, and unconscious thoughts and feelings. These together form the reality that you know. You are hardly at the mercy of a reality, therefore, that exists apart from yourself, or is thrust upon you. You are so intimately connected with the physical events composing your life experience that often you cannot distinguish between the seemingly material occurrences and the thoughts, expectations and desires that gave them birth.

If there are strongly negative characteristics present in your most intimate thoughts, if these actually form bars between you and a more full life, still you often look through the bars, not seeing them. Until they are recognized they are impediments. Even obstacles have a reason for being. If they are your own, then it is up to you to recognize them and discover the circumstances behind their existence.

Your conscious thoughts can be great clues in uncovering such obstructions. You are not nearly as familiar with your own thoughts as you may imagine. They can escape from you like water through your fingers, carrying with them vital nutrients that spread across the landscape of your psyche—and all too often carrying sludge and mud that clog up the channels of experience and creativity.

An examination of your conscious thoughts will tell you much about the state of your inner mind, your intentions and expectations, and will often lead you to a direct confrontation with challenges and problems. Your thoughts, studied, will let you see where you are going. They point clearly to the nature of physical events. What exists physically exists first in thought and feeling. There is no other rule.

(9:40.) You have the conscious mind for a good reason. You are not at the mercy of unconscious drives unless you consciously acquiesce to them. Your present feelings and expectations can always be used to check your progress. If you do not like your experience, then you must change the nature of your conscious thoughts and expectations. You must alter the kind of messages that you are sending through your thoughts to your own body, to friends and associates.

Each thought has a result, in your terms. The same kind of thought, habitually repeated, will seem to have a more or less permanent effect. If you like the effect then you seldom examine the thought. If you find yourself assailed by physical difficulties, however, you begin to wonder what is wrong.

Sometimes you blame others, your own background, or a previous life—if you accept reincarnation. You may hold God or the devil responsible, or you may simply say, "That is life," and accept the negative experience as a necessary portion of your lot.

You may finally come to a half-understanding of the nature of reality and wail, "I believe that I have caused these ill effects, but I find myself unable to reverse them."

If this is the case, then regardless of what you have told yourself thus far, you still do not believe that you are the creator of your own experience. As soon as you recognize this fact you can begin at once to alter those conditions that cause you dismay or dissatisfaction.

(A one-minute pause at 9:49.) No one forces you to think in any particular manner. In the past you may have learned to consider things pessimistically. You may believe that pessimism is more realistic than optimism. You may even suppose, and many do, that sorrow is ennobling, a sign of deep spiritualism, a mark of apartness, a necessary mental garb of saints and poets. Nothing could be further from the truth.

All consciousness has within it the deep abiding impetus to use its abilities fully, to expand its capacities, to venture joyfully beyond the seeming barriers of its own experience. The very consciousnesses within the smallest molecules cry out against any ideas of limitation. They yearn toward new forms and experiences. Even atoms, then, constantly seek to join in new organizations of structure and meaning. They do this "instinctively."

Man has been endowed, and has endowed himself, with a conscious mind to direct the nature, shape and form of his creations. All deep aspirations and unconscious motivations, all unspoken drives, rise up for the approval or disapproval of the conscious mind, and await its direction.

Only when it abdicates its functions does it allow itself to become swayed by "negative" experience. Only when it refuses responsibility does it finally find itself at the seeming mercy of events over which it appears to have no control.

Now you may take your break.

(*"Thank you."*

(*10:00. Jane was out of trance easily. "I've got a feeling," she said, "that that's the start of Chapter One." Her impression stemmed from the way Seth had called his material an "essay" tonight—which is something he hasn't done before. It developed that she was partially correct. Resume at 10:07.)*

Now: Books on positive thinking alone, while sometimes beneficial, usually do not take into consideration the habitual nature of negative feelings, aggressions, or repressions. Often these are merely swept under the rug.

The authors instead tell you to be positive, compassionate, strong, optimistic, filled with joy and enthusiasm, without telling you what to do to get out of the predicament you may be in, and without understanding the vicious circle that may seem to entrap you. Such books, again, while sometimes of value, do not explain how thoughts and emotions cause reality. They do not take into consideration the multidimensional aspects of the self or the fact that ultimately each personality, while following definite general laws, must still find and follow his or her own way of adapting these to personal circumstances.

If you are in poor health, you can remedy it. If your personal relationships are unsatisfactory, you can change them for the better. If you are in poverty, you can instead find yourself surrounded by abundance.

Whether or not you realize it, you have pursued your present course with determination, using many resources, for ends or reasons that at one time made sense to you. You may say, "Poor health makes no sense to me," or, "A fractured relationship with my mate is hardly what I was after," or, "I certainly have not been pursuing poverty after all my hard work."

If you were born poor, or born sick, then it certainly seems to you that these circumstances were thrust upon you. Yet they were not, and to some extent or another they can be changed for the better.

This does not mean that effort is not required, and determination. It does mean that you are not powerless to change events and that each of you, regardless of your position, status, circumstances or physical condition, is in control of your own personal experience.

You see and feel what you expect to see and feel. The world as you know it is a picture of your expectations. The world as the race of man knows it is the materialization en masse of your individual expectations. As children come from your physical tissues, so is the world your joint creation.

(10:26. Pause. Then softly, with a smile:) I am writing this book to help each individual solve his or her own personal problems. I hope to do this by showing you exactly the way in which you form your own reality, by explaining the ways in which you can alter it to your advantage.

The existence of so-called negative thoughts and feelings will not be glossed over, but neither will your ability to handle these. Period. For they are quite under your control. There are methods of using these as springboards for creativity. At no time will you be told to repress them, to ignore them. You will be shown how to recognize those within your experience, to discover which of them has been allowed to run away with you, and how to manage those that seem to be beyond your control.

The methods that I will outline demand concentration and effort. They will also challenge you, and bring into your life expansion and alterations of consciousness of a most rewarding nature.

I am not a physical personality. Basically, however, neither are you. Your experience now is physical. You are a creator translating your expectations into physical form. The world is meant to serve as a reference point. The exterior appearance is a replica of inner desire. You can change your personal world. You do change it without knowing it. You have only to use your ability consciously, to examine the nature of your thoughts and feelings and project those with which you basically agree.

They coalesce into the events with which you are so intimately familiar. I hope to teach you methods that will allow you to understand the nature of your own reality, and to point a way that will let you change that reality in whatever way you choose.

(Louder:) End of dictation.

("Okay. You're pretty tricky, starting your book like that."

(Pleasantly:) That is my way. I will give you the title and other pertinent information in a later session, and if you want it an outline of intent.

("I guess Jane would like to see that.")

Let us have this one as simple as possible . . . Give us a moment . . .

(Still in trance, Jane took a long pause at 10:37. Her eyes closed, she sat rocking back and forth with one foot upon the edge of the coffee table.)

The book will explain how personal reality is formed, with great stress laid upon the ways of changing unfavorable aspects of individual experience.

It will, hopefully, avoid the Pollyanna attributes of many self-help books, and tease the reader into an enthusiastic desire to understand the characteristics of reality if only to solve his or her own problems. The methods given will be highly practical, workable, and within the abilities of any person genuinely concerned with those problems inherent in the nature of human existence.

The point will be made that all healings are the result of the acceptance of one basic fact: That matter is formed by those inner qualities that give it vitality, that structure follows expectation, that matter at any time can be completely changed by the activation of the creative faculties inherent in all consciousness.

Please title what we have done this evening as my preface. The dictated portion, that is. I bid you a fond good evening.

("Thank you very much, Seth. Good night."

(End at 10:47 P.M. Jane's delivery as Seth had been quiet but

rather fast, considering the modest speed I can attain while taking verbatim notes in my homemade shorthand. "I think I've got half of the title," she said as soon as she was out of trance. "It's The Nature of Personal Reality—*hyphen or colon—then something else, but I didn't get that part. All of a sudden I'm exhausted," she added, laughing, "but don't write that down."*

(A few notes, added later: Six months were to pass before we learned the rest of the title for Seth's book. While Jane was resting before supper on October 25, 1972, the full name popped into her conscious mind: The Nature of Personal Reality: A Seth Book. *We held the 623rd session, bridging Chapters Four and Five, that evening.*

(We never did ask Seth for an outline, per se. Once the book was under way we realized it wasn't necessary. This decision also gave Jane as much freedom as possible.)

THE NATURE of
PERSONAL REALITY:
A Seth Book

PART ONE

Where You and the World Meet

CHAPTER 1

The Living Picture of the World

SESSION 610, JUNE 7, 1972,
9:10 P.M. WEDNESDAY

(A number of events, foremost among them the death of Jane's mother after an illness of many years, caused us to lay these sessions aside after Seth finished his preface on April 10. Jane did manage to hold her ESP and writing classes part of the time; she also worked on her novel, The Education of Oversoul 7, *which she discusses in her Introduction.*

(Through it all, however, we looked forward to our daily participation in Seth's new book. Jane hadn't looked at Seth Speaks *for long periods during its production in order to avoid conscious involvement with it—but, she said recently, smiling, she plans to read and use this work session by session as she delivers it. Whatever nervousness she'd felt about producing it was minimal by now. I encouraged her new free attitude.*

(I'll indicate Jane's various states of consciousness as I usually do in these sessions, but the notes can only be hints from an interested observer. The true variety and depth of the various

realities and personalities she reaches are qualities that are uniquely hers, and they often defy the written word.)

Good evening.

("Good evening, Seth.")

Now for dictation. The first chapter is entitled: "The Living Picture of the World."

The living picture of the world grows within the mind. The world as it appears to you is like a three-dimensional painting in which each individual takes a hand. Each color, each line that appears within it has first been painted within a mind, and only then does it materialize without.

In this case, however, the artists themselves are a portion of the painting, and appear within it. There is no effect in the exterior world that does not spring from an inner source. There is no motion that does not first occur within the mind.

The great creativity of consciousness is your heritage. It does not belong to mankind alone, however. Each living being possesses it, and the living world consists of a spontaneous cooperation that exists between the smallest and the highest, the greatest and the lowly, between the atoms and the molecules and the conscious, reasoning mind.

All manner of insects, birds and beasts cooperate in this venture, producing the natural environment. This is as normal and inevitable as the fact that your breath causes a mist to form on glass if you breathe upon it. All consciousness creates the world, rising out of feeling-tone. It is a natural product of what your consciousness is. Feelings and emotions emerge into reality in certain specific ways. Thoughts appear, growing on the bed already laid. The seasons spring up, formed by ancient feeling-tones, having deep and abiding rhythms. They are the result, again, of innate creative aspects that are a portion of all life.

These ancient aspects lie, now, deeply buried in the psyches of all species, and from them the individual patterns, the specific blueprints for new differentiations, emerge.

(9:29. Intently:) The body of the earth can be said to have its own soul, or mind (whichever term you prefer). Using this

3

analogy the mountains and oceans, the valleys and rivers and all natural phenomena spring from the earth's soul, as all events and all manufactured objects appear from the inner mind or soul of mankind.

The inner world of each man and woman is connected with the inner world of the earth. The spirit becomes flesh. Part of each individual's soul, then, is intimately connected with what we will call the world's soul, or the soul of the earth.

The smallest blade of grass, or flower, is aware of this connection, and without reasoning comprehends its position, its uniqueness and its source of vitality. The atoms and molecules that compose all objects, whether it be the body of a person, a table, a stone or a frog, know the great passive thrust of creativity that lies beneath their own existence, and upon which their individuality floats, distinct, clear and unassailable.

So does the human individual rise up in victorious distinctiveness from the ancient and yet ever-new fountains of its own soul. The self rises from unknowing into knowing, constantly surprising itself. As you read these sentences, for example, some of your knowledge is conscious knowing and is instantly available. Some is unconscious, but even the unconscious knowledge is knowing in its own unknowing.

You always know what you are doing, even when you do not realize it. Your eye knows it sees, though it cannot see itself except through the use of reflection. In the same way the world as you see it is a reflection of what you are, a reflection not in glass but in three-dimensional reality. You project your thoughts, feelings, and expectations outward, then you perceive them as the outside reality. When it seems to you that others are observing you, you are observing yourself from the standpoint of your own projections.

Now you may take a break.

(9:46 to 10:09.)

Now: You are the living picture of yourself. You project what you think you are outward into flesh. Your feelings, your conscious and unconscious thoughts, all alter and form your

4

physical image. This is fairly easy for you to understand

It is not as easy, however, to realize that your feelings and thoughts form your exterior experience in the same way, or that the events that appear to happen to you are initiated by you within your mental or psychic inner environment.

Your body does not just happen to be thin or fat, tall or short, healthy or ill. These characteristics are mental, and are thrust outward by you upon your image. I do not mean to be facetious, but you were not born yesterday. Your soul was not born yesterday, in those terms, but before the annals of time as you think of time.

The characteristics that were yours at birth were yours for a reason. The inner self chose them. To a large extent, the inner self can even now alter many of them. You did not arrive at birth without a history. Your individuality was always latent within your soul, and the "history" that is a part of you is written within unconscious memory that resides not only within your psyche, but is faithfully decoded in your genes and chromosomes,* and fulfilled in the blood that rushes through your veins.

You are aware, alert, and participating in many more realities than you know as your soul expresses itself through you. That consciousness of your usual daylight hours, the ego consciousness, rises up like a flower from the ground of the "underneath," the unconscious bed of your own reality. Though you are not aware of it, this ego itself emerges, then falls back again into the unconscious, from which another ego then rises as a new bloom from the springtime earth.

(10:27.) You do not have the same ego now that you had five years ago, but you are not aware of the change. Ego rises out of what you are, in other words. It is a part of the action of your being and consciousness, but as the eye cannot see its own

*For those who have forgotten: Chromosomes are microscopic bodies into which the protoplasmic substance of a cell nucleus separates during cell division. They carry the genes, the "blueprints" that determine hereditary characteristics. Occasionally a footnote like this will be included in order to point up Seth's own material. Often he'll "take off" from such standard definitions in his own way.

5

shifting colors and expressions, as it is not aware that it lives and dies constantly as its atomic structure changes, so you are not aware that the ego continually changes, dies, and is reborn.

Physically the structure of a cell retains its identity, even while the matter that composes it is continually altered. The cell rebuilds itself in line with its own pattern of identity, yet is always a part of emerging action, alive and responding even in the midst of its own multitudinous deaths.

So psychological structures form to which various names are given. The names are meaningless, but the structures behind them are not. Such psychological structures also retain their identity, their pattern of uniqueness, even while they change constantly, die and are reborn.

The eye rises out of the physical structure. The ego rises out of the structure of the psyche. It cannot see itself, as the eye cannot. Both look outward—in one case away from the physical body, and in the other case away from the inner psyche to the environment.

The creative body consciousness creates the eye. The creative inner psyche creates the ego. The body forms the eye in the splendid wisdom of its great unconscious knowing. The psyche brings forth the ego that perceives psychologically as the eye perceives physically. Both the eye and the ego are formations focused toward perception of exterior reality.

You may take your break.

(10:36 to 10:45.)

Now: This is not [book] dictation.

Ruburt was correct in the insight of a few moments earlier *(during break)*. In my book we will be going deeper into the nature of the unconscious and the psyche, bringing out some concepts that are of greatest value.

Ruburt himself, unconsciously but also to some extent consciously, has been more intrigued with questions concerning consciousness and personality—the role of the ego consciousness, for example—since beginning his novel, *Oversoul 7 (in late March, 1972).*

Much is not as yet known. Your psychologists are not able to think in terms of a soul, and your religious leaders are not able, or refuse, to comprehend it psychologically even to its simplest degree. Metaphysics and psychology have not met, in other words.

Now: I am, as I have told you often myself, independent of Ruburt. As you know there are connections between us.* He does not understand as yet the true nature of his own creativity. Few people do. There are always psychological reasons for all such phenomena—for any phenomena at all. In some respects of course Ruburt's children are his books. His psyche is enormously creative. Part of what I seem to be as I speak through him is as deeply and unconsciously a phenomenon as the birth of a child would be. In a different way so is *Oversoul 7* as he thinks of it.

These are not physical children at the mercy of time and the elements, but eternal ones, more knowledgeable than the parent; gods springing from the human psyche, half-human, half-divine. And on this level the parent is astonished, delighted at the superior accomplishments of its children, the superiority of the offspring, and yet also jealous to some extent.

If the books are children symbolically, then in those same terms his representation of my reality is a far more living, three-dimensional aspect. He has at various times wondered about schizophrenia, for example. He does not realize that on this level, now, and regardless of my independence and other issues involved, that he creates the personalities free of time, organizes them under the leadership of the conscious mind, and assigns them tasks of great validity and importance, which are then carried out.

This is creativity of a most specialized nature and allows him to probe, if he will, into the nature of consciousness, the

*A note, added later: *The Seth Material* and *Seth Speaks* contain some references to the reincarnational connections that Seth postulates involving himself, Jane, and me. Such personal data is outside the scope of this book; but in Chapter Nineteen, Seth does go into his ideas on reincarnation, time, etc., in a more objective way.

psyche, and creativity in a way that few can. Now he himself set up the conditions that would make such results possible. A certain part of my reality is a portion of a certain part of his reality, and here the creation of what I seem to be takes place. Beyond that is my own independent reality.

I will have more to say, and add to these notes so that they will build up by themselves.

("They're very interesting.")

If Ruburt would regard his problems as challenges then he would get much better results. That is all for now, and I bid you a fond good evening.

("The same to you, Seth. Thank you.")

Come to our class sometime.

("Okay." End at 11:10 P.M. Jane holds her ESP class on Tuesday night each week. Since I'm more solitary by nature, however, I usually type Monday's session then or work on filing and correspondence.

(In answer to many queries, I'll explain here why I prefer to write these sessions down instead of using a recorder. Shortly after Seth began to speak through Jane in late 1963 we tried recording the material, but I soon learned that I can type a session from my notes a lot faster than I can from a tape.

(This is very important, since all of our psychic work is done at night, after we've already put in a full day writing and painting, and carrying out all those other actions connected with just living in an organized way. [Yet I've had to modify my schedule in order to find the additional time required for the preparation of this manuscript: I paint in the mornings and do this work in the afternoons.]

(When Jane speaks to me as Seth her delivery is slower than it is during a class session, for instance. This, along with Seth's own instructions, makes punctuation easy. The copy is concise; after an occasional correction it's ready for publication. Moreover, I think the fact that such high-quality work is obtained this way says important things about these sessions.)

SESSION 613, SEPTEMBER 11, 1972,
9:10 P.M. MONDAY

(After holding the first session for this chapter, Jane wrote intently on Oversoul 7 *and did some work on a long-range project that she tentatively calls* Aspect Psychology. *Then, just before we were to resume work on Seth's book, the great flood of Friday, June 23, 1972, took place.*

(The flood was the worst on record in this section of the country. It grew out of Tropical Storm Agnes—which, somewhat ironically, had lost its hurricane status by the time it began its erratic course up the East Coast from Florida. Agnes was preceded by days of heavy rain that extended on a broad front for hundreds of miles. The storm unexpectedly veered inland after picking up new strength off the Virginia Capes, and when it stalled over New York and Pennsylvania flooding became inevitable.

(Jane and I decided to remain behind when, finally, last-minute requests to evacuate our section of Elmira were made before dawn. Our decision, of course, contained deeply symbolic meanings for us that we still only partially understand. The Chemung River passes less than a block from our apartment house on its way through the center of the city, but since we lived on the second floor we thought we'd be secure. The house was solid, we decided. The neighborhood emptied itself except for us, and became extremely quiet.

(The water, thick with topsoil, exuding a near-suffocating odor of petroleum effluents, became one foot deep in the yard, then three, then five . . . Jane and I found ourselves experiencing a drastic new world, and although Seth hasn't said so yet, I believe that to be one of the reasons we stayed. We sipped wine and used light self-hypnosis to take the edge off our tension, but as we watched the water crawl up the side of the old red-brick house next door, our new reality threatened to turn into a terrifying one indeed. Had we made the right decision?

9

(By now escape was probably impossible. I suggested that Jane "tune in" psychically to see what she could learn about our situation. "It's hard to be calm when you're really scared," she said, but began to compose herself. Gradually she attained a very relaxed state. She told me that the water would reach its highest level late that afternoon; incredibly, it would become almost ten *feet deep in the yard and reach halfway up the first-floor windows of the house next to ours. We would be safe as long as we stayed where we were. Jane sounded awed, though, when she said that the Walnut Street Bridge would "go." I was awed too, since the old steel bridge crossed the Chemung River less than half a block from us. We couldn't see it because of the houses across the street.*

(As soon as Jane had "picked up" this information we began to feel better. We ate, played cards, and periodically checked the water level. Several hours passed. The flood crested within fifteen minutes of the time Jane had given, and within three inches of her projected high-water mark. We slept that evening knowing that the water was dropping quickly. The next morning I walked over to the Walnut Street Bridge. It had been destroyed; several of its spans had been washed out.

(We were lucky compared to many others in the city. We'd lost our car, but we had a place to live and had all of our paintings, manuscripts and records, including the fifty-three volumes of the Seth material, intact. Since we occupy two apartments in order to have enough living and working space, we had room to take in a couple who had been flooded out. The weather was cold and rainy. Our days became a routine of actions devoted to survival, although Jane finished Oversoul 7 *early in July, and resumed her classes. This book was put aside for a long time.*

(In August Jane held one session on the flood—in which Seth had time to just touch upon the reasons behind our personal involvement in it—and late that month and in September we had several house guests in connection with psychic work. One

10

of them was Richard Bach, author of the very successful book, Jonathan Livingston Seagull.*

(When she felt it was time to resume work on Seth's book, Jane discovered to her surprise that she was somewhat nervous about it. Yet, speaking for Seth, she resumed dictation so smoothly that it seemed there hadn't been any such thing as a three-month lapse . . .)

Good evening.

("Good evening, Seth.")

Now: Give us a moment *(softly)*, and we will resume dictation.

("All right.")

Your experience in the world of physical matter flows outward from the center of your inner psyche. Then you perceive this experience. Exterior events, circumstances and conditions are meant as a kind of living feedback. Altering the state of the psyche automatically alters the physical circumstances.

There is no other valid way of changing physical events. It might help if you imagine an inner living dimension within yourself in which you create, in miniature psychic form, all the exterior conditions that you know. Simply put, you do exactly this. Your thoughts, feelings and mental pictures can be called incipient exterior events, for in one way or another each of these is materialized into physical reality.

You change even the most permanent-seeming conditions of your life constantly through the varying attitudes you have toward them. There is nothing in your exterior experience that did not originate within you.

Interactions with others do occur, of course, yet there are none that you do not accept or draw to you by your thoughts, attitudes, or emotions. This applies in each area of life. In your terms, it applies both before life and after it. In the most miraculous fashion are you given the gift of creating your experience.

*New York, N.Y.: The Macmillan Company, 1970.

In this existence you are learning to handle the inexhaustible energy that is available to you. The mass condition of the world, and the situation of each individual in it, is the materialization of man's progress as he forms his world.

(9:24.) The joy of creativity flows through you as effortlessly as your breath. From it the most minute areas of your outer experience spring. Your feelings have electromagnetic realities that rise outward, affecting the atmosphere itself. They group through attraction, building up areas of events and circumstances that finally coalesce, so to speak, either in matter as objects—or as events in "time."

Some feelings and thoughts are translated into structures that you call objects; these exist, in your terms, in a medium you call space. Others are translated instead into psychological structures called events, that seem to exist in a medium you call time.

Space and time are both root assumptions, which simply means that man accepts both, and assumes that his reality is rooted in a series of moments and a dimension of space. So your inner experience is translated in those terms.

Even the duration of an event or object in space or time is determined by the intensity of the thoughts or emotions that gave it birth. Duration in space is not the same as duration in time, however, though it may seem that this is the case. I am speaking in your terms now. An event or object that exists briefly in space may have a much greater duration in time. It may have far greater importance and intensity, existing in your memory, for example, long after it has disappeared in space. Such an event or object does not merely exist symbolically within your mind or memory—but in your terms its actual reality continues as a time event.

Nor is its reality in space annihilated as long as it exists within your mind. Let us take a very simple example. A child has been told not to play with a doll. The order is disobeyed. The child, wittingly or unwittingly, breaks the doll, and it is finally thrown away. The doll exists in time quite vitally as long as the child or the adult-to-be remembers it.

12

(9:40.) If the doll sat on a bureau and this is also vividly recalled, then the space in which the doll sat still carries the impression of the doll, though other objects may be placed there. You react, therefore, not only to what is visible to your physical eyes in space, or to what is directly in front of you in time, but also to objects and events whose reality is still with you, though they may seem to have disappeared.

Basically you create your experience through your beliefs about yourself and the nature of reality. Another way to understand this is to realize that you create your experiences through your expectations. Your feeling-tones are your emotional attitudes toward yourself and life in general, and these generally govern the large areas of experience.

(Pause.) They give the overall emotional coloration that characterizes what happens to you. Period. You are what happens to you. Your emotional feelings are often transitory, but beneath there are certain qualities of feeling uniquely your own, that are like deep musical chords. While your day-to-day feelings may rise or fall, these characteristic feeling-tones lie beneath.

Sometimes they rise to the surface, but in great long rhythms. You cannot call these negative or positive. They are instead tones of your being. They represent the most inner portion of your experience. This does not mean that they are hidden from you, or are meant to be. It simply means that they represent the core from which you form your experience.

If you have become afraid of emotion or the expression of feeling, or if you have been taught that the inner self is no more than a repository of uncivilized impulses, then you may have the habit of denying this deep rhythm. You may try to operate as if it did not exist, or even try to refute it. But it represents your deepest, most creative impulses; to fight against it is like trying to swim upstream against a strong current.

Now you may take your break.

(9:57 to 10:06.)

These feeling-tones, then, pervade your being.

They are the form your spirit takes when combined with flesh. From them, from their core, your flesh arises.

Everything that you experience has consciousness, and each consciousness is endowed with its own feeling-tone. There is great cooperation involved in the formation of the earth as you think of it, and so the individual living structures of the planet rise up from the feeling-tone within each atom and molecule.

Your flesh springs about you in response to these inner chords of your being, and the trees, rocks, seas and mountains spring up as the body of the earth from the deep inner chords within the atoms and molecules, which are also living. Because of the creative cooperation that exists, the miracle of physical materialization is performed so smoothly and automatically that consciously you are not aware of your part in it.

(10:16.) The feeling-tone then is the motion and fiber—the timber—the portion of your energy devoted to your physical experience. Now it flows into what you are as a physical being and materializes you in the world of seasons, space, flesh, and time. Its source, however, is quite independent of the world that you know.

Once you learn to get the feeling of your own inner tone, then you are aware of its power, strength and durability, and you can to some extent ride with it into deeper realities of experience.

The incredible emotional richness and variety and splendor of physical experience is the material reflection of this inner feeling-tone. It pervades the events in your life, the overall inner direction, the quality of perception. It fills up and illuminates the individual aspects of your life, and largely determines the persuasive subjective climate in which you dwell.

It is the essence of yourself. Its sweeps are broad in range, however. It does not determine, for example, specific events. (Pause.) It paints the colors in the large "landscape" of your experience. It is the feeling of yourself, inexhaustible.

In other terms it represents the expression of yourself in pure energy, from which your individuality rises, the You of

14

you, unmistakably given identity that is never duplicated.

This energy comes from the core of BEING (in capital letters), from All That Is (with our usual capitals), and represents the source of never-ending vitality. It is Being, Being in You. As such, all of the energy and power of Being is focused and reflected through you in the direction of your three-dimensional existence.

You may take your break.

(10:35 to 10:47.)

While your feeling-tone is uniquely yours, still it is expressed in a certain fashion that is shared by all consciousnesses focused in physical reality. So in those terms you spring from the earth as all the other creatures and natural living structures. You are, while physical, a portion of nature, therefore, not apart from it.

Trees and rocks possess their own consciousness, and also share a gestalt consciousness, even as the living portions of your body. The cells and organs have their own awarenesses, and a gestalt one. So the race of man also has individual consciousness and a gestalt or mass consciousness, of which you individually are hardly aware.

The mass race consciousness, in its terms, possesses an identity. You are a portion of that identity while still being unique, individual and independent. You are confined only to the extent that you have chosen physical reality, and so placed yourself within its context of experience. While physical, you follow physical laws, or assumptions. These form the framework for corporeal expression.

Within this framework you have full freedom to create your experience, your personal life in all of its aspects, the living picture of the world. Your personal life, and to some extent your individual living experience, help create the world as it is known in your time.

(11:00.) In this book we will be speaking about your own subjective world, and your part in the creation of events both private and shared. It is important before we continue that you realize that consciousness is within all physical phenomena,

however. It is vital that you realize your position within nature. Nature is created from within. The personal life that you know rises up from within you, yet it is given. Period. Since you are a part of Being, then in a certain fashion you give yourself the life that is being lived through you.

(*Pause.*) New paragraph: You make your own reality. There is no other rule. Knowing this is the secret of creativity.

I have spoken of "you," yet this must not be confused with the "you" that you often think you are—the ego alone, for the ego is only a portion of You; it is that expert part of your personality that deals directly with the contents of your conscious mind, and is concerned most directly with the material portions of your experience.

The ego is a very specialized portion of your greater identity. It is a portion of you that arises to deal directly with the life that the larger You is living. The ego can feel cut off, lonely and frightened, however, if the conscious mind lets the ego run away with it. The ego and the conscious mind are not the same thing. The ego is composed of various portions of the personality—it is a combination of characteristics, ever-changing, that act in unitary fashion—the portion of the personality that deals most directly with the world.

(*Very slowly at 11:18:*) The conscious mind is an excellent perceiving attribute, a function that belongs to inner awareness but in this case is turned outward toward the world of events. Through the conscious mind the soul looks outward. Left alone, it perceives clearly.

In certain terms, the ego is the eye through which the conscious mind perceives, or the focus through which it views physical reality. But the conscious mind automatically changes its focus throughout life. The ego, while appearing the same to itself, ever changes. It is only when the conscious mind becomes rigid in its direction, or allows the ego to take on some of its own functions, that difficulties arise. Then the ego allows the conscious mind to work in certain directions and blocks its awareness in others.

16

And so it is from your larger identity that you form the reality that you know. It is up to you to do this with joy and vigor, clearing your conscious mind so that the deeper knowledge of your greater identity can form joyous expressions in the world of the flesh.

(11:25.) End of the chapter. End of dictation.

Now: The book will enable others to help themselves, and will reach a far greater audience and help more people than Ruburt could meet alone, or than I could help through individual sessions. Those who request help should be put on a list to make sure they know of the book.

("That's a good idea." By mail and telephone, Jane has been getting more requests for help than she can handle.)

Ruburt does not need to feel he must have individual sessions, then, for people who must work this through alone. And now, I bid you a fond good evening.

("Thank you, Seth, and good evening. It's been very pleasant to sit in on a session again.")

If you have questions, you may ask them.

(I paused, considering the late hour, then asked Seth for his opinion about the recent visit of a young scientist from a Western state. Jane, both as Seth and as herself, had made a good start at tuning-in on certain technical information. I felt however that a great amount of time and effort would be needed, on a regular basis over a period of years, probably, for Jane to make full use of her abilities in such specialized endeavors.)

The effect of the visit was good, particularly on Ruburt. We will get to his [scientific] questions. For Ruburt's confidence, I wanted this book decently begun. Other sessions may take over from dictation now and then, but the main project will be the book.

The flood material will be used as an example in the book later on, when natural disasters are discussed; so you will have that material, and others may use and understand it.

And now, a fond good evening.

("Thanks once again, Seth."

(End at 11:32 P.M. Jane was quickly out of an excellent dissociated state." I'm glad Seth's working on his book again," she said. "I know it's silly, but I feel a lot better. I was even wondering if my own attitude was holding the thing up now, after all of those other interruptions . . ." And so, like Seth Speaks, this is really two books in one: It's not only about the nature of personal reality, but the circumstances surrounding Jane's production of the material and the many ideas she has concerning it.

(I was happy to learn that Seth plans to incorporate flood data in his book—I've been concerned lest that subject be pushed aside by other events, then perhaps forgotten.)

CHAPTER 2

Reality and Personal Beliefs

SESSION 614, SEPTEMBER 13, 1972,
9:36 P.M. WEDNESDAY

(Jane was very pleased now that Seth's book was firmly under way after so many delays. Her energy has been "up" these days. After her long session Monday night, she had come back with an even longer one in ESP class Tuesday evening—and with Sumari* added, too. Now a third session was due tonight.

(She wasn't tired, though, Jane said. Her only complaint concerned the excessive humidity, since she is very sensitive to the weather; today had been hot, with rain after supper. We walked around the block just before session time.)

Good evening.

("Good evening, Seth.")

We will resume dictation. Chapter Two: "Reality and Personal Beliefs."

You form the fabric of your experience through your own beliefs and expectations. These personal ideas about yourself

---

*See Jane's Introduction for material on the development of her Sumari abilities.

and the nature of reality will affect your thoughts and emotions. You take your beliefs <u>about</u> reality as truth, and often do not question them. They seem self-explanatory. They appear in your mind as statements of fact, far too obvious for examination.

Therefore they are accepted without question too often. They are not recognized as beliefs <u>about</u> reality, but are instead considered characteristics of reality itself. *(Pause.)* Frequently such ideas appear indisputable, so a part of you that it does not occur to you to speculate about their validity. They become invisible assumptions, but they nevertheless color and form your personal experience.

Some people, for example, do not question their religious beliefs but accept them as fact. Others find it comparatively easy to recognize such inner assumptions when they appear in a religious context, but are quite blind to them in other areas.

(9:45.) It is far simpler to recognize your own beliefs in regard to religion, politics or similar subjects, than it is to pinpoint your deepest beliefs about yourself and who and what you are—particularly in relationship with your own life.

Many individuals are completely blind to their own beliefs about themselves, and the nature of reality. Your own conscious thoughts will give you excellent clues. Often you will find yourself refusing to accept certain thoughts that come to your mind because they conflict with other usually accepted ideas.

Your conscious mind is <u>always</u> trying to give you a clear picture, but you often allow preconceived ideas to block out this intelligence. It has been fashionable to blame the subconscious for personality problems and difficulties, the idea being that early events, charged and mysterious, lodged there. In this country several generations grew up believing that the subconscious portions of the personality were unreliable, filled with negative energy, and contained only locked-up unpleasant episodes best forgotten.

(9:54.) They grew up believing that the conscious mind was

relatively powerless, that adult experience was set in the days of infancy. These concepts themselves set up artificial divisions. People learned that they should not be aware of "subconscious" material.

The doors to the inner self were to be shut tight. Only lengthy psychoanalysis could or should open them. The normal individual felt that he had best leave such areas alone, so in cutting off these portions of the self, barriers were also set up against the joy of the inner spontaneous self. People felt divorced from the core of their own reality.

The concept of original sin was a very poor, limited and distorted one, but at least along with it went rather simple procedures: Through baptism you might be saved, or through certain words or sacraments or rituals redemption could be found. *(See the Gospel according to Mark, 1:1-11, for instance.)*

The idea of the tainted subconscious, however, left man no such relatively easy way out. The few rituals possible required years of analysis, which only the very wealthy were privileged to experience.

About the same time that the idea of the unsavory subconscious arose so strongly, the idea of the soul went out the window. Millions of people therefore believed in a reality in which they were deprived of the idea of a soul, and burdened by the concept of a very unreliable, if not definitely evil, subconscious. They saw themselves as vulnerable solitary points of egos, riding perilously and unprotected upon the tumultuous waves of involuntary processes.

(Pause at 10:05. Certainly these sessions aren't "spiritual" in usual terms. Still in trance, Jane lit a cigarette. Her beer was gone, but since I had a little left in my glass she reached over and helped herself. *)*

*Jane learned on her own some time ago that a very moderate amount of alcohol goes well with the sessions. So does tobacco. Subsequent reading informed us that both substances depress the central nervous system. We think Jane combines the resulting spontaneity with her natural psychic abilities in these sessions. She doesn't begin tasting any beverage, however, until the session is under way.

At about the same time many intelligent persons were realizing that organized religions' ideas of God, and of heaven and hell, were distorted, unjust, and smacked of children's fairy tales. For these individuals there was no place to look for help.

Under the circumstances, to look within would have seemed foolhardy, for they had been taught that this within contained the source of their problems to begin with. Those who could not afford therapy tried the harder to inhibit any messages from the inner self, for fear they would become swallowed by the savage infantile emotions.

Now first of all, there are no limitations or divisions to the self, though for purposes of discussion a word like "ego" may be used here because you understand what you think it means. You can indeed depend upon seemingly unconscious portions of yourself. As you will see later, you can become more and more consciously aware, therefore bringing into your consciousness larger and larger portions of yourself.

(10:12.) You breathe, grow, and perform multitudinous delicate and precise activities constantly, without being consciously aware of how you carry out such manipulations. You live without consciously knowing how you maintain this miracle of physical awareness in the world of flesh and time.

The seemingly unconscious portions of yourself draw atoms and molecules from the air to form your image. Your lips move, your tongue speaks your name. Does the name belong to the atoms and molecules within your lips or tongue? (Pause.) The atoms and molecules move constantly, forming into cells, tissues and organs. How can the name the tongue speaks belong to them?

They do not read or write, yet they speak complicated syllables that communicate to other beings such as yourself anything from a simple feeling to the most complicated information. How do they do this?

The atoms and molecules of the tongue do not know the syntax of the language they speak. When you begin a sentence you do not have the slightest conscious idea, often, of how you will finish it, yet you take it on faith that the words will make sense, and your meaning will flow out effortlessly.

All of this happens because the inner portions of your being operate spontaneously, joyfully, freely; all of this occurs because your inner self believes in you, often even while you do not believe in it. These unconscious portions of your being operate amazingly well, frequently despite the greatest misunderstanding on your part of their nature and function, and in the face of strong interference from you because of your beliefs.

Each person experiences a unique reality, different from any other individual's. This reality springs outward from the inner landscape of thoughts, feelings, expectations and beliefs. If you believe that the inner self works against you rather than for you, then you hamper its functioning—or rather, you force it to behave in a certain way because of your beliefs.

The conscious mind is meant to make clear judgments about your position in physical reality. Often false beliefs will prevent it from making these, for the egotistically held ideas will cloud its clear vision.

I suggest a break.

(*10:31. Jane's trance had been deep. She felt better now, she said, because the weather had lost some of its oppressive quality. I told her that in my opinion the material tonight represented her and Seth at their best—and that it also had a deceptive simplicity. Jane was pleased, saying she felt quite free now about the production of the book.*)

Are you ready?

(*"Yes." I was just finishing my notes when Jane took off her glasses and resumed speaking for Seth. 10:53.*)

Your beliefs can be like fences that surround you.

You must first recognize the existence of such barriers— you must see them or you will not even realize that you are not free, simply because you will not see beyond the fences. (*Very positively:*) They will represent the boundaries of your experience.

There is one belief, however, that destroys artificial barriers to perception, an expanding belief that automatically pierces false and inhibiting ideas.

Now, separately:

The Self Is Not Limited.

That statement is a statement of fact. It exists regardless of your belief or disbelief in it. Following this concept is another:

There Are No Boundaries or Separations of the Self.

Those that you experience are the result of false beliefs. Following this is the idea that I have already mentioned:

You Make Your Own Reality.

To understand yourself and what you are, you can learn to experience yourself directly apart from your beliefs about yourself. What I would like each reader to do is to sit quietly. Close your eyes. Try to sense within yourself the deep feeling-tones that I mentioned earlier *(in the 613th session in Chapter One)*. This is not difficult to do.

Your knowledge of their existence will help you recognize their deep rhythms within you. Each individual will sense these tones in his or her own way, so do not worry about how they should feel. Simply tell yourself that they exist, that they are composed of the great energies of your being made flesh.

Then let yourself experience. If you are used to terms like meditation, try to forget the term during this procedure. Do not use any name. Free yourself from concepts, and experience the being of yourself and the motion of your own vitality. Do not question, "Is this right? Am I doing it correctly? Am I feeling what I should feel?" This is the book's first exercise for you.

You are not to use other people's criteria. There are no standards but your own feelings.

No particular time limit is recommended. This should be an enjoyable experience. Accept whatever happens as uniquely your own. The exercise will put you in touch with yourself. It will return you to yourself. Whenever you are nervous or upset, take a few moments to sense this feeling-tone within you, and you will find yourself centered in your own being, secure.

When you have tried this exercise several times, then feel these deep rhythms go out from you in all directions, as indeed they do. Electromagnetically they radiate out through your physical being; and in ways that I hope to explain later, they form the environment that you know even as they form your physical image.

(11:14.) I told you that the self was not limited, yet surely you think that your self stops where your skin meets space, that you are inside your skin. Period. Yet your environment is an extension of your self. It is the body of your experience, coalesced in physical form. The inner self forms the objects that you know as surely and automatically as it forms your finger or your eye.

Your environment is the physical picture of your thoughts, emotions and beliefs made visible. Since your thoughts, emotions and beliefs move through space and time, you therefore affect physical conditions separate from you.

Consider the spectacular framework of your body just from the physical standpoint. You perceive it as solid, as you perceive all other physical matter; yet the more matter is explored the more obvious it becomes that within it energy takes on specific shape (in the form of organs, cells, molecules, atoms, electrons), each less physical than the last, each combining in mysterious gestalt to form matter.

(11:25.) The atoms within your body spin. There is constant commotion and activity. The flesh that seemed so solid turns out to be composed of swiftly moving particles—often orbiting each other—in which great exchanges of energy continually occur.

The stuff, the space outside of your body, is composed of the same elements, but in different proportions. There is a constant physical interchange between the structure you call your body and the space outside it; chemical interactions, basic exchanges without which life as you know it would be impossible.

To hold your breath is to die. Breath, which represents the most intimate and most necessary of your physical sensations, must flow out from what you are, passing into the world that seems to be not you. Physically, portions of you leave your body constantly and intermix with the elements. You know what happens when adrenalin is released through the bloodstream. It stirs you up and prepares you for action. But in other ways the adrenalin does not just stay in your body. It is cast into the air and it affects the atmosphere, though it is transformed.

Any of your emotions liberate hormones, but these also leave you as your breath leaves you; and in that respect you can say that you release chemicals into the air that then affect it.

Physical storms, then, are caused by such interactions. I am telling you that you form your own reality once again, and this includes the physical weather—which is the result, *en masse,* of your individual reactions.

I will elaborate much more specifically on this particular point later in the book. *(A note added later: Seth does—in Chapter Eighteen.)* You are in physical existence to learn and understand that your energy, translated into feelings, thoughts and emotions, causes all experience. There are no exceptions.

Once you understand this you have only to learn to examine the nature of your beliefs, for these will automatically cause you to feel and think in certain fashions. Your emotions follow your beliefs. It is not the other way around.

I would like you to recognize your own beliefs in several areas. You must realize that any idea you accept as truth is a belief that you hold. You must, then, take the next step and say, "It is not necessarily true, even though I believe it." You will, I hope, learn to disregard all beliefs that imply basic limitations.

You may take your break.

(11:40. Jane was surprised to learn that almost fifty minutes had passed. Her delivery had become increasingly energetic and intent, and the session had turned into one of those occasions when she—and Seth—appeared to be quite capable of continuing half the night. I'd also picked up an infusion of energy. Because I was willing to continue, Jane changed her mind about ending the session here. Resume in the same manner at 11:56.)

Now: Later we will discuss some of the reasons for your beliefs, but for now I simply want you to recognize them.

I am going to list some limiting false beliefs. If you find yourself <u>agreeing</u> with any of them, then recognize this as an area in which you must personally work.

1. Life is a valley of sorrows.
2. The body is inferior. As a vehicle of the soul it is automatically degraded, tinged.

You may feel that the flesh is inherently bad or evil, that its appetites are wrong. Christians may find the body deplorable, thinking that the soul descended into it—"descent" automatically meaning the change from a higher or better condition to one that is worse.

Followers of Eastern religions often feel it their duty, also, to deny the flesh, to rise above it, so to speak, into a state where nothing is desired. *("Emptiness" in Taoism, for instance.)* Using a different vocabulary, they still believe that earth experience is not desirable in itself.

3. I am helpless before circumstances that I cannot control.
4. I am helpless because my personality and character were formed in infancy, and I am at the mercy of my past.
5. I am helpless because I am at the mercy of events from past lives in other incarnations, over which I now have no control. I must be punished, or I am punishing myself for unkindnesses done to others in past lives. I must accept the negative aspects of my life because of my karma.*

*In Hinduism and Buddhism, karma is thought of as the total moral sum of an individual's acts in any one life—thus determining the person's fate or destiny in the next. Seth sees reincarnational lives as all existing at once, so there is constant give-and-take among them. A "future" life, then, can affect a "past" one, so karma as it is usually considered does not apply.

27

6. People are basically bad, and out to get me.

7. I have the truth and no one else has. Or, my group has the truth and no other group has.

8. I will grow frailer, sicker, and lose my powers as I grow old.

9. My existence is dependent upon my experience in flesh. When my body dies my consciousness dies with it.

Now: That was a rather general list of false beliefs. Now here is a more specific list of more intimate beliefs, any of which you may have personally about yourself.

1. I am sickly, and always have been.

2. There is something wrong with money. People who have it are greedy, less spiritual than those who are poor. They are unhappier, and snobs.

3. I am not creative. I have no imagination.

Next: I can never do what I want to do.

Next: People dislike me.

Next: I am fat.

("That would be number 6.")

Then 7: I always have bad luck.

(12:15.) These are all beliefs held by many people. Those who have them will meet them in experience. Physical data will always seem to reinforce the beliefs, therefore, but the beliefs formed the reality. We are going to attempt to knock down such limiting concepts.

First of all, you must realize that no one can change your beliefs for you, nor can they be forced upon you from without. You can indeed change them for yourself, however, with knowledge and application.

Look about you. Your entire physical environment is the materialization of your beliefs. Your sense of joy, sorrow, health or illness—all of these are also caused by your beliefs. If you believe that a given situation should make you unhappy, then it will, and the unhappiness will then reinforce the condition.

Within you is the ability to change your ideas about reality and about yourself, to create a personal living experience that is fulfilling to yourself and others. I would like you to write down your beliefs about yourself as you become aware of them. Later you can use this list in a way that you do not now suspect.

Break or end of session, whatever you prefer.

(*"Well, I guess we'd better end it, then."*

(*End at 12:25 A.M. Both of us felt much better now than we had before the session began.*

SESSION 615, SEPTEMBER 18, 1972,
9:32 P.M. MONDAY

(*Jane has already had one session—a short one—today. The mail had brought us good news early this afternoon; we'd celebrated with a drink, then Seth had come through.*

(*While we were eating supper this evening Jane received a long-distance call from one of our visitors of last August. Regretfully, she had to tell him she'd had little time to work on the scientific projects discussed then, although she was still interested. While she was doing the dishes and thinking about this she received an amusing flash from Seth: She was to stop worrying about such things and "adopt a position of divine nonchalance."*

(*Jane was quite ready for her regular session at 9:00, although because of the call we weren't sure what it would cover. By 9:30, however, the session still hadn't started, and she was impatient. Yet when she did take off her glasses and begin speaking for Seth her voice was quiet, her pace leisurely, her eyes closed often.*)

Now: Dictation.

(*"Good evening, Seth."*)

Your conscious beliefs direct the functioning of your body. It is not the other way around.

Your inner self adopts the physically conscious, physically focused mind as a method of allowing it to manipulate in the world that you know. The conscious mind is particularly

29

equipped to direct outward activity, to handle waking experience and oversee physical work.

Its beliefs about the nature of reality are then given to inner portions of the self. These rely mainly upon the conscious mind's interpretation of temporal reality. The conscious mind sets the goals and the inner self brings them about, using all its facilities and inexhaustible energy.

The great value of the conscious mind lies precisely in its ability to make decisions and set directions. Its role is dual, however: It is meant to assess conditions both inside and outside, to handle data that comes from the physical world and from the inner portions of the self. It is not a closed system, then.

To be human necessitates fine discrimination in the use of such consciousness. Many people are afraid of their own thoughts. They do not examine them. They accept the beliefs of others. Such actions distort data from both within and without.

There is no battle between the intuitive self and the conscious mind. There only seems to be when the individual refuses to face all the information that is available in his conscious mind. (Pause.) Sometimes it seems easier to avoid the frequent readjustments in behavior that self-examination requires. In such cases an individual collects many secondhand beliefs. Some contradict each other; the signals given to the body and to the inner self are not smoothly flowing or clear-cut, but a muddied jumble of counter-directions.

These will immediately set off alarms of various natures. The body will not function property, or the overall emotional environment will suffer. Such reactions are actually excellent precautions, meant to be taken as a sign that change is needed.

At the same time, the inner self will transmit to the conscious mind insights and intuitions meant to clear its sight. But if you believe that the inner self is dangerous and not to be trusted, if you are afraid of dreams or any intrusive psychic material, then you deny this help and turn aside from it.

30

(9:50.) If you <u>believe</u>, moreover, that you must accept your difficulties, then this belief alone can deter you from solving them.

I repeat: Your ideas and beliefs form the structure of your experience. Your beliefs and the reasons for them can be found in your conscious mind. If you accept the idea that the reasons for your behavior are forever buried in the past of this life, or any other, then you will not be able to alter your experience until you change that belief. I am speaking now of more or less normal experience. Later we will discuss more particular areas, such as circumstances in which illnesses date from birth.

The realization that you form your own reality should be a liberating one. You are responsible for your successes and your joys. You can change those areas of your life with which you are less than pleased, but you must take the responsibility for your being.

Your spirit joined itself with flesh, and in flesh, to experience a world of incredible richness, to help create a dimension of reality of colors and of form. Your spirit was born in flesh to enrich a marvelous area of sense awareness, to feel energy made into corporeal form. You are here to use, enjoy, and express yourself through the body. You are here to aid in the great expansion of consciousness. You are not here to cry about the miseries of the human condition, but to change them when you find them not to your liking through the joy, strength and vitality that is within you; to create the spirit as faithfully and beautifully as you can in flesh.

The conscious mind allows you to look outward into the physical universe, and see the reflection of your spiritual activity, to perceive and assess your individual and joint creations.

In a manner of speaking, the conscious mind is a window through which you look outward—and looking outward, perceive the fruits of your inner mind. Often you let false beliefs blur that great vision. Your joy, vitality and accomplishment do not come from the outside to you as the result of events that "happen to

31

you." They spring from inner events that are the result of your beliefs.

(10:06. Seth-Jane, deep in thought, paused.) Much has been written about the nature and importance of suggestion. One of the current ideas in vogue holds that you are constantly at the mercy of suggestion. Your own conscious beliefs are the most important suggestions that you receive. All other ideas are rejected or accepted according to whether or not you believe they are true, in line with the steady conscious chattering that goes on within your mind most of the day—the suggestions given to you by yourself.

You will accept a suggestion given by another only if it fits in with your own ideas about the nature of reality in general, and your concepts about yourself in particular.

If you use your conscious mind properly, then, you examine those beliefs that come to you. You do not accept them willy-nilly. If you use your <u>conscious</u> mind properly, you are also aware of intuitive ideas that come to you from within. You are only half conscious when you do not examine the information that comes to you from without, and when you ignore the data that comes to you from within.

(10:13.) Many false beliefs therefore are indiscriminately accepted because you have not examined them. You have given the inner self a faulty picture of reality. Since it is the function of the conscious mind to assess physical experience, it [the inner self] hasn't been able to do its job properly. If the inner portions of the self were supposed to have that responsibility, then you would not need a conscious mind.

(Emphatically:) When the inner self is alerted, it will <u>immediately</u> try to remedy the situation by an influx of self-corrective measures. On occasion, when the situation gets out of hand, it will bypass those restrictive areas of the conscious mind, and solve the problem by shooting forth energy in other layers of activity.

It will manage to work around the blind spots in the reasoning mind, for example. Often it will sift out from the barrage of conflicting beliefs the particular set that is the most life-giving, and send these forth in what then appears as a burst of revelation. Such revelations result in new patterns that change behavior.

You must be aware of the contents of your own reasoning mind. Find the ambiguities. Regardless of the nature of your beliefs they are indeed made flesh and material. The miracle of your being cannot escape itself. Your thoughts blossom into events. If you think the world is evil, you will meet with events that seem evil. There are no accidents in cosmic terms, or in terms of the world as you know it. Your beliefs grow as surely in time and space as flowers do. When you realize this you can even feel their growing.

You may take a break.

(10:29 to 10:44.)

Now: Resume dictation.

The conscious mind is basically curious, open. It is also equipped to examine its own contents. Because of the psychological theories of the last century, many Western people believed that the primary purpose of the conscious mind was to inhibit "unconscious" material.

Instead, as mentioned *(in this session),* it is also meant to receive and interpret important data that comes to it from the inner self. Left alone, it does this very well. It receives and interprets impressions. What has happened, however, is that man has taught it to accept [only] data coming from the outside world, and to set up barriers against inner knowledge.

Such a situation denies the individual his full strength, and cuts him off—consciously, now—from the important sources of his being. These conditions inhibit creative expression in particular, and deny the conscious self the continually emerging insights and intuitions otherwise unavailable.

Thought and feeling then seem separate. Creativity and intellect do not show themselves as the brothers that they are, but often as strangers. The conscious mind loses its fine edge. It cuts out from its experience the vast body of inner knowledge available to it. Divisions, illusionary ones, appear in the self.

Left alone, the self acts spontaneously as a unit, but as an ever-changing one. Listening to voices both within and without, the conscious mind is able to form beliefs that are in league with the self's knowledge as received from material and non-material sources. Then examination of beliefs takes its place along with other activities—naturally, easily, without effort. Once the conscious mind has accepted a collection of conflicting beliefs, however, a definite attempt is necessary to sort these out.

Remember, even false beliefs will seem to be justified in terms of physical data, since your experience in the outside world is the materialization of those beliefs. So you must work with the raw material of your ideas, even while your sense data may tell you that a given belief is obviously a truth. To change your experience or any portion of it, then, you must change your ideas. Since you have been forming your own reality all along, the results will follow naturally.

(Pause.) You must be convinced that you can alter your beliefs. You must be willing to try. Think of a limiting idea as a muddy color and your life as a multidimensional painting that is marred. You change the idea as an artist would his palette.

The artist does not identify with the colors he uses. He knows he chooses them, and applies them with a brush. So you paint your reality with your ideas in the same manner. You are not your ideas, nor even your thoughts. You are the self who experiences them. If a painter finds his hands stained with pigment at the end of a day, he can wash the stain off easily, knowing its nature. If you think that limiting thoughts are a portion of you, permanently attached therefore, you will not think of washing them off. You would behave instead like a mad artist who says, "My paints are a part of me. They have stained my fingers, and there is nothing I can do about it."

There is no contradiction, though there may seem to be, between spontaneously being aware of your thoughts, and examining them. You do not have to be blind to be spontaneous.

34

You are not being spontaneous when you indiscriminately accept as your own, for a fact, every bit of data that comes to you.

(11:10.) Many beliefs would automatically fall away quite harmlessly if you were being truly spontaneous. Instead you often harbor them.

Previous limiting ideas, accepted, figuratively form a restraining bed, gathering other such material so that your mind becomes filled with debris. When you are spontaneous, you accept the free nature of your mind and it spontaneously makes decisions as to the validity or nonvalidity of data it receives. When you refuse to allow it this function it becomes cluttered.

No apple tree tries to grow violets. Quite automatically it knows what it is, and the framework of its own identity and existence. *(Pause.)* You have a conscious mind, but this is only the "topmost" portion of your mind. Much more of "it" is available to you. Much more of your knowledge can be conscious, therefore; but a false belief, a limiting one, is as ambiguous to your nature as any apple tree's idea that it was a violet plant.

It could not produce violets, nor could it be a good apple tree while it tried to. The mistaken belief is one that does not fit the basic conditions of your inner being. So if you believe that you are at the mercy of physical events, you entertain a false belief. If you feel that your present experience was set in circumstances beyond your control, you entertain a false belief.

You had a hand in the development of your childhood environment. You chose the circumstances. This does not mean that you are at the mercy of those circumstances. It means that you set challenges to be overcome, set goals to be reached, set up frameworks of experience through which you could develop, understand and fulfill certain abilities.

(11:29.) The creative power to form your own experience is within you now, as it has been since the time of your birth and before. You may have chosen a particular theme for this existence, a certain framework of conditions, but within these you

35

have the freedom to experiment, create, and alter conditions and events.

Each person chooses for himself the individual patterns within which he will create this personal reality. But inside these bounds are infinite varieties of actions and unlimited resources.

The inner self is embarked upon an exciting endeavor, in which it learns how to translate its reality into physical terms. The conscious mind is brilliantly attuned to physical reality, then, and often so dazzled by what it perceives that it is tempted to think physical phenomena is a cause, rather than a result. Deeper portions of the self always serve to remind it that this is not the case. When the conscious mind accepts too many false beliefs, particularly if it sees that inner self as a danger, then it closes out these constant reminders. When this situation arises the conscious mind feels itself assailed by a reality that seems greater than itself, over which it has no control. The deep feeling of security in which it should be anchored is lost.

The false beliefs must be weeded out so that the conscious mind can become aware of its source once again, and open to the inner channels of splendor and power available to it.

(11:40.) The ego is an offshoot of the conscious mind, so to speak. The conscious mind is like a gigantic camera with the ego directing the view and the focus. Left alone, various portions of the identity rise and form the ego, degroup and reform, all the while maintaining a marvelous spontaneity and yet a sense of oneness. (See both sessions in Chapter One.)

The ego is your idea of your physical image in relation to the world. Your self-image is not unconscious, then. You are quite aware of it, though often you reject certain thoughts about it in favor of others. False beliefs can result in a rigid ego that insists upon using the conscious mind in one direction only, further distorting its perceptions.

Often you quite consciously decide to bury a thought or an idea that might cause you to alter your behavior, because it does not seem to fit in with limiting ideas that you already

36

hold. Listen to your own train of thought as you go about your days. What suggestions and ideas are you giving yourself? Realize that these will be materialized in your personal experience.

Many quite limiting ideas will pass without scrutiny under the guise of goodness. You may feel quite virtuous, for example, in hating evil, or what seems to you to be evil; but if you find yourself concentrating upon either hatred or evil you are creating it. If you are poor you may feel quite self-righteous in your financial condition, looking with scorn upon those who are wealthy, telling yourself that money is wrong and so reinforcing the condition of poverty. If you are ill you may find yourself dwelling upon the misery of your condition, and bitterly envying those who are healthy, bemoaning your state—and therefore perpetuating it through your thoughts.

If you dwell upon limitations, then you will meet them. You must create a new picture in your mind. It will differ from the picture your physical senses may show you at any given time, precisely in those areas where changes are required.

Hatred of war will not bring peace—another example. Only love of peace will bring about those conditions.

You may take a break, or end the session as you prefer.

("Then we'll call it a night."

(11:56 P.M. Jane was out of an excellent trance before I finished writing. She didn't remember any of the material. "My God, Rob, it's almost midnight," she exclaimed. Actually she could have continued the session—she's been extremely active psychically lately—but I wondered about her being tired tomorrow. She has ESP class tomorrow night, a session Wednesday night, and writing class on Thursday.)

SESSION 616, SEPTEMBER 20, 1972,
9:28 P.M. WEDNESDAY

(As we sat waiting for the session to begin at 9:20, Jane told me she'd just "picked up" the heading for Chapter Three of Seth's book: "Telepathy and Belief Gathering"—or "Idea

Gathering"; she wasn't sure which. We'll see how close she came. At 9:25 she said, "I'm getting ready to start now. I can tell..." She lit a cigarette and looked off to one side and down, her attention already turned inward as she prepared to psychically join a very familiar "energy personality essence," as Seth calls himself.)

Good evening.

("Good evening, Seth.")

Now: We will resume dictation.

I quite realize that many of my statements will contradict the beliefs of those of you who accept the idea that the conscious mind is relatively powerless, and that the answers to problems lie hidden beneath.

Obviously the conscious mind is a phenomenon, not a thing. It is ever-changing. It can be concentrated or turned by the ego in literally endless directions. It can view outward reality or turn inward, observing its own contents.

There are gradations and fluctuations within its activity. It is far more flexible than you give it credit for. *(Pause.)* The ego can use the conscious mind almost entirely as a way of perceiving external or internal realities that coincide with its own beliefs. It is not that certain answers do not lie openly accessible, therefore, but that often you have set yourself on a course of action in which you believe, and you do not want to open yourself to any material that may contradict your current beliefs.

If you are sick, for example, there is a reason. To recover thoroughly without taking on new symptoms, you must discover the reason. You may dislike your illness, but it is a course you have decided upon. While you are convinced that the course is necessary you will keep the symptoms.

Now these may be the result of one specific belief, or caused by a complex of beliefs held together.

The beliefs of course will be accepted by you not as beliefs, but as reality. Once you understand that you form your reality, then you must begin to examine these beliefs by letting the conscious mind freely examine its own contents.

38

(9:40.) We will speak about health and illness more specifically later in the book. I would like to make one point here, however—that often psychoanalysis is simply a game of hide-and-seek, in which you continue to relinquish responsibility for your actions and reality and assign the basic cause to some area of the psyche, hidden in a dark forest of the past. Then you give yourself the task of finding this secret. In so doing you never think of looking for it in the conscious mind, since you are convinced that all deep answers lie far beneath —and, moreover, that your consciousness is not only unable to help you but will often send up camouflages instead. So you play that game.

When and if you manage to change your beliefs in that self-deceptive framework, then any suitable "forgotten" event from the past will be used as a catalyst. One would do as well as another.

(Pause at 9:45, one of many. Now rock music began to blare out from one of the apartments below us. I felt the very floor vibrate, but Jane, in trance, didn't seem to be bothered.)

The basic beliefs however were always in your conscious mind, and the reasons for your behavior. You simply had not examined its contents with the realization that your beliefs were not necessarily reality, but often your conceptions of it.

At the same time, in psychoanalysis you are often programmed to believe that the "unconscious," being the source of such dark secrets, cannot be counted upon as any bed of creativity or inspiration, and so you are denied the help that the inner portions of the self could give to your consciousness.

(9:50.) Usually when you do examine your conscious mind you do so looking through, or with, your own structured beliefs. The knowledge that your beliefs are not necessarily reality will allow you to be aware of all the data that is consciously available to you. I am not telling you to examine your thoughts so frequently and with such vigor that you get in your own way, but you are not fully conscious unless you are aware of the contents of your conscious mind. I am also

emphasizing the fact that the conscious mind is equipped to receive information from the inner self as well as the exterior universe.

I am not telling you to inhibit thoughts or feelings. I am asking that you become aware of those you have. Realize that they form your reality. Concentrate upon those that give you the results that you want.

If you find all of this difficult, you can also examine your physical reality in all of its aspects. Realize that your physical experience and environment is the materialization of your beliefs. If you find great exuberance, health, effective work, abundance, smiles on the faces of those you meet, then take it for granted that your beliefs are beneficial. If you see a world that is good, people that like you, take it for granted, again, that your beliefs are beneficial. But if you find poor health, a lack of meaningful work, a lack of abundance, a world of sorrow and evil, then assume that your beliefs are faulty and begin examining them.

We will later discuss the nature of mass reality, but for now we are dwelling upon the personal aspects. The main point I wanted to make in this chapter was that your conscious beliefs are extremely important, and that you are not at the mercy of events or causes that dwell far beneath your awareness.

That is the end of the chapter, and you may take a break.

("Thank you. Very good."

(10:01. There were several developments during break, and I'll try to discuss them in order before we get into Chapter Three. To begin with, Jane left her excellent trance easily, saying she had barely heard the music. It still boomed up from below us, but she wasn't interested in that. Instead she talked about "feeling sort of funny," without being able to elaborate.

(While we had a quick snack I asked her if she thought the recent strange behavior of our cat, Willy, could stem from his reactions to our own psychic states. We'd seen this happen before, although not recently. Early this month Willy had picked up a case of fleas that was stubbornly resisting treatment. He'd taken to staying outside all night as well as most of the day. He was also losing weight. Our other cat, Rooney, had always seemed to be immune to us in such matters, and even now was conducting himself in his usual leisurely fashion.

(Willy was outside now, in a light rain that had begun a couple of hours ago. At supper time he'd actually seemed to feel that the inside of the house was forbidden territory, and had refused to come in. Now I went down the back stairs and called for him as I circled the house. No Willy. I met Jane in the front hall. Here the music was even louder, thundering out from the first floor apartment.

(Once we were back upstairs in our living room, the music led me to talk about peer groups involving young people. We like rock and often dance to it; it's alive and vital. I also believe that Jane uses its energy when we hear it in the house during sessions. I commented upon the value many youths obviously placed upon conforming in their nonconformity. Jane described her own similar, intense concerns in high school and college. I had evidently chosen not to be much influenced by those factors, though; I'd always been something of a loner.

(I asked that Seth comment upon Willy's behavior, if he cared to, after dictation. Then Jane said, "I knew I was feeling funny tonight. Now I get it. It's like I've got three channels from Seth going at once . . .

("I've even got directions." She pointed off to her upper right as she sat in her rocker. "Seth comes through on his book from here, on this channel." Next she indicated her lower right. "Then over here, immediately available, is Seth on you and me and Willy. And also on the portrait you asked me about the other day—the one you just finished.

("Over here now," Jane said, designating her upper left, "is Seth on what you were just saying about peer groups—how young people feel it's so important to fit in with their own kind, and why. And why I felt that way, but you didn't. Hey, I've even got a bunch of history about that, all ready to deliver—a lot of material on each idea . . . I was really confused for a while, yet now I see that each thing's separate, already prepared by Seth. You're not going to get two sentences about one subject, then switch to another one..." Jane laughed. "Which channel do you want?"

("I'm keeping my mouth shut," I said, joking. "How about going back to the book?" I thought doing that would help her control the proliferation of channels until we could learn more about the development. The possibility had been indicated often: witness Seth's ability to discuss a variety of subjects with the members of a group, even if they were strangers to Jane. The new step in her abilities would be her conscious awareness of the blocks of material already prepared and awaiting delivery. Jane promptly agreed to resume book work.

("I've never felt just this way before—like I've been programmed in advance. It's as though I need three voice boxes. That's really weird. I do get it as sound, though. If I could talk three times at once, I could deliver finished material on those three things. Now I have to pick the right channel to get Seth back on his book; and it almost seems that if someone else came here now and mentioned a subject, I'd have that information all ready too.

("Each channel is as clear as a bell. There's no static or bleed-through between them. There: Now I've just got another one"—Jane pointed to her lower left—"and it explains all of this." She laughed again. "Just call me station J-A-N-E ...")

CHAPTER 3

Suggestion, Telepathy,
and the Grouping of Beliefs

(Seth returned in a humorous manner at 10:37.)

Now: Resume dictation. Chapter Three: "Suggestion, Telepathy, and the Grouping of Beliefs."

(Pause. Note the difference between Seth's heading for this chapter and the one Jane gave before the session.)

Ideas have an electromagnetic reality. Beliefs are strong ideas about the nature of reality. Ideas generate emotion. Like attracts like, so similar ideas group about each other and you accept those that fit in with your particular "system" of ideas.

The ego attempts to maintain a clear point of focus, of stability, so that it can direct the light of the conscious mind with some precision and concentrate its focus in areas of actuality that seem permanent. As mentioned *(in Chapter One)*, the ego, while a portion of the whole self, can be defined as a psychological "structure," composed of characteristics belonging to the personality as a whole, organized together to form a surface identity.

Now generally speaking, through the period of a lifetime, this allows for the easy emergence of many tendencies and abilities.

It permits many more potentials to emerge than would otherwise be possible. If this were not the case, for example, your interests throughout life would not change.

The ego, while appearing to be permanent, then, forever changes as it adapts to new characteristics from the whole self,* and lets others recede. Otherwise it would not be responsive to the needs and desires of the entire personality.

Because it is intimately connected with other portions of the self it does not basically feel alienated or alone, but proudly acts as the director of the conscious mind's focus. It is an adjunct of the conscious mind in that respect.

(10:51. Jane's delivery was very intent.)

Basically it understands its source and its nature. It is the portion of the mind, then, that looks out upon physical reality and surveys it in relation to those characteristics of which it is composed at any given time. It makes its judgments according to its own idea of itself.

It is the most physically oriented portion of your inner self; but it is not, however, apart from your inner self. It sits on the window sill, so to speak, between you and the exterior world. (Voice stronger for emphasis:) It can also look in both directions. It makes judgments about the nature of reality in relationship to its and your needs. It accepts or does not accept beliefs. It cannot shut out information from your conscious mind, however—but it can refuse to pay attention to it.

This does not mean that the information becomes unconscious. It is simply thrown into a corner of your mind, unassimilated, and not organized into the parcel of beliefs upon which you are presently concentrating. It is there if you look for it.

(11:00.) It is not invisible, nor do you have to know exactly what you are looking for, which of course would make the

*In larger terms Seth's ideas as to what the "whole self" is take in a great deal—with reincarnation and probable personalities, for instance, being only two of the concepts involved. The safest thing to say would be that each session, even, adds to our knowledge of what a constantly expanding whole self can be. See both *The Seth Material* and *Seth Speaks*.

situation nearly impossible. All you have to do is decide to examine the contents of your conscious mind, realizing that it contains treasures that you have overlooked.

Another way to do this is to recognize through examination that the physical effects you meet exist as data in your conscious mind—and the information that formerly seemed unavailable will be obvious. The seemingly invisible ideas that cause your difficulties have quite obvious visible physical effects, and these will lead you automatically to the conscious area in which the initiating beliefs or ideas reside.

Once more, if you become aware of your own conscious thoughts, these themselves will give you clues for they clearly speak your beliefs. If, for example, you have scarcely enough money on which to live, and you examine your thoughts, you may find yourself constantly thinking, "I can never pay this bill, I never have any luck, I'll always be poor." Or you will find yourself envying those who have more, degrading the value of money perhaps, and saying that those who have it are unhappy, or at best spiritually poor.

(11:10.) When you find these thoughts in yourself you may say, and rather indignantly: "But those things are all true. I am poor. I cannot meet my bills," and so forth. In so doing, you see, you accept your belief about reality as a characteristic of reality itself, and so the belief is transparent or invisible to you. But it causes your physical experience.

You must change the belief. I will give you methods to allow you to do this. You may follow your thoughts in another area, and find yourself thinking that you are having difficulty because you are too sensitive. Finding the thought you may say, "But it is true; I am. I react with such great emotion to small things." But that is a belief, and a limiting one.

If you follow your thoughts further you may find yourself thinking, "I am proud of my sensitivity. It sets me apart from the mob," or, "I am too good for this world." These are limiting beliefs. They will distort true reality—your own true reality.

(11:17.) These are but a few samples of the ways in which your own quite conscious ideas may be invisible to you while being available all the time, and limiting your experience.

Now we have been speaking of the conscious mind, for it is the director of your activities physically. I told you *(at the beginning of this chapter)* that it was important to realize the ego's position as the most "exterior" portion of the inner self, not alienated but looking outward to physical reality. Using this analogy, portions of the self on the other side of the conscious mind constantly receive telepathic data. Remember, there are no divisions, so the terms used are simply to make the discussion easier.

The ego tries to organize all material coming into the conscious mind, for its purposes—the ego's—are those that have come to the surface at any given time in the self's overall encounter with physical reality. As I said, the ego cannot keep information out of the conscious mind but it can refuse to focus directly upon it.

(11:25.) Now: The telepathic information, using our analogy, comes through deeper portions of the self. These parts have such an amazing capacity to receive that some organization is necessary to sift the data. Some is simply not important to you. It concerns people of whom you have no other knowledge.

You are a sender and a receiver. Because ideas have an electromagnetic reality, beliefs, because of their intensity, radiate strongly. Due to the organizing structure of your own psychological nature, similar beliefs congregate, and you will readily accept those with which you already agree.

Limiting ideas therefore predispose you to accept others of a similar nature. Exuberant ideas of freedom, spontaneity and joy automatically collect others of their kind also. There is a constant interplay between yourself and others in the exchange of ideas, both telepathically and on a conscious level.

This interchange follows, again, your conscious beliefs. It is fashionable in some circles to believe that you react physically to telepathically received messages despite your conscious beliefs or ideas. This is not the case. You react only to those telepathic messages that fit in with your conscious ideas about yourself and your reality *(emphatically)*.

Let me add that the conscious mind is itself spontaneous. It enjoys playing with its own contents, so I am not here recommending a type of stern mental discipline in which you examine yourself at every moment. I am telling you about countering measures that you can take in areas in which you are not pleased with your experience.

Do you want a break?

("Yes, I guess so.")

We will indeed then.

(Humorously: "Thank you."

(11:37. Again Jane had really been under. She didn't remember the material, and was amazed that an hour had passed. I told her I'd taken the break because I was still worried about Willy.

(Jane said she believed that "Seth could do three books at once, a chapter at a time on each, and with no confusion among them. Right now I feel that this whole book's just there, ready to be given for the writing down." Her very active dream life had evidently included a lot of preparation for it, she added, but I didn't ask her any questions that might open up more channels.

("Not since the sessions started [in 1963] have I felt that Seth's material was so richly available. I wasn't able to be that open before this—I couldn't accept a lot that was right there because it didn't fit in with my beliefs." Jane pointed to her left. "Hmmm. Now I could get stuff on archaeology, of all things. Wild . . ."

(She had doubts, though, about her ability to come through with the very technical data for the young scientist who had called her before the last session. She felt somewhat "remote" from his questions while she was so involved in producing this book. Resume at 11:55.)

Now: Give us a moment, for Willy.

In an odd way, he is himself somewhat frightened of his behavior. Ruburt has decided to leave the house more often, and be free to go outside whenever he* wishes—not to spend so much time inside because of his work. Now he has sent Willy out as a testing device, and the cat does not know exactly what has happened.

Willy likes to go out, but he is not used to being out all of the time. To an extent he feels banished. He simply picked up Ruburt's feelings, now, which are strong, and Ruburt's growing vehemence of intent. In a way these were not directed at the cat, yet Ruburt also knew the cat would pick them up.

Willy was always the house cat, you see, and Jane stayed in the house all day, writing. So it is the house cat who changes habits, rather than Rooney *(our other cat)*.

To an extent you both acquiesced, the doors being left open. You obviously have only to keep them closed. Do you follow me here?

("Yes."

(The furnace, knocked out in last June's flood, hasn't been repaired yet because of a shortage of skilled workers in the area. Everything in the house is damp and swollen. Doors especially don't work easily, if at all, so we've been taking the easy way out . . .)

Now give us a moment. Ruburt is beginning now to itch to go out, but it is the cat who itches.

("That's what I've been wondering about.")

Your Willy is in no danger, but show him your love, and regulate his ingoing and outgoing. Not that Ruburt need regulate his, but that his distraction or impatience causes the cat to overreact.

Now: Ruburt's sensing of the channels does represent a development and has been possible for some time; but it is only now entering his experience. Do remind him of his success in

---

*A reminder: Seth usually calls Jane by her male entity name, Ruburt—and thus "he," "him," etc.

this and other areas, for the feeling and reality of success can and will be carried over.

I will end our session. I will see to it that I speak about your painting before or after book dictation. *(Louder, jovially:)* I am on channel one this evening. My heartiest regards.

("Thank you.")

Good evening.

("Good evening, Seth.")

(End at 12:07 A.M. After coming out of trance Jane attempted to describe a manifestation which, though invisible, was "hovering before us now like a big oval type of thing." It was made up of a group of energies that could represent a personality like Seth, she said, yet it was nameless. It was just there, and gave her no feeling particularly that it was going to be of assistance. Jane had trouble being precise about the effect and her feelings in connection with it, and I had difficulty translating her narrative into written words. I mention it here in case something develops. She's had similar perceptions occasionally before.

(By now the members of ESP class are staying on top of each session for the book, implementing the material before the chapters are finished. So are Jane and I. It looks like all of us will grow as the book does.

(A note added a few days later: This session was held on Wednesday. We had guests the following Friday evening, and as Jane described the multiple-channel effects to them, she realized that she was tuning into some of Seth's backlog of data about peer groups and the need to conform. Seth hadn't actually given us the material during Wednesday's session, nor did he now—instead Jane verbalized it on her own to some extent. The next morning I asked her to note down what she remembered of it.

("Telling Rob and our friends about the channels that I became aware of in the last session," Jane wrote, "I suddenly began drawing upon the one with the information about conformity and the need for individual expression.

("I realized that Seth had a great amount of information all gathered and there, including the biological foundations of both characteristics. Take the amoeba, a one-celled microscopic animal, for instance: I knew that the protoplasm in the amoeba, the essential living matter, represents the individual needing-to-go-out quality. Yet the protoplasm must conform to its environment—in this case the amoeba's 'body,' which can only move as a unit when directed by the individualistic need to react to stimuli.

("The protoplasm, while reacting 'on its own,' has to take the cell form into consideration; this insures the integrity of the whole unit. To move, the protoplasm must necessarily move the whole thing.

("This is just a sample of the implications called up by Rob's talk about peer groups in the session Wednesday. The material itself has much more available on biological aspects, plus cultural and historical ones. It could also discuss the same question from the view of the growth of the human body and the development, say, of cancer cells that break out of a conforming pattern and superimpose a 'new' one, their own, on the unit structure . . .

("There—I just got that last sentence as I finished this account. That idea is something new for me, too.")

SESSION 617, SEPTEMBER 25, 1972, 9:21 P.M. MONDAY

(While we were eating breakfast this morning Jane and I heard a peculiar multiple "barking" sound that came from the sky. I leaned out of a window just in time to see a large formation of geese fly over, obviously southbound for the winter. They flew low, I thought, their formation unbalanced— one tail of their inverted V was much longer than the other; inside the V, as though being protected, flew a small group that was not in formation.

(I found the spectacle strangely moving, and so did Jane. We marveled at the inherent order in the migration, the loud

honking that so proudly demonstrated its rightness. Others, we saw, were impressed too: men doing flood repair work in a downstairs apartment came outside to stand in the driveway, staring skyward. I took the flight as another sign of nature's amazing variety and vitality—a strong reminder of values I was afraid we humans often denigrated.

(Jane's delivery as Seth was fast from the beginning of the session.)

Good evening.

("Good evening, Seth.")

We will resume dictation . . . You will react, therefore, to all the information that you receive according to your conscious beliefs concerning the nature of reality. The deeper portions of the self do not have to take the ego's idea of time into consideration, so these portions of the self also deal with data that would ordinarily escape the ego's perception, perhaps until a certain "point" of ego time was reached.

The ego, which must manipulate most directly with the everyday world, takes time, clock time, quite seriously. Even the ego however realizes to some extent that clock time is a convention; but it does not like such conventions broken.

It will often neglect any clairvoyant or precognitive material that comes into the conscious mind from the deeper portions of the self. On occasion, when the ego recognizes that such data can be highly practical, it then becomes more liberal in its recognition of it—but only when such information fits in with its concepts of what is possible and not possible.

Now the ego's concepts are your concepts, since it is a part of you. If you dwell on ideas of danger or potential disaster, if you think of the world mainly in terms of your physical survival and consider all those circumstances that may work against it, then you may find yourself suddenly aware of precognitive dreams that foretell incidents of accidents, earthquakes, robberies or murders.

Your own idea of the perilous nature of existence becomes so strong that the ego allows this data to emerge, even though it is "out of time," because your fearful beliefs convince it that you must be on guard. The incidents do not even have to involve you. From all the unconscious telepathic and clairvoyant data available, however, you will be aware of this particular grouping, and it will only serve to reinforce your idea that existence is above all perilous.

If this information becomes available in the dream state you may then say, "I am frightened of dreams. My bad dreams so often come true." So you try to inhibit memory of your dreams. Instead you should examine your conscious beliefs, for they are so strong that they are causing you not only to focus upon calamity in the physical world, but to use your inner abilities to the same end.

(9:37.) Telepathic communication is constant. This is usually at an unconscious level merely because your conscious mind is in a state of becoming. It cannot hold all of the information you possess. As an example, if your conscious ideas are relatively positive you will react to telepathically received information of a similar nature, even if you do so on an unconscious level.

As I mentioned earlier (in the 616th session), you are also sending your own telepathic thoughts outward. Others will react to those according to their own ideas of reality. A family can constantly reinforce its joy (louder), gaiety, and spontaneity by concentrating on ideas of vitality, strength and creativity; or it can let half of its energy slip away (deeper) by reinforcing resentments, angers and thoughts of doubt and failure.

("I get it."

(Seth's clever, somewhat humorous stresses in the above paragraph were intended to make certain points to me personally while he continued work on his book. Involved were discussions between Jane and me today, and some poor perceptions on my part.)

Either way the ideas of reality are reinforced both consciously and unconsciously, not only within the family but among all those with whom the family comes in contact.

You get what you concentrate upon. There is no other main rule.*

It may be easy for you to see beliefs that are invisible to others in themselves. Reading this book, you may be able to point at friends or acquaintances and see clearly that their ideas are invisible beliefs which limit their experience—and yet be blind to your own invisible beliefs, which you take so readily as truth or characteristics of reality.

Your sense data, again, will most definitely reinforce your ideas. You will also react clairvoyantly and telepathically to inner information at an unconscious level that is, once more, "collected" under the organization of your quite conscious concepts concerning existence in general, and your own in particular. So you are locked into physical situations that are corroborated by the great evidence of sense data—and of course it is convincing because it reflects so beautifully, so creatively, and so actively, your own ideas and beliefs, whether they are positive or negative.

In greater terms positive and negative have little meaning, for the physical experience is meant as a learning one. But if you are unhappy then the word negative has a meaning.

(*Pause, one of few, at 9:50.*) I expect that by now my readers have at least begun to examine their beliefs, and perhaps obtained a glimpse of some invisible ones that had been accepted before as definite aspects of reality.

Now if you are honest with your lists, you will finally come to what I call core beliefs, strong ideas about your own existence. Many other subsidiary beliefs, that earlier seemed separate from each other, should now appear quite clearly as being offshoots of core beliefs. They seem logical only in their relationship to a core idea. Once the core belief is understood to be a false one, the others will fall away.

It is the core belief which is strong enough to so focus your

---

*Here Seth quotes himself exactly from an unscheduled session held on February 26, 1972, during our vacation in Marathon, Florida.

53

perception that you perceive from the physical world only those events that correlate with it. It is also the strength of the core belief that draws up from the vast bank of inner knowledge only those events that seem to fit within its organization.

Now let me give you a brief example of a core belief. It is a blanket belief: human nature is inherently evil. This is a core belief. About it will spring events that only serve to reinforce it. Experiences—both personal and global—will come into the perception of a person who holds this belief, that will only serve to deepen it further.

From all the available physical data of newspapers, television, letters and private communication, he or she will concentrate only upon those issues that "prove" that point. Suspicion of others will grow, to say nothing about the individual's personal distrust. The belief will reach into the most intimate areas of his or her life, and finally no evidence will seem to be available to disprove it.

This is a sample of an invisible core belief at its worst. A person holding it will not trust a mate, family, friends, colleagues, country, or the world in general.

Another more personal core belief: "My life is worthless. What I do is meaningless." Now a person who holds such an idea will ordinarily not recognize it as an invisible belief. Instead he or she may emotionally feel that life has no meaning, that individual action is meaningless, that death is annihilation; and connected to this will be a conglomeration of subsidiary beliefs that deeply affect the family involved, and all those with whom such a person comes in contact.

In writing down your list of personal beliefs, therefore, leave nothing out. Examine the list as though it belonged to someone else. I did not want to imply that you make a list of specifically negative ideas, however. It is of supreme importance that you recognize the existence of joyful beliefs, and take into consideration those elements of your own experience with which you have had success.

I want you to capture that feeling of accomplishment, and to

54

translate it, or transfer it, to areas in which you have had difficulty. But you must remember that the ideas exist first and the experience physically follows.

You may take your break.

(10:06 to 10:19.)

You make your own reality. I cannot say this too often. There will be periods where all of your beliefs are at an even par, so to speak. They will agree.

The ideas may be quite limited. They may be false. They may be based upon premises that are not true. Their vitality and strength however will be quite real, and seem to bring excellent results.

"Wealth is everything." Now this idea is far from a truth. The person who accepts it completely, though, will be wealthy and in excellent health, and everything will fit in quite well with his beliefs. Yet the idea is still a belief about reality, and so there will be invisible gulfs in his experience of which he is ignorant.

On the outside the situation will look most advantageous, and while the person seems quite content, beneath there will be the gnawing knowledge of incompletion. On the surface there will be balance.

So as your beliefs change there will be alterations in your experience and behavior, and points of stress, creative stress, while you are learning. Our rich man just mentioned may suddenly realize that his belief is limiting, in that he concentrated upon it exclusively so that money and health became his sole aims. The shattered belief may leave him open to illness, which would seem like a negative experience. Yet through the illness he may be led to areas of perception he had earlier denied, and [he may] be enriched in that particular manner.

The shifting of belief may then open him to question his other beliefs, and he realizes that in the area of wealth, for example, he did very well because of his beliefs; but in those others, perhaps deeper experiences opened by his illness, he learns that human experience includes dimensions of reality that had earlier been closed to him, and that these are also easily within his reach—and without the illness that originally brought them forth. A new conglomeration of beliefs might emerge. In the meantime there was stress, but it was creative.

(10:31.) Now here is another example. Your conscious thoughts regulate your health. The persistent idea of illness will make you ill. While you believe that you become ill because of viruses, infections or accidents, then you must go to doctors who operate within that system of belief. And because you believe in their cures, hopefully you will be relieved of your difficulty.

Because you do not understand that your thoughts create illness you will continue to undergo it, however, and new symptoms will appear. You will again return to the doctor. When you are in the process of changing beliefs—when you are beginning to realize that your thoughts and feelings cause illness—then for a while you may not know what to do.

In the larger context you realize that the doctor can at best give you temporary relief, yet you may not be completely convinced as yet of your own ability to change your thoughts; or you may be so cowed by their effectiveness that you are frightened. So there is a period of stress in between beliefs, so to speak, while you dispense with one set and are learning to use another.

But here you become involved with one of the most meaningful aspects of the nature of personal reality, as you test your thoughts against what seems to be. There may be a time before you learn how to change your thoughts effectively, but you are engaged in a basic meaningful endeavor.

The truth is then that you form your reality directly. You react consciously and unconsciously to your beliefs. You collect from the physical universe, and the interior one, data that seems to correlate with your beliefs.

Believe, then, that you are a being unlimited by nature, born into flesh to materialize as best you can the great joy and spontaneity of your nature.

Now you may take a break. This will be a shorter chapter because of the previous long one.

(10:40. Jane's pace had been consistently faster than in previous sessions on the book. Break was short. Beginning at 10:45, Seth gave several pages of material for me; I'd hardly expected it. Then he wound up the session at 11:20 P.M. with this comment: "Now: Tell Ruburt there will be schools of thought built upon core beliefs. Tell him that.")

SESSION 618, SEPTEMBER 28, 1972,
9:45 P.M. THURSDAY

(The session was witnessed by writer Richard Bach and his editor, Eleanor Friede. They flew into Elmira yesterday after poor weather had delayed their scheduled arrival on Tuesday in time for ESP class. Dick had also visited us in late August, when Seth had Chapter One of this book under way.

(Jane had delivered a rather lengthy but informal session for our guests last night, as we lingered around the supper table after a late meal. Dick recorded it and is to send us a transcript, so later we'll be able to add a few excerpts from that material to this session.

(Earlier this evening Jane had sung quite spontaneously in Sumari, but her manner became more deliberate now as she began speaking for Seth.)

Now: Good evening—

("Good evening, Seth.")

—and we will resume dictation. Give us a moment. *(Pause.)* Core beliefs are those about which you build your life. You are consciously aware of these, though often you do not focus your attention upon them. They become invisible, therefore, unless you become aware of the contents of your conscious mind.

To become acquainted with your own ideas and beliefs you must walk among them, symbolically speaking, without blinders. You must look through the structures that you have yourself created, the organized ideas upon which you have grouped your experience.

To see clearly into your own mind you must first of all unstructure your thoughts, follow them without judging them,

57

without comparing them to the framework of your beliefs.

Structured beliefs collect and hold your experience, packaging it, so to speak; and so when you look at a given experience that seems like another, you put it into the same structured package, often without examination. Such beliefs can hold surprises; when you lift up the cover of one you may find that it has served to hide valuable information that did not belong there. An artificial grouping of ideas, like paper flowers, can be collected about a standard core belief.

The core belief, because of its intensity and because of your habits, will often tend to attract to itself others of a like nature. They will hang on. If you are not accustomed to examining your own mind, then you can allow separate growths of this kind to form about a belief until you cannot distinguish one from the other. This can develop to such an extent that all of your experience is seen only in relationship to this idea-growth. *(Seth called for the hyphen.)* Data that seems unrelated to this core belief is then not assimilated but thrown into the corners of your mind, unused, and you are denied the value of the information.

Separate portions of your mind can contain such chambers of inactive material. This information will not be a part of the organized structure of your usual thoughts; though the data is consciously available you can be relatively blind to it.

(10:00.) Usually when you look into your conscious mind you do so for a particular reason, to find some information. But if you have schooled yourself to believe that such data is not consciously available, then it will not occur to you to find it in your conscious mind. If furthermore your conscious data is strongly organized about a core belief, then this will automatically make you blind to experience that is not connected with it.

A core belief is invisible only when you think of it as a fact of life, and not as a belief about life; only when you identify with it so completely that you automatically focus your perceptions along that specific line.

For example, here is a seemingly very innocent core belief: "I am a responsible parent."

Now on the surface there is nothing wrong with that belief. If you hold to it and do not examine it, however, you may find that the word "responsible" is quite loaded, and collects other ideas that are equally unexamined by you. What is your idea of being responsible? According to your answer you can discover whether the core belief works to your advantage or not.

If responsible means, "I must be a parent twenty-four hours a day to the exclusion of everything else," then you may be in difficulty, for that core belief might prevent you from using other abilities that exist quite apart from your parenthood.

You may begin to perceive all physical data through the eyes of that core belief alone. You will not look out upon physical reality with the wonder of a child any more, or with the unstructured curiosity of an individual, but always through parental eyes. Thus you will close yourself off from much of physical experience.

Now telepathically you will also attract unconscious data that fits into this rigid pattern, according to the strength and stubbornness of this idea and whether or not you are willing to deal with it. You may narrow your life still further, all information of any kind finally becoming relatively invisible to you unless it touches upon your parental reality.

Now we will take a break.

(10:12 to 10:21.)

Now: The core belief just given is of one kind.

You hold some basic assumptions that are also core beliefs. To you they seem to be definitions. They are so a part of you that you take them for granted. Your idea of time is one.

You may enjoy manipulating thoughts of time in your mind. You may find yourself thinking that time is basically different from your experience of it, but fundamentally you believe that you exist in the hours and the years, that the weeks come at you one at a time, that you are caught in the onrush of the seasons.

Naturally your physical experience reinforces this belief. You structure your perception, therefore, in terms of the lapses that seem to happen between events. This in itself forces you to concentrate your attention in one direction only, and discourages you from perceiving the events in your life in other fashions.

You may occasionally employ the association of ideas, one thought leading easily to another. When you do this you often perceive new insights. As the events fall apart from time continuity in your mind they seem to take on fresh vitality. You have unstructured them, you see, from the usual organization.

As you apprehend them through association you come quite close to examining the contents of your mind in a free fashion. But if you drop the time concept and then view the conscious content of your mind through other core ideas, you are still structuring. I am not saying that you should never organize those contents. I am saying that you must become aware of your own structures. Build them up or tear them down, but do not allow yourself to become blind to the furniture of your own mind.

You can stub your toe as easily on a misplaced idea as you can upon an old chair. It will help you, in fact, if you think of your own beliefs as furniture that can be rearranged, changed, renewed, completely discarded or replaced. Your ideas are yours. They should not control you. It is up to you to accept those that you choose to accept.

Imagine yourself then rearranging this furniture. Images of particular pieces will come clearly to you. Ask yourself what ideas these pieces represent. See how well the tables fit together. Open up the drawers inside.

(10:35.) There will be no mystery. You know what your own beliefs are. You will see the groupings, but it is up to you to look inside your own mind and to use the images in your own way. Throw out ideas that do not suit you. If you read this, find such an idea in yourself and then say, "I cannot throw this idea away," then you must realize that your inner remark is in itself a belief. You can indeed throw the idea away, the second one, as easily as the first.

You are not powerless before ideas. Using this analogy, you will certainly find some furniture that you did not expect. Do not simply look in the center of your inner room of consciousness; and make sure that you are on guard against the certain invisibility that was mentioned earlier *(in this chapter)*, where an idea, quite available, appears to be a part of reality instead.

The structuring of beliefs is done in a highly characteristic yet individual manner, so you will find patterns that exist between various groupings, and one can lead you to another.

The idea of being the responsible parent, for example, may lead quite easily to other psychic structures involving responsibility, so that data is accepted on its own value. You may even think that it is wrong to view any situation except through your parental status.

The belief in guilt therefore would be a cementing structure that would hold together other similar core beliefs, and add to their strength. You must understand that these are not simply dead ideas, like debris, within your mind. They are psychic matter. In a sense then they are alive. They group themselves like cells, protecting their own validity and identity.

You feed them, figuratively speaking, with like ideas. When you examine one such belief then you obviously threaten the integrity of the structure; and so there are ways of inserting new supports, so to speak—methods to tide you over. The whole core belief need not fall down upon you as you examine its basis.

Now: I will stop at that for now, and take a break. We will be finished with this chapter shortly, and then we will begin the next. *(To Eleanor and Dick:)* I would speak faster for you, but we need the notes for the book.

(10:46. Jane's trance had been good. We were pleased that others had been present during some book dictation. The rest of the session was given over to our guests; Seth's manner became

more jovial and his pace speeded up considerably. End at about 12:30 A.M.

(Some notes added later: Dick Bach felt that he didn't really write Seagull *himself. By now the story of that book's conception is well known: Late one night in 1959, Dick was walking beside a canal near a West Coast beach when he heard a voice say, "Jonathan Livingston Seagull." No one else was around. He was astonished. He was even more so when, on his return home, the voice initiated images that gave him the bulk of the book in three-dimensional form. Then it stopped. On his own Dick tried unsuccessfully to finish the manuscript. Nothing happened until one day eight years later, when he suddenly wakened to hear the voice again—and with it came the rest of the book.*

(Who wrote it? Dick didn't claim authorship. He came across The Seth Material, *saw similarities in Jane's and his experiences, and came here to see if she or Seth could explain the phenomenon. There are points of correlation, of course, only Jane is presented not with just a voice but with an entire personality, Seth, who then writes books while she is in an altered state of consciousness. So she and Dick were highly interested in what Seth would say.*

(Besides this Jane's novel, The Education of Oversoul 7, *was written under similar [and yet different] circumstances. She describes the processes involved in her Introduction, along with the creation of some of her poetry.* *

(To Jane, these states are all aspects of the same kind of highly accelerated creativity that finally "goes beyond itself" into levels—or aspects—of reality that we don't understand clearly yet. The whole question is also relevant in cases

---

*In this book there are many examples of various kinds of altered states of consciousness on Jane's part. In addition to Seth's volume, these sometimes resulted in very creative products of her "own": Some of the psychic experiences connected with her book of poetry, *Dialogues of the Soul and Mortal Self in Time,* which she began in November, 1972, are described in the 639th session in Chapter Ten. And in the 653rd session in Chapter Thirteen, we go into those involved with the writing of her long poem, *Dialogues of the Speakers,* on April 2, 1973.

involving automatic writing, painting, singing, musical composition, etc.

(Now here are some near-verbatim quotes from the information Seth gave Dick Bach and company on the evening of September 27, 1972: "Information does not exist by itself. Connected with it is the consciousness of all those who understand it, perceive it or originate it. So there are not records in terms of objective, forever-available banks of information into which you tune. Instead, the consciousness that held, or holds, or will hold the information attracts it like a magnet... The information itself wants to move toward consciousness. It is not dead or inert. It is not something you grab for, it is also something that wants to be grabbed, and so it gravitates to those who seek it.

("Your consciousness attracts the consciousness that is already connected with the material. That is one of my goodies for the evening! Information, then, becomes new and is reborn as it is interpreted through a new consciousness, as Seagull was.

("The inner portion of your being, using those abilities that have always been yours, interpreted the information through the kaleidoscope of your own being, using the best portions of yourself—producing, then, a brilliant truth in new clothes—but in clothes that no one could have given it but yourself. Now I will tell you: If you assign the authorship of Seagull to another, then you deny the uniqueness of your own inner self.

("The truth came to you and was given to you, but the originality and uniqueness was provided by your own inner being, which may now be so separated from your conscious self that it seems to be apart from it.

("So other things were also involved—not only the birth of a book, but the emergence of the inner self, through art, into the physical universe. Now part of the focus and the strength comes from those two births, and the intensity behind them is also the reason why the book's nativity strikes the world as strongly as it does. The two are merged in the book. You are looking for the author of Seagull, and I tell you I am looking at him. He may

63

not have the face that you see when you look in the mirror, simply because you cannot see your true identity in a mirror. But I am looking at all that is visible of the author of Seagull, and you should know him best of all. And I will tell you through the years how to become acquainted with him, and more on speaking terms.

("Ruburt already has a head start on this, so I am not spoiling his fun. There are indeed 'aspects' of your own consciousness that operate in completely different environments. Environments, for example, that are not physical. There are aspects of you, therefore, that know many other kinds of information than those available to you at the conscious level now . . ."

(Note that Seth endorsed Jane's theory of Aspects. She's begun a book on the subject. In it she will explore—among other things—the nature, validity, and sources of such personalities as Seth, and the "intrusion" of intuitional or revelatory material. Once again, see her Introduction.)

SESSION 619, OCTOBER 9, 1972,
9:06 P.M. MONDAY

(My mother lives with my brother and his family in a small community in upstate New York, near Rochester, and Jane and I had spent the weekend visiting one and all. During our drive back to Elmira this morning Jane said, "Somebody's working on Seth's book, I can tell you that. I keep getting snatches of it. It's about imagination and beliefs, I think, and how they interact—only there's a lot more to it. Well," she added, pleased, "it's nice to know the work's being done . . .")

Now: I bid you good evening—

("Good evening, Seth.")

—and unless there is something you specifically want me to discuss, we will resume dictation.

("No, go ahead.")

Give us a moment, then . . . Imagination also plays an important part in your subjective life, as it gives mobility to your beliefs. It is one of the motivating agencies that helps transform your beliefs into physical experience. It is vital therefore that you understand the interrelationship between ideas and imagination. In order to dislodge unsuitable beliefs and establish new ones, you must learn to use your imagination to move concepts in and out of your mind. The proper use of imagination can then propel ideas in the directions you desire.

End of Chapter Three.

CHAPTER 4

Your Imagination and Your Beliefs, and a Few Words About the Origin of Your Beliefs

(Pause at 9:12.) Chapter Four: "Your Imagination and Your Beliefs, and a Few Words About the Origin of Your Beliefs."

In physical life, your conscious mind is largely dependent upon the workings of your physical brain. You have a conscious mind whether you are in flesh or out of it, but when you are physically oriented, then it is connected to the physical brain.

The brain to some extent keeps the mind to a three-dimensional focus. It orients you toward the environment in which you must operate, and it is because of the mind's allegiance with the temporal brain that you perceive, for example, time as a series of moments.

The brain channels the information that the mind receives to your physical structure, so that your experience is physically sifted and automatically translated into terms that the organism can understand. *(Seth-Jane spoke emphatically, rapping upon the coffee table between us.)* Because of this, physically speaking and in life as you think of it, the mind is to a large extent dependent upon the brain's growth and activity. There is some information necessary to physical survival that must be taught and handed down from parent to child. There are basic assumptions of a general nature with which you are born, but because the specific conditions of your environment are so various, these must be implemented. So it is necessary that the child accept beliefs from its parents.

These will reinforce the family group when the child most needs protection. This acquiescence to belief, then, is important in the early stages as infant develops into child. This sharing of mutual ideas not only protects the new offspring from dangers obvious to the parents; it also serves as a framework within which the child can grow.

(9:27.) This provides leeway until the conscious mind is able to reason for itself and provide its own value judgments. Later I will discuss greater aspects of the origin of ideas, but for now we will simply speak in terms of this life, the one you know.

The beliefs that you receive, therefore, are your parents' conceptions of the nature of reality. They are given to you through example, verbal communication, and constant tele-pathic reinforcement. You receive ideas about the world in general and your relationship to it; and from your parents you are also given concepts of what you are. You pick up their ideas of your own reality.

Underneath all of this, you carry indelibly within you your own knowledge of your identity, meaning and purpose, but in the early stages of development great care is taken to see that you relate in physical terms. These are directional beliefs that you receive from your parents, orienting you in ways that they feel are safe. Cushioned with these beliefs the child can be safe and satisfy its own curiosity, develop its abilities, and throw its full energy in clearly stated areas of activity.

(9:35.) So it is quite necessary that an acquiescence to belief does exist, particularly in early life. There is no reason, though, for an individual to be bound by childhood beliefs or experi-ence. The nature of some such beliefs is that while seemingly obvious ones are recognized as harmful or foolish, others connected to them may not be so easily understood.

For example: It may seem silly to you that you ever believed in, say, original sin. It may not be so obvious that many of your present actions are caused by a belief in guilt. We will have much to say about the ways in which your beliefs can be connected, simply because you are not used to examining them.

You may say, "I am overweight because I feel guilty about something in my past." You may then try to discover what the charged event was, but in such a case your trouble is a belief in guilt itself.

You do not have to carry such a belief. I am well aware that strong elements of your civilization are built upon ideas of guilt and punishment. Many of you are afraid that without a feeling of guilt there would be no inner discipline, and the world would run wild. It is running quite wild now—not despite your ideas of guilt and punishment, but largely because of them. But we will have more to say about that later in the book.

The early ideas given to you by your parents, then, structure your learning experiences themselves. They set the safe boundaries within which you can operate in early years. Quite without your conscious knowing—because your mind, connected with its brain, is not that developed—your imagination is set along certain roads.

(9:46.) Largely, but not completely, your imagination follows your beliefs, as do your emotions. To some extent there are certain general patterns. A child will cry when it is hurt. It will stop when the hurt stops, and the emotion behind the cry will automatically change into another. But if the child discovers that a prolonged cry after the event gets extra attention and consideration, then it will begin to extend the emotion.

From the earliest stages the child automatically compares its interpretation of reality with its parents'. Since the parents are bigger and stronger and fulfill so many of its needs, it will attempt to bring its experience into line with their expectations and beliefs. While it is generally quite natural for the child to cry or feel "badly" when hurt, this inclination can be carried through belief to such an extent that prolonged

68

feelings of desolation are adopted as definite behavior patterns.

Behind this would be the belief that any hurt was inherently a disaster. Such a belief could originate from an overanxious mother, for instance. If such a mother's imagination followed her belief—as of course it would—then she would immediately perceive a great potential danger to her child in the smallest threat. Both through the mother's actions, and telepathically, the child would receive such a message and react according to those understood beliefs.

Many such beliefs lie quite within the conscious mind. The grown adult, not used to examining his or her own beliefs, however, may be quite unaware of harboring such an idea. The idea itself is _not_ buried or _un_conscious. It is simply unexamined.

So one of the most hampering beliefs of all, as earlier mentioned _(in the 614th session in Chapter Two, for instance),_ is the idea that the clues to current behavior are buried and usually inaccessible. This belief itself closes to you the contents of your own conscious mind and prevents you from looking there for the answers that are available.

Now you may take your break.

(10:01. Jane said she had been really out during her trance, and that now she felt "almost drunk with exhilaration." The times noted as she delivered the material show that she'd marched along at a good pace. "On the one hand," she continued, looking a little bleary, "I could go way under and deliver the book until morning; or I could just go to bed and conk right out." She was quite curious about the reasons behind these feelings.

(I now described an effect that had started to bother me after the session had begun; it's a good little example of the way beliefs can work. No sooner had Seth come through than I became aware of an unaccustomed tightness in my writing hand—a tension that interfered with the automatic formation of the letters and words. I kept the notes going by making an extra effort, but I found it quite distracting to keep thinking about *the mechanics of writing while trying to concentrate upon what Seth was saying. The difficulty persisted through the delivery and into break.*

(I told Jane I'd thought of using the pendulum after the session to get at the cause of the hand phenomenon, since I didn't want to interrupt book dictation by asking Seth about it. [Briefly for those who have asked me: The pendulum is a very old method. I use it, with excellent results, to obtain ideomotor—"subconscious"—responses about knowledge that lies just outside my usual consciousness. I hold a small heavy object suspended by a thread so that it's free to move. By mentally asking questions, I obtain "yes" or "no" answers according to whether the pendulum swings back and forth, or from side to side.]

(As we talked about our individual hang-ups, Jane said that we had a choice: We could get material on them or continue with book work. Both channels were available from Seth, complete. Although we wanted dictation to continue we were also interested in learning more about our personal questions. Feeling somewhat guilty, we opted for the latter course—but as the material unfolded we were glad we'd done so. Resume at 10:20.)

Now: This is your information.

First of all, it is within your conscious mind. The pendulum would be a method of allowing you to view conscious material that is not structured to recognized beliefs. I want you to understand that, for the reader does not have the benefit of my talking to him personally in this way.

The belief is conscious. You are well aware of it, but you are not aware of those that cling to it. The belief is that you do not communicate well with your mother.

(Seth was quite correct. Talk about seeing the proverbial light—suddenly I saw the belief that had been right there all the time . . . Remember that Jane and I had spent the weekend visiting my mother and brother, et al.)

Hinged to this is the belief that this felt lack of communi-cation is wrong, and that for anything wrong you should be punished. In taking dictation for this book you are helping us communicate with many people, while at the same time you feel that you cannot communicate with your own parent.

These beliefs working together, then, bring about a strain in the hand that does the writing. Quite simply, you want to express through the sessions these ideas in which you so believe, and yet you feel or believe yourself guilty for doing so when you cannot describe the same ideas to your own parent.

The conflicting beliefs, then, cause the difficulty in the method. The hand's motion is not as automatically smooth as it should be. You also believe that you communicate through writing far better than you do verbally. To Ruburt you often write notes, saying things easily and beautifully that you find difficult verbally because of your belief.

("Yes . . .")

So this evening you feel guilty in reaching others through transcribing the notes, when you believe that you could not reach your mother vocally. So the method becomes involved with your beliefs.

(With a smile:) I am giving this to you to show you how beliefs work.

("I need the help, too.")

You also believe—*(humorously:)* if you wish you can under-line every "believe" while I am talking to you—that your main method of communication is painting; and here you are taking notes as a form of dissemination instead.

This would not be involved particularly were it not for the fact of two subsidiary current beliefs that conflict, having to do with the weekend. One, that you should be in Rochester, as you were, dealing vocally with your mother. And two, that you should have been here, reaching out to the world at large through your painting.

Instead, on your return you are communicating to the world through your notes—a choice you made consciously, but without being aware of the other contents of your conscious mind, and the "conflicting" beliefs. Do you follow me?

71

("Yes.")

These mentioned beliefs are obvious enough when I tell you of them, but their opposing natures gave confusing data to the body consciousness: Write and do not write.

(10:35.) The idea of punishment, the belief in it, also enters in. You do what you decided to do anyway—have the session—but by punishing yourself with your own personal interpretation.

Your mother's "condition," you <u>believe</u>, involves a lack of communication. Your brother told you about her occasionally faltering speech. Now your quite conscious interpretation of an apt kind of self-punishment was a lack of hand motion. I am trying to put this simply so you can follow the connections.

Because you believe your method of expression is primarily through your hand in painting, and you believe your mother's to be vocal, you tampered with your hand's motion—not, for example, your speech. Can you follow that consciously?

("Yes." And it was very well put, I thought as I wrote.)

Now at various times you made those conscious choices. They escaped your notice but they existed as conscious points of awareness and choice. Now do you have any questions?

(10:40. "No, I'd just like time to think about all of this.")

Now: Ruburt has recently been in the process of recognizing some beliefs that he wants to get rid of. He has been loosening them so that they rattle around within his consciousness. He is becoming aware of them. They are not as invisible as they were. He is facing many of them for the first time.

You should both become equally aware, and consciously and alertly aware, of the beneficial ideas and their importance in your lives—and this will be a portion of the book for others also.

Tonight Ruburt was exhausted, in one way, from comparing your joint beliefs with those of your brother's family; of checking his own body beliefs *(Jane touched her knee)* with theirs and seeing where his were detrimental—but also from contrasting his personal psychic and creative abilities with theirs, and that exhilarated him. The result *(smilingly)* was that he felt both exhausted and exhilarated.

I saw to it that he became aware that I was working on our book *(this morning)*. Ideas about it came into his consciousness. In the past, he did not believe that such bleed-throughs should occur, and so in his experience they did not usually emerge. They were there but his belief prevented his recognition of them.

I will from time to time give subsidiary material for Ruburt and also for you, implementing a chapter in the book for your personal use. It is vital that you realize you are working with beliefs in your mind—that the real work is done there in the mind—and not look for immediate physical results.

They will follow as surely and certainly as the "bad" results followed, and this must be a belief: that the good results will come. But the real work is done in the mind. If you do the work then you can rest assured of the results, but you must not check constantly for them. Do you see the difference?

("Yes.")

Do you have any questions?

("No. I think it's excellent material." As Seth, Jane now did something rather unusual: She turned in her rocker to look at the clock that sits to her left and somewhat behind her, on our combination bookcase and room divider.)

Now: Take a brief break. I will then add some book material to get us further into the chapter, but I will not keep you overlong.

(10:55. After Jane had come out of another "far-out trance," as she put it, I was very pleased to tell her that my writing hand was much improved and that Seth had answered her own questions. I went over the delivery with her. Resume at 11:08.)

Dictation. *(Pause.)* Your beliefs always change to some extent. As an adult you perform many activities that you believed you could not as a child. For instance: You may at [the age of] three have believed it was dangerous to cross a street. By thirty, hopefully, you have dismissed such a belief, though it fit in very well and was necessary to you in your childhood. If your mother reinforced this belief telepathically and verbally through dire pictures of the potential danger involved in street crossing, however, then you would also carry within you that emotional fear, and perhaps entertain imaginative considerations of possible accident.

Your emotions and your imagination both follow your belief. When the belief vanishes then the same emotional context is no longer entertained, and your imagination turns in other directions. Beliefs automatically mobilize your emotional and imaginative powers.

Few beliefs are intellectual alone. When you are examining the contents of your conscious mind, you must learn, or recognize, the emotional and imaginative connotations that are connected with a given idea. There are various ways of altering the belief by substituting its opposite. One particular method is three-pronged. You generate the emotion <u>opposite</u> the one that arises from the belief you want to change, and you turn your imagination in the opposite direction from the one dictated by the belief. At the same time you consciously assure yourself that the unsatisfactory belief <u>is</u> an idea <u>about</u> reality and not an aspect of reality itself.

You realize that ideas are not stationary. Emotions and imagination move them in one direction or the other, reinforce them or negate them.

(Pause at 11:23.) Quite deliberately you use your conscious mind playfully, creating a game as children do, in which for a time you completely ignore what <u>seems</u> to be in physical terms and "pretend" that what you really want is real.

If you are poor, you purposely pretend that you have all you need financially. Imagine how you will spend your money. If you are ill, imagine playfully that you are cured. See yourself doing what you would do. If you cannot communicate with others, imagine yourself doing so easily. If you feel your days dark and pointless, then imagine them filled and joyful.

Now this may sound impractical, yet in your daily life you

use your imagination and your emotions often at the service of far less worthy beliefs; and the results are quite clear—and let me add, unfortunately practical.

As it took a while for the unsatisfactory beliefs to become materialized, so it may be a time before you see physical results; but the new ideas will take growth and change your experience as certainly as the old ones did. The process of imagining will also bring you face to face with other subsidiary ideas that may momentarily bring you up short. You may see where you held two quite conflicting ideas simultaneously, and with equal vigor. In such a case, you stalemated yourself.

You may believe that you have a right to health, and yet with equal intensity believe that the human condition is by nature tainted. So you will try to be healthy and not healthy at the same time, or successful and not successful, according to your individual system of beliefs—for later in the book you will see how your beliefs will generally fall into a system of related ideas.

This is the end for the evening.

("Very good, Seth.")

(Pleasantly:) I am glad you approve.

("Good night.")

I bid you a fond good evening, and a hearty introduction to good beliefs.

("Thank you." End at 11:33 P.M. Once the session was over Jane began to yawn repeatedly, her eyes wet. My writing hand was practically free of tension now.

(The members of Jane's ESP class have been putting the ideas in Personal Reality *to good use. Strangely, this has made Jane somewhat impatient, since she can only proceed with what Seth has given so far. She finds herself in the odd position of envying future readers, who will be able to go through the finished work and make use of it as a unit.*

(The next morning Jane told me that she and/or Seth "worked on the book all night. Each time I woke up, dictation, or stuff like that, was going on. It was pretty insistent—almost

unpleasantly so at times ..." She's experienced such effects before in connection with the book. They aren't a nightly occurrence by any means, but I suggested she tell herself upon retiring that she wouldn't be aware of such activity during sleeping hours. We planned to ask Seth about it also.)

SESSION 620, OCTOBER 11, 1972, 10:00 P.M. WEDNESDAY

(Late this afternoon Jane received a call from a senior editor of Time *magazine. He wants to talk to her later this week in connection with a cover story he is to write about Richard Bach. Dick's book has become a national phenomenon. See the 618th session in Chapter Three.)*

Good evening.

("Good evening, Seth."

(Humorously:) I hope you have time for me.

("I get it. Yes.")

We will then resume dictation. *(Pause.)* Your beliefs generate emotion. It is somewhat fashionable to place feelings above conscious thoughts, the idea being that emotions are more basic and natural than conscious reasoning is. The two actually go together but your conscious thinking largely determines your emotions, and not the other way around. Your beliefs generate the appropriate emotion that is implied. A long period of inner depression does not just come upon you. Your emotions do not betray you. Instead, over a period of time you have been consciously entertaining negative beliefs that then generated the strong feelings of despondency.

If emotion could be trusted above conscious reasoning then there would be little point in aware thought at all. You would not need it.

You are not at the mercy of your emotions, either, for they are meant to follow the flow of your reasoning. Your mind is meant to perceive the physical environment clearly, and its judgments about the environment then activate the body's mechanisms to bring about proper response. If your beliefs

76

about existence are fearful, then the emotional reactions will be those leading to stress. Your own value judgments need examination in such a case.

Your imagination of course fires your emotions, and it also follows your beliefs faithfully. As you think so you feel, and not the other way around.

Later we will have some comments regarding hypnotism. Here let me mention that in those terms you hypnotize yourself constantly with your own conscious thoughts and suggestions. The term hypnosis merely applies to a quite normal state in which you concentrate your attention, narrowing your focus to a particular area of thought or belief.

You concentrate with great vigor upon one idea, usually to the exclusion of others. It is a quite conscious performance. As such it also portrays the importance of belief, for using hypnosis you "force-feed" a belief to yourself, or one given to you by another—a "hypnotist"; but you concentrate all of your attention upon the idea presented.

Here, as in normal life, your emotions and actions follow your beliefs. If you believe you are sick then for all intents and purposes you are sick. If you believe that you are healthy then you are healthy. There is much written about the nature of healing, and there will be material in this book dealing with it, but there is also healing-in-reverse, in which case an individual loses a belief in his or her health and accepts instead the idea of personal illness.

(Pause at 10:22.) Here the belief itself will generate the negative emotions that will, indeed, bring about a physical or emotional illness. The imagination will follow, painting dire mental pictures of a particular condition. Before long physical data bears out the negative belief; negative in that it is far less desirable than a concept of health.

I mention this here simply because in the overall development of an individual, an illness may also be used as a method to achieve another, constructive, end. In such a case belief would also be involved. Such a person would have to believe that an unhealthy condition was the best way to serve another purpose.

Other means would seem closed to him because of various personal beliefs that would form a vacuum in his experience—that is, he would see no other way, perhaps, to achieve the same end. This will be discussed much more thoroughly later in the book.

One belief, of course, can be dependent upon many others, each generating its own emotion and imaginative reality. The belief in illness itself depends upon a belief in human unworthiness, guilt and imperfection, for example.

The mind does not hold just active beliefs. It contains many others in a passive state. These lie latent, ready to be focused upon and used; any of them can be brought to the fore when a conscious thought acts as a stimulus.

If you are focusing upon ideas of poverty, illness or lack, for example, your conscious mind also holds latently concepts of health, vigor and abundance. If you divert your thoughts from the negative ideas to the positive ones, then your concentration will begin to alter the balance. The vast reservoir of energy and potential within you is called into action under the leadership of your conscious mind.

Because you _are_ reasoning as creatures, because you have available such varieties of experience, the [human] species developed reasoning abilities that are meant to evolve and grow as they are used. Your consciousness expands as you use it. You become "more" conscious as you exercise these faculties.

A flower cannot write a poem about itself. You can, and in so doing your own consciousness turns around about itself. It literally becomes more than it was. Existing in such diversified, rich environment-possibilities, the human psyche needed and developed a conscious mind that could make fairly concise and accurate "minute by minute" judgments and evaluations. As the conscious mind grew, now, so did the range of imagination. The conscious mind is a vehicle for the imagination in many ways. The greater its knowledge the further the reach of imagination.

78

In return imagination enriches conscious reasoning and emotional experience.

(*Slowly:*) You have not learned to use your consciousness properly or fully, so that it seems that imagination, emotions and reasoning are separate faculties, or sometimes set against each other. The mature conscious mind, once more, accepts data from the exterior world and from the interior one. It is only when you believe that consciousness must be attuned only to exterior conditions that you force it to cut itself off from inner knowledge, intuitional "voices," and the depths from which it springs.

You may take your break.

(*10:48. Jane had spoken for Seth at a deliberate pace throughout the delivery, in a rather dry voice. Her trance had been good. This proved to be the end of book work for the evening. Seth came through with five additional pages of material for Jane and me, however, and the session ended at 11:45 P.M.*)

SESSION 621, OCTOBER 16, 1972,
9:40 P.M. MONDAY

(*Seth spoke through Jane five times last week. On Monday and Wednesday evenings he furnished material on this book, plus some personal material for us; discoursed at length Tuesday night in ESP class; spoke briefly Friday afternoon to a visiting editor from* Time *magazine—subject, Freudian psychology; and on Saturday evening talked informally to a group of our friends about daily life in Italy during the time he had been a minor pope in the fourth century A.D. [Reincarnation-wise, Seth had first mentioned his papal experience in an ESP class session in May, 1971. See Chapter Twenty-two of* Seth Speaks.*]*)

(*I made just a few notes on the Saturday night material after our guests left. We'd been discussing current population problems when Seth came through to tell us that in the fourth century, infanticide—at least to his knowledge—had been quite common. Before a child was baptized it was considered to be the property of its parents, who could do with it as they wished, with no stigma attached.*

(Surplus children, who would have been "an impossible burden" upon the economy of the times, its housing, food supply, etc., were simply killed before baptism. Once the child was baptized, however, it became a sacred being, possessing a soul and the right to life . . .

(Seth added that our records of those early centuries are confused as far as the Church, baptism and children are concerned. There was quite a bit more to the session but I didn't think my memory of it was clear enough for accurate notes.)

Good evening again.

("Good evening, Seth.")

Dictation: I am not minimizing the importance of the inner self. All of its infinite resources are placed at the disposal of your conscious mind, however, and for your conscious purposes.

(Pause.) There has been on the one hand a too-great reliance upon the conscious mind—while its characteristics and mechanisms were misunderstood—so that proponents of the "conscious-reasoning-mind-above-all" theories advocate a use of intellect and reasoning powers, while not recognizing their source in the inner self.

The conscious mind was [therefore] expected to perform alone, so to speak, ignoring the highly intuitive inner information that is also available to it. It was not supposed to be aware of such data. Yet any individual knows quite well that intuitive hunches, inspiration, precognitive information or clairvoyant material has often risen to conscious knowledge. Usually it is shoved away and disregarded because you have been taught that the conscious mind should not hold with such "nonsense." So you have been told to trust your conscious mind, while at the same time you were led to believe it could only be aware of stimuli that came to it from the outside physical world.

On the other hand there are those who stress the great value of the inner self, the emotional being, at the expense of the

80

conscious mind. These theories hold that the intellect and usual consciousness are far inferior to the inner "unconscious" portions of being, and that all the answers are hidden from view. (Pause.) The followers of this belief consider the conscious mind in such derogatory terms that it almost seems to be a supercilious cancer that sprouted like a growth upon man's psyche—impeding rather than aiding his progress and understanding.

Both groups ignore the miraculous unity of the psyche, the fine natural interworkings that exist between the so-called conscious mind and the so-called unconscious—the incredibly rich interaction as each gives and takes.

The "unconscious" simply contains great portions of your own experience in which you have been taught not to believe. Again, your conscious mind is meant to look into the exterior world and into the interior one. The conscious mind is a vehicle for the expression of the soul in corporeal terms.

(A one-minute pause at 9:59.) It is your method of assessing temporal experience according to the beliefs that it holds about the nature of reality. It automatically causes the body to react in certain ways. I cannot say this often enough: Your beliefs form your reality, your body and its condition, your personal relationships, your environment, and en masse your civilization and world.

Your beliefs automatically attract the appropriate emotions. They reinforce themselves through imagination; and at the risk of repeating myself, because this is so important: Imagination and feeling follow your beliefs. It is not the other way around.

If—now, a brief innocuous-enough example—you meet an individual often enough and think, "He gives me a pain in the neck," it is surely no coincidence that you find yourself with a painful neck in future encounters with this person. The suggestion is quite a conscious one, however (emphatically), given by yourself and carried out not symbolically but most practically, most literally. In other words, the conscious mind gives its orders and the inner self carries them out.

81

In this existence you _are_ physically oriented. Surely then the conscious physically oriented mind is the one that is meant to make deductions about the nature of physical reality. Otherwise you would have no free will.

_(10:10.)_ In Western culture since the Industrial Revolution _(after about 1760)_, the idea grew that there was little connection between the objects in the world and the individual. Now this is not a history book so I will not go into the reasons behind this idea, but will merely mention that it was an overreaction, in your terms at least, to previous religious concepts.

Before that time man did believe that he could affect matter and the environment through his thoughts. With the Industrial Revolution, however, even the elements of nature lost their living quality in man's eyes. They became objects to be categorized, named, torn apart and examined.

You do not dissect a pet cat or dog, so when man began to dissect the universe in those terms he had already lost his sense of love for it. It became soulless for him. Only then could he examine it, you see, without qualm, and without being aware of the living voice that protested _(Jane now spoke in a much louder and deeper voice temporarily);_ and so in his great fascination for what made things work, in his great curiosity to understand the heredity of a flower, say, he forgot what he could [also] learn by smelling a flower, looking at it, watching it be itself.

So he examined "dead nature." Often he had to kill life in order, he thought, to discover its reality.

You cannot understand what makes things live when you must first rob their life. And so when man learned to categorize, number and dissect nature, he lost its living quality and no longer felt a part of it. To some important extent he denied his heritage, for spirit is born into nature and the soul, and for a time resides in flesh.

Man's thoughts no longer seemed to have any effect upon nature because in his mind he saw himself apart from it. In an ambiguous fashion, while concentrating upon nature's exterior aspects in a very conscious manner, he still ended up denying the conscious powers of his own mind. He became blind to the connection between his thoughts and his physical environment and experience.

Do you want a break?

(*"No."*)

Nature became then an adversary that he must control. Yet underneath he felt that he was at the mercy of nature, because in cutting himself off from it he also cut himself off from using many of his own abilities.

It was at this point that the nature of the conscious mind itself became so misunderstood, and those unrecognized or denied powers were assigned to unconscious portions of the self by ensuing schools of psychology. (*With emphasis:*) Very natural functions of the conscious mind, therefore, were assigned to the "underground" and cut off from normal use.

Now you may take your break.

(*10:29. Jane had been very well dissociated, with her delivery intense and often fast. She shook her head as she came out of trance. "Wow, was he ever going strong. Boy . . . I didn't have the slightest idea of what he was going to talk about tonight, but then I saw that he had one whole block of stuff to get through before he gave us any break . . ."*)

(*Resume in the same active manner at 10:40.*)

Now: Resume dictation. Then I will have a remark to make.

(*"Okay."*)

Give us a moment . . . Because the conscious mind has been so stressed (while stripped of many of its characteristics), there is now an overreaction occurring in which normal consciousness is being put down, colloquially speaking.

Emotion and imagination are being considered as far superior. The displaced powers of consciousness are still being assigned to the unconscious, and great efforts are being made to reach what seem to be normally inaccessible areas of awareness. To this end drugs are utilized, cults set up, and there are methods and training manuals galore. Period. Yet there is nothing basically inaccessible about such "inner knowledge or experience." It can all be quite conscious, and utilized to enrich the reality that you know. The conscious mind is not some prodigal child or poor relative of the self. It can quite freely focus into inner reality when you understand that it can. You, again, _have_ a conscious mind. You can change the focus of your own consciousness.

There have been tyrannies propagated for various reasons by the race of man upon itself. One of the greatest, however, is the idea that the conscious mind does not have any touch with the fountains of its own being, that it is divorced from nature, and that the individual is therefore at the mercy of unconscious drives over which he has no control.

Man therefore feels himself powerless. If the purpose of civilization is to enable the individual to live in peace, joy, security and abundance, then that idea has served him poorly.

(_Pause at 10:55._) When a man or a woman feels no connection between personal reality and experience and the surrounding world, then he [or she] loses even an animal's sense of pure competence and belonging. Your beliefs, once more, form your reality, shaping your life and all of its conditions.

All of the powers of your inner self are set into activation as a result of your conscious beliefs. You have lost a sense of responsibility for your conscious thought because you have been taught that it is not what forms your life. You have been told that regardless of your beliefs you are terrorized by unconscious conditioning.

The whole following sentence to be underlined: And as long as you hold that conscious belief you will experience it as reality.

(_All through these pages Jane's delivery was most absorbed and energetic. I easily felt Seth staring at me through her wide-open eyes._)

Some of your beliefs originated in your childhood, but you are not at their mercy unless you believe that you are. Because your imagination follows your beliefs, you can find yourself in a vicious circle in which you constantly paint

84

pictures in your mind that reinforce "negative" aspects in your life.

The imaginative events generate appropriate emotions, which automatically bring about hormonal* changes in your body or affect your behavior with others, or cause you to interpret events always in the light of your beliefs. And so daily experience will seem to justify what you believe more and more.

The only way out of it is to become aware of your beliefs, aware of your own conscious thought, and to change your beliefs so that you bring them more in line with the kind of reality you want to experience. Imagination and emotion will then automatically come into play to reinforce the new beliefs.

As mentioned (*in the 614th session in Chapter Two*), the first important step is to realize that your beliefs about reality are just that—beliefs about reality and not necessarily attributes of reality. You must make a clear distinction between you and your beliefs. You must then realize that your beliefs are physically materialized. What you believe to be true in your experience is true. To change the physical effect you must change the original belief—while being quite aware that for a time physical materializations of the old beliefs may still hold.

If you completely understand what I am saying, however, your new beliefs will—and quickly—begin to show themselves in your experience. But you must not be concerned for their emergence, for this brings up the fear that the new ideas will not materialize, and so this negates your purpose.

I mentioned (*in the 619th session*) a game in which you playfully adopt an idea that you want to materialize, then imagine it happening in your mind. Know that all events are mental and psychic first and that these will happen in physical terms, but do not keep watching yourself. Continue with the game.

*Hormones are the secretions formed by the ductless glands of the endocrine system—the adrenals, thyroid, pancreas, etc. These complex compounds are then carried by body fluids to other organs or tissues, where they have certain effects. Here, as always, Seth maintains that we're not at the mercy of such involuntary processes.

(11:10.) You are doing the same thing now constantly and automatically with whatever beliefs you have, and they are being as constantly and automatically translated. It is the separation of self from beliefs that is so important initially, however.

You are not to hammer at yourself consciously. Imagination and emotion are your great allies. Your conscious direction will automatically bring them into play. You can see why it is so important that you examine all of your beliefs about yourself and the nature of your reality; and one belief, if you let it, will lead you to another.

Now: Much has been written saying that if imagination and will power are in conflict, imagination will win. Now I tell you, if you examine yourself you will find *(deeper and louder)* that imagination and will power are never—underlined twice—in conflict. Your beliefs may conflict, but your imagination will always follow your will power and your conscious thoughts and beliefs.

If this is not apparent to you, then it is because you have not as yet completely examined your beliefs. Let us take a simple example: You are overweight. You have tried diets to no avail. You tell yourself that you want to lose weight. You follow what I have said so far. You change the belief. You say, "Because I believe I am overweight, I am, so I will think of myself at my ideal weight."

But you find that you still overeat. In your mind's eye you still see yourself as overweight, imagine the goodies and snacks, and in your terms "give in" to your imagination—and you think that will power is useless and conscious thought powerless.

But pretend that you go beyond this point. In sheer desperation you say, "All right, I will examine my beliefs further!" Now this is a hypothetical case so you may find one of innumerable beliefs. You may, for instance, find that you believe you are not worthy, and hence should not look attractive. Or that health means physical weight and it is dangerous to be slim.

86

Or you may find that you feel—and believe that you are—so vulnerable that you need the weight so people will think twice before they shove you around. In all of these cases the ideas will be conscious. You have entertained them often and your imagination and emotions are in league with them, and not in conflict.

(As Seth, Jane looked at the clock on our bookcase.)

Do you want a break, or do you want to end the session?

("We'll take a break.")

As you will.

(11:26. To me, Jane's very deep trance had seemed to be quite impervious, her delivery fueled by a driving energy. She confirmed that she hadn't been bothered in the slightest by anything, and added that Seth was really able to continue until dawn. It certainly seemed so.

(Moreover, she sat waiting for me to finish these notes so that Seth could return. He was ready with some personal data for us, she said, and this would be followed by more book dictation if we stayed up for it.

(Seth did return at 11:35 with some information deleted here. He also gave some unrecorded material during a freer exchange between the two of us; I described this to Jane after the session while it was fresh in my memory. At 11:52 Jane sat quietly, still in trance, while I wrote a few lines. Then she resumed book dictation at 11:55.)

Now: You may be poor. Following my suggestions, you may try to alter the belief and say, "My wants are taken care of and I have a great abundance." Yet you may still find yourself unable to meet your bills.

Imaginatively you may see the next bill coming, with you unable to pay it. "I will have enough money," you say. "This is my new belief." But nothing changes so you think, "My conscious thoughts mean nothing." Yet upon examination of your beliefs you may find a deep conviction of your own unworthiness.

You may find yourself thinking, "I am no one to begin

with," or "The rich get richer and the poor get poorer," or, "The world is against me," or, "Money is wrong. People who have it are not spiritual." You may discover, again, one of numerous beliefs that all lead to the fact that you do not want to have money or are afraid of it. In any case your imagination and your beliefs go hand in hand.

You may be trying to remember your dreams—another example. You may give yourself appropriate suggestions each night, only to awaken again with no memory of them. You may say, "Consciously I want to remember my dreams, but my suggestions do not work. Therefore what I want on a conscious level has little significance."

Yet if you examine your beliefs more carefully you will find one of many possible beliefs, such as, "I'm afraid to remember my dreams," or, "My dreams are always unpleasant," or, "I'm afraid to know what I dream about," or, "I want to remember my dreams but—they may tell me more than I want to know!"

In this case also your reality colors your beliefs, and your experience is a direct result of your conscious attitudes. By such attitudes as these just mentioned you put clamps upon your inner self, purposely hamper your experience, and reinforce beliefs in the negative aspects of your being.

Only by examining these ideas of your own can you learn where you stand with yourself. Now I do not mean to stress the negative by any means, so I suggest that you look to those areas of your life in which you are pleased and have done well. See how emotionally and imaginatively you personally reinforced those beliefs and brought them to physical fruition—realize how naturally and automatically the results appeared. Catch hold of those feelings of accomplishment and understand that you can use the same methods in other areas.

End of dictation.

("Okay.")

And unless you have questions, end of session.

("No, I guess not. It's very interesting.")

It's always a pleasure.

("Thank you. Good night.")

(12:07 A.M. As Jane came slowly out of trance she announced the title for the next chapter, which will be Five. It had just come to her: "The Future and Your Present Beliefs." "But I think there's still a little tail left to this chapter first," she said. Eyes closed, she sank back into her rocker. It took an extra effort for her to rouse herself enough to go to bed.

(A note added later: "I was wrong about this being the title of the next *chapter," Jane wrote in November, "but I know it will be one . . ." However, not only was the end of this chapter not so imminent; Seth never did use Jane's suggested chapter heading.)*

SESSION 622, OCTOBER 18, 1972,
9:40 P.M. WEDNESDAY

("It's funny. I'm still waiting for the session," Jane said at 9:35. By then, we'd been ready for twenty minutes. I hadn't really expected her to have a session tonight—but then, was my belief influencing reality? She had delivered a long and intense one Monday night, and in Tuesday's ESP class she'd "been in and out of trance all night," as she described it. This meant for about three hours; Sumari had been included, too. Jane's energy has been high for some time now.

(Then at 9:38 she said, "At last—I feel Seth around. We'll have a session after all . . .")

Now: Good evening—

("Good evening, Seth.")

—and we will begin with dictation. *(Quietly.)*

You also communicate your beliefs to others, of course. When visitors enter your home, they do not see it exactly as you do because they also view it through the screen of their beliefs. In your own environment however your personal beliefs will usually predominate.

(Pause.) People with like ideas reinforce each other's beliefs. You may meet with some misunderstanding when you suddenly decide to change your reality by changing your beliefs—

according to the circumstances, you may be going in a completely different direction than the group to which you belong. The others may feel it necessary to defend ideas that all of you previously took for granted. In such cases your beliefs merged. Each individual has his or her own ideas about reality for reasons that seem valid. Needs are met. When you abruptly change your beliefs, then in the group you no longer have the same position—you are not playing <u>that</u> game any longer.

In the group, you may suddenly cease to provide for the others a need that you satisfied earlier. This affects both intimate behavior and, say, social interactions.

(Interestingly enough, we're already beginning to hear about such frictions developing, especially from members of ESP class as they work with the ideas in this book. Other people we see regularly have similar episodes to relate.)

For a time then you may experience a feeling of loss as you move from one group of beliefs to another. However, others, sharing your new beliefs, will gravitate toward you and you to them. I will say more about this later in the book, but it explains for example why a diet-watcher, suddenly determined to lose weight, may meet with veiled or even open resistance from family or friends; why the person who makes new resolutions may find himself baffled by associates' ridicule; why the alcoholic trying not to drink finds others tempting him quite openly, or teasing him into indulgence by hidden tactics.

When someone who has been ill starts on the road to recovery through changing his beliefs, he may be quite surprised to find even his dearest allies suddenly upset, reminding him of the "reality" of his dire state for the same reasons.

New paragraph: Because beliefs form reality—the structure of experience—any change in beliefs altering that structure initiates change to some extent, of course. The status quo which served a certain purpose is gone, new elements are introduced, another creative process begins. Because your private beliefs are shared with others, because there is interaction, then any determined change of direction on your part is felt by others, and they will react in their own fashion.

You are setting out to experience the most fulfilled reality that you can. To do this you have, hopefully, begun to examine your beliefs. You may want others to change. In doing so you begin with yourself. I told you *(in the 619th session)* to imagine a game in which you see yourself acting in line with the new desired belief. As you do so, see yourself affecting others in the new fashion.

(10:01.) See them reacting to you in the new way. This is highly important because telepathically you are sending them interior messages. You are telling them that you are changing the conditions and behavior of your relationship. You are broadcasting your altered position.

Some will be quite able to understand you at that level. There may be those who need the old framework, and someone, if not you, to play the part you played before. Those people will either drop out of your experience or you must drop them from yours.

Once more, if you think of daily life as an ever-moving three-dimensional painting with you as the artist, then you will realize that as your beliefs change so will your experience. You must accept the idea completely, however, that your beliefs form your experience. Discard those beliefs that are not bringing you those effects you want. In the meantime you will often be in the position of telling yourself that something is true in the face of physical data that seems completely contradictory. You may say, "I live amid abundance and am free from want," while your eyes tell you that the desk is piled with bills. You must realize that you are the one who produced that "physical evidence" that still faces you, and you did so through your beliefs.

So as you alter the belief, the physical evidence will gradually begin to "prove" your new belief as faithfully as it did your old one. You must work with your own ideas. While there are general categories of beliefs, and general reasons for them, you must become personally aware of your own, for no one person is completely like any other. The old beliefs served a purpose and fulfilled a need.

As mentioned earlier you may have believed that of itself poverty was more spiritual than abundance, or that you were basically unworthy and should therefore punish yourself by being poor. *(See the 614th session in Chapter Two, for instance.)*

You may take your break.

(10:15 to 10:30.)

According to your energy, power and intensity, you can help change the beliefs of many people, of course.

In your daily physical life you are usually concerned simply with changing your beliefs about yourself, and then changing the beliefs others hold about you. You will find conflicting beliefs within yourself and you must become aware of these. As an example, you may believe that you want to understand the nature of your inner self—you may tell yourself you want to remember your dreams, but at the same time still hold a belief in the basic unworthiness of the self, and be quite frightened of remembering your dreams because of what you might find there.

It does no good in such a case to bemoan the situation and say, "I want to understand myself but I'm frightened that I will not like what I find." You yourself must change your beliefs. You must stop believing that the inner self is a dungeon of unsavory repressed emotion. It does contain some repressed emotion. It also contains great intuition, knowledge, and the answers to all of your questions.

Listen to your own conversation as you speak with friends, and to theirs. See how you reinforce each other's beliefs. See how your imaginations often follow the same lines. All of this is quite out in the open if you realize that it is.

Almost everyone in this society is acquainted with the old suggestion, "Every day, in every way, I am getting better and better."* Now that is an excellent suggestion, given by the conscious self to other portions of your being. The results of such a suggestion would also follow your conscious beliefs, however.

Earlier I used, "I am a dependable parent," as an example of a belief. *(See the 618th session in Chapter Three.)* If to you this means, "I give great attention to seeing that my children brush their teeth, eat enough, and perform properly," then you will interpret the "better and better" suggestion in that light.

If the belief means to you that love for children is <u>best</u> expressed in those terms, if you feel that there is something embarrassing about expressing affection directly, then the "better and better" suggestion may only reinforce that belief.

You may become more and more efficient in that manner. This is why it is vital that you examine your beliefs for yourself and understand what they mean to you personally. If, using that example, you suddenly begin to realize your position and begin to express your love to your children directly, you may find them quite surprised, delighted but confused. It may take them a while to understand your reactions, but as the old reality had a cohesiveness so will the new.

You must therefore understand and examine your beliefs, realize that they form your experience, and consciously change those that do not give the effects you want. In such an examination you will be aware of many excellent beliefs that work for you. Trace these through. See how they were followed by your imagination and emotions. If <u>possible, look in your own past</u> for points where recognizable new ideas came to you and beneficially changed your experience.

Ideas not only alter the world constantly, they <u>make</u> it constantly.

Now: We are nearly at the end of Chapter Four. I will give

---

*Seth here referred to the Frenchman Emile Coué's famous autosuggestion. Coué was a pioneer in the study of suggestion, and wrote a book on the subject in the 1920's. His ideas were well received in Europe at the time, but weren't in this country to any large degree. In fact, his lecture tour of the United States turned out to be a failure because of the hostile press reaction.

you both a rest, and we will resume at our next session. My heartiest regards to you both.

(*"Thank you very much, Seth." End at 10:54 P.M.*)

(*No session was held last Monday night.*

(*This afternoon Jane began to experience strong feelings of relaxation. These lasted well into the evening. Also, while lying down before supper she received the last three words of the title for this book:* The Nature of Personal Reality: A Seth Book. *See the notes at the end of Seth's Preface, which we received as the 609th session on April 10, 1972.*

(*Jane said she didn't want to postpone the session even though she felt "so great"—so much like just taking it easy. While we were talking about health in general, I wondered why so many people in our society wore glasses. I mention this here because the subject unexpectedly crops up in the session.*

(*Just before 9:45 Jane told me I could have material from Seth on the glasses idea, or on his book. Both channels were open. I chose this book, of course. "It's funny," Jane said, "but I know that the next [fifth] chapter is there. It's about health and sound, inside sound and outside sound." She proved to be correct, but at the moment she was unable to elaborate.*

(*The house was noisy temporarily: A carpenter in a down-stairs apartment was using an electric saw at frequent intervals as he repaired some of the damage caused by last June's massive flood. Jane's Seth voice was rather quiet, however.*)

Good evening.

(*"Good evening, Seth."*)

Dictation: Let us go on to discuss the relationship between the inner self, your conscious beliefs, and your most intimate physical creation—your human image.

End of Chapter Four.

The Constant Creation
of the Physical Body

Chapter Five. *(Pause.)* "The Constant Creation of the Physical Body."

As mentioned *(in Chapter Four),* the conscious mind is a portion of the inner self; that part that surfaces, so to speak, and meets physical reality more or less directly.

You are mainly concerned now with physical orientation and the corporeal materialization of inner reality. Therefore the conscious mind holds in ready access the information that you require for effective day-to-day living. It is not necessary that you hold in steady consciousness data that does not directly apply to what you consider your physical reality at any given "time."

(Pause, one of many.) As soon as the need for such data—aid, information, or knowledge—arises, then it is immediately forthcoming unless your own conscious beliefs cause a barrier. The exquisite, precise and concentrated focus of your conscious mind is quite necessary in physical life. It is because of this highly selective quality that you can "tune into" the particular range of activity that is physical.

In their own way, animals also possess this selective consciousness. They also focus their attention in very specific directions, perceiving from a vast general field of perception stimuli that is "recognized" and accepted in an organized manner.

Now the animals' conscious minds, connected with their physical brains, make this necessary selectivity possible. Without it there would be an "out of focus" effect that would make physical survival impossible, so certain portions of the inner self come to the foreground of being.

New sentence: Because your mind in life is connected with the brain and the physical organism, it is automatically attuned to corporeal reality, and to some extent of course it ignores some nonphysical data that lies within any given field of perception. Quite simply, it does not allow it into its organizing perceptions. It [the data] is then blocked out.

Again, this is quite necessary. There is some information and data that does not "apply" to physical reality. Some of it is perceived by "nonphysical entities" who organize it into their system of reality, where it does have meaning, but we will not be concerned with it here.

While you are physical then you will always be concentrating upon certain data to the exclusion of other data. In other kinds of realities you may ignore the physical system entirely, however, focusing instead upon those systems of existence that are not now recognized within your own.

In your present life the conscious mind assesses physical reality and has behind it all the energy, power and ability of the inner self at its disposal. Any information that it requires will be available. Its job is to assess that reality effectively, using that fine focus mentioned earlier. (See Chapter Two.) Because of its character, consciousness, or the conscious mind, cannot be swamped by too much detail, too much information. The inner self sends to it only the information it asks for or feels necessary. To a very large extent then conscious beliefs act as great liberators of such inner data, or as inhibitors of it. Are you following me?

("Yes." Seth asked the question because of a prolonged burst of hammering from the apartment below us. 10:16.)

The conscious mind is itself developing and expanding. It is not a thing. It learns through experience and through the effects of its behavior. The inner self brings about whatever results the conscious mind desires.

It does not leave the conscious mind at loose ends nor isolate it from the fountains of its own being. Because the conscious mind is part of the inner self, it is obviously made of the same energy, filled with the same vitality, and revitalized by the deep sources of creativity from which all being emerges.

You must understand that it is not cut off from the inner self. The inner self keeps the physical body alive even as it formed it. The miraculous constant translation of spirit into flesh is carried on with inexhaustible energy by these inner portions of being, but in all cases the inner self looks to the conscious mind for its assessment of the body's condition and reality, and forms the image in line with the conscious mind's beliefs.

So—once more—you form reality through your beliefs, and your most intimate production is your physical body. Your beliefs about it are constantly fed into inner data. You organize on an unconscious level the atoms and molecules that compose your cells to form your body. But the blueprint is made by your conscious beliefs. To change your body you change your beliefs, even in the face of physical data or evidence that conflicts.

You each have a body and you each have a consciousness. You can practice with these ideas by applying them to your body. For now we are taking into consideration the fact that, generally speaking, you are not going to make yourself five physical feet taller if you are a grown adult already, because there are certain physical laws with which you must contend. We will discuss those more fully later.

In that context you can even appear taller, and affect others as if you were—which would usually be what you wanted in any case under the circumstances. But except for some conditions which will be mentioned later, you can become healthy if you are ill, slim if you are overweight, gain weight if you prefer, or alter your physical image in profound fashion through the use of your ideas and beliefs.

They form the blueprint by which you make your body, whether you have known this or not. Your body is an artistic creation, formed and constantly maintained at unconscious levels, but quite in line with your beliefs about what and who you are.

You may take a break.

(10:37 to 10:55.)

Now: Dictation: You constantly give yourself suggestions about your body, your health or ill health. You think about your body often, then. You send a barrage of beliefs and instructions to the inner self that affect your physical image.

As I mentioned earlier, your thoughts have a very definite vital reality. Beliefs are thoughts reinforced by imagination and emotion concerning the nature of your reality.

Now thoughts in general possess an electromagnetic reality, but whether you know it or not, they also have an inner <u>sound</u> value.

You know the importance of exterior sound. It is used as a method of communication, but it is also a by-product of many other events, and it affects the physical atmosphere. Now the same is true about what I will call <u>inner sound</u>, the sound of your thoughts within your own head. I am not speaking here of body noises, though you are usually oblivious to these also.

Inner sounds have an even greater effect than exterior ones upon your body. They affect the atoms and molecules that compose your cells. In many respects it is true to say that <u>you speak your body</u>, but the speaking is interior.

The same kind of sound built the Pyramids, and it was not sound that you would hear with your physical ears. Such inner sound forms your bone and flesh. The sound exists connected with but quite apart from the mental words you use in thinking.

(Pause at 11:05. It might be noted here that Seth devoted a group of sessions last November, December, and January to some of the meanings and uses of inner and outer sound. That material was new to us, and included information on the Egyptians' use of "inaudible" sound to help build the Pyramids; according to Seth the Romans also employed such sound in erecting the enormous, truly awesome city of Heliopolis at Baalbek, in what is now the Middle Eastern country of Lebanon. See the continuation of these notes at the end of the session.)

It does not matter in which language you are addressing yourself, for example. The sound is formed by your intent, and the same intent—I am putting this simply now—will have the same sound effect upon the body regardless of the words used.

(As Seth, Jane paused during her delivery. She evidently changed her mind about just what to say and how to say it.)

But usually you think in your own language, and so in quite practical terms the words and the intent merge. For all practical purposes then the two are one. When you say, "I am tired," mentally you are not only giving silent messages to yourself—I say messages rather than message because the general statement is broken down; many portions of the body must be affected before you feel tired—but beside this the inner sound value of the messages automatically affects the body in just that way.

What should you do, then, if you find yourself feeling tired? This is your conscious assessment of your body's reality at a given time. You want to change it so you do not reinforce it. Instead you say mentally that the body can now begin to rest and refresh itself. You take your initial judgment for granted then without restating it, and instead suggest the remedy be carried out *(positively)*.

You can, if the conditions warrant, physically rest by lying down or making whatever adjustments seem appropriate. If none are possible then several such suggestions—that the body can refresh itself—will give you benefit. To tell yourself over and over that you are tired, however, reinforces the condition.

99

The inner sound value of the countering suggestion automatically begins to refresh the body. It is fashionable now to think about noise pollution, yet the same kind of circumstances occur with inner sound, particularly when your inner thoughts are self-contradictory, scrambled and random.

(11:23.) Diverse and highly conflicting instructions are then given to the body. As you should know, the body's inner environment changes constantly, and it is you who change it. Change is quite necessary and as a rule the body's overall balance is maintained. But the directions that you give are often not clear or advantageous, and your beliefs largely determine the kind of information you send to that environment.

The inner self always attempts to maintain the body's equilibrium and health, but many times your own beliefs prevent it from coming to your aid with even half of the energy available to it. Often only when you are in dire straits do you open up the doors to this great energy, when it is much too clear that your previous beliefs and behavior have not worked.

You have at your disposal the means to insure your health. My friend Joseph *(as Seth calls me)* brought up a point concerning this before our session. He wanted to know why so many in this country wore glasses. He wondered if people unacquainted with glasses and suddenly introduced to them would develop a need for them; and they would.

Many individuals are given glasses to correct an eye difficulty at an early age. Left alone, in many cases, the eyes would correct themselves. The glasses can impede any such self-correction by providing a crutch that further weakens eye muscles, for example, and instead fixes the condition. When you believe that only glasses will correct poor vision then only glasses will.

Instead you must discover the reason for the belief behind the physical poor function or nonfunction, and if this is done the condition will automatically clear up. Now for most people it is easier to get glasses.

We will end dictation.

("Okay.")

We will be going into the medical profession and it is too late for that . . . Now Ruburt should go along with the continuing relaxation sessions as they occur, and try to capture his mental state then in ordinary times. And I bid you a fond good evening.

("Good night, Seth. Thank you very much.")

Tell him that my energy has always been available to him. He can use it freely and fully. It will not negate or block out <u>my</u> existence. It is available at all times, and it is also his by <u>right</u>, and <u>mine</u> by right. It belongs to all beings by right. It is <u>simply</u> manifested in many ways at many times. And good night.

("Good night."

(End at 11:37 P.M. Jane still felt more or less relaxed—"floppy." She laughed. "I haven't done a damned thing since three o'clock this afternoon, except get supper and have the session. And right now I feel pretty fine."

(We think her relaxation follows naturally enough in the wake of her prolonged, intense psychic activity. She had no session Monday night, for instance, nor did Seth come through in ESP class last night—and she's already called off her writing class for this Thursday afternoon.

(Adding to the 11:05 note on sound: The 1971-72 sessions mentioned there also contained much about the inner meanings of sound and Jane's development and use of Sumari—and once again I refer the reader to her Introduction. As Seth told us, "Sumari effectively blocks the automatic translation of inner experience into everyday verbal stereotypes." One of its services will be to teach Jane to free her inner cognitions enough so that she can translate Speaker manuscripts without distorting them out of all proportion.

(As with Sumari, we expect that references to the Speakers will be included in this book from time to time. In reincarnational terms, the Speakers are teaching personalities who reach across the centuries. Seth commented in Chapter Twenty of Seth Speaks: *"The Speakers, more than most, are highly*

active through all aspects of existence, whether physical or nonphysical, waking or sleeping, between lives or at other levels of reality . . ."

(Ironically, many of the very ancient Speaker "manuscripts" are entirely verbal. They weren't put into writing because of the beliefs of the times.)

SESSION 624, OCTOBER 30, 1972, 9:45 P.M. MONDAY

Now: Good evening.

("Good evening, Seth.")

We will continue dictation.

To be healthy you must believe in health. A good physician is a changer of beliefs. He will replace an idea of illness with one of health. Whatever methods or drugs he uses will not be effective unless this change of belief takes place.

Unfortunately, when man became a labeller he also made maps, so to speak, of great complexity, categorizing various diseases with greater effectiveness than ever before. He studied dead tissue to discover the nature of the disease that killed it. Physicians began to think of men as carriers of disease and diseases—which, in certain terms, they [the physicans] did themselves create through some new medical procedures.

The old medicine men often dealt far more directly with the patient himself, and understood the nature of beliefs and the prime importance of suggestion. Many of their techniques were adopted for their psychological shock value, in which the patient was quite effectively "brainwashed" out of the disease he believed that he had.

The present medical profession is sadly hampered because of its own beliefs. Often it operates as a framework in which poor health and disease are not only accepted as normal, but the concepts behind them strengthened. Here you have again, as in psychoanalysis, a hide-and-seek arrangement in which both doctor and patient take part. *(See the 616th session in Chapter Two.)*

Both believe they need the other, of course. Behind this is the psychic pattern of beliefs in which the patient often assigns to the doctor the powers of knowledge and wisdom that his beliefs have taught him he does not have. Knowing otherwise, the patient still <u>wants</u> to consider the doctor omnipotent.

Upon the patient a doctor often assigns and projects his own feelings of helplessness against which he combats. The interactions continue with the patient trying to please the doctor, and at best merely changing from one group of symptoms to another. Far too often the doctor shares the patient's unshakeable belief in poor health and disease.

Not only this, but the medical profession often provides blueprints for diseases, and the patient too often tries them on for size. This is not to say that the medical profession often is not of great aid and benefit, but within the value system in which it operates much of its positive influence is negated.

Because they are held in such high esteem, the suggestions given by doctors are paid particular attention. The patient's emotional condition is such that he or she readily accepts statements made under such circumstances less critically than usual.

The naming and labelling of "diseases" is a harmful practice that to a large extent denies the innate mobility and ever-changing quality of the psyche as expressed in flesh. You are told that you have "something." Out of the blue "it" has attacked you, and your most intimate organs, perhaps. You are <u>usually</u> told that your emotions or beliefs or system of values <u>have nothing to do</u> with the unfortunate circumstances that beset you.

(10:08.) The patient, therefore, often feels relatively powerless and at the mercy of any stray virus that might come along. The facts are that you choose even the <u>kind</u> of illness that you have according to the nature of your beliefs. You are immune from ill health as long as you believe that you are.

These are quite practical statements. Your body has an overall body consciousness filled with energy and vitality. It automatically rights any imbalances, but your conscious beliefs also affect this body consciousness. Your muscles believe what you tell them about themselves. So does every other portion of your physical body.

While you believe that only doctors can cure you, you had better go to them, because in the framework of your beliefs they are the only people who can help you. But the framework itself is limiting; and again, while you may be cured of one difficulty, you will only replace it with another as long as your beliefs cause you to have physical problems.

Now the same applies to what is frequently called spiritual healing. If through the concentrated use of psychic energy your body is cured by such a healer, you will also simply trade those symptoms for others unless you change your initial beliefs. Now sometimes a healer or a doctor, with his effectiveness in healing a condition, will show you by inference that the healing energy was always within yourself, and this realization may be enough to allow you to change your beliefs about health entirely.

In such a case you will realize that your previous ill health was caused by your belief. If you have any physical problems, concentrate instead upon the healthy portions of your body and the unimpeded functions that you have. In the healthy areas, your beliefs are working for you.

As I mentioned *(in the last session),* inner sounds are extremely important. Each of the atoms and molecules that compose your body has its own reality in sound values that you do not hear physically. Each organ of your body then has its own unique sound value too. When there is something wrong the inner sounds are discordant.

The unharmonious sounds have become a part of that portion of the body as a result of the inner sound of your own thought-beliefs. That is why it is vital that you not reinforce these inner sounds through repeating the same negative suggestions to yourself. Verbal suggestions are translated into inner sound. This passes through your body in somewhat the same way that some kinds of light do.

You may take a break
(10:25 to 10:35.)

Now: While you are physical creatures, then your perceptions must be <u>largely</u> physically oriented. Even your bodies exist in other terms than you usually suppose.

You perceive them as objects, with bulk, composed of bone and flesh. They also have "structures" of sound, light, and electromagnetic properties that you do not perceive. These are all connected with the physical image that you know. Any physical disabilities will show themselves in these other "structures" initially.

The sound, light, and electromagnetic patterns give strength and vitality to the physical form that you recognize. They are more mobile than the physical body, and even more susceptible to the changing pattern of your own thought and emotion.

I told you that thoughts are translated into this inner sound, but thoughts always attempt to materialize themselves also. As such they are incipient images, collectors of energy. They build up their own embryonic form until it is in one way or another physically translated.

Mental images therefore are extremely powerful, combining inner sound and its effects with a clear mental picture which <u>will</u> seek physical form. Your imagination adds motivating and propelling power to such images, and so you will find that many of your beliefs are entertained by you in an inner visual manner. They will have mental pictures connected with them.

One such image may represent one particular belief or it may stand for several. As you make lists of your beliefs you will find some of these pictures coming into your mind. Look at them as you would a painting you have created. If you do not like what you see then quite consciously change the picture in your mind.

These images are interior, yet because they are so a part of your beliefs you will see them exteriorized also in your experience.

(10:48.) Let me give you a simple example. You have a sore toe. Now and then you see it quite clearly in your mind. You

may find yourself looking at the toe more frequently than usual, and you may also find yourself picking out from the populace anyone who is not walking properly. These people might escape your notice ordinarily, but suddenly the world seems to be full of sore toes.

We are dealing to make a point with a belief already made physical. But if you continued such concentration the toe either would not heal or would develop into a worse condition. Behind all this, of course, would be the belief that caused the difficulty; but once you have brought about a group of symptoms you must be very careful that you do not begin to view your field of reality from that position. When you do, you add both inner and outer images that reinforce the condition.

There is light then that you do not see with physical eyes, as there is sound that you do not hear with your ears. These combine to mentally form the physical image that you know, so you must work from the inside out. Your beliefs are your palette, using the analogy of a painting again.

Your thoughts give the general outline of the reality that you physically experience. Your emotions will fill in the patterns with light. Your imagination will forge these together.

The sound of your inner thoughts is the medium that you actually use. This is far more than an analogy, however, for in simple terms it explains quite clearly the way in which your beliefs form your reality. In quiet moments the word "O-O-O-Q-O-M-M-M-M-M," said slowly, mentally or aloud, will be of benefit in toning up your general physical condition. The sounds contain within them a built-in impetus toward energy and well-being, as I will explain shortly.

Now—I am going to end for this evening. I will resume however at our next session. If you have questions I will answer them.

(*"No . . ."*)

Then I bid you a fond good evening.

(*"The same to you, Seth."*

(*Louder:*) And my heartiest regards to you both.

("Thank you. Good night." End at 11:05 P.M. Jane remembered none of the material she'd delivered since last break.)

SESSION 625, NOVEMBER 1, 1972,
9:03 P.M. WEDNESDAY

(Jane's delivery was leisurely and quiet as the session began.)
Now: Good evening.

("Good evening, Seth.")

Dictation: The body reacts not so much to physical sound as to the interior sounds into which the physical sounds are translated. As mentioned *(in the last two sessions),* it also reacts to sounds that have no physical "counterparts."

There are certain properties within the structure of the chromosomes that must be activated by specific internal sound values. If this activation does not take place then the "attributes" latent within the chromosomes remain so.

There are chains of influence that are actually composed of inner values of sound that thread together, as it were, the complicated interweavings of both the genes and chromosomes.

I am taking this slowly to explain it as simply as possible.

("Yes." See the definitions of genes and chromosomes in the 610th session in Chapter One.)

These sound values are literally interwoven in an electromagnetic pattern. The sounds weave *(gesturing)* themselves through, and help form this pattern. The activity of cells within the body also causes what you might call minute explosions of interior sound. *(Long pause.)* The electromagnetic and inner sound patterns are impinged upon by certain kinds of light. Together these all form the prototype upon which, and out of which, the physical body is formed.

Now: When you create a mental image in your mind it is composed of the same properties just mentioned. A mental image then is also a pattern of internal sound with electromagnetic properties imbued with certain light values. In a sense, and a very real one, the mental image <u>is</u> incipient matter; and

107

any structure so composed, combining the electromagnetic sound and light values, will automatically try to reproduce itself in physical existence, or materialization. *(Long pause.)* There is a definite connection, then, with the nature of such images and the way in which your body itself is composed.

(Pause at 9:25.) Electrons, atoms, and molecules* all have their independent interior sound and light values. There are definite sounds produced when messages leap from your nerve ends.** It is very difficult to explain some of this, but there is "invisible" light, then, and inaudible sound, that affects your body and helps form the pattern about which it <u>constantly</u> emerges.

The body is obviously continually created during your present lifetime, in your terms. It is not a mechanism once created, then left to fend for itself. You were not given a certain amount of "life force" at birth that you use up as you go along, contrary to many schools of thought.

(9:28.) The atoms and molecules within you are quite literally dying and being completely replaced all the time. You are being created physically each instant. Period. The body reacts to exterior sounds and to the stimuli brought to it by the physical senses. These patterns of reaction can be clearly shown. They are <u>all</u> that is presently observable, however, of far greater interactions that also occur.

The atoms and molecules that compose your cells and your flesh, for instance, do not react to the physical sounds that you hear or to the light patterns that your physical eyes perceive. In times of danger your entire body must be able to move swiftly. The hormonal system must react with great rapidity, sometimes completely changing the balance of a moment earlier. The

---

*There is a steady progression in complexity involving the three. Electrons are negatively charged particles circling a nucleus on which there are an equal number of positive charges; together these make up an atom; groups of atoms combine to form molecules.

**Seth tells us in Chapter Nineteen of *Seth Speaks:* "Molecular structures send out their own messages, and unless you are tuned in to perceive them, they may be interpreted as meaningless noise."

muscles must be immediately alert, and the entire body flexible enough to respond as a whole. This includes every organ and the most minute portion.

Say you are in the middle of a street and suddenly a car is about to hit you. It has come seemingly from nowhere. The cells that compose your intestines, your heart, your muscles obviously do not see the car as "you" do. Yet the whole system must be instantly activated, and the data that "you" perceive must be translated in terms that will energize every portion of your body.

This is done by translating exterior stimuli into interior stimuli, but the physical carriers of the data are all that scientists or physicians have been able to follow thus far. The greater interactions have not been perceived, and the true story of the decoding of such messages *(much louder abruptly)* <u>has not been understood</u>—and take your break.

(9:40. Jane's trance had developed into quite a profound one but, typically, she was soon out of it. "Wow, he's going to town tonight," she exclaimed. "He gave me a break now only because he's going into something more, and he doesn't want to interrupt it. I couldn't tell you what that was about, and yet I have an idea . . . I think Seth wishes I had a better vocabulary for body things."

(Resume in the same manner at 9:57.)

Now: *(Pause.)* The nerves are also composed of the same kind of interior structures as mentioned earlier *(in this chapter)*: around, or rather from which, the physical nerves form. Here the exterior data is translated and broken down into inner terms. That is, it is decoded in terms of the internal sound, light, and electromagnetic patterns discussed before.

It then becomes usable information, even in terms of the atoms and molecules that compose the cells. The physical lapse that occurs between an incoming message *(pause, frowning)*, and its intended destination does not occur on these other levels. The "interior message" gets to its destination ahead of the physical one.

By the time the organism responds the inner patterns have already reacted, and this must and always does precede any physical response to stimuli. Therefore the invisible body pattern, composed of its interior light, sound and electromagnetic properties, reacts first, and actually initiates the later physical response.

(Slowly:) There is always this translation of exterior stimuli. The perceived lapse noted by scientists is of course the physical one (leaning forward, hand to closed eyes), caused by the "time" it takes the message to leap the nerve endings.* The interior translation however is simultaneous.

Now return in your mind to the situation of the near accident. That event with the car, its driver, and your own precarious position, exists as another structure beside the one that you physically see. It also—the event—exists in the terms mentioned earlier, in a reality composed of invisible light, inaudible sound, and electromagnetic patterns.

Consciously you react to the physical data—the noise, the squeal of brakes perhaps, the visual shock of seeing the car so close, but the entire inner reality of that scene or event is instantly "recognized" by what I refer to as your inner senses. (See the note at the end of the session.) These respond to the interior patterns I've told you about. The physical data is carried through the nerves with the necessary time lapses that must occur. These represent the temporal end of the spectrum of perception.

Because you are flesh and blood creatures, the interior aspects of perception must have their physical counterparts. But material awareness and bodily response to it would be impossible were it not for these internal webworks.

Now before you see anything physically, you do so through these inner pathways. The interior perception activates the outside one. When you experience physical motion or activity,

*Here Seth refers to the way the nervous impulse passes from one neuron, or nerve cell, to the next as it traverses the body's nervous system. The junction between two neurons is called the synapse.

110

events or phenomena, you are becoming aware of the tail end of a long "series" of interior comprehensions. I am saying that all exterior events, including your own bodies with their insides, all objects, all physical materializations, are the outside structures of inside ones that are composed of interior sound and invisible light, interwoven in electromagnetic patterns.

(10:28.) Beneath temporal perception, then, each object and event exists in these terms, in patterns that interact with each other. On a physical level you seem to be separated from everything that is not yourself. This is not true, but in your day-to-day existence it seems to be, and it is an assumption that you usually take for granted.

(Pause.) On the interior level of which I have been speaking, all happenings and objects are connected. A movement or change in one affects others. You will physically respond to and recognize some of this alteration, as in the example of the near accident. But whether or not you are consciously aware of such activity, it changes the interior environment of your body through these inner pathways.

Your own thoughts and beliefs, having the same kind of inner reality, also transform the interior environments of others. The near-accident mentioned was a physical event but it was initially a mental one. It existed in this nontemporal reality then before, in your terms, it was physically materialized, perceived and reacted to.

It was propelled from inner reality to outward reality through belief, emotion and imagination. Because you cannot see them, it may seem to you that these qualities are not as real, say, as an object. Physically you can only see the results of an emotion, for instance. You cannot hold it in your hands as you can a stone.

Ideas represent your psychic intent. They generate emotion and imagination. These activate the interior patterns. They are the motive force of action *(pause),* the means by which all interior events are exteriorized. They are energy formed and directed, formulations of interior and exterior patterns of

111

reality. They are a part of the creative force from which all realities spring. Again, we run into difficulties in explanation simply because there are few verbal equivalents for what I am trying to say.

(*Deliberately:*) Imagination and emotions are the most concentrated forms of energy that you possess as physical creatures. Any strong emotion carries within it far more energy than, say, that required to send a rocket to the moon.

(*Very forcefully:*) Emotions, instead of propelling a physical rocket, for example, send thoughts from this interior reality through the barrier between nonphysical and physical into the "objective" world—no small feat, and one that is constantly repeated.

You may take a break.

(*10:47. "Boy, I'm telling you I was out that time, I really was," Jane said. "The house could have fallen down, I think . . . I had that thing again where you're in it so deep that you're a part of it—the feeling where you're in the guts of things.*

(*"It's a real weird kind of inner focus. There's a great kind of fulfilling sense of triumph, doing it, like you're pulling stuff out of the secret nature of things. I can't say where you go or what you do. After all this time I'm still amazed that [this book] comes out all finished," she said. "Usually I don't want anybody else around for this. You cut out everything else—other people would cause you to pick up on them, or be distracting . . ."*

(*Seth had something to say about this last thought not long ago. The following quotes are extracted from some deleted material: "Generally speaking, it is better if book dictation is done alone, or with those with whom you are well acquainted and easy. This is simply because there are less psychic distractions, and it is easier for Ruburt to focus into one clear channel.*

(*"The needs and desires of others naturally enter in," Seth continued, "and some energy must be used to close them out. The more interested and excited [witnesses] are, of course, the more their own concerns ring out. It is difficult for Ruburt to block out these additional psychic distractions . . . With strangers the sessions are often personal, however, because their own emotional reactions are so vibrant initially . . ."*

(*Supplementing Seth's mention of the inner senses during the last delivery: He's told us about nine of these so far, and a list of them can be found in Chapter Nineteen of* The Seth Material. *There are more to come, too.*

(*This break, it developed, marked the end of book dictation. Seth returned with other material, though, and the session lasted until 11:45 P.M.*)

SESSION 626, NOVEMBER 8, 1972,
9:06 P.M. WEDNESDAY

(*No session was held last Monday evening.*

(*Yesterday Jane and I read the* Time *magazine cover story for November 13, 1972, featuring Richard Bach and his book,* Jonathan Livingston Seagull. *We were very pleased for Dick. The article also included information about the Seth material. See the 618th session in Chapter Three for an account of Seth's meeting with Dick and the latter's editor, Eleanor Friede.*

(*It isn't necessary to go into dates and other details here; but several days before we were told that the Bach story's originally scheduled appearance in late October had been postponed, Jane had a vivid dream giving her that literal information. She wrote Dick about it and told others. Her dream was also fairly accurate concerning the magazine's cover painting for the piece: a montage featuring "a bird that was somehow a part of a man's head, or face," as she described it. Actually* Time's *design showed a seagull superimposed over Dick Bach's head, partially obliterating it.*

(*Monday night, Jane had another vivid dream involving the Seth material, herself, and a certain kind of magazine story. She's written it down, and we'll see how it turns out.*)

Good evening.

(*"Good evening, Seth."*)

Dictation. (*Pause. Then humorously:*) An aside to you: Now,

you see, I can speak in Time or out of it. Underline "Time."
  ("*Yes.*")

The physically alive body, its activities and condition, are directed through the beliefs of the conscious mind. The body, as explained in this chapter, also has "invisible" counterparts composed of the electromagnetic properties and the interior sound and light qualities.

These invisible structures preceded the emergence of the physical body. They also exist after the body's death. While the condition of the body is directed by the conscious mind in life, then, the idea or mental pattern for the body existed before the conscious mind's connection with the physical brain.

The genes and chromosomes do not just happen to have within them the precisely definite coded information that will be needed. The data is impressed upon them from within. The identity exists before the form. You could say that the identity, existing in another dimension entirely, plants the seed into the medium of physical reality from which its own material existence will spring.

Therefore the inner self forms, first, the "invisible" body structure which will "later" emerge in flesh. At the event of this mental seeding, the conscious mind, in your terms, is obviously not connected with the brain, which has not yet been formed in flesh. The idea of the body is held and made physical by a conscious mind.

New paragraph: Consciousness then is not dependent upon physical perception, though this attribute does require an awareness immersed within a material form. While physical consciousness is sifted through the bodily apparatus, you are usually unaware of noncorporeal kinds because of that process. The general framework, properties and characteristics of the body exist, therefore, before its formation. In simple terms, you choose ahead of time the kind of body you will inhabit and impress. It may seem to you that you do not have any conscious control over your body's condition in life as you know it, much less before your birth. You have been taught that there is little connection between your thought and your body's activities.

(9:29.) A man believing he has heart trouble will finally, through his own anxiety, affect the functioning of his "involuntary" system until his heart is definitely harmed if the belief goes unchecked. The conscious mind directs the so-called involuntary systems of the body, and not the other way around. No idea slips insidiously past your awareness to affect your involuntary system unless it fits in with your own conscious beliefs. Once more, you will not be sick if you think you are well—but there may be other ideas that make you believe in the necessity for poor health.

You are not aware of how the body performs its many involuntary functions. The conscious mind could not handle all that data, but those functions perfectly mirror your consciously held ideas and beliefs.

As I also mentioned *(in the 614th session in Chapter Two),* the conscious mind is not basically cut off from the inner self or from those deep inner sources of knowledge available to it. The aware mind is not any one event, for that matter; it represents various portions of the inner self that "surface" at any given time.

Within the basic framework of the body chosen before physical birth (for reasons that will be discussed later), the individual has full freedom to create a perfectly healthy functioning form. The form is, however, a mirror of beliefs, and will accurately materialize in flesh those ideas held by the conscious mind.

(Jane's delivery was very serious, and somewhat loud. She leaned forward and tapped upon the coffee table between us, her eyes wide and dark.)

That is one of the body's primary functions. A sick body is performing that function then, in its way, as well as a healthy one. It is your most intimate feedback system, changing with your thought and experience, giving you in flesh the physical counterpart of your thought. So it is futile to become angry at a symptom, or to deride the body for its condition when it is presenting you with the corporeal replica of your own thought, as it was meant to do.

Your environment and your experience in the physical world also provide you with the same kind of feedback. It is just as useless to berate your environment or your experience in it as it is to deride your body, for the same reasons.

It often seems, when such ideas as these are presented, that the ideal results in your terms would be perfection—"heaven on earth"—a state in which everyone would be healthy, wealthy, and wise.

(*Now Seth asked me to open a beer for Jane. "I don't want to give him a break yet," he added—the "him" stemming from Jane's male entity name, Ruburt. It was obvious that Jane was in a very deep trance. Our house was turning noisy but she showed no signs whatever of unease. Instead, she sat quietly waiting for me to pick up my notebook . . .)*

You are, however, in physical existence using your body as a medium for learning and expression. You are each unique. (*Pause.*) Many of you for your own reasons pursue courses that do not involve an even development of abilities, an overall balanced picture, for example, but choose to express and experiment with certain qualities to the exclusion of others. Such a course would not, in physical reality, present you with anything like a balanced picture of perfection.

(*9:50.*) Later in the book we will discuss other kinds of existence in which you are also involved; and these to some extent color your intents and purposes in physical life as you now understand it.

If all of your beliefs, not just your "fortunate" ones, were not materialized, you would never thoroughly understand on a physical level that your ideas create reality. If only your "positive" beliefs were materialized then you would never clearly comprehend the power of your thought, for you would not completely experience its physical results.

116

The conscious mind exists before material life and after it. In corporeal existence it is intertwined with the brain, and during physical life your earthly perceptions—your precise and steady focus within your particular space and time system—are dependent upon that fine alliance.

(Pause.) Before physical birth then you form a mental concept of the body you will have. This image is impressed into matter in this way: You tune yourself into a highly specific dimension of reality. You form a physical structure that will have existence within that intensely concentrated area, that will have validity and actuality—that will come alive within those "frequencies" (very positively).

Now it is here that the seeming division in the self occurs, for in physical life the conscious mind must be connected with the brain, and in terms of time that organ itself must grow and develop. So all of your consciousness cannot be physically aware. The portion that must "wait for" the brain's development is the part you call in life "the conscious mind."

The other portions can be called the inner self. Now all of this inner self cannot become expressed even with its connection with the brain, since the brain must sift perception through the physical apparatus.

You may take your break. Because of the noise distractions in the house I kept Ruburt in trance longer—it is easier that way.

(10:06. Jane's hour-long trance had indeed developed into a profound one. "Man, have I been out," she said, trying to keep her eyes open. She finally gave up and leaned back in her rocker. "Are you tired of writing?" I said I wasn't.

("Well, I guess we'll go on, then," she said. She took her glasses off. Seth returned in a few moments. As soon as he did Jane's eyes came wide open, and her manner grew animated and intense once more. Resume at 10:10.)

The brain with its bodily connections must deal with the time lapses that sensual perception always imply. The interior workings of the body, to be conscious, would have to deal with

117

time sequences that would present the physically attuned consciousness with "mathematical" deductions and calculations far too numerous for it to handle. For example, it would have to keep conscious track of all the muscles, nerves, organs, cells, molecules and atoms, while manipulating the body in space and time.

Therefore a seeming division occurs, in which a portion of the invisible conscious mind is connected with the physical brain, and a portion of it is free of that connection. That [latter] part forms what you think of as the involuntary system of the body.

Again, it is important that you realize the initial nonphysical reaction to stimuli that sparks off all physical reactions. There is constant interplay and communication between the areas of consciousness that are connected to the brain and those that are not. The "deeper" purposes of the consciousness involved "circulate," sometimes arising in the awareness that is joined with the brain. Information coming from those deeper sources of the self, reaching the areas connected to the brain, will be interpreted according to the beliefs of that most physically focused segment of the self.

To some degree, such inner data will be colored by the current beliefs of that part of the self most directly confronting the physical world. Those beliefs, however, are also constantly being examined by the inner self.

And now, I suggest that you end the session—

("All right," I said, in some surprise.)

—but we have a good portion of the material through. So *(smiling)* count your blessings.

(End at 10:27 P.M. Jane slowly emerged from a deeply dissociated state. The rather abrupt end of the session came, she finally said, just because she had been tiring. This proved to be the end of Chapter Five.)

118

CHAPTER 6

*The Body of Your Beliefs,
and the Power Structures of Beliefs*

SESSION 627, NOVEMBER 13, 1972,
9:21 P.M. MONDAY

*(Over the last few days Jane has received a number of tele-
phone calls—as well as letters—from people about the country,
asking for help from her and/or Seth. Some of the problems
cited are quite severe, and often they're beyond any reasonable
[let alone quick] therapy that Jane, Seth, or I can offer.
Because of our own sympathetic reactions Jane and I often end
up feeling frustrated; also, to help but a few people with any
thoroughness means that we'd have no time left for the rest.
Apropos of Jane's efforts to personally do what she can, she
received a visitor recently who displayed signs of a secondary
personality . . .)*

*(As we waited for the session tonight, Jane said two
channels from Seth were open: Seth could speak on the people
who have been seeking her out, or give book dictation. She
chose to continue with the book, saying that it will help
numbers of people far beyond anything she can do
individually.)*

119

Good evening.

(*"Good evening, Seth."*)

Dictation: Chapter Six: "The Body of Your Beliefs, and the Power Structures of Beliefs." This is the heading.

Quite literally, you live in the body of your beliefs. You perceive through the body of your beliefs. Your beliefs can increase your vision or diminish it. They can increase or diminish your hearing, or any sense function.

If, for example, you believe that after a certain time of life hearing will fade, then so it will. You will begin to use the faculty less and less, unconsciously transfer your attention to the other senses to compensate, and rely less and less upon your ears until the functions themselves do atrophy. Period.

Functions in this particular regard are habits. You simply forget how to hear properly, following your belief. All of the minute manipulations necessary to hearing are unconsciously repressed. The actual physical deterioration then does indeed follow. The deterioration however does not occur first, but after.

The same kind of development can occur in almost any physical category. Usually more than one belief is involved. Parallel with the belief that vision will fail, you may have the before-mentioned belief that hearing will dim, and these two ideas may be reinforced by a belief that age automatically makes you less a person, turning you into an individual who can no longer relate in the daily pattern of environment. The belief, you see, would work to insure the materialization of that state. (*Pause.*) On the other hand you may believe that wisdom grows with age, that self-understanding brings a peace of mind not earlier known, that the keen mind is actually far better able to assess the environment, and that the physical senses are much more appreciative of all stimuli. And so those conditions will be physically met in your experience. The physical apparatus itself, following your beliefs, will continue in health.

You must understand, again, that your ideas and thoughts do not exist as phantoms or shadow images without substance.

They are electromagnetic realities. They affect your physical being and they are automatically translated by your nervous system into the stuff of your flesh and of your experience.

(9:36.) Your conscious mind is meant to assess and evaluate physical reality, and to help you chart your course in the corporeal universe of which you are presently part. Other portions of your being, as mentioned *(in the last session, for example)*, rely upon you to do this. All energy at the inner self's disposal is then concentrated to bring about the results asked for by the conscious mind.

Your effective power of action follows the lines of your beliefs. To believe in your own weakness is to deny yourself the power of action. To accept uncritically all beliefs that come to you is to open yourself to a barrage of conflicting data at best, in which the clear lines of action and power become blurred. Contradictory demands and assessments are then sent in to the inner self, which by various methods will try to tell you that something is wrong. Beliefs of like nature attract each other, for you are bound to look for consistencies in your behavior and experience.

(Pause.) You must learn to deal with your own beliefs directly or you will be forced to deal with them indirectly—by reacting to them quite without knowing it in your physical experience. When you rail against an unfavorable environment, or a situation or condition, basically—and underline the following phrase—you are not acting independently, but almost blindly reacting. You are reacting to events that seem to happen to you, and always in response to a situation.

To act in an independent manner, you must begin to initiate action that you want to occur physically *(emphatically)* by creating it in your own being.

This is done by combining belief, emotion and imagination, and forming them into a mental picture of the desired physical result. Of course, the wanted result is not yet physical or you would not need to create it, so it does no good to say that your physical experience seems to contradict what you are trying to do.

(*Pause.*) Because ideas and beliefs have this electromagnetic reality, then, constant interplay between those strongly contradictory beliefs can cause great power blocks, impeding the flow of inner energy outward. At times a polarization can occur. Unassimilated beliefs, unexamined ideas, can seem to adopt a life of their own. These can effectively dominate certain areas of activity.

You may take your break.

(*9:50 to 10:10.*)

Now, dictation: Not long ago Ruburt was presented with a demonstration embodying the nature and power of beliefs.

He received a phone call from a man who lived in another state. There was a request for an interview. Without knowing why, Ruburt felt an impulse to see the man, and set up an appointment. The visitor arrived from the airport with his wife in tow.

He was a study, a living example, of the effects of conflicting unexamined beliefs, a fierce and yet agonized personification of what can happen when an individual allows his conscious mind to deny its responsibilities—i.e., when an individual becomes afraid of his own consciousness.

Here was a young man whose beliefs were alive with their own life while he was relatively powerless. No effort had been made to reconcile directly opposing beliefs, until the personality itself was quite literally polarized.

(*10:20.*) You were faced with what could be called a classic instance of secondary personality. I am discussing it here because it so beautifully illustrates the nature and power of beliefs, and the conflicts that can arise when an individual does not accept responsibility for his own thoughts. This is not a usual case—but to some extent or another, such a division occurs physically or mentally when the contents of the conscious mind are not examined.

Entering, the man bristled with belligerence and hostility. Having requested help, he then hated himself for the weakness that he believed caused such a need. He glowered at our friend

Ruburt with great vehemency, projecting all of the energy at his command to show that he would not be cowed, and that if anyone took over the situation he would be the one to do so. He spoke of another personality far more powerful than he—though, he said, he could force a roomful of a hundred-and-fifty people to follow his commands. The other personality, however, originated in another galaxy, and came as a friend to help and protect him.

At his behest [he said] this invisible friend killed a lawyer. The lawyer not only did not understand the condition, according to the story, but hurt the feelings of the man under discussion. We will call the man Augustus.

Take a break for Ruburt . . .

(10:30. Jane had begun coughing intermittently after last break. Now she coughed so steadily that Seth interrupted the delivery—which is a pretty rare occurrence. While Jane rested, I suggested that if Seth returned it would be better if he discussed the reasons behind her coughing. This was done. Surprisingly, the material received ran to several pages. The session ended at 11:43 P.M.)

SESSION 628, NOVEMBER 15, 1972, 9:29 P.M. WEDNESDAY

(In Monday's session Seth had started a discussion of Jane's recent visitor, "Augustus," who had shown definite signs of a subordinate or secondary personality. As we sat for tonight's session Jane said, "I know what Seth's going to call Augustus's other personality: 'Augustus Two.' " We were amused, thinking of Seth and Seth Two.* Now, Jane began speaking slowly in trance.)

Good evening—

("Good evening, Seth.")

---

*For more extensive material on Seth Two, see Chapter Seventeen of *The Seth Material*, and Chapter Twenty-two of *Seth Speaks*. In the latter Seth tells us: "Seth Two stands relatively in the same position to me as I stand to the woman [Jane] through whom I am now speaking."

—and we will resume dictation . . .

To begin with, Augustus was brought up to believe that the inner self was dangerous, that individuals reacted because of inner conflicts over which they had little conscious control. *(Gesturing:)* He believed that the individual personality was relatively powerless to understand itself and that it stood precariously alone and undefended, with a chasm of evil beneath and with an unattainable, cold, just, but not compassionate Good (with a capital "G") above.

He felt bewildered in a world of opposites. Conflicting beliefs were uncritically accepted. *(Pause.)* The conscious mind will always attempt to make sense out of its beliefs, to form them into patterns and sequences. It will usually organize ideas in as rational a way as possible, and dispense with those that seem to contradict the overall system of its beliefs.

Augustus had been taught to fear his own thoughts, to avoid self-examination. Beliefs or ideas that frightened him were not faced, therefore, but initially shoved into corners of the conscious mind, where they lay relatively harmlessly in the beginning.

As time went on the number of unexamined, frightening beliefs began to accumulate. Ideas and beliefs do feed upon themselves. There is within them a built-in impetus toward growth, development and fulfillment. Over the years two opposing systems of beliefs built up strongly, vying for Augustus's attention. He believed that he was utterly powerless as an individual, that despite all his efforts he would come to nothing, go unnoticed. He felt completely unloved. He did not feel worthy of love. At the same time he let his conscious mind wander, and to compensate saw himself as all-powerful, contemptuous of his fellow human beings, and able to work greater vengeance upon them for their misunderstanding of him. In this line of beliefs he was able to do anything—cure mankind's ills if he chose, or withhold such knowledge from the world to punish it. Period.

Now all of these ideas were quite conscious, but he held each group separately. The conscious mind, again, tries to obtain overall integrity and unity, lining up its beliefs into some kind of consistent system. When opposing beliefs that directly contradict each other are held for any length of time, and little attempt is made to reconcile them, then a "battle" begins within the conscious mind itself.

(Pause at 9:50.) Since it is the beliefs of the conscious mind that regulate the involuntary bodily motions and the entire physical system, then contradictory beliefs obviously set up adverse physical reactions and imbalances. Before Augustus's opposing beliefs lined themselves up into separate camps, so to speak, the body was in continual turmoil; contradictory messages were constantly sent to the muscular system and the heart. The hormonal system teetered. Even his physical temperature varied rather drastically.

Because like ideas do attract like, both electromagnetically and emotionally, the conscious mind found itself with two complete contradictory systems of belief, and two self-images. *(Pause.)* To protect the integrity of the physical structure, Augustus's conscious mind neatly divided itself up. No longer were the minute-to-minute messages to the body scrambled.

(Slowly:) The part of Augustus who felt powerful and alien became personified. When Augustus felt threatened then the conscious mind switched over, accepting as operating procedure the system of beliefs in which Augustus saw himself as all-powerful, secure—but as alien. This part of his beliefs, therefore, and this particular self-image, took over his conscious mind and became what we will here call Augustus Two. When Augustus Two assumed leadership then the physical body itself was not only strong and powerful, but capable of physical feats far surpassing those of Augustus One.

(10:01.) Augustus Two, you see, believes that his body is nearly invincible, and following this belief the body <u>does</u> perform much better. Augustus Two believes that he is an alien. In this case the rationale—because there must be one—is that he is a being from another planet, in fact from another galaxy. His

125

purpose in this case is quite clear and simple: He is to help Augustus One, to use his power on the latter's behalf, rewarding his friends and terrifying his enemies. Augustus One quite deeply believes he needs this kind of help.

Now this is a split of the conscious mind. It does not originate within the inner self. When Augustus Two takes over he is quite conscious. He simply views physical reality through an undeviating system of beliefs. The messages sent to the body are not in the least contradictory. The body is under excellent control.

Augustus One's moods of course were a direct result of the ideas he was entertaining. It was this unceasing swing from high states of exaltation and power to low ones of powerlessness and depression that the body could not tolerate, because of the vast alterations entailed. For the greater periods of time Augustus One predominates, since his ideas of worthlessness, in your terms, were adopted earlier; and worse—are only reinforced by the contrast between him and Augustus Two. Augustus Two comes on sometimes for as long as a week at a time.

He does all the things and says all the things that Augustus One would dearly love to do and say, with only certain safeguards. Augustus One, however, is not literally unconscious during this time, but quite aware of the "vicarious" activities and fulfillments. Again, it is a game of hide-and-seek, in which the so-called unconscious mind is relatively innocent.

Augustus Two can therefore rant and rave, lie and cheat, assert himself, show his contempt for his fellows, and absolve Augustus One of any responsibility.

You may take your break and we will continue.

(10:19 to 10:30.)

Now: There is nothing evil in the nature of Augustus Two. In spiritualistic circles however he would most certainly be interpreted as an evil spirit or guide.

His nature is protective. The basic ideas and beliefs that have been personified into his being, that became his being, were formed to protect Augustus One from the destructive ideas given to him in his childhood, to combat the beliefs in power-lessness and futility. To that degree they were added onto the original ideas, but still at an early age; so it was from the child's concept of a powerful being that Augustus Two sprang.

The greater the feelings of weakness then the greater the compensating feelings of power and strength—but, again, with no attempt at conscious reconciliation.

(Pause.) Augustus's mother noted only that her son seemed highly changeable. Augustus Two did not present himself as obviously "another personality" until after Augustus's marriage, when the demands of fatherhood and making a living were placed upon him. He could not cope.

His beliefs in his unworthiness prevented him from using his abilities, or even pursuing a course of effective action, with any persistence. It was then that Augustus Two began to assert himself—and to Augustus's wife. In his own way Augustus Two would prove to her that she was married to quite an unusual, powerful man, a paragon of virility and strength; but to do so Augustus One must appear as Augustus Two to her. This con-tinued for some time. Augustus One would first develop a splitting headache, and then this alien from outer space would arrive: the commanding male that Augustus One was not.

(Pause.) Here, however, the "deception" brought about certain difficulties. Not only was Augustus Two more sexually promiscuous, but by contrast Augustus One seemed very pallid indeed. Augustus Two was originally intended to help Augustus One. It's true that the exotic conditions spilled over, casting some glamor on Augustus One when Augustus Two left for a time, but the contrast was too blatant, too out in the open. Augustus One, still the primary personality, became even more frightened. He knew that gradually Augustus Two was outliving his purpose, showing him up, and had to go.

(10:46.) In fact, once Augustus Two obviously "took over" the body of Augustus One, it was all out in the open in the family. The wife began to take notes of what was done and said. When these events were repeated to Augustus One later, the

127

lying and cheating was evident. So was the infantile nature of the "personality"; yet Augustus Two purported to be all-wise, from a galaxy far surpassing Earth in every category of endeavor. And here he was making predictions that never happened, and boasting and lying like a trouper.

The beliefs whose energy generated this "alternate self-image" then appeared in the daylight, acting out their natural results in physical reality. Augustus One, now in manhood, was forced to perceive the nature of these beliefs to some extent, yet when he was here visiting Ruburt he still would not examine them.

Augustus Two has not taken over now for two and one-half months. Augustus is in a dilemma, for he still holds intact the beliefs in his own powerlessness, and the contradictory beliefs of omnipotence are not now being expressed through Augustus Two. Yet expressed they will be; and so in the interview Augustus One—who we will now simply call Augustus—at one moment came through with his gigantic belligerence, staring at Ruburt and telling him that he could annihilate anyone who hurt him. In the next moment the great plea for help would surface, the love of his wife and child. In one sentence Augustus would make a statement, and ten minutes later make it clear with another remark that the first fact had not been true.

Here the polarity between Augustus One and Two had dissolved, so that the two opposing systems of belief operated alongside each other. Still Augustus would not examine his own words, his own thoughts, or see the contradictions so obvious to others.

The nature and importance of belief appeared so eloquently that Ruburt was astounded, and found himself forced into some complicated psychological footwork. The two "personalities" were no longer separate, but merging.

(Pause at 11:00.) Augustus said, "My friend killed a neighbor of mine who was against me by giving him pneumonia. He looks out for me." Another neighbor has ulcers, and Augustus told Ruburt that after he touched this neighbor the ulcers seemed to have been healed. So he said, "I would like to know how much of this great ability belongs to me." And looking briefly away: "Perhaps I do not need my friend to protect me after all." Now this was definitely to the good, in that Augustus was beginning to feel that perhaps he was not powerless. His own personality, however, is left to handle the definitely unsavory characteristics of an Augustus Two who is no longer personified.

He is left with the questions: "If I am so powerful, how is it that I am so weak, and cannot even support my family? If I am so great, why cannot I effectively use my energy?"

For the body of Augustus is once again under the sway of beliefs about himself that are highly contradictory. Before, he was physically powerful when he was Augustus Two, and weak when he was Augustus One. Now as Augustus he is alternately strong and weak, and the body stresses are apparent. As Augustus Two he could stay up night and day and perform physical tasks quite difficult for the normal human being to do, for he operated under the indivisible idea of power and strength.

It has taken some courage for him to let Augustus Two vanish. Because the neat division of beliefs no longer exists, however, he will seem even more difficult to his wife since the characteristics of Augustus Two now "bleed into" his own. He will lie for example where before only Augustus Two lied.

Here then is a case where directly opposing beliefs dominated the conscious mind at various times, each operating the body in its own manner. Physically the body has the same capacity for strength regardless of which group of ideas were dominant; but practically speaking, Augustus One was incapable of performing the feats of Augustus Two.

Augustus Two once leaped from a second-story window to the ground in anger, and without injury—a highly unusual feat. Augustus, however, is so exhausted that he can barely get through a normal day. You had a situation in which an individual, through beliefs, put his power and energy literally beside himself He could use it only when he switched beliefs completely.

It was only because the childlike characteristics of Augustus Two finally appeared so blatantly that Augustus Two had to be dispensed with. Augustus's wife made the difference, for it was obvious that she did not have the same opinion of this "friend" that her husband had. Her beliefs then became the new foundation, the one point of change that allowed Augustus to view this alternate self-image with any kind of detachment at all.

(*Humorously:*) You may take your alternate break.

(*11:22. Jane remembered nothing of what Seth had said. But as soon as she came out of trance—which was quickly, as usual—she told me, "I can tell that Seth's got more on that right there, all ready and waiting . . . In between sessions I don't feel aware of that usually, though I dream about it sometimes . . ."*

(*This was the end of book work for the evening. After break Seth came through with two pages about a matter I'd brought up earlier tonight. Thus the recorded session ended at 11:51 P.M.*

(*The session resumed, however, after I had put my notebook aside. During a spontaneous exchange, Seth delivered some insights concerning his own origin and creative aspects, and why Jane's personality would make the emergence of a Seth possible. There was more. I didn't write down what was said, and as usual ended up wishing I had—perhaps we'll take the time to recoup it during a session.*

(*I've always found that the material seems to fly away unless it's recorded at once in some fashion. One of the reasons for this, I've often thought, is because Jane isn't the only one who's in a trance during a session—the receiver [myself, for instance] is too, in his or her own way. When the connections between Seth and his audience are broken, the material is to some degree "left behind" in that common meeting area.*)

SESSION 629, NOVEMBER 29, 1972,
9:28 P.M. WEDNESDAY

(*As usually happens at this time of year, we've begun to miss some regularly scheduled sessions. Jane and I figure that from now on they'll probably be held irregularly into January, 1973; partly because of our holiday activities, which we enjoy, but also because this seems to be a natural time of rest for us— although Jane plans to keep her ESP and writing classes going as usual.*

(The first portion of this session is deleted. Seth resumed book dictation on Chapter Six at 9:59.)

There is no real adequate framework in your society in which people like Augustus can be treated with any effectiveness.

An analyst might consider Augustus as schizophrenic and label him neatly, but such terms are basically meaningless. If the analyst, over a period of time, should convince Augustus that his condition in the present resulted from some specific inhibited event in the past, and if the analyst was an intuitive and understanding man, then Augustus might change his beliefs enough so that some kind of "cure" was worked. He would then conveniently remember such an event and display the expected emotions as he re-experienced it. Unfortunately in his present state, powerless as it were without Augustus Two, he might also simply call on his "alter ego" to show the good doctor that he was no one to trifle with.

Then there would be the matter of helping Augustus to face the implications of his other-self's behavior in such a way that he could accept it as a portion of his whole identity.

When Augustus Two was in control of the body the chemical makeup varied considerably. It showed significant differences over Augustus's usual hormonal status. The chemical changes were caused by the transition in beliefs that operated, and not the other way around.

(Pause at 10:08. See the material on hormones and beliefs in the 621st session in Chapter Four.)

If chemical alteration were made in Augustus Two he <u>would</u> return to the Augustus One personality, but the change would be artificial—not permanent, and possibly quite dangerous.

The chemically inhibited tendencies would to some extent be forcefully blanketed through medication. The problem would

131

remain, though, and it is quite possible that overt suicidal tendencies could result; or more insidious hidden suicidal inclinations, where vital organs would be attacked.

Sometimes such cases are handled within another framework, in which Augustus would be considered possessed by an independent "evil" entity whenever Augustus Two took over. Now again, if Augustus somehow changed his beliefs it is possible that even within that framework some kind of cure would be effected. But at the same time the dangers and difficulties would make such a cure relatively impossible.

If a practitioner who believed that Augustus was possessed then convinced Augustus of the "fact," their joint charged beliefs might possibly work for a while. Convincing Augustus that he was under the domination of an evil entity would be step one. Step two, getting rid of the intruder, could at least follow. The trouble is that working within that framework, the self-structure is further weakened, for the normally repressed characteristics of Augustus Two are forever denied. Augustus must then always be "good," and yet he would always feel vulnerable to another such invasion of evil. The same results as those given could be possible: the growth of suicidal tendencies or other self-destructive behavior.

You may take your break.

(*10:23. "When all this started [in late 1963] about speaking in trance," Jane said, "I used to feel that there was just one word available at a time, with nothing before it or after it—but now I sense whole blocks of material there just waiting to be given. Like the stuff on the Speakers tonight, earlier.* * *It's like that more and more often . . ." Before the session Jane had again been aware of several channels of information available from Seth.*

(*Resume at 10:45.*)

*Jane referred here to the deleted part of tonight's session, and Seth's discussion therein of the work we are to do in translating early Speaker material: "The Speaker manuscripts are in your future, and will involve as I told you considerable work—a labor of love." See the notes following the 623rd session in Chapter Five. Also consult Chapter Seventeen in *Seth Speaks*.

Dictation: Luckily the human mind and body are far more flexible, durable and creative than ever given credit for. Many cases like Augustus's never come to light. The individuals involved cure themselves. Sometimes this is done when such a person chooses to undergo a traumatic experience—often one part of the personality will plan this quite deliberately while the other portion closes its eyes. These events can seem to be disasters or near disasters, and yet they can sufficiently mobilize the entire personality for survival's sake. In a moment of high critical tension the personality may put itself together again.

Such critical-uniting episodes usually do not involve long sicknesses, though they may, but instead events such as bad accidents. The difficulty may be exteriorized as a broken limb, for example, instead of a broken self, and as the body is repaired the necessary assimilation of belief takes place.

There are various kinds and stages in such cases. Each individual is unique. Sometimes the framework includes another method of cure, in which portions of each conflicting side of the personality break off to form a clearer psychological structure which can communicate with the other two, act as a referee, and reconcile the opposing beliefs held by each.

This is done many times without the main personality realizing what is really going on. On occasion automatic writing is utilized, or the Ouija board. Both are methods to uncover invisible conscious beliefs—that are accepted by you consciously at any given time, say, and deliberately ignored at another given time.

When people using such methods are told that their writing comes through from a demon or the devil, or an evil spirit, then those invisible beliefs are shoved farther away. Any search into the mind becomes frightening and dangerous, since it might lead to further such "invasion."

Now such invasion is usually the sudden appearance of previously unacceptable beliefs, quite conscious but invisible, tucked away. Then they suddenly appear as alien. In most instances the possession concept makes it all the more upsetting. Easier to face, often, is the idea that the responsibility for such ideas must belong to another entity or being. In all cases of this nature involving Augustus-type episodes, the problem is one of unassimilated beliefs. Instead of such comparatively drastic behavior, however, such beliefs can be expressed through various parts of the body. Unfortunately, a system of medicine that largely deals with symptoms only encourages a patient to project such beliefs on new organs, for instance, after already sacrificing others in operations.

The solutions lie in the conscious mind—I cannot emphasize this too strongly—and in those beliefs that you accept about the nature of reality and, specifically, about the nature of your being.

While the most basic work must be done by the individual, help is always available from a variety of sources, both within and without. You will literally interpret and use almost any data that comes to you as helpful, and it will be highly effective—unless your beliefs lead you to think, perhaps, that everyone is against you, or that you are beyond help, or that you do not deserve it. Other such ideas can also close you off from help, of course, but you will instinctively look for it and use it when possible.

You may take a break or end the session as you prefer.

("We'll take the break."

(11:15 P.M. I chose a break in order to see if Jane still wanted me to ask Seth about the ideas she'd talked about before the session. She had been tired earlier, but had revived considerably by now; nevertheless she decided to forego the questions and end the session.)

SESSION 630, DECEMBER 11, 1972,
9:26 P.M. MONDAY

(Jane and I sat for the session at about 9:15. At 9:25 she abruptly told me that she'd just "received" the title of a book I am to write: Through My Eyes. *She was very surprised—and so was I. At first, Jane said, she interpreted her information [from*

134

Seth?] to mean that I would be writing a chapter with that title for one of her own books. But then she quickly realized that this is to be a work of my own.

(It's supposed to express my views of the Seth experience, and how it has influenced or changed my ideas on art, life, and so forth. Then, as Jane told me about all of this, she announced that Seth was coming through right away—a most unusual procedure as far as our regular sessions are concerned. She took off her glasses . . .)

Now: The book title should be: "Through My Eyes," and it should be your own book, covering in your own way many important areas. You have writing ability, as you know.

. The book should cover your version of our joint experience—your own philosophical explanation of it, the questions it arouses within your own mind, your observations of Ruburt as Jane and in our trance states. Other portions should explain your own ideas concerning creativity as you <u>feel</u> it in yourself—the differences and similarities between your experience when you paint a picture from "usual" inspiration and when first of all you perceive the psychic impression that leads to a painting. Some illustrations from an initial sketch to a completed painting should be included.

Give some thought to experimentation, observing the nature of color in usual consciousness and in altered states. Pay attention to color in your dreams also. You should go into your own ideas about the people you paint, and why, being fascinated with portraits, you often do not use models.

The book can include some of the material I have given you on art through various channels, and how you have applied it. This work can be followed by one utilizing sessions concerned with art mainly but covering some other artistic areas as well, such as the nature and origin of inspirations.

I have given you an outline that I am sure you can follow. The book should be fun to write besides, and combine your writing and painting abilities. The title is a good one and the book will sell. You will be able to get a contract on it, with advance, and writing it will also serve as a spurt for your painting. I am being tricky here.

(*"Are you?" I tried to bait Seth a little here.*)

I am indeed. For this will short-circuit some of your hang-ups as far as painting is concerned and will lead to new spontaneous painting power (*humorously*). You will also consider it a work of merit, and you will be doing your own thing with your experience. I know that the impetus alone will quite slyly and automatically produce some excellent paintings. You will want to use them. I will not tell you in what particular way this sneaks by some of your problems now, or which ones are involved. I suggest that you do up a prospectus, an outline, and some few beginning pages—say a chapter or so.

Now we will have a break, and that is my little surprise for both of you.

(*"I'll say. Thank you."*

(*9:42. "I'm so surprised I haven't even put my glasses back on yet," Jane exclaimed after she'd come out of trance. Neither of us have been thinking of such a project, which isn't to say the idea of my doing a book involving Seth, at least in part, hasn't occurred to me occasionally.*

(*"I'm really surprised when something like this happens to me in a session," Jane said. "It's so different from what I've been thinking about, or doing. I can see a center section of the book right now, with your illustrations. And I can see Seth's portrait on the back cover." She pointed over her right shoulder to where the painting—which is reproduced in* The Seth Material—*hangs on our living room wall just in back of her rocker.*

(*Resume in the same active manner at 9:58.*)

Now: This book will be a good advertisement for the later book that I will do—and if you insert what I have told you in the book I am doing now, people will already begin to look forward to your book.

(*"That's pretty crafty."*)

So include it in *The Nature of Personal Reality*, for it is the birth of the book in your personal reality.

I had several things in mind this evening. Some of Ruburt's questions will be answered in our next chapter, which we will begin. Then I will have some other personal comment.

CHAPTER 7

The Living Flesh

(Pause at 10:01. Our telephone began to ring. The sound penetrated the two closed doors between Jane's study and the living room, where we were. I disliked interrupting the session so I let it ring—feeling uneasy all the while. Jane, in trance, seemed not to hear it.

(She receives more and more calls these days. Now when either of us picks up the telephone we're prepared to talk to a person from any part of the country. Earlier this evening, for instance, Jane took a call from the High Sierra country in California.)

Dictation: Chapter Seven: "The Living Flesh."

Give us a moment . . . Often individuals go overboard, forgetting that ideas have their own vitality. Such people make divisions where basically there are none. They consider ideas as completely mental properties, separate from their concept of the body. They think ideas reside in their heads. Who, for example, imagines that an idea is alive in his elbow, or knee, or toe?

Generally, people believe that ideas have little to do with the living flesh. The flesh seems physical and ideas do not. Those given to love of the intellect often make an unnecessary separation between the world of concepts and that of the flesh.

While it is true that the body is the living materialization of idea, it is also true that these ideas form an active, responsive, alive body. The body is not just a tool to be used. It is not just a vehicle for the spirit. It is the spirit in flesh. You impose your ideas upon it and largely affect its health and well-being through your conscious beliefs. But the body is composed of living, responding atoms and molecules. These have their own consciousnesses alive in matter, their drive to exist and be within the framework of their own nature. They compose the cells, and these combine to form the organs. The organs possess the combined consciousnesses of each of the cells within them, and in their way the organs sense their own identity.

They have a purpose—that function they provide within the organism as a whole. This cooperation of consciousness continues so that you have a body consciousness that is vital, that strives to maintain its own equilibrium and health.

The stuff of the body should not be considered as some metaphysical result, then, but as a living gestalt of responsive flesh. Your body is composed of other living entities, in other words. Though you organize this living material it has its own right to fulfillment and existence. You are not a soul encased in inert clay.

The "house of clay" does not immediately deteriorate when you leave it. It disintegrates at its own rate. It is no longer organized by your own domain. The life of its atoms and molecules and cells is translated into other living natural forms. Your perception is merely that which you are aware of. Even the atoms and molecules have their own fine vision and appreciate their environment in their own way. The same power that moves your mind forms your body.

There is no difference between the energy that shapes your ideas and the energy that grows a flower, or that heals your finger if you burn it. The soul does not exist apart from nature.

It is not thrust into nature. Nature is the soul in flesh, in whatever its materializations. The flesh is as spiritual as the soul, and the soul is as natural as the flesh. In your terms the body is the living soul. Now the soul can live, and does, in many forms—some physical and some not, but while you are material, the body is the living soul. The body constantly heals itself, which means that the soul in the flesh heals itself. The body is often closer to the soul than the mind is because it automatically grows as a flower does, trusting its nature.

You may take your break.

(10:27. Jane's pace had been good. This was the end of book work. After break Seth delivered two pages of data for Jane and me, and the session ended at 11:01 P.M.)

SESSION 631, DECEMBER 18, 1972,
9:37 P.M. MONDAY

(We had spent the earlier part of the evening trimming our Christmas tree. Now that it was done, with the multicolored lights shining through the branches and the tinsel, we prepared for the session. Beneath our living room windows, a carpenter pounded on an outside door frame as he repaired damage done to the ground floor of the house by the flood of last June [see the 613th session in Chapter One]. Beside this, the sound of additional hammering inside the house rose up through our floor; but none of this lasted long or interfered with the session.)

Now—

("Good evening, Seth.")

—to begin dictation: Physical existence is valuable for many reasons, one being that the flesh is so responsive to thought and yet so resilient. There are built-in guidelines so that the body consciousness itself, while mirroring your negative images at times, will also automatically struggle against them.

You must remember that you dwell always in a natural framework—which means that your thoughts themselves are as natural, say, as the locks of your hair. In what may seem to you

140

to be an odd analogy I will compare your thoughts with viruses,* for they are alive, always present, responsive, and possess their own kind of mobility. Physically speaking at least, thoughts are chemically propelled, and they travel through the universal body as viruses travel through your temporal form.

Thoughts interact with the body and become part of it as viruses do. Some viruses have great therapeutic value. The physical body will often let down its own barriers to these, knowing they will counteract certain others that are not beneficial at the time.

So-called harmful viruses are ever-present within the body. You are very rarely vulnerable to any but a small percentage, though you carry within you traces of the most deadly of them all of the time. Viruses themselves undergo transformations completely unsuspected by medical men. If one virus disappears and another is found, it is never suspected that the first may have changed into the second; and yet through certain alterations of quite natural character such is the case.

So viruses can be beneficial or deadly according to the condition, state, and needs of the body at any given time. It is known that one disease can often cure another; sometimes, left alone, an individual will go from a serious disease through a series of less severe ones that are seemingly unrelated to the original problem.

Now in the context of usual Western learning, and with the introduction of modern drugs, you are in somewhat of a quandary. The body knows how to handle "natural" drugs coming directly from the earth—whether ground or boiled, minced or steamed. A large variety of "manufactured" drugs offer an unfamiliarity to the body's innate structure, which can lead to strong defense mechanisms. These are often aimed directly against the drug instead of the disease itself. Such a

---

*According to scientists, viruses are ultramicroscopic units that can cause diseases in plants and animals. They multiply only in connection with live cells, and are thought of both as living organisms and as complicated proteins. Few scientists would grant thoughts the same kind of validity, though.

situation means that you must then use another drug to counteract the one just given.

(Pause at 9:58.) I am not suggesting that you not visit doctors or not take drugs of that nature, as long as you believe in the structure of medical discipline that the Western world has evolved. Your bodies have been conditioned to it through the use of such medications since birth. There are many casualties, but this is still a system that you have chosen, and your ideas still form your reality. No one dies who has not made the decision to do so—and no disease is accepted blindly. Put simply, your thoughts can be regarded as invisible viruses, carriers, sparks setting off reactions not only within the body but the entire physical system as you know it.

Your thoughts are as natural as the cells within your body, and as real. They interact with one another as viruses do. While you are in this reality there is no division between the mental, the spiritual, and the physical. If you think there is, then you do not sufficiently understand the spirituality of the flesh or the physical reality of your thought.

You may take a break.

(10:06 to 10:29.)

Now: As stated, thoughts are as natural as any portion of the body. They are as much a part of nature as feelings are, but if you set up an arbitrary division—considering thoughts mental as distinguished from the physical—then your body may give a truer reflection of your being than your thoughts do.

In the body's spontaneous functioning you see the easy mobility of the soul, the "going with that which I am," which is an indication of the soul's inner freedom and yet innate sense of direction. All portions of the body's reality are versions in flesh of the soul's reality, even as all segments of the exterior universe mirror an internal one. The latter is as alive and natural and changing as the exterior world. Physical phenomena is only a portion of what nature is, and all realities are natural.

In your terms, probabilities are extensions and variations on the growth principle that is quite obvious in your daily reality.

Such growth is a natural manifestation flourishing within your particular area of actuality, observable to your senses. Again, other entirely natural manifestations of that principle exist. Some can only be glimpsed in distorted form because of other "natural" conditions that you cannot perceive. Probabilities involve you with a rich psychological growth and development, present but not observable in your "home ground." Any kind of existence happens within the context of nature, and nature includes the soul. Your definition of nature has simply been too limiting.

It is natural to live after death, and natural to return the body to earth and [then to] form another. It is natural for your thoughts to be as quick, responsive, and alive as viruses. It is natural for you to have probable selves as well as reincarnational existences.*

When you consider ideas as mental and apart from nature, then you feel separated from nature itself. When you imagine a life after death as unnatural or supernatural then you feel divorced, cut off and bewildered. You must try to understand that there are different kinds of nature within Nature—and a capital for the last one. Your physical life—your human nature—is, in your terms, dependent upon a time when you were not. You must realize that not being in that connotation is quite as natural as physical being. Your existence before and after death is as much a normal phenomenon as your present life.

End of dictation. Now do you want a break?

("Yes.")

Then I will continue on another line.

(10:55. Jane had been well dissociated. The house had long since fallen quiet—a somewhat unusual situation these days, it seemed. After break, Seth discussed my painting and gave some

---

*I didn't finish this little note until June, 1973: Seth discusses probabilities in Chapters Fourteen and Fifteen, and reincarnation in Chapter Nineteen, although both subjects are mentioned elsewhere in this book. Also see The Seth Material and Seth Speaks.

material for others who aren't involved with this book. The session ended then at 11:35 P.M.)

SESSION 632, JANUARY 15, 1973,
9:00 P.M. MONDAY

(We've had a series of brilliant warm days this month, and the ground is bare of snow. Our Christmas tree is gone, although we kept it up through last week. Jane has her classes back in action now. Although we had a few shorter sessions on different matters during the holiday season, this is the first material Seth has given on his book since December 18—and as he resumed dictation on Chapter Seven so easily, we were reminded that he's impervious to our ideas of time.

(Jane's psychic work has resulted in a steady, if modest, increase in mail, and gradually we've fallen far behind in answering it. Recently Seth told us he'd dictate "a nice letter" that we could send to those who write along with any personal note we might add, but we haven't obtained this yet.)

Good evening.

("Good evening, Seth.")

For now, dictation: As most of you know, the atoms that compose your cells, as well as the cells themselves, constantly die and are replaced. The stuff of the internal organs changes and yet they always retain their form. Their identity is intact.

So is your own identity secure in the midst of all these births and deaths of which your conscious self is unaware. The memory of all of its experiences is retained. Each cell remembers its past though all of its parts have been and are being continually replaced.*

As your cells have their own memories, so the conscious mind has a more overt kind of memory. Your conscious thoughts act as triggers, bringing both kinds of memory into activation. Within your physical being then each joyful,

---

*Let's define the cell in ordinary terms as a tiny, very complex unit of proto-plasm. It's usually made up of a nucleus, a semifluid living matter, and a membrane. Seth's ideas of cellular memory, however, add many new dimensions . . .

expanding, traumatic and tragic "past" event lies indelibly written. In your terms this is your working material, the memory of your physical being since the time of its <u>conception</u> in corporeal form. There are [in your memory] the most complex organizations and associative frameworks, that exist both in the depths of your cellular structure and in the highest reaches of your conscious activity.

Earlier I compared your thoughts to viruses *(in the last session).* Think of them now as living electromagnetic cells, differing from the physical cells in your body only in the nature of their materialization. Your thoughts direct the over-all functioning of your body's cells, even though you do not consciously know how those cells operate. That work <u>is</u> unconscious.

Each physical cell is in its way a miniature brain, with memory of all of its personal experiences and of its relationship with other cells, and with the body as a whole. In your terms this means that each cell operates with an innate picture of the body's entire history—past, present, and future.

Now this picture is ever-changing and mobile. An alteration in just one cell is instantly noted by the body consciousness (the combined consciousnesses of the cells), and the future effect perceived. This information is used together with all other data from the body, and a prediction made.

(9:21.) This body prediction is then assessed, and on more levels than it is possible for me to explain. Briefly, the picture is "shown" in the invisible arena where flesh and spirit meet. This arena is not a place, of course, but an inner state of gestalt consciousness. The state is brought about through certain inter-actions that occur deep within the body. Magnetic structures are formed. They are created on a physical level through certain activations of the nerves in which the normal patterns are jumped, so to speak, and images are formed. The nerves and the cellular structures at their tips take pictures. These are all assembled and used to form the larger picture of the body's condition.

These are not images as you think of them but highly coded information, electromagnetically imprinted, that would not appear as images to the physical eye. In any case they cannot be perceived except by the body. But this procedure is so far superior to anything that you know that the body, therefore, actually takes precognitive pictures of its future condition—as if the body situation at the time were projected into the future.

(Seth-Jane paused often while delivering the last sentence, obviously searching for just the right words.)

This predictive picture is then set against two models. First it is checked against the body's ideal standard of health in its individual case—its own greatest fulfillment. Then it is checked against the image of the body sent to it by the conscious self. Correlations are made instantaneously. In an organizational framework that would certainly be envied by the most advanced technological concern, communications spring back and forth with great rapidity. The body makes whatever changes are necessary in order to bring the two images in line with the present corporeal condition.

You may take your break.

(9:35. "Seth gave us a break just to give us a break," Jane said. "He's got a lot more there, all ready. I think he might talk about that book we bought last week, too—at least a little."

(The book Jane referred to is a compendium of experiments with animal and human biological rhythms. We haven't read all of it yet, but from our points of view we're already questioning some of the conclusions drawn within it. We think Seth is continually offering larger insights into such rhythms. Resume at 9:42.)

There is a built-in equilibrium to some extent. The body is so responsive to conscious thought that it has its own innate system of self-preservation and its own guiding image of fulfillment.

Say that at the age of four you were severely injured. An accident took place at 3:20 in the afternoon. It was snowing. Your mother was roasting a turkey. Imagine that you burned a hand severely. Though all of the tissue in that hand has often been completely replaced by the time you are twenty-seven, for example, the identity within each of those present cells remembers that injury.

There were countless other events that happened to you on different afternoons at the same hour, both before and after that one. The cells within your hand contain within themselves memories your conscious mind would be dazzled to behold. Yet remember that the cells in your twenty-seven-year-old hand are in no physical way the same cells that experienced any of those events. In some underground of sensation, however, the buried evidences of stimuli and reaction experienced during those numberless "past" afternoons still exist. Some of those memories will certainly be played back, to affect what you think of as your current experience at twenty-seven. Your conscious thoughts and habits regulate which of them will intermix into the maelstrom of the present.

You consciously give the signals for reaction. It is not the other way around. Past events do not intrude in this manner unless they are beckoned by the conscious expectations and thoughts that exist within your mind. *(Pause.)* Those unconscious memories will be activated according to your current beliefs. You will be replenished and renewed as your thoughts motivate joyful body sensations and physical events, or you will be depressed as you bring into your awareness unpleasant past body happenings.

At times of course both can be highly beneficial. A conscious realization of danger, for example, will call up all information dealing with similar situations, so that the body can deal with it at once from the vast bank of its living memory. But constant unpleasant thoughts put the body into a state of turmoil that is "unrealistic," and, in turn, force it to reactivate such old patterns.

(Long pause at 10:01, eyes closed.) The living flesh is quite aware of certain facts that escape you on a conscious level. It knows it dies and is reborn constantly, and yet retains itself. I

147

use the terms "dies" and "is reborn" because you make sense of them, but the body does not. The body, while being always itself, comes and goes. It does not feel less or diminished when a cell dies, for it is also in the process of forming a new one.

For a moment, think of your body as one large cell in the moment of its being. You, the larger self, have many bodies, each turning into the other as one dies and is reborn; yet You (capital Y) maintain your identity and your memory even as the smallest cell in your present body does.

This is merely an analogy but it will explain your body's concept of itself; for as a whole it knows it "dies," as now its portions do, but is also aware of its "future" transformation. Within this framework it protects and maintains its own stability and survival.

At one level of your being there is a common ground where body consciousness merges with that higher consciousness from which your own identity springs. This is the ground of your being where soul and flesh meet, both in time and out of it.

You may take your break.

(10:13 to 10:25.)

Now: Because you are conscious of being, you form your physical reality through conscious thought.

I am quite aware that I am repeating myself again and again when I make that statement, but you need to be reminded that you are not at the mercy of unconscious events. You have the body's innate wisdom behind you and it will always try to correct your errors.

These suggestions will appear in numberless ways—some quite physical to your way of thinking, and some through other means. The body may of itself begin to crave certain foods, for example, or fresh air or exercise. These are simple instances, and later we will be more specific.

You may have dreams urging you to move in such and such a direction, or pointing out areas in which corrections should be made. Often such dreams bring about behavior changes whether or not you remember them in the morning. You may request

148

dreams in which proper direction is given, and you will receive them. If you ask on the one hand, however, and do not believe in the therapeutic nature of dreams on the other, you will short-circuit any such activity. In such a case you are not being honest with the contents of your conscious mind. Instead you are saying, "I will have a dream to help me, and yet I do not believe I can have such a dream."

In all cases when you are concerned about your health, there is a choice of directions for you to follow. The living flesh is yours. It is the materialization of your soul, and through the body the soul will provide you with those answers you require. In the next chapter we will begin to discuss those methods that can be used to refresh and heal the body, and that will help you arouse from within the physical form those memories and experiences most to your advantage. For best results, you must remember that ideas are as alive as the cells within your hand.

End of chapter. That was a transitional chapter. We will take a brief break, and you can have the beginning of the next chapter, or personal material as you request.

("We'd better make it personal then, I guess."

(10:40. During break Jane received some insights from Seth as to what would follow in Chapter Eight—that, for instance, when good thoughts from an individual's present life were activated, they would draw upon similar ones from his or her reincarnational personalities. This was a very interesting idea, aside from being a comforting one. I couldn't recall Seth presenting the concept in just that way before. [A note added later: But as things developed, he didn't begin alluding to it until Chapter Ten.]

(As often happens, the "personal" material that followed break has good general application, and Jane decided she'll use it to make certain points in ESP class. End at 11:26 P.M.

(When she read the first page of this session after I'd typed it, Jane said, "It looks like I distorted that bit about atoms 'dying.' I don't think it should be put that way, I guess. Seth must have a lot on that. All I remember is that matter can't be created or

destroyed. And those particles that break off atoms and are released as radiation don't 'die' as far as I know—although they might evolve . . . ?"

(In our reality, the first law of thermodynamics tells us that energy [matter] can be changed from one form to another but that it can't be created or destroyed. Although a chemical change results in a new substance the total weight of the ingredients involved remains practically the same; in such ordinary reactions the amount of matter converted into heat is infinitesimal. In mathematical terms Einstein revealed that mass and energy are equivalent to each other—when one is "destroyed" the other is "created."

(We've been especially interested in such material since Seth referred to the "deaths" of atoms and molecules in the 625th session in Chapter Five, but we haven't asked for more details because the subject matter is somewhat outside the scope of this book. In physics it is "known," for instance, that the proton, an elementary particle in the atomic nucleus, has an exceptionally long life in years—the number one followed by twenty-four [or more] zeros. When Seth finishes Personal Reality we plan to ask him to reconcile such data from our world with the root assumptions, or basic agreements, in his own reality.

(At the same time, Jane and I read these days that physicists are beginning to question the immutability of such rigid "laws" as those applying to thermodynamics, causality, etc., saying that they are either in error after all or need to be modified . . .

(Those who care to might see Seth's discussion of internal electromagnetic sound and light values in the 625th session referred to earlier, as well as his material on EE [electromagnetic energy] units in Chapter Twenty of Seth Speaks.

CHAPTER 8

Health, Good and Bad Thoughts, and the Birth of "Demons"

SESSION 633, JANUARY 17, 1973,
9:14 P.M. WEDNESDAY

(Tonight I asked Jane if Seth would deliver his promised letter for correspondents. We sat for the sessions at 9:05. At the same time the city fire whistle began to sound insistently; then we heard several other sirens.

(A note: Jane spent a large part of her working time today rereading her manuscript, The Physical Universe as Idea Construction, *and writing new material related to it. She received the original in a transcendent state on the evening of September 9, 1963. This event initiated her psychic development; almost ten years after its conception the work still serves as a "touchstone" for her—and today Jane discovered concepts in it that she'd been blind to earlier. For more on Idea Construction see* The Seth Material *and* Seth Speaks.*)*

Good evening.

("Good evening, Seth.")

Now: We will begin with a letter.

Dear Friend:

I appreciate your interest in my work and sessions. I also am aware of your quite natural and human need to translate philosophy into daily life and action.

The ideas however are tools given to you for your use, in your own way. The more often you use these mental implements, the more proficient you become in developing and fulfilling your own unique gifts. There are those in your world to whom you can turn for help, often—friends, confidants, or doctors, psychologists and psychics. According to "where you are," any of these persons may be of assistance.

While such help may be welcomed, the kind of value I offer is of a different nature. In larger terms one of my most important messages is simply this: "You are a multidimensional personality, and within you lies all the knowledge about yourself, your challenges and problems, that you will ever need to know. Others can help you in their own way, and at certain levels of development such help is necessary and good. But my mission is to remind you of the incredible power within your own being, and to encourage you to recognize and use it."

To this end, through Ruburt, I am producing the continuing body of the Seth material, and books, each in a different way geared to these goals. In my present book, *The Nature of Personal Reality: A Seth Book,* I am including techniques that will allow you and thousands of others to use these ideas in normal daily living, to enrich the life that you know and to help you understand and solve your problems.

While it may not seem so at the present, the greatest gift I can give you is to reaffirm the integrity of your own being. I say this also because I am aware of your present status even as other portions of your own entity are.

Ruburt has only so much time available, and much must be taken into consideration. I am personally aware of your letter. Ruburt cannot answer all mail personally, however, or his work and mine could suffer. I am composing this note therefore to let you know that I hold you in my mind, and that energy is automatically sent out to you when your letter is received, and when this reply is sent. The energy will help release your own understanding and healing abilities, or help you in whatever particular area help is required.

Such energy is <u>always</u> available, whether you write to me or not. Such energy is constantly at your own command. If you believe me, then you will realize that others at best can only act as intermediaries, middlemen, and are in that respect not needed, for the energy is always available in your life. I simply give you that which is your own.

Seth

("Thank you.")

Now give us a moment; and that is the end of our letter. Some people you will want to send it to, and some you will not. Others you can take care of yourselves.

(Pause at 9:36. We think it of interest to include Seth's letter in his book, since it stresses the importance of beliefs.)

Dictation: Try a simple experiment. The results will be self-explanatory. Think of a sad event from your life. Similar feelings will soon follow, and with them memories of other such unpleasant episodes strung together through association. Scenes, odors, words, perhaps half-forgotten, will suddenly come upon you with new freshness.

Your thoughts will activate the appropriate feelings. Beneath your awareness, however, they will also trigger the cells' ever-present memory imprints of stimuli received when those events occurred. There is, to some extent now, a cellular memory playback—and on the part of the entire body, the recognition of its state at that time.

If you pursue such sorrowful thoughts persistently you are reactivating that body condition. Think of one of the most pleasant events that ever happened to you and the reverse will be true, but the process is the same. This time the associated memories are pleasant, and the body changes accordingly.

Remember, these mental associations are living things. They are formations of energy assembled into invisible structures, through processes quite as valid and complicated as the organization of any group of cells. Comparing them with cells, they are of briefer duration, generally speaking, though under certain conditions this does not apply. But your thoughts form structures as real as the cells. Their composition is different in that no solidity is involved in your terms.

As living cells have a structure, react to stimuli and organize according to their own classification, so do thoughts. Thoughts thrive on association. They magnetically attract others like themselves, and like some strange microscopic animals they repel their "enemies," or other thoughts that are threatening to their own survival.

(Two automobiles equipped with blaring sirens sped past our apartment house, but Jane didn't seem to be disturbed. Similar alarms had been audible in the background since session time.)

Using this analogy, your mental and emotional life forms a framework composed of such structures, and these act directly upon the cells of your physical body.

Now let us return to Augustus; for here we find again in one individual an excellent example of the way in which seemingly nonphysical thoughts and beliefs can affect and alter the corporeal image. And you may take a break.

(9:55. Jane was out of trance quickly. She repeated the idea she'd voiced several times lately—that although Seth had ended the Augustus data rather abruptly in Chapter Six, he planned to return to it occasionally through the book.

(I asked about the title for Chapter Eight. Jane thought it had come through; although she had glimmerings of it now, she couldn't get it clearly. The sirens continued, reminding me of animals prowling about in the distance. As we listened to them I picked up a book which an ESP class member had left behind last night. It was about philosophy and religion in India. "Oh, put it down," Jane said as I began to leaf through it. "This is one of those times when Seth could give a whole bunch of stuff on that book"—meaning, of course, that now she had more than one channel available.

(She went on to explain that to her way of thinking the book was "more insidious than a lot of outright lies, because the truth that you instinctively feel it contains could lead you to accept the greater distortions that are also in it . . ."

(Resume in a fast manner at 10:14.)

Now: First of all, Augustus had been told in various ways, quote: "You think too much. You should be doing something physical, involved in sports, more outgoing." Such repeated remarks, with other childhood conditions, made him afraid of his own mental activity. He also felt unworthy, so how could his thoughts be good?

Feelings of violence accumulated early, but in his family there were no acceptable ways of releasing normal aggressive feelings. When these built up into felt, violent eruptions, Augustus was only the more convinced of his unacceptable nature. For some time in his normal state as a teenager, he tried harder and harder to be "good." This meant the banishing of thoughts or impulses that were sexually inspired along various lines, aggressive, or even just unconventional. Considerable energy was used to inhibit these portions of his inner experience. The denied mental events did not disappear, however. They increased in intensity and were kept apart from his "safer" usual thoughts.

In such a way, Augustus actually created a mental structure whose organization followed the principles I mentioned before your break. Under other circumstances and possessing different characteristics, another individual could damage a physical organ by literally attacking it, as surely as it might be assaulted by a virus *(emphatically)*. Because of Augustus's particular temperament and nature, however, and his native though conventionally undeveloped creativity, he formed a structure rather than destroying one.

In his normal state he accepted only the beliefs he considered were expected of him. As mentioned *(in the 628th session in Chapter Six)*, there was a time before his condition developed when his "good-self thoughts" and his "bad-self thoughts" vied for his attention, and the body tried desperately to react to constant, alternating and often contradictory concepts.

(Pause.) What developed was a situation in which the conflicting sets of thoughts and feelings finally took turns, though

155

Augustus maintained his own integrity for <u>most</u> of the time. But those beliefs that he shoved away were, by attraction, instantly seized by the other mental structure—again, composed of ideas and feelings combined into what you might think of as an invisible cellular organization, with all capabilities of reaction.

. In his normal condition Augustus thought of his own power-lessness—for he had denied himself normal aggressive action—and felt this weak. The beliefs activated the body's cellular memory, weakening the body and impeding its function. Yet for a time, while performance was dulled it was steady. A balance was maintained that suited his purposes.

He became afraid that the body would go out of control and commit violent action, because he was of course aware of the strength of the denied thoughts and feelings. When a crisis situation arose or when he became lost in despair, an acceleration began that he pretended not to notice, and Augustus Two would appear.

(10:35.) Augustus Two was filled with a sense of power—because Augustus considered power wrong and set it aside from what he thought of as his normal self. Yet Augustus knew the body needed the vitality that he had denied it. Therefore enter Augustus Two with his great ideas of extraordinary power, vigor and superiority—*(louder and smiling:)* <u>I</u> am keeping my Augustuses straight. I hope you are too.

("Yes.")

—and with fantasies of exceptional heroism and the memories of all of those denied by Augustus himself.

Aggressive action conveniently forgotten by Augustus was now recalled with exuberant glee by Augustus Two. As a result the chemical nature of the body was instantly revitalized. Muscular tone was greatly improved. There were changes in the amount of sugar in the blood and an alteration in the flow of energy throughout the body.

I knew when Ruburt interviewed Augustus that the young man identified Augustus Two with the left side of himself. In

156

his normal state that side of the body contained more tension than the right.

In Augustus Two, the tension found release and the energy flow became more even after initial bursts of activity. The longer Augustus Two stayed, however, the weaker his position became—a fact recognized by Augustus <u>and</u> Augustus Two. Augustus, you see, had to build up sufficient repressed thought and emotion because of a situation with which he could not cope. This threat would then bring about the emergence of Augustus Two. The body behaves as you think it must behave, so Augustus and Augustus Two, with their alternating patterns of behavior, caused the body to react in quite different ways.

Forget now that in this case such a division occurred, and imagine instead the successive thoughts and feelings that you possess. When you feel weak you are weak. When you feel joyful your body benefits and becomes stronger. Augustus's case simply shows in exaggerated form the effects of your beliefs upon your physical image. If you think, "Aha, then from now on I will only think good thoughts—and therefore be healthy, and inhibit my 'bad' thoughts, or do anything at all with them but think them," then in your own way you are doing what Augustus did. He began by believing that some of his thoughts were so evil that they must somehow be made nonexistent. So inhibiting what you consider as negative thoughts, or assuming that they are so terrible, is no answer.

The chapter is to be called, "Health, Good and Bad Thoughts, and the Birth of 'Demons.' " And you may take your break.

(*10:55. Jane's trance had been deep, her pace good, yet she remembered hearing the sirens. They continued now although we couldn't see any glow—say from a fire—in the sky over the western section of the city. Resume in the same active manner at 11:15.*)

Now: Your beliefs about what is desirable and what is not, what is good and what is evil, cannot be divorced from the condition of your body. Your own ideas of values can help you

157

achieve good health or bring about disease, can bring into your experience success or failure, happiness or sadness. Yet each of you will interpret that last remark in line with your own value system. You will have definite ideas about what success or failure means, or what good or evil is.

Your own value system then is built up of your beliefs about reality, and those beliefs form your experience. Suppose you believe that to be "good" you must try to be perfect. You may have been told, or read, that the spirit is perfect, and hence thought that your duty was to reproduce that perfect spirit in flesh as best you could. To this end you attempt to deny all imperfect thoughts and emotions. Your own "negative" thoughts appall you. You may believe also what I have told you—that your thoughts create your reality—so you become all the more frightened at mental or actual expressions of an aggressive nature. You may be so concerned about hurting someone else that you hardly dare move. Trying to be perfect all the time can be far more than a nuisance: It can be disastrous because of your misunderstanding.

The word "perfect" holds many pitfalls. In the first place it presupposes something completed and done beyond change, and so beyond motion, further development, or creativity.

The spirit is always in a state of becoming, ever-changing, supple, and in your terms without end, as it was and is without a point of beginning. Ruburt said recently that if he was sure of one thing about physical reality, it was [that it was] not anywhere near perfect in those terms. But in the same meaning of the word neither is the spirit, which to fulfill the requirement of perfection would have to be set in some state of completion beyond which no fulfillment or creativity was possible.

Your thoughts are. Your may approve or disapprove of them, in the way that you think of a storm, for example. Left alone, your thoughts are as various, magnificent, trivial, frightening, or glorious as a hurricane, a flower, a flood, a toad, a raindrop or the fog. Your thoughts are perfectly themselves. Left alone, they come and go.

You with your conscious mind are to discriminate among those thoughts as to which ones you want to form into your system of beliefs (intently), but in so doing you are not to pretend blindness. You may at times wish that a rainy day were a sunny one, but you do not stand at the window and deny that the rain is falling, or that the air is cold and the sky dark.

Because you accept the rain as a present reality does not mean, either, that you must believe that all days are stormy, and make that obvious misconception a part of your beliefs about reality. So you do not have to pretend that a "dark" thought doesn't exist. You do not have to take it as fact that all of your thoughts would be murky, left alone, and try to hide them.

Some people are afraid of snakes, even of the most harmless variety, and blind to their beauty and place in the universe. Some are afraid of certain thoughts, and so are oblivious to their beauty and their place in mental life.

Since you have all kinds of thoughts there are reasons for having them, as you have all kinds of geography. Within your reality it is as foolish to deny the existence of certain thoughts as it would be, say, to pretend that deserts do not exist. In following such a course you deny dimensions of experience and diminish your reality. This does not mean that you have to collect what you think of as negative thoughts, any more than it means that you should spend a month in a desert if you do not like them. Period. It does mean that within nature as you understand it, nothing is meaningless or to be pretended out of existence.

That will do. Now you may end the session or take a break if you prefer.

("I hate to say it, but we'd better end it then.")

(Jovially:) Then I will add: I told you there would be no trouble with the book. Tell Ruburt I said so—but who listens to me? Though he is listening better lately, and on the right track . . . I wish you a hearty good evening.

("Thank you, Seth. Good night."

(11:44 P.M. Only our own weariness prompted me to end the session; I could tell that Seth was capable of continuing indefinitely. It had been a long day for us. Now even the sirens had fallen silent.

(Seth's joking remarks about "the book" refer to this one. In some recent deleted material he had discussed Jane's initial uncertainty about signing a contract for the publication of psychic work before it had been produced. Tam Mossman, Jane's editor at Prentice-Hall, has read the first six chapters of Personal Reality *[as we call it], and has written her a very encouraging letter.)*

SESSION 634, JANUARY 22, 1973,
9:19 P.M. MONDAY

(Since I hadn't finished typing the 633rd session yet, Jane asked me to read her the last couple of pages of it from my notes.)

Now: Dictation: Each individual will have a slightly different definition for "negative" emotions. One person may find sexually stimulating thoughts delightful and a most enjoyable kind of diversion. Another may consider them impure, bad, unhealthy, or otherwise disadvantageous.

Some individuals can with ease and exuberance imagine themselves in a fistfight, a brawl, unmercifully beating "the devil" out of an adversary. The same thoughts may fill another man with intense terror and grave feelings of guilt. This same man, however, who would not purposely entertain fantasies of such nature under normal conditions, may in time of war imagine himself killing the enemy with the greatest feelings of holy joy and righteousness.

(Pause.) What is usually forgotten is the real nature of aggressiveness, which in its truest sense simply means forceful action. This does not necessarily imply physical force, but instead the power of energy directed into a material action.

Birth is perhaps the most forceful aggression, in your terms, of which you are capable in your system of reality *(emphatically).*

160

In the same way, the growth of any idea into temporal realization is the result of creative aggression. It is impossible to try to erase true aggressiveness. To do so would obliterate life as you know it.

(Pause at 9:34.) Any attempt to impair the flow of true aggression results in a distortive, uneven, explosive pseudo-aggression that causes wars, individual neurosis, and a great many of your problems in all areas.

Normal aggressiveness flows with strong patterns of energy, giving motive power to all of your thoughts whether you consciously regard them as positive or negative, good or bad. *(Very definitely:)* The same thrusting creative surge brings them all forth. When you consider a thought good you usually do not question it. You allow it its life and follow through. Usually if you regard a thought as bad or beneath you, or if you are ashamed of it, then you try to deny it, stop its motion and hold it back. You cannot restrain energy, although you may think you can. You simply collect it, whereupon it grows, seeking its fulfillment.

This will lead you to say, "Supposing I feel like killing my boss, then, or putting poison in my husband's tea; or worse, hanging my five children on the clothesline instead of the towels? Are you saying that I should merely follow through?"

I sympathize with your predicament. The fact is that before being "assailed" by what may seem to be such terrifying unnatural ideas, you have already blocked off an endless variety of far less drastic ones, any of which you could have expressed quite safely and naturally in daily life. Your problem then is not how to deal with normal aggressiveness, but how to handle it when it has remained unexpressed, ignored, and denied over a long period of time. Later in this book we will deal specifically with methods to that end. Here I simply want to point out the difference between healthy natural aggressiveness, and the explosive, distorted emergence of repressed aggression.

You will each have to discover for yourself those areas in

which you strongly repress your thoughts, for many energy blockages will be found there. All of this will be covered in the later section.

For now consider this blocked energy. Consciously, most people are already afraid of it—they did not repress it because they considered it good. When I use the word "repressed" I do not mean forgotten, or shoved into the unconscious, or beyond reach. You may pretend that such material is hidden but it is quite within your conscious awareness. You have only to honestly look for it and organize what you find.

It is very possible to "see" such information and not see it at the same time, simply because you do not add all of the data together. No one can make you do that, of course. To do it you must have a sense of courage and adventuresomeness; and tell yourself that you refuse to be cowed by ideas that after all belong to you, but are not you.

Now: It is often said that man believes in devils because he believes in gods. The fact is that man began to believe in demons when he started to feel a sense of guilt. The guilt itself arose with the birth of compassion.

Animals have a sense of justice that you do not understand, and built-in to that innocent sense of integrity there is a biological compassion, understood at the deepest cellular levels.

In your terms man is an animal, rising out of himself, from himself evolving certain animal capacities to their utmost; not forming new physical specializations of body any longer (again in your terms), but creating from his needs, desires and blessed natural aggressiveness inner structures having to do with values, space and time. To varying degrees this same impetus resides throughout all creaturehood.

(Pause at 10:02.) Do you want a break? I forgot.

("No, I'm okay." Seth-Jane's pace was rather slow.)

Such a task meant that man must break out of the self-regulating, precise, safe and yet limiting aspects of instinct. The birth of a conscious mind, as you think of it, meant that the species took upon itself free will. Built-in procedures that had beautifully sufficed could now be superseded. They became suggestions instead of rules.

Compassion "rose" from the biological structure up to emotional reality. The "new" consciousness accepted its emerging triumph—freedom—and was faced with responsibility for action of a conscious level, and with the birth of guilt.

A cat playfully killing a mouse and eating it is not evil. It suffers no guilt. On biological levels both animals understand. The consciousness of the mouse, under the innate knowledge of impending pain, leaves its body. The cat uses the warm flesh. The mouse itself has been hunter as well as prey, and both understand the terms in ways that are very difficult to explain.

(As Seth-Jane delivered this material, my mind flashed back many years to a summer day when I was about eleven years old. With my two brothers I sat in the back yard of the house in which we grew up, in a small town not far from Elmira. Our next-door neighbor's cat, Mitzi, had caught a field mouse. She played with it in the grass; with conflicting feelings I watched Mitzi, of whom I was very fond, block off each attempt of the terrified mouse to escape—until finally, having had her sport, she ate it . . .

(The Mitzi episode in turn reminded me of a series of little poems Jane wrote a few years ago. Many people call them Haiku—the Japanese verse form—but they are only reminiscent of that category. We have several of them pinned up on our walls, among them this one:

> The cat eats the mouse.
> Neither exist.
> Do not tell them.

(The weather has been exceptionally warm for days. A light rain had started at session time, and now there was lightning, followed by thunder resounding across the city.)

At certain levels both cat and mouse understand the nature of the life energy they share, and are not—in those terms— jealous for their own individuality. This does not mean they will not struggle to live, but that they have a built-in unconscious sense of unity with nature in which they know they will not be lost or immersed (*quietly intent*).

Man, pursuing his own way, chose to step outside of that framework—on a conscious level. The birth of compassion then took the place of the animals' innate knowledge; the biological compassion turned into emotional realization.

The hunter, freed more or less from animal courtesy, would be forced to emotionally identify with his prey. To kill is to be killed. The balance of life sustains all. He must learn on a conscious level then what he knew all along. This is the intrinsic and only real meaning of guilt and its natural framework.

(*Long pause.*) You are to preserve life consciously, then, as the animals preserve it unconsciously.

You may take your break. I am sorry.

(*"That's all right. It's very interesting."*

(*10:27. This had been one of Jane's longer trances. It had been a deep one, too—yet she remembered hearing the thunder when I asked her about it. She was eager to have me read Seth's material back to her, but then: "Oh, wait a minute ... I'm already starting to get more, and I want to get up and move around first." To give her a break, I went outside to look for our oldest cat, Willy. The younger one, Rooney, was in. Resume at 10:44.*)

Now: The interpretations and uses to which this quite natural guilt has been put are horrendous.

Guilt is the other side of compassion. Its original purpose was to enable you to empathize on an aware level with yourselves and other members of creaturehood, so that you could consciously control what was previously handled on a biological level alone. Guilt in that respect therefore has a strong natural basis, and when it is perverted, misused or misunderstood, it has that great terrifying energy of any runaway basic phenomenon.

(*Pause.*) If you think you are guilty because you read one kind of book or another, or entertain certain thoughts, then you run particular risks. If you believe something is wrong then

164

in your experience it will be, and you will consider it negative. So you will collect an "unnatural" guilt, one that you do not deserve but accept and so create.

You will not usually form a creation of it of which you are proud. If you believe firmly in poor health you may use this repressed energy to attack a physical organ—a gall bladder may become "bad." According to your own belief system, you may trust the integrity of your body and instead project this guilt out upon others—onto a personal enemy, or a particular race, creed or color.

If you are religious-minded and fundamental in your beliefs, you may blame a devil who causes you to behave in such and such a manner. As the body creates antibodies* to regulate itself, so you will set up mental and emotional "antibodies," certain thoughts that are "good," to protect you from the fantasies or ideas that you consider bad.

If its built-in instincts are left alone the body is basically self-regulating. It does not kill off all red blood cells if there are too many of them at a given time. It has better sense. But in your fear of negative thoughts you often attempt to deny all normal aggressiveness, and at the first glimpse of it bring up your mental antibodies prepared for action. In so doing you try to repudiate the validity of your own experience. If you do not feel your individual reality, then you can never realize that you form it, and so can change it. It is this denial of experience, and the energy blockages involved, that build up the accumulation of unnecessary "unnatural" guilt. The body itself cannot understand these blocked messages, and cries out to express its own corporeal knowledge of the moment as it experiences it. (*Intently:*) You mentally shout in such situations that you do not feel what you feel.

Over a period of time the conscious mind, because of its position, can override the body's messages. Yet the backed-up

---

*Antibodies are proteins manufactured in the body in order to neutralize toxic substances. Here again, Seth postulates inner mental counterparts of organic phenomena.

accumulation of energy will seek outlet. The smallest, most innocent symbol for the repressed material may then bring about behavior on your part that seems out of all proportion to the stimulus.

On ten justified occasions you may have felt like telling someone to leave you alone, but refrained, not wanting to hurt their feelings; afraid that you would be rude even though the occasion was one where your remark might well have been understood and taken calmly. Because you did not accept your feelings, much less express them, on the next occasion you might explode seemingly without reason and initiate a spectacular argument, completely unjustified.

(11:10.) In this case the other person has no idea as to why you reacted in such a fashion, and is deeply hurt. And your guilt grows. The trouble is that ideas of right and wrong are intimately involved with your chemistry, and you cannot separate your moral values from your body.

When you believe that you are good, your body functions well. I am sure that many of you will say, "I try constantly to be good, yet I am in miserable health, so how can that be?" If you examine your own beliefs the answer will be apparent: You try to be so good precisely because you believe you are so bad and unworthy.

Demons of any kind are the result of your beliefs. They are born from a belief in "unnatural" guilt. You may personify them. You may even meet them in your experience, but if so they are still the product of your immeasurable creativity, though formed by your guilt and your belief in it.

If you shed the distorted concepts of unnatural guilt and accepted the wise ancient wisdom of natural guilt instead, there would be no wars. You would not kill each other mindlessly. You would understand the living integrity of each organ in your body and have no need to attack any of them.

This obviously does not mean that the time of the body's death would not come. It does mean that the seasons of the body would be understood as following those of the mind,

166

ever-changing and flowing, with conditions coming and going but always maintaining the splendid unity within the body's form. You would not have <u>chronic</u> illnesses. Generally speaking, and ideally, the body would wear our gradually while still showing far greater endurance than it does now.

There are many other conditions, though, all having to do with your conscious beliefs. You may think it is better to die quickly of a heart attack, for example. Your individual purposes are not the same so you will manage your body experiences in a great variety of ways.

Generally speaking, you are here to expand your consciousness, to learn the ways of creativity as directed through conscious thought. The aware mind can change its beliefs, and so to a large extent it can alter its bodily experience . . .

(I sat with my eyes closed momentarily, and Seth caught me.

(Smiling:) You may change your experience: You may take a break or end the session as you prefer.

("We'll take the break."

(11:32 to 11:48.)

Natural guilt then is the species' manifestation of the animals' unconscious corporeal sense of justice and integrity. It means: Thou shalt not kill more than is needed for thy physical sustenance. Period.

It has nothing to do with adultery or with sex. It does contain innate issues that apply to human beings, that would have no meaning for other animals in the framework of their experience. Strictly speaking, the translation from biological language to your own is as given in this session; but the finer discrimination reads thusly: Thou shalt not violate.

The animals do not need such a message, of course, nor can it be <u>literally</u> translated, for your consciousness is flexible and leeway <u>had</u> to be left for your own interpretation.

An outright lie may or may not be a violation. A sex act may or may not be a violation. A scientific expedition may or may not be a violation. Not going to church on Sunday is not a violation. Having normal aggressive thoughts is not a violation.

Doing violence to your body, or another's, is a violation. Doing violence to the spirit of another is a violation—but again, because you are conscious beings the interpretations are yours. Swearing is not a violation. If you believe that it is then in your mind it becomes one.

(12:01.) Killing another human being is a violation. Killing while protecting your own body from death at the hands of another through immediate contact is a violation. Whether or not any justification seems apparent, the violation exists.

(Long pause.) Because you believe that physical self-defense is the only way to counter such a situation then you will say, "If I am attacked by another person, are you telling me that I cannot aggressively counter his obvious intent to destroy me?"

Not at all. You could counter such an attack in several ways that do not involve killing. You would not be in such a hypothetical situation to begin with unless violent thoughts of your own, faced or unfaced, had attracted it to you. But once it is a fact, and according to the circumstances, many methods could be used. Because you consider aggression synonymous with violence, you may not understand that aggressive—forceful, active, mental or spoken—commands for peace could save your life in such a case; yet they could.

Usually there are a variety of physical actions, not involving killing, that would suffice. As long as you believe that violence must be met with violence you court it and its consequences. On individual terms, your own body and mind become the battleground, as does the physical body of the earth in mass terms. Your material form is alive through natural aggression, the poised, forceful and directed action that is the carrier for creativity.

(Long pause at 12:11, eyes closed.) If you cut your finger it bleeds. In so doing the blood clears away any poisons that may have entered. The bleeding is beneficial and the body knows when to stop it. If the flow continued it would be wrong or detrimental in your terms, but the body would not think the blood was bad because it continued its course of action. It

168

would not attempt to cut off all blood, considering it evil. It would instead make whatever adjustments were necessary to bring the emission to a natural halt.

When you consider aggressive thoughts wrong, using this analogy, you do not even begin to allow the system to clear itself. Instead you shut up the "poisons" inside.

As an accumulation would occur in the flesh, so the same thing might happen in your mental experience. Physically you could end up with a very serious condition; and mentally and emotionally such a clamping down on natural forces can result in "diseased" idea structures that are isolated from other more healthy concepts. These can be like growths—not lacking oxygen, for example, but free access and flow with other portions of your conscious experience.

We will now end the session. My heartiest regards to you both, and a fond good evening.

("Thank you very much, Seth. Good night.")

(End at 12:25 A.M. "Wow," Jane said when she was out of another excellent trance, "I'm tired now but Seth's still got plenty left . . .")

SESSION 635, JANUARY 24, 1973,
9:44 P.M. WEDNESDAY

(Soon we'll be able to start sending out Seth's own letter to some of our correspondents; he dictated it in the 633rd session. I've prepared the typewritten camera copy so that it has just the look Jane and I want it to have, and now a local printer is making several hundred copies for us.)

Good evening.

("Good evening, Seth.")

Dictation. Now (smiling:) You do not need to put in my first now's. (But I had already done so.)

Natural guilt is also highly connected with memory, and arose hand in hand with mankind's excursion into the experience of past, present and future. Natural guilt was meant as a preventive measure. It needed the existence of a sophisticated memory system in which new situations and experiences could be judged against recalled ones, and evaluations made in an in-between moment of reflection.

Any previous acts that had aroused feelings of natural guilt were to be avoided in the future. Because of the multitudinous courses open to the species, not only did the highly specific nature of many kinds of animalistic instinct no longer apply, but a curious balance had to be maintained. The conscious options that opened as man's mental world enlarged made it impossible to allow sufficient freedom, and yet necessary control, on a biological level alone.

(*Long pause at 9:56.*) So controls were needed lest the conscious mind, denied full use of the animals' innate taboos, run away with itself. Guilt, natural guilt, depends upon memory then.

It does not carry with it any built-in connection with punishment as you think of it. Once more, it was meant as a preventive measure. Any violation against nature would bring about a feeling of guilt so that when a like situation was encountered in the future, man would, in that moment of reflection, not repeat the same action.

I have used the phrase "moment of reflection" several times because it is another attribute peculiar to the conscious mind and, again in your terms, is largely denied to the rest of creaturehood. Without that pause—in which man can remember past in the present, and envisage a future—natural guilt would have no meaning. Man would not be able to recall past acts, judge them against the present situation, or imagine the future sense of guilt that might result.

To that extent natural guilt projected man into the future. This is of course a learning process, natural within the time system that the species adopted. Unfortunately, artificial guilt takes on the same attributes, utilizing both memory and projection. Wars are self-perpetuating because they combine both natural and unnatural guilt, compounded and reinforced by memory. Conscious killing beyond the needs of sustenance is a violation.

170

(Long pause at 10:08.) We are taking this slow . . .

("All right." Jane's delivery has been leisurely since the start of the session.)

The collection of unrecognized artificial guilts, built up through the centuries, has led to such an accumulation of repressed energy that its release has resulted in violent action. Thus the hatred of one generation of adults whose parents were killed in a war helps generate the next one.

Thou shalt not violate. Again, the injunction had to be flexible enough to cover any situations in which the conscious species could become involved. The animals' instincts and their natural situations kept their numbers in bounds; and with unconscious, unknowing courtesy they made room for all others.

Thou shalt not violate against nature, life, or the earth. In your terms creaturehood, while striving for survival and longing for life, while abundant and rambunctious, is not inherently gluttonous. It follows the unconscious order that is within it even as there is a definite order, relationship and limit to the number of chromosomes. A cell that becomes omnivorous can destroy the life of the body.

Thou shalt not violate. So the principle applies to both life and death. You may take your break.

(10:18 to 10:37.)

There is hardly anything mysterious in the idea that life can kill. On a biological level all death is hidden in life, and all life in death.

Viruses are alive, as I mentioned in another connection *(in the 631st session in Chapter Seven),* and can be beneficial or detrimental according to other balances in the body. In cancer cells the growth principle runs wild; within creaturehood each of the species has its place, and if one multiplies out of its proper order then all life and the body of the earth itself comes into peril.

In those terms overpopulation is a violation. In the cases of both war and of overgrowth, the species has ignored its natural guilt. When a man kills another, regardless of his other beliefs a

171

certain portion of his conscious mind is always aware of the violation involved, justify it though he may.

When women give birth in a crowded world they also know, and with a portion of their conscious minds, that a violation is involved. When your species sees that it is destroying other species and disrupting the natural balance, then it is consciously aware of its violation. When such natural guilt is not faced there are other mechanisms that must be employed. Again at the risk of repeating myself: Many of your problems result from the fact that you do not accept the responsibility of your own consciousness. It is meant to assess the reality that is unconsciously formed in direct replica of your thoughts and expectations.

When you do not embrace this conscious knowledge, but refuse it, you are not using one of the finest "tools" ever created by your species, and you are to a large extent denying your birthright and heritage.

(*Most intently:*) When this happens, the species by default must fall back upon vestiges of old instincts—that were not geared to operate in conjunction with a conscious reasoning mind, and do not comprehend your experience; that finds your "moment of reflection" an impertinent denial of impulse. So man loses full use of the animals' regulated, graceful instinct, and yet denies the conscious and emotional discrimination given him instead.

(*10:52.*) The messages sent as a result are so highly contradictory that you are caught in a position where true instinct cannot reign, nor can reason prevail. Instead a distorted version of instinct results, along with a bastard use of sense as the species tries desperately to regulate its course.

Presently you have a condition in which overpopulation is compensated for by wars (*pause*), and if not by wars then by diseases. Yet who must die? The young who would be the parents of children. An understanding of the nature of natural guilt's integrity would save you from such predicaments.

The "demons," your projections, are then placed upon a national enemy, or the leader of another race; sometimes whole masses of population will project upon other large groups the images of their own unfaced frustrations. Even in Augustus you find the hero and the villain, separate and diversified. As a man can be so divided, so can a nation and a world. So can a species. And a brief break.

(11:02 to 11:12.)

Now, dictation: So, therefore, can a family be so divided, and one member always appear as a hero and one the villain or the demon.

You may have two children, one of whom, generally speaking, behaves like Augustus One, and one who acts like Augustus Two. Because one seems so compliant and docile and one is so violent and unruly, you may never see the connections between their behavior, thinking them so obviously different. Yet if being "good," polite, and compliant is not the usual state of normal children, neither is incessant violent activity. In such cases what you usually have is a situation in which one child is acting out unfaced aggressive behavior for the whole family. Such unreconciled patterns of activity also mean that love is not being freely expressed.

Love is outgoing, as aggression is. You cannot inhibit one without similarly affecting the other, so under such conditions the docile loving child is usually projecting and expressing the restrained love for the family as a whole. Both the villain and the hero will be in trouble, however, for each are denying other legitimate aspects of their experience.

The same applies then to nations. Natural guilt is a creative mechanism, meant to serve as a conscious spur in the solving of problems that, in your terms, no other animals ever had. By taking advantage of it you leap still further through unknown frontiers, and break through into dimensions of awareness that were always latent since the birth of the conscious mind.

Natural guilt, followed, is a wise guide that brings along with it not only biological integrity, but triggers within consciousness aspects of activity that must otherwise remain closed.

Give us a moment. *(Pause.)* End of chapter.

CHAPTER 9

Natural Grace, the Frameworks of Creativity,
and the Health of Your Body and Mind.
The Birth of Conscience

(11:30.) Chapter Nine: "Natural Grace, the Framework of Creativity, and the Health of Your Body and Mind. The Birth of Conscience."

(I had to ask Seth to repeat the heading so I could be sure I had it right.)

With animals, there are varying degrees of division between the self who acts and the action involved. With the birth of the conscious mind in man, however, the self who acts needed a way to judge its actions. Again we come to the importance of that period of reflection, in which the self, with the use of memory, glimpses its own past experience in the present and projects its results into the future.

Now that is all. I simply wanted to begin.

("All right.")

I bid you a fond good evening.

("Thank you. Good night." 11:35 P.M. The ending of the sessions was abrupt.)

SESSION 636, JANUARY 29, 1973,
9:28 P.M. MONDAY

(I hadn't finished typing the 635th session by tonight, so I read Jane the last page or so of Chapter Eight and the beginning of Chapter Nine from my notes. Jane has been on a creative "binge" all month. Seth's material has been infused with a driving energy. This same intentness has shown up in her sessions and Sumari for ESP class—and it has been very evident in her poetry.

(Jane is still writing her book of poetry, Dialogues of the Soul and Mortal Self in Time.* *Last week she taped some of this material. She's also working on her autobiography,* From This Rich Bed; *this has been under way for some months.*

(From one of the apartments below us came the very faint sounds of classical music. Seth's manner was quiet to begin with this evening.)

Now: Good evening.

("Good evening, Seth.")

Dictation: The state of grace is a condition in which all growth is effortless, a transparent *(pause),* joyful acquiescence that is a ground requirement of all existence. Your own body grows naturally and easily from its time of birth, not expecting resistance but taking its miraculous unfolding for granted; using all of itself with great, gracious, creatively aggressive abandon.

You were born into a state of grace, therefore. It is impossible for you to leave it. You will die in a state of grace whether or not special words are spoken for you, or water or oil is poured upon your head. You share this blessing with the animals and all other living things. You cannot "fall out of" grace, nor can it be taken from you.

You *can* ignore it. You can hold beliefs that blind you to its existence. You will still be graced but unable to perceive your

---

*A note added a little later: For more on *Dialogues,* altered states of consciousness, creative processes, etc., see the notes following the 618th session in Chapter Three, and those for the 639th session in Chapter Ten.

own uniqueness and integrity, and blind also to other attributes with which you are automatically gifted.

Love perceives the grace in another. Like natural guilt, the state of grace is unconscious in the animals. It is protected. They take it for granted, not knowing what it is or what they do, yet it speaks through all their motions and they dwell in the ancient wisdom of its ways. They do not have conscious memory, again, but the instinctive memory of the cells and organs sustains them. All of this applies in degrees according to the species, and when I speak of conscious memory I am using words that are familiar to you—I mean a memory that can at any time look back through itself.

In some animals, for instance, the rising of such conscious memory is apparent, yet still highly limited, specialized. A dog may remember where he saw his master last, but without being able to summon the memory, and operating without the kind of mental associations that you use. His connections will be of a more biological nature and will not provide the leeway *(pause)*, that your own mental conditions allow you.

The dog does not recall joyful appreciation of his own state of grace from a past, nor anticipate a recurrence in any future. With the large freedom provided by the conscious mind, however, man could stray from that great inner joy of being, forget it, disbelieve in it, or use his free will to deny its existence.

The splendid biological acceptance of life could not be thrust or forced upon his emerging consciousness, so to be effective, efficient, to emerge in the new focus of awareness, grace had to expand from the life of the tissue to that of the feelings, thoughts and mental processes. Grace became the handmaiden of natural guilt, then.

Man became aware of his state of grace when he lived within the dimensions of his consciousness as it was turned toward his new world of freedom. When he did not violate, he was aware of his own grace. When he violated, it fell back into cellular awareness, as with the animals, but he felt consciously cut off from it and denied.

The simplicity of natural guilt does not lead to what you think of as conscience, yet conscience is also dependent upon that moment of reflection that in a large measure sets you apart from the animals. Conscience, as you think of it, is caused by a dilemma and a misunderstanding of the conditions set upon your physical existence. Conscience arose with the emergence of artificial guilt. Give us a moment . . .

Now: Artificial guilt is still highly creative in its way, an offshoot made in man's image as his conscious mind began to consider and play upon the natural innocent guilt that originally implied no punishment.

You may take your break.

(10:04. Jane was out of trance quickly. Surprisingly, she had been bothered by the music from below, muted as it was; she has very acute hearing. Her delivery had been intent but on the slow side. Resume at a faster rate at 10:20.)

The conscious mind is a maker of distinctions. It brings to the surface of awareness whole gestalts of previously unconscious material, then assembles and organizes it in ever-changing form. Through purposeful focus, a literally infinite amount of such data can be unconsciously sorted; then only the desired elements will emerge.

The conscious mind is endlessly creative. This applies to all areas of conscious-mind thinking. It is also the organizer of physical data, so natural guilt became the basis for all kinds of variations. These closely followed man's religious and social groupings. The latter are also the result of the aware mind's capacity to play upon, mix and merge, and rearrange perception and experience.

Man is innately good. His conscious mind must be free, with its own will. He can, therefore, consider himself bad. He is the one who sets those standards in his own image.

The mind is also equipped to see its own beliefs, reflect upon them and evaluate their results, so using this tool as it was meant to be used would automatically help man in recognizing both his beliefs and their effects. Part of this great permissiveness has to do with the fact that man is to realize that he creates his own reality. Free will is a necessity. The leeway given allows him to materialize his ideas, meet them in physical experience, and evaluate for himself their particular kind of validity.

(*Pause at 10:34.*) The animal has no such need. It nestles safely within the confines of its instincts while exploring other aspects of awareness with which man is not so intimately familiar. Yet natural grace and natural guilt are given you, and these will also grow more fully into conscious awareness. If you can sit quietly and realize that your body parts are replacing themselves constantly—if you turn your conscious mind into the consideration of such activity—then you can realize your own state of grace. If you can sense your thoughts steadily replacing themselves then you can also feel your own elegance.

You cannot feel guilty and enjoy such recognition, however; not on a conscious level. If you find that you are berating yourself because of something you did yesterday, or ten years ago, you are not being virtuous. You are most likely involved with artificial guilt. Even if a violation occurred, natural guilt does not involve penance. It is meant as a precautionary measure, a reminder before an event.

"Do not do this again," is only the afterward message. I am placing these concepts within your time scheme because in your terms they were born out of it. But the fact is that all "time" is simultaneous.

In a simultaneous time, punishment makes no sense. The punishment as an event, and the event for which you were being punished, exist at once; and since there is no past, present and future, you could just as well say that the punishment came first.

We have mentioned reincarnation hardly at all (*but see the 631st session in Chapter Seven*), yet here let me state that the theory is a conscious-mind interpretation in linear terms. On the one hand it is highly distorted. On the other hand it is a creative interpretation, as the conscious mind plays with reality as it

178

understands it. But in the terms used there is no karma to be paid off as punishment unless you believe that there are crimes for which you must pay (*as indicated in the 614th session in Chapter Two*).

In larger terms there is no cause and effect either, though these are root assumptions in your reality.*

(*Slowly:*) I use these concepts, again, because of their familiarity to you. In the world of time they appear as real. We return once more to that moment of reflection, for it is here that both causes and effects first appear. Dimly, in your terms, it can be traced by observing the animals that even now roam the earth, for each in its own degree—far less than yours—shows that reflection. In some, for all intents and purposes, it does not exist at all. Yet it is there, latent.

You may take your break.

(*10:56. Jane didn't have "the slightest glimmering of what that was all about." Since she was so curious, I read the last few paragraphs to her. Nor do I always try to keep material in mind. Instead I'm usually concentrating on recording it, checking with Seth when I'm in doubt about a word, asking that worthy to repeat a phrase when I fall behind in the notes . . .*

(*Resume at a faster rate at 11:11.*)

Now: The greater your "period" of reflection, the greater the amount of time that seems to pass between events.

You seem to think that there is an expanse of time between reincarnational existences, that one follows the other as one moment seems to follow another. Because you perceive a reality of cause and effect, you hypothesize a reality in which one life affects the next one. With your theories of guilt and punishment you often imagine that you are hampered in this existence by guilts collected in the last life—or worse, accumulated through the centuries.

*Seth notes in part, in Chapter Three of *Seth Speaks*: "Root assumptions are those built-in ideas of reality . . . those agreements upon which you base your ideas of existence. Space and time, for example, are root assumptions. Each system of reality has its own set of such agreements. When I communicate within your system, I must use and understand the root assumptions upon which it is based."

These multiple existences, however, are simultaneous and open-ended. In your terms the conscious mind is growing toward a realization of the part it has to play in such multidimensional reality. It is enough that you understand your part in this existence. When you fully comprehend that you form what you think of as your current reality, all else will fall into place.

Your beliefs, thoughts and feelings are instantly materialized physically. Their earthly reality occurs simultaneously with their inception, but in the world of time, lapses between appear to occur. So I say one causes the other, and I use those terms to help you understand, but all are at once. So are your multiple lives occurring as the immediate realization of your being in the natural extension of its many-faceted abilities.

"At once" does not imply a finished state of perfection nor a cosmic situation in which all things have been done, for all things are still happening. You are still happening—but both present and future selves; and your past self is still undergoing what you think is done. Moreover, it is experiencing events that you do not recall, that your linear-attuned consciousness cannot perceive on that level.

Your body has within it the miraculous strength and creative energy with which, in your terms, it was born. You most probably take this to mean that I am implying the possibility of an unending state of youth. While youth can be physically "prolonged" far beyond its present duration, that is not what I am saying.

(11:32.) Physically, your body must follow the nature into which you were born, and in that context the cycle of youth and age is highly important. In some ways, the rhythm of birth and death is like a breath taken and exhaled. Feel your own breath as it comes and goes. You are not it, yet it comes into you and leaves you, and without its continuous flow you could not physically exist. Just so your lives go in and out of you—you and yet not you. And a portion of you, while letting them all go, remembers them and knows their journey.

Imagine where your breath goes when it leaves your body,

180

how it escapes through an open window perhaps and becomes a part of the space outside, where you would never recognize it—and when it has left you it is no longer a part of what you are, for you are already different. So the lives you have lived are not you, while they are of you.

Close your eyes. Think of your breaths as lives, and you the entity through which they have passed and are passing. Then you will feel your state of grace, and all artificial guilts will be meaningless. None of this negates the supreme and utter integrity of your individuality, for you are as well the individual entity through whom the lives flow, and the unique lives that are expressed through you.

No one atom of air is like another. Each in its own way is aware and capable of entering into greater transformations and organizations, filled with infinite potential. As your breath leaves you and becomes part of the world, free, so do your lives leave you and continue to exist in your terms. You cannot confine a personality that you "were" to a particular century that is finished and deny it other fulfillments, for even now it exists and has fresh experience. As your moment of reflection gave birth to consciousness as you think of it—for both really came together—so then can another phenomenon and kind of reflection give birth to at least some dim conscious awareness of the vast dimensions of your own reality.

The animal moves, say, through a forest. You move through psychic, psychological and mental areas in the same way. Through his senses the animal gets messages from distant areas that he cannot directly perceive, and of which he is largely unaware. And so do you.

Am I speaking too softly?

(*"No." Although I'd had to ask Seth to repeat several phrases.*)

End of dictation (*louder*), end of session—

(*"It's been very interesting."*)

—and my heartiest good wishes.

(*"Thank you. Good night."*

(11:50 P.M. Jane's trance had been very deep, her pace steady and intent. She yawned several times. Seth was right there, she said, ready with more material, "but I'm tired. I wish I were in bed this minute . . .")

SESSION 637, JANUARY 31, 1973,
9:05 P.M. WEDNESDAY

(Before Seth began book dictation, he spent fifteen minutes answering two questions we had for others.)

Now give us a moment, for dictation.

(Pause at 9:20.) The you that you consider yourself is never annihilated. Your consciousness is not snuffed out, nor is it swallowed, blissfully unaware of itself, in some nirvana.* You are as much a part of a nirvana now as you will ever be.

To some extent, we have discussed your body and its composition of cells *(in the 632nd session in Chapter Seven, for instance).* All of the cells that now make up your physical form obviously exist at once. Imagine that you have many lives enduring in the same fashion. Instead of cells then you have selves. I told you that each cell has its own memory. The self-memory is, of course, of far greater dimension.

Think of the greater you—call it the entity if you want to—as forming a psychic structure quite as real as your physical one, but composed of many selves. As each cell of your body has its position within your corporeal space and boundaries, so each self within the entity is aware of its own "time" and dimension of activity. The body is a temporal structure. The cells, however, while a part of this body, are not aware of the entire dimension in which your consciousness dwells. They do not perceive all of the elements that are available even in three-

---

*In Buddhism, nirvana—a state of heavenly perfection—is achieved by the extinction of individual life and the soul's absorption into the supreme spirit.

In a recent ESP class session, however, Seth said: "There is nothing more deadly than nirvana. At least your Christian concepts give you some twilight hopes of a stifling and boring paradise, where your individuality can at least express itself, and nirvana extends no such comfort. Instead it offers you the annihilation of your personality, in a bliss that destroys the integrity of your being. Run from such bliss!"

dimensional experience, yet your present consciousness—seemingly so much more sophisticated—physically rests upon cellular awareness.

So the entity or "greater" psychic structure of which you are a part is aware of much larger dimensions of activity than you are, yet in the same way its more sophisticated consciousness rests upon your own, and one is necessary to the other.

In physical life there is a lapse while messages leap the nerve ends. *(See the 625th session in Chapter Five.)* In other terms and on other levels, this was represented in that "moment of reflection" that took place as man's consciousness emerged from that of the animals. (Note: I did not say that <u>man</u> emerged from the animals.)

In still other terms and at different levels this lapse occurs—this moment of reflection extends itself—as the <u>self</u> leaps clear of physical form (even as the cell at one time deserts the body).

(9:39.) In this regard now, and for the sake of our analogy only, think of the life of the self as one message leaping across the nerve cells of a multidimensional structure—again, as real as your body—and consider it also as a greater "moment of reflection" on the part of such a many-sided personality.

I make these analogies because they <u>are</u> pertinent, yet I am aware that they can make you feel small or fear for your identity. You <u>are</u> more than a message, say, passing through the vast reaches of a superself. You are not lost in the universe. In a book we must use words, but such analogies can, if you let them, conjure up within your imagination some feeling of your intimate relationship with all other reality. To some extent, the feeling of grace is your emotional recognition of the necessity, purpose and freedom, the innate appreciation, of your rightness and your place in existence.

Do you want a break?

("No.")

Remember also, in your terms now, the great gulf that separates you as a self from those cells that physically compose you. Your own present identity contains the knowledge and "memory" of all those simultaneous existences, even as the cells in their way retain memory of all those physical structures which they (have) formed. Consciously, because of your time concepts, you will interpret those simultaneous lives in reincarnational terms, one seemingly before the other.

You may take your break.

(9:52 to 10:07.)

Now: Your conscious ideas, expectations and beliefs direct the health and activity of the cells. Period.

The cells do not have free will in your terms. They have the innate capacity to form other organizations, but not while affiliated with you. To leave you they must change their form. To some extent you determine their "good health" within the framework of their nature. They also help maintain yours. *(Pause.)* In terms of consciousness, the entity or greater you knows as much more than you know, as you know more than your cells.

(Humorously, Seth made sure I noted down the last sentence correctly.)

You however do have free will, for while the entity's psychic structure can be compared to the body, it is a part of and inhabits far greater dimensions. All of this may seem to have little to do with your personal reality. Yet your daily experience is as connected with your self or entity *(abruptly louder, briefly)*, as it is with the cells of your physical form.

There is an obviously intimate relationship between each cell and another. There is a constant give-and-take and grouping of awareness within the body's own miraculous corporeal structure. Your idea of reality and its experience is much different than that of any cell, yet each is interconnected.

(Pause at 10:20.) A group of cells forms an organ. A group of selves forms a soul. I am not telling you that you do not have a soul to call your own. *(Again louder, with a smile:)* You are a part of your soul. It belongs to you, and you to it. You dwell within its reality as a cell dwells within the reality of an organ. The organ is temporal in your terms. The soul is not.

The cell is material in your terms. The self is not. The entity then, or greater self, is composed of souls. *(Pause.)* Because the body exists in space and time, the organs have specific purposes. They help keep the body alive and they must stay "in place." The entity has its existence in multitudinous dimensions, its souls free to travel within boundaries that would seem infinite to you. As the smallest cell within your body participates to its degree in your daily experience, so does the soul to an immeasurably greater extent share in the events of the entity.

You possess within yourself all of those potentials in which consciousness creatively takes part. The cell does not need to be consciously aware of you in order to fulfill itself, even though your expectations of health largely influence its existence, but your recognition of the soul and entity can help you direct energies from these other dimensions into your daily life.

You, dear reader, are in the process of expanding your psychic structure, [of] becoming a conscious participator with the soul, in certain terms, [of] becoming what your soul is. As cells multiply and grow—within their own nature and the physical framework—so do selves "evolve" in terms of value fulfillment.*

Souls are also creative psychic structures, ever-changing and yet always retaining individual integrity *(pause)*, and all are dependent one upon the other. Souls make up the life of the entity in those terms. Yet the entity is "more" than the soul is. Take a break.

(10:37. Jane's trance had been very deep. She seemed to pop out of it quickly; yet: "I am so far out . . ." Her voice was

---

*I've always thought Seth's term, "value fulfillment," a particularly evocative one. He was using it not long after these sessions began. In the 44th session for April 15, 1964, I find him saying, in part: "Growth in your camouflage [physical] universe involves the taking up of more space. Actually in our inner universe . . . growth exists in terms of the value or quality expansion of which I have spoken, and does not—I repeat—does not imply any sort of space expansion. Nor does it imply, as growth does in your camouflage universe, a sort of projection into time.

"I am giving it [this material] to you in as simple terms as possible. If growth is one of the most necessary laws of your camouflage universe, value fulfillment corresponds to it in the inner-reality universe."

getting rough. "I feel like we've gotten a fantastic amount of material through—not in terms of time but in content..." Resume at 11:01.)

Now: When you are aware of the existence of the entity and of the soul, you can consciously draw upon their greater energy, understanding and strength.

It is <u>inherently</u> available, but your conscious intent brings about certain changes in you that automatically trigger such benefits. The results will be felt down to the smallest cells within your body, and will affect even the most seemingly mundane events of your daily life.

You are growing in consciousness; therefore using it expands its capabilities. It is not a thing, but an attribute and characteristic. That is why your understanding and desire are so important. The processes initiated are beyond your normal awareness. They occur automatically with your intent if you do not block them through fear, doubt or opposing beliefs.

(Long pause.) <u>Imagine</u> yourself as a <u>portion of an invisible universe</u>, but one in which all the stars and planets are conscious and full of indescribable energy. You are aware of this. Think of this universe as having the form of a body. If you want to, visualize its outline brilliant against the sky. The suns and planets are your cells, each filled with energy and power but awaiting your direction.

Then see this image exploding into your own consciousness, which is unbelievably bright. Realize that it is a portion of a far greater multidimensional structure, spread out in an even richer dimension. Feel the entity sending you energy as you send energy to your cells. Let it fill your being and then direct it physically any place within your body that you choose.

If instead there is a physical event that you strongly desire, then use that energy to imagine its actual occurrence as vividly as you can. If you follow these directions and understand the meaning for them as given, you will find the results most startling and effective. Energy may be directed to any portion of the body, and if you do not block its actions by disbeliefs, that portion will be cured. Remember, however: If you hold the belief that you are a sickly person, that can hinder you. [In that case, then, to] change that particular kind of belief is your first concern. *(Pause.)* One of the purposes of this book is to tell you that no one is born to be a sickly person, so reading it can help you there.

In your terms, if you believe that you chose illness to compensate for a past-life deficiency, then it will help you to realize that you form your reality now in your present, and can therefore change it.

Later we will discuss such matters as birth defects. Here we are speaking about conditions that can be physically corrected—but not the growth of an arm if you were born without one, for example, or the correction of other lacks in the body at birth.

(Pause at 11:27.) Do you want a break?

("No.")

Your body is the basic product of your creativity on a physical level. From its integrity all other constructions in your lifetime must come. Your greatest artistic endeavors must arise out of the soul-in-flesh (with hyphens). You create yourselves on a daily basis, changing your form according to the incalculable richness of your multitudinous abilities. *(Very positively:)* So out of the soul's resplendent psychic richness do you spring with your free will and desire. You in turn create other living creatures. You also produce forms of art—fluid living constructs that you do not understand, in terms of societies and civilizations—and all of these flow through your alliance with flesh and blood.

This creativity, the strongest force within all reality, reaches from sources we have not as yet discussed in this book, down to the smallest atom and molecule. Your health is an extension of your creativity. So is your relationship with your mate, your boss, and the kinds of events with which you are uniquely familiar.

Now give us a moment; and if you want to, rest your hand.

(A pause at 11:34.) Next chapter heading. This one I believe is Nine.

("Yes.")

All right. *(With pauses:)* "Your Body as Your Own Unique Living Sculpture. Your Life as Your Most Intimate Work of Art, and the Nature of Creativity as It Applies to Your Personal Experience."

("That's it?")

That is all heading. Do you have it clearly?

("Yes." A note added later: Seth made a mistake here, as will be seen in the 639th session. This is actually the heading for Part Two, rather than Chapter Ten. The error led to some confusion on our parts for a while.)

You may end the session or take a break as you prefer.

(Reluctantly: "We'd better end it, I guess.")

Then I bid you a fond good evening—

("The same to you.")

—and Ruburt is on the right track, and with your help.

("All right." Here Seth referred to Jane's daytime writing projects.)

My fondest regards.

("Thank you. Good night, Seth."

(End at 11:40 P.M. When Jane woke up the next morning, this passage of Seth's from last night's session was on her mind: "A group of selves forms a soul." See the paragraph of material following the 10:20 pause. We're used to thinking, very conveniently, that each of us has our own individual soul. Was Seth saying that we share a soul with others?

(Jane was sure that she'd spoken correctly in delivering the material, and checking, we found that my notes backed her up. Even considering the rest of the paragraph under discussion, she wanted to learn more; she wasn't taken with the idea of a group soul, say, or of sharing a soul. We decided to ask Seth to elaborate—a request we don't make too often.

(A rereading of Chapter Six in Seth Speaks, *"The Soul and the Nature of its Perception," helped remind us of the truly unlimited attributes of the soul.*

(A session had been mandatory Monday evening, February 5, since we'd scheduled it for an out-of-state visitor some time ago, but we didn't feel much like it when the time came. Jane and I were saddened Monday morning to discover that our black cat, Rooney, had died unexpectedly during the night. We'd taken him in as a stray kitten some four years ago. I buried him in the garden. As far as we knew, this neighborhood had been his home territory.

(Because of his particular disposition, Rooney had furnished ideal companionship for our other cat, Willy, who is several years older, and Jane and I had often speculated about the special relationship between the two. Willy had always been the boss. Rooney, incidentally, can be seen in a photograph with Jane on the jacket of The Seth Material, *hard cover edition.*

(Monday evening's session concerned the use of hallucinogenic drugs, including LSD, as therapy; no book dictation was involved. Actually, once Jane began speaking for Seth the session went very well indeed, and lasted until midnight. Our visitor is to send us transcripts of the tapes he made. At day's end Jane and I were exhausted.

(Even so, her use of energy in ESP class Tuesday night was remarkable once again; she alternated between Seth and singing in Sumari throughout the evening.

(Seth had already given the heading for Chapter Ten, but as we sat for the session now I reminded Jane of her questions about group souls, as described at the end of the 637th session. It was another unusually warm night; we had a window open, and were aware of traffic noise. Jane's delivery was comparatively fast to begin with.)

Now: good evening.

("Good evening, Seth.")

Give us a moment for dictation. *(Once again on Chapter Nine.)*

I can see that my analogy comparing the soul to an organ within a multidimensional psychic structure of the entity is confusing you. We will clear it up by comparing the same properties, changing the word "soul" to read "oversoul."

As earlier mentioned (*at 10:20 in the 637th session*), and simply following the analogy, each self has its own soul within the oversoul, and the oversoul is itself a part of the entity's multidimensional structure.

The earlier statement makes perfect sense to me, for each self would call that portion of its greater reality within the whole unit its own soul. Now, does that explanation clear up the matter for you?

(*"Yes, I think so . . ."*)

If it does for you, then it also will for the reader.

(*Even though I said yes, at first break I checked the dictionary definition for oversoul, just in case it might lead me to ask Seth for more clarification. The dictionary discussed the oversoul as the spirit infusing all living things, resulting in the perfect realization of an ideal nature. This is a concept in the nineteenth-century transcendentalist philosophy of Ralph Waldo Emerson* and others.*)

All of this material, I understand, is complicated. It is also difficult to explain. It becomes highly pertinent, however, in many instances of your lives, and affects your daily being and experience. I gave the information [in this chapter] purposely when I did, knowing that our visitor from the psychiatric clinic would be here.

I want to discuss the state of grace in some detail and in different ways throughout this book. (*Pause.*) The young man who came here described in some detail the way in which LSD is used in therapy work with patients. The psychologists hoped

---

*An aside: This was unexpectedly interesting. According to Seth, Emerson is one of the "Speakers"—personalities who, both in the physical state and out of it, speak to man through the ages, reminding him of inner knowledge so that it is never really forgotten. Check Jane's Introduction to this book, the notes for the 623rd session in Chapter Five, and (added later) the 653rd session in Chapter Thirteen. Also see Chapter Twenty in *Seth Speaks*.

to bring about a cure for various emotional difficulties, to literally introduce a "state of grace." Period.

The material that I have just given you is necessary for any understanding of the ways in which massive doses of LSD can affect the individual. Here we are dealing with an artificial and forced method of, hopefully, bringing about physical, psychic and spiritual illumination. Such enlightenment is supposed to lead to better health, self-knowledge, and provide an inner state of peace. Through such therapy, conscience is to be encountered and conquered once and for all.

("Do you mean 'conscience' or 'consciousness'?")

Conscience. Am I speaking clearly enough?

("Yes." Although once in a while I have to ask that a word or phrase be repeated.)

It is believed that the self must shed its ego and die symbolically in order that the inner self can be free.

(9:29.) A discussion involving LSD, conscience, the "death and birth of the self," mental health and spiritual illumination, may not seem applicable to those of you who have not taken drugs. But all of you do hope for illumination, greater vitality and understanding in one way or another, and wonder what methods might help you achieve these ends. Much of this book will be devoted to various techniques that will help you change your own reality for the better.

The next chapter will, actually, deal with a further discussion of some subjects that have been mentioned in this one: How aware can you be, as an individual, of your own greater reality? Can you use such knowledge beneficially to improve your daily life? If you are in serious difficulty can LSD, with therapy, help you? Can a chemical open up the doorways to the soul?

Now: End of chapter.

(Pause at 9:35.) Your time was not sidetracked the other evening. That is not for dictation.

("Okay." In retrospect, Jane and I had been wondering if Monday's session should have consisted of book dictation—yet Seth was putting that material to use tonight . . .)

PART TWO

Your Body as Your Own Unique Living Sculpture. Your Life as Your Most Intimate Work of Art, and the Nature of Creativity as It Applies to Your Personal Experience

CHAPTER 10

The Nature of Spontaneous Illumination,
and the Nature of Enforced Illumination.
The Soul in Chemical Clothes

Next chapter.

(*As Seth, Jane sat quite motionless in her rocker for well over
a minute. Her eyes were closed. She's often told me that she
isn't aware of such long pauses while in trance.*)

"The Nature of Spontaneous Illumination, and the Nature of
Enforced Illumination. The Soul in Chemical Clothes."

Now you may take a break and we will then begin.

(*9:40. I didn't realize until the session was over that this was
the* second *heading Seth had given for Chapter Ten. Perhaps my
own lapse came about because we'd skipped book dictation on
Monday. [See the material near the end of the 637th session.]
Resume at 9:52.*)

Now: The young man, an assistant to a famous doctor, wrote
and requested a session (*on November 13, 1972*). He came here a
few evenings ago (*Monday, February 5*), and then attended
Ruburt's class the next night. I spoke to him on both occasions.

He had been working with the drugs in a therapeutic
framework for some time. Before this he had wandered through
India, finally following a guru. He left the guru to follow the

doctor. Like many young men all through the ages he was on his individual journey, looking for truth, overturning all stones in an effort to find those methods that would help him discover—in capitals—THE WAY.

Meditation had brought him some enlightenment, yet the guru [in India] told him that he must follow blindly in obedience. The doctor offered greater freedom and the hope that perhaps chemically the doors to truth, within his own soul at least, could be opened. So our searcher returned to this country and became part of a large organization.

He saw the sick, unhappy and neurotic brought to this new temple of truth in which chemicals take the place, say, of communion of bread. He felt that some good had been done, yet he also feared that some unnecessary and dangerous tampering might also be accomplished.

He himself took drugs under controlled conditions several times, first small doses and then larger ones. He encountered some particularly frightening material. The doctor suggested that he face himself by taking another massive dose, and though he did not want to, he acquiesced.

The experience was so shattering that he pleaded for a counter drug, knowing as he did so that this was against all the rules. The drug was refused him in any case. He said that he was glad that he was forced to see the thing through, yet grave doubts brought him here, and will finally lead him into other areas away from such therapy.

Many have come to me, or written after "bad trips"; the young especially, always great searchers after truth, and very tempted to look to the chemical, LSD now,* as the latest method of finding it. I am not speaking of marijuana at all, which is a different thing altogether and is a natural product of the earth. I am talking about a chemical that is a result of your technological knowledge.

*Lysergic acid diethylamide-25. A "trip" can last for five to eight hours, or even longer. But there isn't any one psychedelic experience for all, either in terms of time or content—the whole thing is too intensely personal. Note, though, that Seth's statements here refer only to LSD, used under certain conditions. There are other chemical hallucinogens, for example, that are not mentioned above.

When you are fairly happy and content in your daily life, you can be said to be in a state of grace. On those occasions when you feel at one with the universe, or come upon an exceptional experience in which you seem to go beyond yourself, you can be said to be in a state of illumination, and this has many degrees and levels. In any such state your physical health benefits, generally speaking, though there may be some beliefs blocking in that direction.

(10:14.) These natural states activate within your cells "past" memory having to do with joyful cellular response, brought about by particular events in your lifetime whether you are aware of them or not.

This personal kind of cellular memory in turn triggers other layers within the cells to varying degrees. Again, each atom and molecule contains within it "memory" of its "previous" experiences. According to the state of illumination or grace, those mass memories may be activated that do not necessarily involve your personal experience—though your own involvement and the events of your life may appear within them in an entirely different framework than the one with which you are familiar.

Any event of your life is written in the memory of the universe, for example, as you think of it. *(Pause.)* So in a state of illumination private cellular memory may be animated, and beyond this, a deeper level of knowing in which your own birth and death may or may not be explained.

Do you want a break?

("No.")

Naturally, left alone, you will at various times spontaneously experience such states of grace or illumination, though you may not use those terms. You will feel at peace with yourself and your world, or you will surpass yourself, suddenly feeling a part of events and phenomena usually considered not yourself. But to one extent or another such experiences are natural and a part of your heritage.

Your conscious mind, again, is a part of your inner self, and ever-changing. In terms of species consciousness it is a development of great significance. It draws strength from such sources of vitality and rejuvenation. They come naturally up to consciousness. Psychologists usually see people who are already in difficulty. The happy man has no need for such a visit. Few studies have been done to discover why the happy man is happy, yet his answers would be highly pertinent.

In therapy using massive doses of LSD, a condition of chemically enforced insanity takes place. By insanity, I mean a situation in which the conscious mind is forced into a state of powerlessness. There is a literal assault made not only upon the psyche, but upon the organizational framework that makes it possible for you to exist rationally in the world that you know. The ego, of course, cannot be annihilated in physical life. Kill one and another will, and must, emerge from the inner self which is its source.

Take your break.

(10:34 to 10:39.)

Now: Under such enforced conditions, you are literally facing egotistical consciousness with its own death in an encounter that need not occur—and while the physical body is fighting for its own life and vitality. You are bringing about a dilemma of great proportions.

The landscape of the psyche is indeed revealed, bringing good data to the psychiatrist. But the experiences undergone by the patients—and all of this applies to massive doses—represent the enactment, through terrible encounter, of the species' birth into consciousness, and its death as consciousness falls back annihilated; followed by its <u>rebirth</u> as the individual patient struggles to emerge again from dimensions not native under those conditions.

The deepest biological and psychic structures are <u>altered</u>. I did not say they were damaged, though they may be according to the situation. Consciousness is assaulted at its roots. When periods of transcendence <u>are</u> felt under such conditions, they represent the psychic birth of a new personality from the sources of the old, and from the death, psychically, of the old.

In some cases the genetic messages have changed, in that they are different. *(Strongly:)* This is psychic slaying in a technological framework.

Under LSD you are highly suggestible. If you are told that the ego must die then you will kill it. You will telepathically follow the ideas of your guide under even the best of conditions. *(Long pause.)* The psychic "rebirth" may leave you with a completely new set of problems, rising on the bed of the old and as yet undecipherable.

The new ego is quite aware of the conditions of its birth. It knows it was born out of the death of its predecessor, and for all its feelings of transcendent joy, natural enough at its birth, it fears that annihilation from which it sprang.

The natural creature-integrity is not the same. The physical world will never be trusted in quite the same way. The alliance with it is not as secure. *(Still very positively:)* The "self" that was born into the body, and grew with it, has gone, and another "self" has risen from that previous organization.

Now: Such self-changes happen naturally as life progresses, and when the self modulates at any given time, it is different from what it was. When this occurs "all by itself" it is an innate reflection of the psyche's creativity and happens with its own rhythm—connected to seasons of the mind and blood and consciousness and cells in ways that you do not as yet understand. But the whole structure and its subsidiary relationships change together, and the conscious mind is able to assimilate what is happening.

You grow and live through deaths that happen in you constantly, and travel through births within your lifetime that you do not comprehend. *(Jane leaned forward for emphasis:)* Such massive doses of LSD chemically activate all levels of cellular memory to such an extent that in certain terms they are no longer in charge of themselves, and the memories can then emerge unpredictably when the system is under stress. The fine biological and psychological alliance is now weakened.

Take a break.

(11:02 to 11:24.)

Now: It is only because you believe that the ego is such a stepchild of the self that you go to such great lengths to bring out inner knowledge.

It is just because individuals are not aware of the resiliency of their own consciousnesses that they agree to such proceedings. So patient and therapist share the belief that the conscious mind does not have easy access to the needed knowledge.

They also share other beliefs, for example: That the inner self is a repository for repressed fears, terrors, and uncivilized savagery; that the inner self must be forced to get rid of such material before it is possible for it to express its power, energy and strength in creative, positive terms; and that, therefore, the self must first encounter and deal with all those terrors of its past before it can be free of the fears of the present.

Now this is simply another system of belief in which patient and therapist operate. The spontaneity of such sessions <u>do</u> indeed <u>seem</u> to present psychiatrists and psychologists with a map of the psyche. Statistically the individual experiences, while different, will of course follow a pattern—the pattern of beliefs consciously acknowledged and telepathically reacted to.

Beneath this a definite, though distorted, landscape of the psyche <u>can</u> be glimpsed in symbols. These [symbols] are consciousness's attempt to portray cellular memory. Psychic motion always excites the molecules. The latent, easily flowing innate "knowledge" of the molecules builds up the "knowledge" of the cells *(smiling).* They work smoothly together. Under the enforced psychic assault of massive doses of LSD, the very comprehension of the molecules tries to split open. Now this is not something you can physically perceive. Cellular integrity itself <u>can</u> be threatened. Ruburt is quite right in thinking that this is far worse than any physical shock therapy.

Worst of all, there is no need for it. All of this treatment rests upon the idea that the conscious mind is highly inadequate, that deep problems are unknown to it, that it is meant to be simply analytical, and is unable to handle very intuitive or psychic material. Your beliefs alone make this so.

(11:38.) Assaults upon your consciousness in such a manner challenge the stability of your species, and insult the integrity of your creaturehood. You may say that such chemicals are natural because they exist within the reality that you know, but the body is equipped to deal with ingredients that come from the earth. Great doses of such "artificial" drugs are not easily assimilated, and bring about biological confusion.

Within their native framework, some American Indians use peyote in their own way—but not as gluttons, stunning and annihilating their systems. They accept it as a natural ingredient belonging to their earthly structure. They do not try to blast themselves out of existence. They use it to increase the innate perceptions that they have.

They become part of All That Is—as they should—without dying as they are. They are able to assimilate their knowledge, to purposefully direct it into both their individual lives and their social structure. They also use it within their own system of beliefs, of course, in which their creaturehood is understood and taken for granted. The conscious mind is seen as a complement, rather than a detriment, to biological being.

As mentioned earlier *(in the 621st session in Chapter Four)* there are, simply speaking, two schools of thought in current favor.

One believes that the conscious mind and the intellect have all the answers, but to this school this means that the conscious mind is analytical above all, and that it can find all the answers through reason alone. The other school believes that the answers are in feelings and emotion. Both are wrong. Intellect and feeling together make up your existence, but the fallacy is particularly in the belief that the aware mind must be analytical above all, as opposed to, for example, the understanding or assimilation of intuitive psychic knowledge.

Neither school understands the flexibility and the possibilities that are inherent within the conscious mind, and mankind has barely begun to use its potentials.

Now: I will end dictation. Do you have any questions?

("No.")

The material on your cat is there when you want it.

("Yes. Thank you." It was too late now; both of us were bleary. Seth had also mentioned the availability of the data about Rooney's life and death in last Monday's deleted session.)

And I am pleased with our contract—

("So are we." Tam Mossman, Jane's editor at Prentice-Hall, has notified her by telephone that within a few days she will receive a contract for the publication of this book.)

—but then *(smiling)*, I knew about it, you see.*

("Yes. Good night, Seth.")

(Louder and jovially:) And do not worry about time. We can have three sessions a week if you want them.

("Okay." This manuscript is tentatively due next October.)

I can do everything but the typing.

(End at 11:55 P.M. "Now I've got all this energy left over," Jane said, after quickly coming out of trance. "I feel it going through me. I could go for a long walk or play badminton—or even have a session," she joked.

(It isn't contradictory to say that Jane did *have energy, even though she was tired. At midnight she sang a short song to me in Sumari. The song was very clear, lyrical and restful; I had been in a low mood today and now she tried to cheer me up. As always, I thought she seemed transported as she sang so beautifully, sitting in her rocker with her head tipped back and her eyes closed. She uses real power in Sumari at times, then contrasts it with very delicate passages. Her breath control is excellent. She's had no musical training.*

(Jane discusses Sumari in her Introduction to this book. She's included a selection of Sumari prose and poetry in the

---

*This reminded me that before Seth Speaks was even contracted for, Seth told Tam that it would be published.

Appendix of her novel, The Education of Oversoul 7, *which Prentice-Hall is to publish this fall.)*

SESSION 639, FEBRUARY 12, 1973,
9:05 P.M. MONDAY

(After the last session, I told Jane that I was most intrigued by Seth's assigning two headings to Chapter Ten, but the dilemma was hardly very complicated.)

Now: I bid you good evening.

("Good evening, Seth.")

Part One of the book is to be called: "Where You and the World Meet." The heading that you asked about is for Part Two of the book *("Your Body as Your Own Unique Living Sculpture," etc., given in the 637th session in Chapter Nine).* The heading referring to the soul in chemical clothes is for the next chapter *(Ten),* which is the first chapter in Part Two.

("All right.")

Now: Those are directions for you. *(Pause.)* Dictation: Your body is you in flesh. As I have mentioned in other books, the soul cannot affirm itself fully through bodily experience at any given "time," so in those terms there are always portions of you that are unexpressed.

All of your physical experience must, of course, be pivoted in the corporeal reality of the body. The energy that moves your image comes from the soul. Through your own thoughts you direct the body's expression, and it can be of health or of illness. Out of a knowledge of the contents of your own conscious mind you can definitely heal most maladies of the body, within conditions to be given later.

Your ideas themselves follow certain laws of creativity. They have their own rhythms. The associative processes of your mind, working through the brain, have great connection with the minute behavior of your cells. As you learn to use your thoughts, or even as they naturally change, resulting alterations take place within the cells. There is an orderly progression, an intimate relationship.

When massive doses of LSD are used, you are artificially creating a disaster area from which you hope to salvage an efficient working self. It is true that the old interactions between an associative pattern of thought and its habitual action may be broken down, but it is also true that the inner-ordered structure has been shocked psychically and biologically.

(A one-minute pause at 9:21.) In normal daily life, considerable natural therapy often takes place in the dream state, even when nightmares of such frightening degree arise that the sleeper is shocked into awakening. The individual's conscious mind is then forced to face the charged situation—but after the event, in retrospect. The nightmare itself can be like a shock treatment given by one portion of the self to another, in which cellular memory is touched off much as it might be in such an LSD session.

But the self is its own best therapist. It knows precisely how many such "shocks" the psyche can take to advantage, which associations to animate through such intense experience and imagery, and which ones to leave alone.

Nightmares in series are often inner-regulated shock therapy. They may frighten the conscious self considerably, but after all it comes awake in its normal world, shaken perhaps but secure in the framework of the day.

Other dream events, though forgotten, may also cushion the individual to withstand the effects of such "nightmare therapy." In the same way that some LSD treatment finally results in a feeling of rebirth (that is often only temporary, however), so a period of such nightmares often leads quite naturally to dreams in which the self finally makes new and greater connections with the source of its own being.

(9:32.) If scientists studied the body and the mind in terms of natural healing abilities, they could learn how to encourage these, for such processes—and I have mentioned only one of them—are continuous through your lifetime.

When large doses of chemicals are used, the conscious mind is confronted full blast with very potent experiences that it was not meant to handle, and by which it is purposely made to feel powerless. *(Pause.)* Faced with the exterior nightmares of wars and natural disasters, the conscious mind is still directed outward into that world with which it knows it was formed to cope. In periods of great physical stress it draws upon the powers of the body and inner self to perform remarkable feats of heroism—that leave it wondering afterward at the power and energy of the self in crisis.

Its own stability and awareness can be vastly deepened and strengthened. In times of seemingly calamitous encounters with nature, individuals may find themselves amazed at their capacity to relate with other people, but in the artificially induced psychic disaster area of massive LSD therapy, the situation is reversed. Consciousness finds itself in a crisis situation; not [because of one coming] from the exterior world, but because it is forced to fight on a battleground for which it was never designed and cannot understand, where basically counted-upon allies of association, memory and organization, and all the powers of the inner self, are suddenly turned into enemies.

It is made vulnerable to all those forces it was meant to lead, while being stripped of its natural logical abilities—indeed, of its very sense of identity. *(Intently:)* There is nothing exterior against which it can work, and no framework in which it can get balance.

Ruburt has been working on a book of poems called *The Dialogues,* and in it recently he wrote of the double worlds. One night he stood at the kitchen window, and quite without drugs saw a rainy puddle below suddenly turn into an alive, beautifully fluid creature who stood up and walked while the rain slid off its liquid sides.

He was filled with joy as he observed this reality. He knew that in the physical world the puddle was flat, but that he was perceiving another just-as-solid reality; a larger one, in fact, in which that rain creature had its being.

For a moment he saw double worlds with his physical vision. While the experience was exhilarating, it could have turned into a "nightmare" had his conscious mind not clearly understood; had he walked outside, for example, and found himself encountering living creatures rising out of each rainy puddle; and if for the life of him he could not have turned the creatures back. As it was, it was a beneficial experience.

But when the conscious mind is forced to face far less pleasant encounters, and is robbed of its power to reason at the same time, then you do indeed insult the basis of its being.

You may take your break.

(*9:51. Jane's trance had been really deep, her pace as fast as it's been since Seth began this book. She yawned repeatedly now.*

(*When she had her experience involving the puddle—as well as another one, described immediately below—I asked her to write an account of both events in case Seth referred to them sometime. Her material is presented, with the appropriate selection of poetry from* Dialogues, *in the notes at next break. Resume at a bit slower rate at 10:20.*)

Dictation. (*A whisper, humorously.*

(*I whispered back: "Okay."*)

Now: A few moments following Ruburt's experience with the rain creature, he had another. His eyes were wide open and he stood in the exceedingly small kitchen—when suddenly there appeared before him a round soft yellow light.

He saw it physically, yet could find no physical cause for it. It lasted several seconds and disappeared. As soon as Ruburt saw it he leaped back. The last line in the poem he had completed just before dinner spoke of a light that would illuminate both worlds, one of the soul and one of the flesh. Consciously he thought the light must have been caused by lightning, even while he knew with another portion of himself that that was not the case.

A moment later the line from his poem came to him, and he made the proper connection. The conscious mind was disturbed for a moment but it assimilated the data. The meaning of the light will become even clearer through Ruburt's dreams,* the intuitive continuation of the poem, and physical example.

The meaning of the light will normally become unfolded as he is ready to fully perceive it. While the event has happened, therefore, like any event it is not completed. In the drug experience mentioned before *(in the last session),* startling, enforced symbols and occurrences are suddenly thrust upon the conscious mind; and more, within a context in which time as it knows it has little meaning. It [the conscious mind] cannot reflect upon phenomena subjectively. They happen too quickly.

Within their happening there may be a distorted—to it—grotesque duration in which action may be seemingly impossible. No separation between self and experience may be allowed. Even an exalted experience can be an assault upon consciousness if it is forced. The price paid is much too high as far as the entire personality is concerned.

The feelings that are often realized in later sessions, say of rebirth, are indeed that. The old organizations of the self have fallen, and the new structures do indeed rejoice in their oneness and vitality.

A strong suicidal base frequently exists here. The knowledge is present that the "old self" did not make it—so what assurance does the so-called new self have? *(Pause.)* Again, the body is a living sculpture. You are in it and you form it, and it is to all intents and purposes you while you are physical. You must identify your material being with it. Otherwise you will feel alienated from your biological identity.

This identity is your physical self through which now, in your terms, all expression must come. You are <u>more</u> than your temporal being alone. Your life as a creature is dependent upon your alliance with flesh. You <u>will</u> exist when your body is dead, but practically speaking, you will always be working through an image of yourself.

*As of several months later, though, Jane hasn't remembered any dreams about the light . . .

(10:42.) If you identify with your body alone, then you may feel that life after death is impossible. If you consider yourself a mental being only, however, you will not feel alive in the flesh, but separated from it. Think of yourself as a physical creature now. Know that later you will still operate through another form, but that the body and the material world are your present modes of expression.

These attitudes are highly important. In a strong drug experience you take physical demonstration out of its natural framework, presenting it in such a way that its usual reactions make no sense. A world may be tumbling down upon you, for example, yet there is no adequate physical defense or retaliation possible.

The psychiatrist may say, "Go along entirely with the experience. If necessary become annihilated." This flies directly in the face of your biological heritage, and the common sense of the conscious mind.

(Smile:) I am quite aware of the distorted religious connections made here: Die to yourself and you will be reborn; you will not kill yourself. What you think of as the self dies and is reborn constantly, as the cells of your body do. Biologically and spiritually, new life relies upon these innumerable changes and transformations, deaths and births that occur naturally both in the seasons of the earth and those of the psyche.

(Slowly at 10:54.) Change flexibly with the gracious dance of all being that is reflected in the universe of the body and mind. This does not include the crucifixion of the ego.

It is always because you do not trust the natural self that you resort to such drug therapy. The individuals who seek out treatment fear the nature of their own identity more than anything else. They are then only too willing to sacrifice it. *(Pause, then smiling:)* Your thoughts and beliefs form your reality. There is, as Joseph *(Seth's name for me)* said in our break, no magic therapy—only an understanding of your own great creativity, and the knowledge that you yourself make your world.

In physical life the soul is clothed in chemicals, and you will use the ingredients you take into your body to form an image that is in line with your beliefs. Some of these ideas will undoubtedly be accepted by you from your culture. Others will be your own private interpretation of yourself in flesh. Your beliefs about any chemical will affect what it does to you. Under LSD therapy you expect a drastic reaction and are told to prepare yourself. Your experience will follow your beliefs and your therapist's, communicated verbally and telepathically.

If you believe, however, that the chemicals in certain foods will harm you drastically and bring about disastrous consequences, then even small doses of these can do you harm.

You may take your break.

(*11:05. Jane had no recollection of the material she'd delivered for Seth since last break.*

(*Now here are excerpts from the account she wrote for me of her experiences involving the rain-puddle creature and the light on the evening of February 2. Jane's narrative and poetry supplement Seth's own words, and show how she became consciously aware of the unique transformation of her original poetic ideas into visual reality—and how she then carried the creative process* another *step by converting her new perceptions into more poetry. We think these bleed-throughs between realities are common, if largely automatic in most cases, in any area of "life." In the arts they're often called inspiration.*

(*"Friday, February 2, 1973.*

(*"I'd been working all day," Jane wrote, "on my book of poetry,* Dialogues of the Soul and Mortal Self in Time. *Working like crazy, really on a creative 'high.' Just before supper time I'd been writing about the single yet double universe of self and soul, and the last line had quoted the mortal self:*

> '*Let us, using our double vision,*
> *travel two worlds in one and form*
> *a single double song*
> *that splashes out in ripples*
> *of thought and blood*

that eddy, wrinkle and wake
through the double skies
of our single universe, and break
into rainbow vowels that sing
soft lullabies,
and fall as light
in both our worlds.'

("After supper Rob went out to get groceries. I don't
know the time but it was dark and raining hard, with flashes
of soundless lightning. It was quite warm for February. I
thought about going for a walk, but didn't . . . Immediately
after the two experiences that Seth describes in this session,
involving the rain creature and the light, I added this section to
Dialogues:

The mortal self,
sometime later says,
'That light, striking,
what did it touch
and was it real?
Just now I stood
by the open kitchen window,
looking down again at the rainy street.
Only now it's dark.
I've written all day long
and done my chores,
and company is coming,
so my mind was blank.

Yet I was caught, transfixed—
The raindrops fell
in thousands of separate sparkling dots
into a puddle far below,
and as I watched,
the puddle rose up, thickened
into prickly tissue like an air-filled lung
or porcupine of light,
with the raindrops growing out of it
as much as in.

209

It drank the reflections
from the passing car headlights,
and they rushed into it blindly
till it was so full it pulsed—
a shining fluid living thing.
The rain slid off its smooth liquid skin
and there stood a creature so mobile,
each part moving and alive, sliding, shimmering,
that I closed my eyes.

I opened them almost instantly.
The creature'd flattened out again
but just began to rise
when everything I saw
went through my soul.
Our worlds merged and I cried out;
and as I did, a soft sudden
circle of light appeared,
right in front of me,
well-defined, between the refrigerator
and the stove.

It startled me so
that I leapt back—
a softly glowing circle
waist-high in the air
to above my head,
not a ball of fire, but a silent
round, unmoving light,
and no illumination spread
outward from its edges,
so the rest of the room
was still dark.
Lightning, of course,
but no flash leapt out
from the refrigerator or stove,
and there was no beam of light
inside the room or without
from which it came.

It hung in the air
like a sudden flat sunflower,
larger than life,

minus seeds or stem.
An omen? The light you spoke of
that would unite our double
single worlds, appearing
in my universe from yours?
Whatever its cause or origin
I felt it appeared for a reason,
and I'd like to know
what that reason is.

I know the puddle was natural,
and in this world flat,
while with other vision
I saw its counterpart
rise up all shining
and nearly walk,
but if that light came
from the world I know,
than I have to admit
that I don't know how.

But, dear soul,
I'm afraid I can't wait
for your reply just now.
I hear my company,
and I'm glad to just sit and chat
this stormy night,
while that rainy wind blows.'

("*With the puddle creature I saw both realities—the puddle in physical terms, and the creature in larger than physical terms—and could switch from one reality to the other if I wanted to, I think. But the light didn't have a physical counterpart. I think it came . . . from that other reality directly here, because I had my 'windows' open.*"

(*Resume at 11:25.*)

Now: In the normal cycle of the death and rebirth of cells, and the usual pattern in which the ego constantly changes, there in a smooth flow and no loss of orientation. Previous cellular memory is carried along easily from one cell generation to another.

211

As mentioned earlier *(in the 610th session in Chapter One)*, what you call the ego is a portion of the inner identity that rises to face the world of physical existence. In the regular course of events it will change into another ego, but while losing its "dominant" status it will not die to itself. It will alter its organization as a part of the living psyche.

Under enforced annihilation, there is a frantic attempt at reorganization as the inner self tries to "send up" alternate egos to handle the situation—and in those terms, the more egos you kill the more will emerge.

In all of this the body's situation is highly agitated, and the physical organism is forced to respond as best it can to a series of disastrous events—which, however, it realizes it cannot be experiencing physically. It knows a "mock" battle is going on, but cannot stop itself from sending forth those chemicals and hormones necessary to a physical situation of like degree. There is a great wear and tear on the body, and an inexcusable exhaustion of its native energies.

Ideas form reality, so the body is used to reacting to some "imaginary" situations in which, for example, the mind conjures up dire circumstances which do not physically exist; but these still force the organism into an over-activation, setting up a state of stress. In massive drug therapy the body feels in greatest threat, for it is forced to use all of its resources while its own signals tell it that the messages it is getting do not have a correlation—and yet they are of the most urgent nature.

(11:40.) To some extent there is also an assault upon simple creaturehood. Its images and experience, furthermore, are seldom forgotten, and the so-called new ego is born with the memory of their imprint. Some psychologists like to say that you cry out unconsciously against the natural method of your birth.* But here you have the situation where a self is faced with its own annihilation, while another "self" arises after conscious participation with its death.

---

*Jane and I heartily disagree with this idea.

212

(Long pause.) I am aware that many psychologists and psychiatrists feel that they are charting the course of the psyche with these methods. It is one thing, and unfortunate enough, to dissect a frog to see what <u>did</u> make it live. It <u>is triply dangerous</u> to dissect a psyche, hoping to put it back together again.

That is the end of dictation. We will end the session unless you want to ask questions.

("You said you'd give us some information about Rooney when I asked for it."

(Our cat, Rooney, died a week ago, as described at the beginning of the 638th session. This material is included because many correspondents have asked us about the roles pets can play in family groups and their belief systems. Seth's data proved to be unexpectedly penetrating and intimate—so much so that what follows is edited to some degree. Enough remains, however, to show that such relationships can be complicated indeed.)

Give us a moment . . . The cat would have died that winter. In your terms it was a probable death. In a part of his reality he did die that winter. In your reality, you kept him alive. He had been closed up in that house over there, and went wild and terrified.

(The house in question, one of those decaying turn-of-the-century Victorian piles, had squatted on the corner diagonally across the street from us. Jane often sketched it from our living room windows.

(Four years ago this winter it was damaged by fire. The family living in it was moved and the shell boarded up—with Rooney, as a kitten, trapped inside. A passer-by heard his cries days later and freed him. The house has since been torn down.)

Ruburt was somewhat afraid of the cat, considering him wild and caged originally, as his own mother had been in his interpretation. Ruburt therefore felt obligated to help Rooney, who did not really have any love for him—just as in his earlier years he [Jane] had felt obligated to help his mother.

The cat was aware of this in its terms. It became heavy like

213

Ruburt's mother, but no longer threatening. You finally had it fixed. If Ruburt's mother had been unable to bear a child, then Ruburt would have had a different mother and a different background, granting that Ruburt had come <u>alive</u>.

The cat was a male. You and Ruburt originally called it Katherine, however, when it was still a kitten, and before you finally succeeded in coaxing it into your house. Rooney got into neighborhood scrapes, as Ruburt's father did in bars in various parts of the country. The cat knew of the identification but was willing to trade this for several years of additional physical life, in which he also learned to relate to gentleness for the first time.

Rooney even learned to be on terms with another cat; Willy, your older cat, in his way served as mentor.

Ruburt's mother was very much afraid of cats, particularly black ones. Now and then Rooney and Ruburt passed symptoms back and forth. The cat was not a passive receptor, however, and also learned from his encounters with your neighbor downstairs (who also has a cat). Many of Ruburt's feelings about his mother are buried in Rooney's grave. Rooney, though, is free of a distrust that he had carried with him this time, having to do with his background in that house across the way, and was grateful for those additional years you gave him.

He was also symbolic of Ruburt's own harsh childhood, and to some extent then conquered simply through the natural passage of events.

With the death of Ruburt's mother last year, Rooney's purpose was fulfilled for Ruburt. Rooney even did a final service, for through his death Ruburt faced the nature of pain and creaturehood that his mother's <u>life</u> had so frightened him of.

That is enough.

("Thank you.")

My heartiest wishes.

("The same to you, Seth. Good night."

(12:08. Jane didn't remember any of that material. Seth had

referred to probabilities and hinted at reincarnation in connection with Rooney, I realized as I scanned the notes, but before I could ask about such relationships he returned with a page of information for Jane on a different subject. Then when she came out of trance again, Jane said, "He's got stuff on Willy, too," but she was tiring. The session ended at 12:21 A.M.)

SESSION 640, FEBRUARY 14, 1973, 9:27 P.M. WEDNESDAY

(A wet snow had begun after supper. By session time the fall looked like it might be the heaviest of the year. The neighborhood was muffled and serene; even the traffic passing our apartment house was slowed to a crawl for a change.)

Good evening.

("Good evening, Seth.")

Now: Dictation: There are natural feedback systems within the body and psyche that operate to set up optimum frameworks of balance, in which your growth and development can take place. There is some difference here, which was mentioned earlier *(in the 636th session in Chapter Nine)*, between you and the animals and the particular <u>way</u> in which you create your reality . . .

(Pause.) I am trying to get a rhythm here that will be a good one for you to take notes by . . .

("I'm doing all right." Seth-Jane's flow of cadences had been uneven since the beginning of the session, and I'd started to wonder if I should interrupt to ask what was going on. After this exchange, though, Jane's delivery resumed its usual, rather deliberate rhythm.)

In man, conscious thoughts are highly important as the directors of unconscious activity. You become more responsible, then, in a particular way for physical effects that, comparatively speaking, are "instinctive" in the animal. This gives you both a conscious and unconscious feedback system against which to test your experience and alter its nature.

Therapeutic systems are an important part of this interrelationship, and they operate constantly. In one way, a state of grace or illumination happens where there is the greatest poised balance of the conscious mind with other levels of the psyche and body—a biological and spiritual recognition of the individual's wholeness within himself and his relationship with the universe at large.

Such states lead to a condition of mental, psychic and physical health and efficiency. The aware mind's great leeway through the intellect, and its connection with the senses, makes it possible for any singly insignificant event to trigger such experience. Intense focus is a characteristic of the conscious mind, and you can call it narrow because it includes only the physical dimension; but within the scope of that corporeal field it has great freedom to interpret the given dimension in any way it chooses.

The conscious mind can, for instance, see a rose as a symbol of life or death, or joy or sadness, and under certain conditions its interpretation of a simple flower can trigger deep experiences that call up power and strength from the inner resources of being. Since the attributes of egotistical consciousness have been so misinterpreted, you usually consider it only in its analytical breaking-down functions. These are very important as it separates larger fields of perception into smaller ones that can be physically understood. But the conscious mind is also a great synthesizer. It brings together diverse elements from your experience and unites them in new patterns.

These organizations then serve as awakeners or stimulation to inner portions of the self, always providing it with fresh experience. The inner self responds through the richness of its own psychic fabric, sending up, so to speak, ever-new particularized abilities to meet the exterior circumstances.

(9:45.) When your body and mind are working together then the relationship between the two goes smoothly, and their natural therapeutic systems place you in a state of health and grace. 1 told you earlier *(in the 614th session in Chapter Two, for instance)* that your feelings follow the flow of your beliefs,

and if this does not seem true to you it is because you are not aware of the contents of your conscious mind. You can close your physical eyes. You can close the eyes of your conscious mind also, and pretend not to see what is there. It is because you do not trust your own basic therapeutic nature, or really understand the conscious or unconscious mind, that you run to so many therapies that originate from without the self.

It seems that technologies and inventions have done a lot of harm, and so they have. On the other hand technology brings within your reach the great therapy of music; this activates the inner living cells of your body, stimulates the energy of the inner self and helps to unite the conscious mind with the other portions of your being.

Music is an exterior representation, and an excellent one, of the life-giving inner sounds that act therapeutically within your body all the time. (*See Chapter Five.*) The music is a conscious reminder of those deeper inner rhythms, both of sound and of motion. Listening to music that you like will often bring images into your mind that show you your conscious beliefs in different form.

The natural healing of sound can happen also when you do such a simple thing as listen to the rain. You do not need drugs, hypnotism, or even meditation. You only need to allow and direct the freedom of your conscious mind. Left alone, it will flow through thoughts and images that provide their own therapy.

You often avoid this natural treatment, however, and run from frightening conscious thoughts that would in their turn lead you to the source of "negative" beliefs, where they could be faced; you could then travel through them, so to speak, into feelings of joy and victory. Instead, for example, many of you accept the way of drugs, where such feelings and thoughts are thrust upon you, or forced out of you while you are denied the stabilizing comforts of the conscious mind.

You may take your break.

(*10:01 to 10:16.*)

Dreams are one of your greatest natural therapies, and one of your most effective assets as connectors between the interior and exterior universes.

Usually they are not analyzed according to your [own] current beliefs. You have been taught to interpret them along the lines of very ritualized procedures. You are told, for instance, that certain objects or images in your dreams have a definite meaning—not necessarily your own, but following whatever psychological, mystical or religious school of thought in which you happen to be interested.

Some of these systems do touch upon legitimate portions of reality, but they all overlook the great individualistic and highly private nature of your dreams, and the fact that you create your own reality.

Fire has one meaning if you are afraid of it, another if you consider it a source of warmth; and either of these two meanings will also be colored by any of the endless variations of personal events that any individual might have encountered with it. Your own knowledge of dream symbols and their personal meaning is so opaque simply because you are not used to examining them with your conscious mind. You have been taught that it cannot understand. The great interconnections between waking and dreaming experience then escape you. You do not realize the many physical problems that are solved for you, and by you, in your dreams.

This happens very frequently when you consciously set the problem before yourself, state it clearly, and then drift into sleep. The same thing happens, however, even without such a conscious set. Dreams give you all kinds of information concerning the state of your body, the world at large, and the probable exterior conditions that your present beliefs will bring about.

The dream state provides you with a trial framework in which you explore probable actions and decide upon the ones you want to physically materialize. Not only nightmares, as mentioned earlier (*in the last session*), but many other dreams follow rhythms of a therapeutic nature far more effectively than any that are drug-induced. Sleeping pills can interfere with this activity.

I will have quite a bit to say in this book concerning the creative and healing nature of dreams, and the easy methods that can be used to help you utilize those conditions more effectively. Here I merely want to point out some of the natural doorways to self-illumination and states of grace. These can be alternative courses to those who believe that there is no other way but to browbeat the ego—either through the use of chemicals or by other methods calculated to strip it of its powers at least momentarily, rather than teaching it to use those great abilities of assimilation that it does possess.

Your nature, beside possessing natural, general healing abilities, has its own unique and particular private triggers arising from your experience. They can be learned, recognized and utilized by you.

In this area certain events really matter. Singular circumstances, meaningless to others, can be used to open your own storehouse of energy and inner strength. These will include both waking and dreaming events. If you remember having certain dream experiences and waking refreshed, then before sleep consciously think about those dreams and tell yourself they will return.

If any activity, odd or silly as it might seem, brings you a sense of satisfaction, pursue it. Any of these natural healing methods can even lead beyond feelings of well-being and strength, physical health and vitality, to those sublime experiences of illumination and grace.

(10:42.) Enjoyment of an art is also very therapeutic, and its creation springs from an exquisite wedding of the conscious and unconscious minds. I will try later to explain the deep interweaving that exists between dreams, creativity, and the nature of the reality of your experience.

The most rejuvenating idea of all, and the greatest step to any true illumination, is the realization that your exterior life springs from the invisible world of your reality through your conscious thoughts and beliefs, for then you realize the power of your individuality and identity. You are immediately presented with choices. You can no longer see yourself as a victim of circumstances. Yet the conscious mind arose precisely to open up choices, to free you from a one-road experience, to let you use your creativity to form diversified, varied comprehensions.

Let us make a clear distinction here: Your conscious beliefs direct the flow of unconscious processes which bring your ideas into physical reality, so while your thoughts cause your experience, you are not consciously aware of how this takes place (*forcefully*).

You cannot, as an instance, tell yourself vehemently, "I want to receive illumination," and expect it to happen if all of your beliefs actually go in the other direction.

You may feel unworthy or believe such a state impossible for you to achieve, in which case you are sending contradictory messages. Nor can you become concerned with the ways in which your conscious purposes will be unconsciously produced, for the inner workings are not aware phenomena.

The framework of sex is another natural therapeutic system if you have not already hampered its effectiveness by contrary beliefs. Natural "mystical" experience, unclothed in dogma, is the original religious therapy that is so often distorted in ecclesiastical organizations, but it represents man's innate recognition of his oneness with the source of his own being, and of his own experience.

Do you want a break?

(*10:56. "No."*)

The soul is not only dressed in chemical clothes, but wears the apparel woven from all of the elements of the earth. As physical creatures you will be partially changed by any chemical or element, or food or drug that becomes part of your living system, but those effects will follow the nature of your beliefs.

Your dreams and the physical events of your lives constantly alter the chemical balances within your body. A dream may be purposely experienced to provide an outlet of a kind that is missing in your daily life. It will mobilize your resources and fill your body with a rush of needed hormones, creating a dream state of stress that will bring the organism's healing abilities into combat and result in an end to particular physical symptoms.

Another dream might provide a "dreaming" peaceful interlude in which all stress is minimized, with the overactive output of certain hormones and chemicals quieted as a result.

Such dreams will be greatly effective, but only for a short period of time unless the conscious mind faces the beliefs that have been causing the imbalance. The heavy doses of chemicals introduced from the outside, however, give you an entirely different kind of situation and add new stresses. These dilemmas condition consciousness to believe its position to be even more precarious than it was before, and its sense of power and effectiveness is greatly reduced.

Consciousness's experiences following such therapy may be those of elation, but it feels that any of its adventures rest on issues that it cannot understand, and its capacity to deal with physical reality is less secure than before. This is not the case with natural inner treatments that are carried on in individual behavior. These are the ones that should be understood and encouraged, say, by the psychologists.

Take your break.

(11:13. Jane's trance had been good, her delivery even and very intent for the most part. It was snowing heavily. Resume in the same manner at 11:28.)

Now: Your body is your own living sculpture—not only the shape, structure and nature of its form, but the miraculous sense-knowledge of its being and the unique effect it has upon others. The sculpture itself is also endowed with the power of creativity given to it by yourself.

(Long pause.) Those innate bodily abilities also help sustain you as you continually create the image. *(Pause.)* The source for all of this creativity springs from your own inner identity, which is never completely materialized in flesh, and so you

always have unused portions of creativity at your command. You react to the body even though you form it. In those terms there is a constant interaction between the creation and the creator, and in three-dimensional reality the creator is so a part of his handiwork that it is difficult to tell one from the other.

A painter puts part of himself into a painting. You put all of you of which you are aware into your body, so that it becomes you in flesh. An artist loves his painting. In physical terms it is completed when he puts down his brush—at least for him, though its effects continue. But you are creating your material image as long as you live, and manifesting yourself in it.

A painter does not look out of his creation's eyes into the room upon whose wall the painting hangs. But you peer out through your own eyes at the universe. (Pause.) You create not only the body, then, but its entire experience, the context in which it takes place. You endow yourself with a three-dimensional existence. It is the framework in which you have your experience, created by you as the artist gives his paintings their dimension.

The trees in a landscape painting cannot physically move with the wind that may blow through the three-dimensional room. The head in a portrait cannot close its eyes if they are open, but you move within the framework of the temporal space that you have created for yourself.

(11:44.) The features in a portrait are painted on canvas or board, but your soul is not painted on your body. It enters into and becomes part of it. Physically, you cannot contain all of your identity, and that "free" portion unconsciously creates the flesh, in your terms. Again, you direct its form through your beliefs, but the unconscious part of you does the "work" of producing it.

That is the end of the session.

("Thank you."

(Actually it wasn't quite the end. Seth returned to deliver a page of material in which he briefly discussed Jane's own work with beliefs, her poetry, and her latest ideas about her psychic

222

abilities; from there he went into our relationship with each other and with our parents.

(Assembling all of these elements into a psychological whole, he declared that "the sessions, among other things, were generated by your own experiences as creatures, and your desires to look for personal answers—but more basically, to seek out the answers [asked for] by all of your race." End at 11:50 P.M.)

SESSION 641, FEBRUARY 19, 1973, 9:42 P.M. MONDAY

(Beginning at 8:30 this evening, Jane received two long telephone calls from other states—hence the later start of the session.)

Now: Good evening.

("Good evening, Seth.")

(Amused:) Are you ready for dictation?

("More or less." I was only half joking in return. For some reason it was difficult to get my mind on the business at hand.)

A man who makes a statue uses his conscious mind, his creative abilities, his physical body, and the inner resources of his own being.

Deliberately he decides to create a sculpture, and automatically focuses his energies in that direction. When you form the living sculpture of your body, which is far more important to you than any work of art, you should certainly follow the same course. In other words, direct your energies toward the creation of a healthy functioning body. You form your image constantly; as many of the artistic processes are hidden, so the inner mechanisms by which you create your material self lie beneath the surface of your conscious mind. They are highly effective, nevertheless.

As the creation of any art is intimately connected with the dream state, so is the living art of your body. Its breathing form is influenced by the great therapy of dreams. If there are chemical imbalances they are often corrected quite automatically

223

in the dream state, as you act out situations calling up the production of hormones, say, that would be summoned in a like waking situation. *(See the footnote about hormones in the 621st session in Chapter Four.)*

The role-playing in the dream drama would be one in which you creatively worked out the problems that caused the imbalances to begin with. Dreams of a strongly aggressive nature in this context may be very beneficial to a given individual, allowing the release of usually inhibited feelings and freeing the body from tension. By such constant dream therapy, both body and mind regulate themselves to a large degree. So your flesh is affected by your dreams.

In them of course one object may be a symbol, but there is no such thing as an overall statement of dream symbolism, in which a given symbol will have a general meaning. There are too many variations in personal experience. It is true that in dreams you do reach some of the deepest sources of your being at times, but even there, the expression of that being is far too individualistic to assign the same kind of "unconscious" meaning to overall symbols.

(9:54.) Again, there can be a useful analogy in the field of art. While artists all use the same "material"—the human experience—it is still the brilliant uniqueness or individuality pointing out and riding upon that shared human performance that makes a work "great." Afterward the critics may point out patterns, assign the work to a certain school, connect the images or symbols to those in other paintings—and then make the mistake of believing the symbols to be general, always apt, meaning the same thing wherever they are found. But all of this may have little to do with the artist's interpretation of his own symbols, or with his personal experience, so he may wonder how the critics could read this into his work.

(Too true. An as artist myself, I've experienced this "critical" phenomenon more than once. Sometimes the results have been laughable—but more often they've been frustrating. I've also been praised or criticized for elements that I hadn't realized

existed in a painting, while my conscious intentions were ignored or unperceived. That can be even more mystifying: "Are they talking about my painting?")

With dreams the same is true. No one really knows their meaning but yourself. If you read books in which you are told that a certain object always represents such and such, then you are like the artist who accepts the critic's idea of the symbols in his own work. You will feel alienated from your dreams since you are trying to make them follow a pattern that is not yours.

In any case, interpretation involves but one part of the task as you try to consciously assess a dream's meaning. The real work of the dream is done during the event itself, on deep psychic and biological levels.

The dream's happening affects your entire physical condition, and so has this constant therapeutic effect. This result stems from the psychic situation set up within any dream drama (pause), and in it the problems or challenges of your existence are worked out. Many probable actions are taken; these are then projected into the probable future.

As you come to understand the nature of your own beliefs, you can learn to use the dream state more effectively for your conscious purposes. It is one of the most efficient natural therapies, and the inner framework in which much of your physical body building actually takes place.

You may take a brief break.

(10:14. Jane's pace had been steady. The reference to probabilities in the material reminded me of Chapter Sixteen in Seth Speaks. In that chapter Seth voices one of my favorite quotes: "Each mental act opens up a new dimension of actuality. In a manner of speaking, your slightest thought gives birth to worlds." Resume at 10:33.)

Now: There is one point here that I would like to make. Some of the drugs given to "mental" patients impede the natural flow of dream therapy to varying degrees.

There is another consideration involving medicine; though as I mentioned earlier (in the 624th session in Chapter Five), if

225

you accept Western medical beliefs I am not suggesting that you suddenly forsake all doctors. But naturally and left alone, any chemical upsets in the body will right themselves after the inner problems causing them are worked out through any of a variety of innate healing methods.

The new balance signals the organism that an inner problem has been resolved. The body, mind and psyche are then more or less operating together. When new psychic challenges arise, another round of natural therapy begins in rhythmic pattern. When imbalances of a physical nature are removed by the introduction of drugs, however, the body signals say that the inner dilemma must have been taken care of also—while this may not be the case at all *(very positively)*.

The whole organism is not at one with itself under such conditions. The problem manifested itself in a given way, and the drugs then block that normal expression of the psychic disorder. Other pathways of demonstration will be sought.

If these are blocked in the same manner also, then the entire mind-body relationship becomes alienated from itself. The inner mechanics are disturbed. The basic challenge not only is not faced, but is constantly denied the physical expression that, left alone, would bring about its natural solution.

Obviously there are many ramifications here, and in your society your own belief systems must also be taken into consideration. If you do not believe in the natural healing processes you will simply block them. Your fear of not seeing a doctor then will only cause more damage. On the other hand, if you have faith in medical help, this alone will bring therapeutic benefit.

This can only go so far, though, if the inner problems are not dealt with. Often they _are_ resolved regardless of what you do or believe, simply as a result of the vast creative energies within your being, and the system of checks and balances with which you provided your body at birth.

(10:49.) The same applies to mental conditions, which have a way, sometimes, of working themselves out better _without_ your

professional therapies than with them—often cures happen in spite of your best-intentioned treatment. One of the latest ideas is that certain mental conditions are caused by chemical imbalances. Supplying these does result in some improvement, but such inequalities do not cause any disease. Your beliefs about the nature of your own reality do. If medication of that sort improves the immediate situation, the inner problem of beliefs must still be worked out. Otherwise other illnesses will be substituted.

It is extremely difficult to work with yourself in the natural manner when you are surrounded everywhere by the belief that certain drugs, or foods, or doctors will provide the answers. So, in the barrage of mass ideas to the opposite, those who try to allow themselves the benefit of their own innate healing must usually face the stress of wondering whether or not they are right.

Unfortunately, the more you rely upon exterior methods the more it seems you must rely upon them, and the less you trust your own natural abilities. You will often become "allergic" to a drug simply because the body realizes that if the drug was accepted, all recourse to the solution of a particular problem would be cut off, or another more severe illness would result from the physical "cover-up" of the dilemma.

Natural therapy, therefore, is difficult to achieve to its fullest benefit in your society, because it is constantly interfered with from the time of your birth. Yet it operates regardless of interference, and is always at your command to give health and vitality to the living sculpture in which you have your present experience.

Take your break.

(11:02. During break there was an outburst of heavy noise from one of the other apartments. Several people seemed to be dragging furniture back and forth. The racket was so loud and prolonged that I was surprised when Jane went back into trance. Resume at a slower pace at 11:14.)

Now. *(Pause.)* Mental "diseases" often point out the nature of your beliefs as they agree or conflict with those held by others. Here the belief systems are different than those of society to such a degree that obvious effects show in terms of behavior. There are crisis points here as with many physical illnesses, and left alone an individual may well work through to his own solution.

Even with so-called mental disorders, however, orientation with the body is very important, as are the individual's beliefs about his own form and its relationship with others and with time and space. *(Pause.)* There will often be chemical imbalances in such a situation, unconsciously produced by the individual, sometimes in order to allow him to work out a series of "hallucinary" events. Such sustained "objectified dreaming" necessitates a change, chemically, from the normal state of waking consciousness. It is important to note that regardless of the mental or physical illness adopted, it is chosen for a reason, and is a natural method that the individual himself knows he is physically and mentally equipped to handle.

(11:28. Now all was quiet . . .)

Personality differences then obviously have a great deal to do with the kind of illness adopted, or the "mars" you may inflict upon your own living sculpture.

Now the inner problems that you encounter are always constructive—challenges leading you toward greater fulfillment.

A problem caused by guilt, for example, physically materialized as a malady, is meant to lead you to face and conquer the idea of guilt, the belief in it that you hold in your conscious mind. The body itself is always in a state of becoming. You think of it as reaching a certain peak and then deteriorating, or becoming less. That is because you do not understand it as the expression of your being in flesh.

It reflects the seasons of the earth and of the flesh. In what you think of as you, it mirrors one condition with great faithfulness and abandon. In old age it does the same thing. It shows you in flesh, both as you come into it and leave it, and here you see great variation. Many cease creating their bodies

228

and die at a young age for a great variety of reasons, of course, but some die because they <u>believe</u> that old age is shameful and that only a young body can be beautiful.

Your beliefs about age, therefore, will affect your body and all of its capacities. As mentioned earlier in this book *(in the 627th session in Chapter Six)*, you may become hard of hearing because you firmly believe that this must come with age. You will alter the chemical composition of your body according to your beliefs about its activity through the various portions of your life.

Elements, chemicals, cells, atoms and molecules—these partially compose your living sculpture, but you are the one who directs their activity through your conscious beliefs, which then initiate all of those great creative powers that give your body its life, and insure its constant reflection of the self that you believe you are.

(Louder, smiling after an intent delivery:) End of session, and very near the end of the chapter. Unless of course you have questions.

("I guess not.")

Then I bid you a fond good evening—

("Thank you very much, Seth.")

—and my heartiest regards to you both.

("Good night." 11:40 P.M.)

SESSION 642, FEBRUARY 21, 1973,
9:11 P.M. WEDNESDAY

Good evening.

("Good evening, Seth.")

Dictation: The natural therapies of the body can be called upon with great effectiveness, as you will see in the next chapter. We will discuss the ways in which this can be encouraged, as well as the role of the conscious mind as the director of "the soul in chemical clothes."

End of chapter.

CHAPTER 11

*The Conscious Mind
as the Carrier of Beliefs.
Your Beliefs in Relation
to Health and Satisfaction*

(9:12.) Now: The next chapter, Eleven, to be titled: "The Conscious Mind as the Carrier of Beliefs. Your Beliefs in Relation to Health and Satisfaction." That is the heading.

(Pause.) The nature of your personal beliefs in a large measure directs the kinds of emotions you will have at any given time. You will feel aggressive, happy, despairing, or determined according to events that happen to you, your beliefs about yourself in relation to them, and your ideas of who and what you are. You will not understand your emotions unless you know your beliefs. It will seem to you that you feel aggressive or upset without reason, or that your feelings sweep down upon you without cause if you do not learn to listen to the beliefs within your own conscious mind, for they generate their own emotions.

One of the strongest general causes of depression, for example, is the belief that your conscious mind is powerless either in the face of exterior circumstances thrust upon you from without, or before strong emotional events that seem to be overwhelming from within.

Psychology, religion, science—in one way or another, all of these have added to the confusion by stripping the conscious mind of its directing qualities, and viewing it as a stepchild of the self. *(Pause.)* The schools of "positive thinking" try to remedy the situation, but often do more harm than good because they attempt to force beliefs upon you that you would like to hold, but do not in your present state of confusion.

Many such philosophies make you cower at the idea of entertaining "negative" thoughts or emotions. In all cases the clues to your emotional experience and behavior lie in your systems of belief: some more evident to you than others, but <u>all</u> available to you consciously. If you believe that you are of little merit, inferior and filled with guilt, then you may react in several ways according to your personal background and the framework in which you accepted those beliefs. You may be terrified of aggressive feelings because [it seems] others so much more powerful than you could retaliate. If you believe that all such thoughts are wrong you will inhibit them and feel all the more guilty—which will generate aggressiveness against yourself and further deepen your sense of unworthiness.

(9:34.) Now if you read a book in your situation that instructs you to contemplate goodness, to turn your thoughts immediately to love and light when you feel irritated, you are in for trouble. Such practices will only serve to make you more frightened of your natural emotions. You will not understand why you have them any better than you did before. You may only hide them more cleverly, and perhaps become ill if, given the situation, you are not already.

The harder you try to be "good" in such a case the more inferior you will become in your own mind. What do you think of yourself, your daily life, your body, your relationships with others? Ask yourself these questions. Write down the answers or speak them into a recorder. But in one way or another objectify them.

When you feel the rise of unpleasant emotions, take a moment and make an effort to identify their source. The answers are far more available than you may have previously believed. Accept such feelings as your own in the moment. Do not shove them underneath, ignore them or try to substitute what you think of as good thoughts.

First be aware of the reality of your feelings. As you become more aware of your beliefs over a period of time, you will see how they bring forth certain feelings automatically. A man who is sure of himself is <u>not</u> angry at every slight done him, nor does he carry grudges. A man who fears for his own worth, however, <u>is</u> furious under such conditions. The free flow of your emotions will always lead you back to your conscious beliefs if you do not impede them.

Your feelings always change the chemical balance of your body and alter its hormonal output, but the danger comes only when you refuse to face the contents of your conscious mind. Even the intent to know yourself, to face the reality of your experience, can be of great benefit, generating emotions that will provide an energy, an impetus to begin.

(Pause.) No one can do this for you. You may believe that good mental health means being always cheerful, resolute and kind, and never crying or showing disappointment. That belief alone can lead you to deny quite natural dimensions of human experience, and to impede the flow of emotions that could otherwise cleanse both your body and your mind. If you are convinced that feelings are dangerous, then again that belief itself will generate a fear of all of them, and you may become almost panic-stricken if you display anything but the most "reasonable" calm behavior.

Your emotions then may strike you as highly unpredictable, extremely powerful, and to be kept down at all costs. Such an attempt to strangle natural feeling is bound to take its toll, but it is <u>the belief itself</u> that is to blame, and not the emotions. Any of the conditions mentioned puts you out of touch with your inner sense of balance. The natural grace of your being becomes disturbed.

Now—take a break and we will continue.

(9:54. Jane's trance had been excellent, her delivery fast considering my writing speed. Seth's material, especially that given around 9:34, was quite apropos in light of an amusing incident involving Jane shortly before the session: Idly, it seemed, she had picked a book from one of our shelves. It turned out to be a self-help treatise written by a prominent medical man. Leafing through it, Jane became so angered at the poor suggestions it contained that she threw it across the room.

(During break, I wondered aloud if she might have selected the book because she intuitively knew Seth was going to discuss its kind tonight—or did Seth use the incident, once it transpired, to make his points in a fresh way? Jane didn't know, adding that she hadn't "looked at the book in four or five years." Nor had I. Yet I remembered how we'd believed in it so implicitly at the time of purchase . . .

(Resume in the same fast manner at 10:05.)

The conscious mind is meant to align all of your capabilities in accordance with its beliefs about the nature of reality. Those resources are considerable, for they include the deepest aspects of your creativity, and powers far beneath consciousness of which you are only dimly aware.

You cannot will yourself to be happy while believing that you have no right to happiness, or that you are unworthy of it. You cannot tell yourself to release aggressive thoughts if you think it is wrong to free them, so you must come to grips with your beliefs in all instances.

If you have been told, again, that the spirit is good, in fact perfect, and that you must then be perfect in all of your ways, while at the same time you believe in the imperfection of the body, you will always be in conflict with yourself.

If it seems to you that the soul is degraded by its alliance with the flesh then you will not be able to enjoy your own sense of grace, for you will not consider it possible. Your beliefs will dictate your very interpretation of various kinds of emotions. Many people, for example, are convinced that anger is always negative. It can be the most arousing and therapeutic emotion under certain circumstances. You can then realize that you have cowered before contradictory beliefs for years, rise up in anger against them, and quite literally begin a new life of freedom. Normal aggressiveness is basically a natural kind of communication, particularly in social orders; a way of letting another person know that in your terms they have transgressed, and therefore a method of preventing violence—not of causing it.

In animals natural aggression is used with the greatest biological integrity. It is on the one hand ritualized, and on the other hand perfectly spontaneous. Its signals are understood. The various degrees, postures, and indications of natural animal aggressiveness are all steps in a series of communications in which the animal encounters are made clear.

To a large extent, a highly involved series of symbolic actions are carried out long before any battle takes place, if it does finally. The display of the aggressive behavior, however, far more frequently prevents an actual combat situation. Man has highly charged contradictory attitudes about aggression, and his beliefs about it cause many of his mass and private problems.

(Jane paused, still in trance. She had picked up a fresh cigarette, then discovered that she was out of matches. "Wait a minute," I said, "I'll get you a light . . . " I was glad of the chance to rummage around; the pace had been fast.)

He and I both thank you.

To some degree we will touch upon those dilemmas in this book. In your society and to some extent in others, the natural communication of aggression has broken down. You confuse violence with aggression, and do not understand aggression's creative activity or its purpose as a method of communication to prevent violence.

You deliberately make great effort, in fact, to restrain the communicative elements of aggression while ignoring its many positive values, until its natural power becomes dammed up, finally exploding into violence. Violence is a distortion of aggression.

234

(Pause at 10:28.) Give us a moment . . .

Birth is an aggressive action—the thrust outward with great impetus of a self from within a body into a new environment. Any creative idea is aggressive. Violence is not aggressive. It is instead a passive surrender to emotion which is not understood or evaluated, only feared, and at the same time sought.

Violence is basically an overwhelming surrender, and in all violence there is a great degree of suicidal emotion, the antithesis of creativity. *(Pause.)* Both killer and victim in a war, for instance, are caught up in the same kind of passion, but the passion is not aggressive. It is its opposite—the desire for destruction.

Know that yearning is made up of feelings of despair caused by a sense of powerlessness, not of power. Aggressiveness leads to action, to creativity and to life. It does not lead to destruction, violence or annihilation.

Let us take a very simple example involving a kind and good man in a fairly ordinary environment within your society. *(Pause.)* He has been taught that it is manly to be aggressive, but he believes that this means fighting. As an adult, he frowns upon fighting. He cannot hit his boss, though he may want to. At the same time his church may tell him to turn the other cheek when he is upset, and to be kind, gentle and understanding.

His society teaches him that such qualities are feminine. He spends his life trying to hide what he thinks of as aggressive—violent—behavior, and trying to be understanding and kind instead. The stereotype is of course unrealistic, having to do with distorted concepts concerning the male and the female, but here we will merely consider the aspects of aggressiveness. Because he is trying to be so understanding our man inhibits the expression of many of the normal irritations that would serve as a natural system of communication between, say, his superior and himself at work, or perhaps with the members of his family at home.

Simultaneously all of these inhibited reactions seek release, for the manifestation of aggressive feelings sets up natural

235

balances within the body itself, as well as serving as a communication system with others. When his system has had enough, our friend may then indeed react with violent behavior. He might suddenly find himself in a fight—initiating one—and the smallest incident may serve as a trigger. He could seriously hurt himself or someone else.

As a rule the animals have better sense. Your mind and your body, therefore, are quite equipped to handle aggression. Violence occurs only when the natural expression of aggression has been short-circuited. The sense of power felt during such episodes is the result of repressed energy suddenly released, but the individual is always at the mercy of that energy then—submerged within it, and passively carried with it.

The fear of your own emotions can do far more damage than their expression, because the apprehension builds up a charge that intensifies the energy behind them.

Now you may take your break.

(10:52. Jane had been "way out . . . I think we're going to get more on animals and aggression . . . Boy, Seth's still here. I just got the next sentence," she laughed, but my writing hand was lame so I asked her to wait. "It's funny," she added, "but part of me is already into the session while the rest is still here on break . . ." Resume in the same manner at 11:05.)

Now: Because you have conscious minds you have great leeway in the manner in which you can express aggression, but the animals' heritage is still retained in its own way. A frown is a natural method of communication, saying, "You have upset me," or, "I am upset." If you tell yourself to smile when you feel like scowling, then you are tampering with your natural expression and denying to another a legitimate communication that tells how you feel.

When a man or a woman always smiles at you, the smile can be like a mask. You do not know whether or not you are communicating with such a person. The sound of the voice, again, follows its own patterns, and natural aggression should and will color it at times.

There are many biological signs shown by the body, all meant as communications to others on a creative basis—as warnings to whatever degree. Each is automatic in its own way, and yet ritualistic, a dance of muscle in motion with its own meaning, and biologically understood. These are all constructive. They are meant to elicit reactions from others and to arrive at new points of understanding, a balance of rights. When your conscious thoughts interfere with such processes, you are in deep trouble.

The animal's behavior pattern is more limited than your own, in a way freer and more automatically expressed, but narrower in that the events an animal encounters are not as extensive as your own. *(Pause.)* You cannot appreciate your spirituality unless you appreciate your creaturehood. It is not a matter of rising above your nature, but of evolving from the full understanding of it. There is a difference.

You will not attain spirituality or even a happy life by denying the wisdom and experience of the flesh. You can learn more from watching the animals than you can from a guru or a minister—or from reading my book. But first you must divest yourselves of the idea that your creaturehood is suspect. Your humanness did not emerge by refusing your animal heritage, but upon an extension of what it is.

(11:25.) When you try to be spiritual by cutting off your creaturehood you become less than joyful, fulfilled, satisfied natural creatures, and fall far short of understanding true spirituality. Many who say they believe in the power of thought are so afraid of it that they inhibit it in themselves, avoiding any that appear negative or harmful. The slightest "aggressive" expression is blocked. Thoughts can kill, these people think—as if the individual against whom such an impulse was directed had no protective life-giving energies of his or her own, and no natural defense.

Here, often, and for various reasons, you find a hidden and distorted sense of power that says, "I am so powerful that I could kill you with my thought, and yet I refuse to do so." No one, and no one thought, is that powerful. If thoughts alone could kill, you would not have the overpopulation problem!

Each person has his own built-in energy and protection. You accept only those ideas and thoughts that fit in with your own system of beliefs, and even then there are various safeguards. No man dies unless he wants to die, and for a much better reason than that you may want him to.

(Pause.) Sometimes you think of suicide as ignominious and passive, but of war as aggressive and powerful. Both are equally the result of passivity and distorted aggression, and of natural pathways of communication not used or understood. You think of flowers in terms of gentleness, beauty and "goodness," and yet every time a new bud opens there is a great thrust of joyful aggression that is hardly passive, and a daring and courage that reaches actively outward. Without aggression your body would be denied its growth, the cells within it caught in inertia. Aggressiveness is at the base of the magnificent bursting of creativity.

Now: That is the end of dictation, and the end of our session. If you want something on probabilities I will give it to you at another time, and it will be, though briefly, discussed along with some material on reincarnation in this book.

(Lately I've been asking Jane if she thought Seth would give at least a short dissertation on probabilities for this book. I've been especially curious about this since we received his information on the death of our cat, Rooney, in the 639th session. [A note added later: Seth kept his word. See Chapters Fourteen and Fifteen.]

(Now Seth made some suggestions about how the members of ESP class could, by following the data in this session, write down their individual beliefs for group discussion.)

Then I will give a progress report at a later time.

("All right.")

I bid you a fond good evening. And have Ruburt show you his latest paper.

("Yes. Thank you, Seth. Good night.")

(11:40 P.M. Jane yawned again and again. "I feel exhausted—and yet I'm charged with energy at the same time," she said. The paper Seth had referred to concerned some of her own work with beliefs. My writing hand ached.)

SESSION 643, FEBRUARY 26, 1973, 9:20 P.M. MONDAY

(Both of us have been very busy since the last session was held. I had only one page of it typed from my notes, and now neither of us could remember the rest of it. "Well, since I was in trance when it was delivered, I can say that I haven't heard it," Jane laughed, "so that's my excuse. What's yours?" I didn't have any. I read a few pages of notes to her while we waited for this session to begin.)

Good evening.

("Good evening, Seth.")

Dictation: Today Ruburt received a call from a young woman I will name Andrea. She is a lovely young blonde. I would like to use this instance as an excellent example of the ways in which conscious beliefs affect your feelings and behavior.

Andrea is in her early thirties, divorced, with three children. She called to tell Ruburt that she had lost her job this morning; but more than this, that she was involved in a week of very negative circumstances and emotional encounters. A young man she had been seeing began to avoid her. A salesman placed her in what seemed to be a very humiliating situation, and yelled at her in front of a crowd of people. All of her other encounters of late had seemed to follow the same pattern. Finally she became ill and emotionally overwrought. She stayed home from work, and that situation culminated in the loss of her job.

She told Ruburt that she felt herself to be an inferior person, unable to cope, an individual who was not able to hold her own with her co-workers or the world at large.

She had carried those beliefs of course throughout that period of time, and they were expressed unconsciously through

239

her body—through gestures, expressions, tones of voice. The whole physical self expected rebuffs. The events of those days, whatever they were, would be interpreted in the light of that mental set (*intently*).

All of the available data coming into the organism would be sifted, weighed and valued in a precise search for the material that would give physical emphasis to those beliefs. Information or events running counter would be ignored to a large degree, or distorted in such a fashion that they would be made to fit in with what the mind <u>said</u> was reality.

Conscious beliefs focus your attention, channel it and direct your energy so that you can swiftly bring the ideas into your physical experience. They also act as blinders, throwing aside data that cannot be assimilated while preserving the integrity of the beliefs. So our Andrea did not see, or ignored, the smiles that came her way, or the encouragement; and in some cases she even perceived some potentially beneficial events as "negative"—these then were used to further reinforce the belief in her own inferiority.

Over the phone Ruburt reminded Andrea of her own basic uniqueness, and also of the fact that she was creating her reality through beliefs. Ruburt reinforced other ideas that Andrea had momentarily forgotten—the fact, among others, of her own true worth; and because Ruburt believed in Andrea's worth, and because Andrea knew it, this more positive belief rose up to shove the others aside.

During the day, Andrea was able to look at both beliefs and see them as opposing ideas that she had held about herself. She believed she was unique and good—and also that she was inferior and bad. At various times one belief would color her experience nearly to the exclusion of the other. Just before this session Andrea called back. She realized that she had indeed set up the situation by not dealing honestly with her own conscious ideas.

She had wanted to leave her job for another one but was afraid of taking the step, so she created circumstances in which

240

the decision was seemingly taken out of her hands; it would appear as if she were the victim of unfeeling co-workers, jealous and misunderstanding, and a boss who would not stand up for her.

(Pause at 9:42.) Now she understood that she was not a victim but the originator of those conditions. During the time involved, her feelings faithfully mirrored her conscious beliefs. She was lost in self-pity and self-condemnation. These brought about the weakened body state. In speaking to her the second time Ruburt gave Andrea excellent advice, explaining the way in which such feelings can be handled to advantage. In his or her own way, each reader can easily utilize the method.

Ruburt advised Andrea to accept the validity of such feelings as feelings—not to inhibit them, but to follow their flow with the understanding that they are feelings about reality. As themselves they are real. They express emotional reactions to beliefs. The next time Andrea feels inadequate, for example, she is to actively experience that feeling, realizing that even though she feels inferior this does not mean that she is inferior. She is to say, "I feel inferior," and at the same time to understand that the feeling is not a statement of fact but of emotion. A different kind of validity is involved.

Experiencing your emotions as such is not the same as accepting them as statements of fact about your own existence. Andrea is then supposed to ask, "Why do I feel so inferior?" If you deny the validity of the emotion itself and pretend it away, then you will never be led to question the beliefs behind it.

(Long pause at 9:56.) I am simply giving you a moment to rest your hand . . . You're not resting it—

("Yes I am," I said jokingly, putting my pen down after I had finished these notes. As Seth, Jane stared at me soberly.)

At this point Andrea believes that her life must be difficult. She has been told often that a woman without a man is in a very difficult situation, particularly a woman with children. She believes that a new mate will be almost impossible to find. She has been informed that children need a father, and feels at the same time that no man wants to become involved with a woman with children.

In her thirties, it seems to her that youth is fast fleeing, and in line with her beliefs she cannot see a woman who is much older being desirable. So her beliefs put her in a state of crisis. Change them and no crisis exists. The body would then cease reacting to such stress, and almost immediately the exterior situation itself would be altered.

At the same time all beliefs are communicated to others, not only through quite unconscious bodily mechanisms, but telepathically. You will always try to correlate your ideas with exterior experience. *(Pause.)* All of the abilities of the inner self will be brought to bear to materalize the image of your beliefs, regardless of what they ought to be. The "proper" emotions will be generated, bringing about those body states that exist in your conscious mind.

(Louder:) Now you may take a break.

("Thank you.")

(10:03. Jane had been "really out, not aware of anything," she said—but Seth promptly returned when I voiced some doubts about using this material in his book.)

Now: This was a way of assisting the young woman involved, and others too. Show her this session. There will be no problem. The situation is one in which many young women are involved, and this material can help them solve dilemmas of which they may have been unaware previously. They do not know a Ruburt, but they can learn through this book. Now you may take your break.

("All right.")

(10:06. Jane laughed when I said I'd been hoping Seth would respond to my comments in that manner. Resume at a slower pace at 10:33.)

I have used Andrea because so many typical Western beliefs coincide in her reality—the idea that aging is disastrous; that women are relatively powerless without a man beside them; that life is, practically speaking, highly difficult while it should be ideally simple. All of these ideas obtain their charge from a basic belief in the powerlessness of the conscious self to form and regulate its experience.

Luckily Andrea is working with her own system of beliefs. Presently, however, while she tells herself that age does not matter, she still believes that her desirability as a woman decreases with the passage of each day. So she feels and acts less attractive—when that belief holds sway. She is fortunate enough to be able to check her physical experience against her beliefs, and astute enough to see areas in which she has made great advances. But let us look at some of those beliefs and apply them to others generally.

Often, of course, those who try the hardest to be "good" do so because they fear for their basic worth, and those who speak of having youthful minds and bodies do so because they are so terrified of age. In the same way, many who shout about independence are afraid that they are basically helpless. In most instances these opposing beliefs are held quite consciously, but kept apart from each other. Therefore they are not reconciled.

(10:45.) Since your feelings follow your beliefs, various groups of them will appear to be senseless at times if you do not allow them free connection with opposing ideas that you may also hold.

A person may seem to be very open and responsive. Reading this book, for example, any reader might say, "My trouble is that I am too emotional." Yet on some self-analysis, almost all will find areas in which emotions are expressed only to a certain point. They are not followed through.

(Pause, one of many.) No feeling brings you to a dead end. It is in motion, and that always leads into another feeling. As it flows it alters your entire physical condition, and that interchange is meant to be consciously accepted. Your emotions will always lead you into a realization of your beliefs if you do not impede them. Emotional states are always impetuses for action, meant to be physically expressed. Each has a basis in natural aggression.

The connections between creativity and aggression have never been understood in your society. A misunderstanding of true aggression can lead into a fear of all emotion, and cause you to cut yourself off from one of nature's best therapies.

Natural aggression provides the charge for all creativity. Now reading this, many readers will be taken back, for they believe that love is the impetus, and that love is opposed to aggression. There is no such artificial division. Natural aggression is the creative loving thrust forward, the way in which love is activated, the fuel through whose agency love propels itself. *(With emphasis:)* Aggression in the most basic terms has nothing to do with physical violence as you think of it, but with the force through which love is perpetuated and creatively renewed.

(11:01.) When you think in other terms, then you fall into distorted views in which power is assigned to negative elements—and seen as threatening, wrong, or even given demonic connotations. In contrast, good is seen as weak, powerless, passive, and in great need of defense.

You will be afraid of any powerful emotion, therefore; frightened of the dimensions of your own actuality, and to a large extent be led to run away from an acceptance of the power and energy of your own being. You will be forced to dilute your own experience. Such beliefs have a strong depressing characteristic that can lead you to shut down powerful feelings by immediately considering them negative.

You will automatically begin to inhibit any stimulus that might bring about forceful emotions, and so deny yourself needed feedback. You are at the mercy of your emotions only when you fear them. They are the motion of your being. They go hand in hand with your intellect. But when you are unaware of the contents of your conscious mind, and not fair with your emotions, you run into difficulty.

You may take a break.

(11:11. Jane was quickly out of trance. "Somehow I didn't feel quite with it," she said, but I told her the material was as

cogent as ever. As sometimes happens, she'd been bothered by
an outburst of noise in the house during her delivery; so had I.
At break we were still irritated.

(We sat until 11:26 P.M. before Jane decided that it wasn't
worth trying to resume the session: "I hate to say it, but to hell
with it for tonight—")

SESSION 644, FEBRUARY 28, 1973,
9:05 P.M. WEDNESDAY

(We held the session in Jane's study for a change.

(During the last few days, Jane has felt that she's been
picking up "advance" material from Seth on his book. She's
made some notes about it. One of the phrases that we think
evocative is "bridge beliefs."

(Shortly before the session Jane told me that she felt Seth
around, as usual. But then she added, "I feel a source of energy
just above my head—not a cone, nothing that definite, just that
it's there outside my body. I feel a sort of free slide or glide that
isn't ordinary, like I've had perhaps three glasses of wine . . . I
think I know what Seth's going to talk about. My hands feel
light, too, real smooth, as though they're swirling through silky
water. Not that I'm out-of-body, but . . ."

(Jane took her glasses off and closed her eyes as she sat in her
rocker. Then:)

Good evening.

("Good evening, Seth.")

Dictation: Ruburt did receive some information from me, by
using another method. Some advance material was given to him
for his own use ahead of time, so to speak.

It seemed to him that the information "just came," but not
already prepared into words. Instead he received ideas which he
then interpreted and verbalized, and wrote down for himself.
That material is pertinent and belongs in this chapter. I will give
it in my way now.

I have often stated that the mind-body relationship is one
system. The thoughts are as necessary to the whole system as

245

the body's cells are. Ruburt correctly interpreted an analogy I gave him in which I compared thoughts to individual cells, and belief systems to the physical organs, which are composed of cells. The organs obviously are stationary in the body, though the cells within them die and are reborn.

Belief systems are as necessary and natural as physical organs are. In fact, their purpose is to help you direct the functioning of your biological being. You give no conscious thought to the coming and going of cells within your organs. Left alone, your thoughts will come and go through your belief systems just as naturally; and ideally, they will balance out, maintaining their own health and directing your body so that its innate therapies take place.

Your systems of belief will of course attract certain kinds of thoughts, with their trails of emotional experience. A steady barrage of hateful, revengeful thoughts should actually lead you to look for the beliefs from which they are gaining their strength.

You cannot do this by ignoring the validity of the thoughts as your experience, however (very intensely), by trying to shove them under the rug of a superficial optimism. Such habitual, unhappy thoughts will bring about the same kind of physical experience, but it is your own system of beliefs that you must examine.

(9:22. Her eyes closed, Jane sat quite still for over a minute.)

The "negative" subjective and objective events that you meet are meant to make you examine the contents of your own conscious mind. In their way the hateful or revengeful thoughts are natural therapeutic devices, for if you follow them, accepting them with their own validity as feelings, they will automatically lead you beyond themselves; they will change into other feelings, carrying you from hatred into what may seem to be the quicksands of fear—which is always behind hatred.

By going along with feelings you unify your emotional, mental and bodily state. When you try to fight or deny them, you divorce yourself from the reality of your being. Dealing with thoughts and feelings as just directed at least roots you firmly in the integrity of your present experience, and allows its innate <u>motion</u> and natural creativity to thrust toward a therapeutic solution.

When you refute such emotions or become terrified of them, you impede the flow of feeling from one moment to the other. You set up dams. Any emotion will change into another if you experience it honestly. Otherwise you clog the natural movement of your entire system.

Fear, faced and felt with its bodily sensations and the thoughts that go along with it, will automatically bring about its own state of resolution. The conscious system of beliefs behind the impediment will be illuminated, and you will realize that you feel a certain way because you believe an idea that causes and justifies such a reaction.

(9:34.) If you habitually deny the expression of any emotions, to that degree you become alienated not only from your body but from your conscious ideas. You will bury certain thoughts and put up biological armor to prevent you from physically feeling their effects upon your body. In each case the answer lies in your personal system of beliefs, in those strong concepts you hold on an intimate level that brought about the inhibitions to begin with.

If you find yourself running around in a spiritual frenzy, trying to repress every negative idea that comes into your head, then ask yourself why you believe so in the great destructive power of your slightest "negative" thought.

The body and mind together do present a united, self-regulating, healing, self-clearing system. Within it each problem contains its own solution if it is honestly faced. Each symptom, mental or physical, is a clue to the resolution of the conflict behind it, and contains within it the seeds of its own healing.

You may take a break.

(9:44. Jane said that during the delivery she "knew," without being aware of what Seth was saying, that he was talking about

247

*the material she'd received on her own earlier in the week.
Resume at a slower pace at 10:01.)*

Now: It is true that <u>habitual</u> thoughts of love, optimism and
self-acceptance are better for you than their opposites; but
again, your beliefs about yourself will automatically attract
thoughts that are consistent with your ideas. There is as much
<u>natural</u> aggressiveness in love as there is in hate. Hate is a
distortion of such a normal force, the result of your beliefs.

As in the material that Ruburt received ahead of time for his
own use, natural aggression is cleansing and highly creative—the
thrust behind <u>all</u> emotions.

There are two ways to get at your own conscious beliefs. The
most direct is to have a series of talks with yourself. Write down
your beliefs in a variety of areas, and you will find that you
believe different things at different times. Often there will be
contradictions readily apparent. These represent opposing
beliefs that regulate your emotions, your bodily condition and
your physical experience. Examine the conflicts. Invisible
beliefs will appear that unite those <u>seemingly</u> diverse attitudes.
Invisible beliefs are simply those of which you are <u>fully</u> aware
but prefer to ignore, because they represent areas of strife
which you have not been willing to handle thus far. They are
quite available once you are determined to examine the
<u>complete</u> contents of your conscious mind.

If this strikes you as too intellectual a method, then you can
also work backward from your emotions to your beliefs. In any
case, regardless of which method you choose, one will lead you
to the other. Both approaches require honesty with yourself,
and a firm encounter with the mental, psychic and emotional
aspects of your current reality.

(10:12.) As with Andrea *(see the last session),* you must
accept the validity of your feelings while realizing that they <u>are</u>
<u>about</u> certain issues or conditions, and are not necessarily
factual statements of your reality. "I feel that I am a poor
mother," or, "I feel that I am a failure." These are emotional
statements and should be accepted as such. You are to

understand, however, that while the feelings have their own integrity as emotions, they may not be statements of fact. You might be an excellent mother while feeling that you are very inadequate. You may be most successful in reaching your goals while still thinking yourself a failure.

By recognizing these differences and honestly following the feelings through—in other words, by riding the emotions—you will be led to the beliefs behind them. A series of self-revelations will inevitably result, each leading you to further creative psychological activity. At each stage you will be closer to the reality of your experience than you have ever been.

The conscious mind will benefit greatly as it becomes more and more aware of its directing influence upon events. It will no longer fear the emotions, or the body, as threatening or unpredictable, but sense the greater unity in which it is involved.

The emotions will not feel like stepchildren, with only the best-dressed being admitted. They will not need to cry out for expression, for they will be fully admitted as members of the family of the self. Now, again, some of you will say that your trouble is that you are too emotional, too sensitive. You may believe that you are too easily swayed. In such cases you are afraid of your emotions. You think their powers so strong that all reason can be drowned within them.

(10:27.) No matter how open it may seem that you are, you will nevertheless accept certain emotions that you think of as safe, and ignore others, or stop them at particular points, because you are afraid of following them further. *(Pause.)* This behavior will follow your beliefs, of course. *(Long pause.)* If you are over forty, for instance, you may tell yourself that age is meaningless, that you enjoy much younger people, that you think young thoughts. You will accept only those emotions that appear to be in keeping with your ideas of youth. You become concerned with the problems of the young. You accept what you think of as optimistic health-giving thoughts. You consider yourself quite emotional, perhaps.

Underneath however you are very much aware, as indeed you should be, of your reality in creaturehood. Yet you firmly ignore any changes in your appearance from the time you were, say, thirty—and in so doing lose sight of your validity as a creature in space and time.

You will inhibit any thoughts of death or dying, or of old age, and so close out quite natural feelings that are meant to lead you beyond your earlier years. You are denying the body's corporeal existence and its focus in the time of the seasons, and cheating yourself of those natural biological, psychic, and mental <u>motions</u> that are meant to take you past themselves.

You may take your break.

(10:37 to 10:54.)

Now: In this particular context, one of the problems arises out of the connotations given to the words "older," or "old." In your culture you believe that to be young is to be flexible alert and aware. To be old or older is considered a disgrace, generally speaking; rigid, out of style, and passé.

If you desperately try to remain young, it is usually to hide your own beliefs about age, and to negate all of those emotions connected with it. *(Pause.)* Whenever you refuse to accept the reality of your creaturehood, you also reject aspects of your spirit. The body exists in the world of space and time. The experiences you may encounter in your sixties are as necessary as those in your twenties. Your changing image is supposed to <u>tell</u> you something. When you pretend alterations do not occur you block both biological and spiritual messages.

In old age the organism is, in certain terms, preparing for a new birth. The combined events of spirit, mind and body involve not only the passing of one season but preparation for the beginning of another. The situation includes all of those supports necessary to carry you through, not only with acceptance but with the great aggressive drive toward new experience.

To refute your reality in time, therefore, results in your being stuck <u>in</u> time and obsessed by it. Accepting your integrity in time allows the body to function until its natural end, in good

250

condition, free from those distorted, invisible concepts about age. If you believe that youth is the ideal and struggle for it while simultaneously believing that old age must involve infirmities, then you cause an unnecessary dilemma, and hasten aging according to the negative aspects of your mind.

Each individual must examine his or her individual beliefs, or begin with feelings which will inevitably lead to them. In this area, as in all others, those of you who are proficient verbally might use the method of writing. Either write down your beliefs as they come to you, or make lists of your intellectual and emotional assumptions. You may find that they are quite different.

If you have a physical symptom, do not run away from it. Feel its reality in your body. Let the emotions follow freely. These will lead you, if you allow them to flow, to the beliefs that cause the difficulty. They will take you through many aspects of your own reality that you must face and explore. These methods release your withheld natural aggressiveness. You may feel that you are swamped by emotion, but trust it—again, it is the motion of your being, and it arouses your own creativity. Followed, it will seek the answers to your problems.

Ruburt in his *Dialogues* has an excellent example, in the way in which he allowed his feelings to arise, though he was initially frightened of them. Everyone cannot write poetry, but each person is creative in his or her own way, and can follow the emotions as Ruburt did whether or not a poem results.

He will know the passage to which I refer. Use it.

You must realize that your conscious mind is competent, its ideas pertinent, and that your own beliefs affect and form your body and your experience.

You may take your break.

(*11:17. Jane was very surprised to learn that she'd been in trance for almost half an hour; she thought but a few minutes had passed. Here is part of the passage from her book of*

251

poetry referred to by Seth. Jane wrote it five days ago. In this
excerpt the Mortal Self tells the Soul:

"But now
my body trembles and breathes deep.
Ancient angers
rumble up from my toes.
A dull heavy black hole
rises up through my belly to my throat
and empties its load upon my tongue
which turns leaden
with unsaid uncried things,
long forgotten by my mind
but clotted in my blood.
Ashen statues
of unspoken vowels and syllables,
images I should have kicked,
all from my lips go toppling.

The specifics merge,
the icy heavy mass
grows alive in birth
and rushes,
squalling, out
into the universe.
Shapes and colors,
blacks and purples mix
with the skyscape's
great moving picture
and are lost
and redeemed in it.

And I feel you now, even in my anger,
splendid and terrible,
emerging through my flesh
with the rightness of storm winds
and clouds blowing,
devastating the landscape
yet filling it with freshness,
sending debris flying
full blast and releasing
new tubers

which lay hidden under
and are justly served by my anger,
which lifts them
and you and me all together
over repression's frosty land,
surging in giant free swirls
that burst like summer lightning, flashing
and speeding over the countryside,
joyously furious."

(There was no more book work after break, however. Seth returned to deliver a page of material for Jane, and the session ended at 11:34 P.M.)

SESSION 645, MARCH 5, 1973,
9:40 P.M. MONDAY

(After supper Jane began to show signs of going into an altered state of consciousness. She started talking about her "silky" skin, and the luxurious feeling of her sweater against her back. She'd had similar feelings preceding the last session, too, although to a lesser degree; see the appropriate notes. Now, her already acute hearing began to magnify sounds—the rustle of cellophane as she opened a pack of cigarettes, the quality of my voice as I talked to our cat, Willy, the noise of my handling the newspaper. "But words are such poor things to describe the effects," she said more than once. "They're too trite . . ."

(Her situation reminded me of several transcendent states she'd achieved during the last year, so I suggested she go along with it. Jane said she preferred to hold the session. She went into the living room to read, and found the magazine she picked up "heavier" than it should be. Gradually her perception of the beauty in ordinary things became considerably heightened. She'd planned to turn her easy chair around so that she could look out at the street lights, but instead she found herself admiring the bookcase that the chair already faced. By now her voice had acquired a hard-to-define richer quality, joyous but subdued.

(For a while she just sat there, exclaiming over her surroundings.

Willy, our cat, jumped up into her lap. He became especially beautiful, Jane told me; when she stroked him his fur felt marvelously smooth and alive. On inspiration, she simultaneously stroked the air beside *Willy with her other hand—and found* that *sensation to be almost as rich.*

(We had a snack, then Jane moved to her rocker. While we waited for Seth to come through she stared wonderingly about the room, her eyes much darker than usual. "Everything looks so great: you, the room, Willy, but I think I can have a session. I want to . . ." Late in the session, Seth commented upon her state of expanded awareness.

Good evening.

("Good evening, Seth.")

Dictation: As you examine the contents of your conscious mind, it may seem to you that you hold so many different beliefs at different times that you cannot correlate them. They will, however, form into clear patterns. You will find a grouping of core beliefs about which the others gather.

If you think of these as planets, then your other ideas orbit about them. There may be some "invisible beliefs," and there may be one or two invisible core beliefs. These, following the analogy, would be hidden behind the other brighter, more obvious "planets," and yet would show their presence through their effects upon your relationships with all of the other visible core beliefs in your "planetary system."

Questions you cannot seem to answer as you study your own ideas, for example, may lead you to suspect the existence of such invisible core beliefs. Let me emphasize that they are consciously available. You can find them through the approaches mentioned earlier *(in the last session),* working from your feelings or by beginning with the beliefs that become most readily available.

(9:50.) This subject leads to what I will call bridge beliefs, and again Ruburt received some information on this topic ahead of time for his own benefit. *(See the notes prefacing the last session.)* As you examine your ideas you will discover that even

some apparently contradictory ones have similarities, and these resemblances may be used to bridge the gaps between beliefs—even those that seem to be the most diverse. Because you are the individual who holds the beliefs you will stamp them, so to speak, with certain characteristics that you will recognize. These aspects will themselves emerge as bridge beliefs. They contain great motion and energy. When you discover what they are, you will find a point of unity within yourself from which you can, with some detachment, view your other systems of belief.

(*Long pause.*) The emotions connected with these bridge beliefs may indeed surprise you, but standing upon such unifying structures you are also free to let the emotional flow sweep past, feeling it, but aware for the first time, perhaps, of the origin of those feelings in your beliefs, and no longer afraid of being swept away by them.

It is impossible to tell you of the emotional reality of such an experience. You will have to discover it for yourself. Such bridge beliefs often allow you to perceive the "invisible" beliefs mentioned this evening, and these can then appear to you as a revelation. On second thought, however, you will realize that another belief blocked that one from your view, but that you were always aware of it; and that in a strange way it was also invisible because you took it for granted. You did not consider it a belief about reality but as reality itself, and never questioned it.

Andrea never doubted the "fact" that life was more difficult for a woman than for a man. (*See the 643rd session.*) When she examined her beliefs this escaped her. The invisible belief, however, affected her behavior and experience. Now she understands it and can deal with it as belief, and not as a condition of reality over which she has no control.

(*A one-minute pause at 10:05.*) Bridge beliefs may become available to you in the dream state. If so, the conscious knowledge may appear suddenly in the middle of your waking day. A reconciliation will be felt within the self following such a conscious understanding, though the dream itself may not be consciously remembered. In the dream various symbols may be used. Each person will vary in this regard. When such dreams are remembered, however, individual symbols, such as crossing a river safely, or an ocean, or bridging a gap or an abyss, are often involved.

(Pause.) At such times there can also be strong emotional content, as of finally triumphing over psychological chaos, or even of rising from the dead. You can suggest to yourself the emergence of such bridge beliefs. The conscious idea itself represents a statement of intent. Various core beliefs, not well assimilated, will give you conflicting self-images. Now there is a difference between freely experimenting with and enjoying various styles of dress, attitudes and behavior—and finding yourself "lost" in a compulsion to change your appearance, attitude and behavior. The latter usually involves contrary core beliefs that are alternately pulling you one way and then the other.

Usually exaggerated opposing emotions will also be apparent. Once you understand this it is not difficult to look at your beliefs to identify these, and to find a bridge to unite the seeming contradictions.

You may take your break.

(10:17. Jane's trance had been very deep. She hadn't heard the sporadic sounds of flood-repair work being done downstairs.

(Her very pleasant altered state continued at break, as though she had rejoined it. "It's a real richness of sense data. Everything's got such a fantastic unity . . ." Jane explained that the motion of my hand as I wrote was related to the sounds of automobiles passing the house; the rhythmic noises of her rocker were sensually connected to the feel of her slacks beneath her hand; when she ran a finger down a fold in them "amplified long sound" was produced. She was especially loose from the waist up when she got to her feet.

(During break we heard an elderly downstairs tenant, Margaret, call her cat, Susy. Jane said this reminded her of a fish; she had the hilarious image of Margaret's gulping mouth *sending her calls out in physical ripples through the air, to envelop Susy and draw her home.*

(Jane thought she was experiencing the results of her own work with bridge beliefs, since receiving the material in advance, so I asked her if Seth would say something about her personal reactions for this chapter. "All right. I'm waiting now," she said, and closed her eyes. Resume at 10:43.)

Dictation: Since this book was begun, Ruburt has been working with his beliefs, and using methods in his own way as every reader must.

When we began, he found it difficult to believe that so many answers were available in the conscious mind, and was astonished as he proceeded to discover that this was the case. I will use him here as an example to some extent, to show how a bridge belief appeared to assimilate what seemed to be diametrically opposed ideas. The same procedures will operate regardless of the particular beliefs held.

(Pause.) Ruburt is determined, persistent, stubborn, with great energy; creative, intuitive, and endowed with excellent flexibility of consciousness. He built his life around the core belief in himself as a writer.

Through this belief he viewed all of his experience, correlating it; he encouraged those impulses that furthered it, and impeded those that did not. Now: Because of this particular temperament he put all of his eggs in one basket, so to speak. Those of you who do the same thing will see yourselves in one particular way, whatever it is. You will primarily organize your experience along definite lines. It may be your sex role or your professional role. You may see yourself as a mother or a father first of all, as a teacher, an editor, or as a "man's man." You will, however, emphasize one certain quality above all others— your athletic nature, your spiritual bent, whatever it may be.

Now such concentration is excellent if the original concept continues to expand with your experience, and of itself is not limiting to a strong degree. You may see yourself primarily as a mother. Initially, that may simply involve taking care of your

257

children at home. But if that idea of yourself remains limited then it may preclude, say, even being a wife to your husband, deny you many complementary interests, and prevent expansion of your personality in other areas.

In the same way, if your core belief stresses your spirituality to such an extent that it cuts off needed sensual expression, then it has become restrictive and will end up strangling, even, that spiritual experience that it was originally meant to express.

As he worked with his beliefs, Ruburt found himself in a position where he came face to face with two conflicting core beliefs. His "writing self" followed one belief, in which writing certain material was permissable and good. He had schooled himself to refute any opposing impulses, and built his life along those lines from a young age.

With the initiation of psychic experience, he found himself wanting to write about what happened to him, and to use the material creatively. The previous beliefs in himself as a writer, however, clashed with these new urges because he did not consider anything but fiction as the work of a writer, except for poetry.

He proceeded to make two divisions in his life, one "psychic," and the other "the writing self." The writing self looked askance at any creative material that did not come from the kinds of inspiration with which it was previously familiar. It insisted that other creative material come outside of Ruburt's five-hour writing day. These beliefs generated their own emotions, of course, so that Ruburt would become angry when thought of as a "psychic" by others.

The same kind of dilemma can arise in any reader's experience whenever two strongly conflicting core beliefs meet. Ruburt also believed in his psychic work, you see, and was fully committed to it. He developed some physical symptoms, and following through with his beliefs he is working them out on his own. He saw for himself how they perfectly mirrored his inner image of himself.

(11:12.) I gave him helpful information, but this could only be used by him as he _felt_ it for himself and traveled through his own system of beliefs. When you understand the nature of reality and your part in forming it, then you can no longer look to others to solve your problems for you, and you realize that your own beliefs are the rich creative elements that you yourself must mix and match. If you think that certain foods will help you, then they will be effective in that system—because of your beliefs. If you believe in doctors, then they _will_ help you.

If you believe in healers then they can help you, but all of those aids are only temporary at best. Ruburt was in a position where he realized that. He accepted the fact that he formed his own reality, and that there were physical aspects of it that disturbed him deeply. He also understood _(long pause)_, that he could not use me as a crutch.

Dialogues (see the 639th session in Chapter Ten) is now a book, just completed, but it also represented a movement of the self through a question-and-answer format, through which Ruburt recognized and faced many diverse beliefs. Each reader can utilize the same method whether or not artistic achievement is also involved, through objectifying personal beliefs in a dialogue form. This also happens frequently in the dream state, when you allow your natural creativity so much freedom. Often there are dreams in which "you" are two separate people, either strangers or familiar, each asking questions of the other.

The day Ruburt received the "advance" information on bridge beliefs _(see the last session)_, the obvious suddenly became clear. The writing self was finding itself more and more hampered, unable to use excellent material because of its limited beliefs. It focused so defensively on its own material that it was hampering its flow of creativity, while the "unacceptable" aspects of Ruburt merrily went on creating other books, not even including my own.

Ruburt found himself bargaining with the early writing self, and suddenly said, "What am I doing?"

His core belief in himself as a writer, he saw, was really highly constrictive. He had not realized that before. At the same time he had consciously known it, but allowed it to remain invisible. He realized that the writing and psychic aspects each did want to write, and this was the bridge belief.

Using it, he is only now in the process of assimilating the newly available energy. He understands that he is the self who holds all of those beliefs, and does not identify so completely with the one core belief any longer. That association was what had prevented its natural motion and expansion earlier.

(Pause.) The original belief meant that he considered his reality in mental terms, generally identifying a writer with ideas, and using his body as a vehicle rather than thinking of it as the living organism through which creaturehood experience must come. So this evening the senses were allowed their freedom, but the experience was magnified by his psychic sensitivity.

If you consider yourself primarily physical then you may, in line with your beliefs, impede your spiritual or emotional aspects. In that case, working with your beliefs will lead you to greater experience along mental and spiritual paths. But all are interconnected, and you cannot ignore one except at the expense of others.

Now you may take a break.

(11:37. Jane had been far out, she said, but she'd known Seth had been talking about her. During break her "ecstasy feelings"—she didn't know what else to call them—continued. They surged through her. She was acutely conscious of the sensations of her clothing against her skin. "My body's so alive that I almost can't stand it at times—"

(The sound of a passing automobile leaped up her legs, through her body and down to her fingertips. Water running somewhere in the house filled her with a great thrilling. Jane, wanting to continue the session, made strong efforts to quiet her reactions. She lit a cigarette, sat in her rocker, and closed her eyes. Resume at 11:55.)

Now: Ruburt also saw that he believed he had to justify his existence through his writing. This because he did not trust the

260

basic right of his being as it existed, and does, in space and time. These old beliefs had not caught up to his newer ones.

The same artificial need to vindicate being is present in many of my readers, and various core beliefs may be built up to hide this inner insecurity. You may "justify your life" by biological creativity, and then latch onto your children and never want to let them go. You may use your career instead. But in all cases you must come to grips with such unnecessary ideas, face the reality of your creaturehood, and see that you certainly have as much of a place in the universe as a squirrel, an ant or a leaf. You do not question their right to exist. Why question your own?

(Louder, smiling:) And that is the end of our passionate session, and you may delete the word.

("Thank you, Seth. Good night."

(12:02 A.M. "Those feelings even came up a couple of times while Seth was talking," Jane said. And her richly sensual responses continued. The feel of the bedsheets against her body was "almost too much" for an hour or so after the session. Traces of the experience lingered into the next day.

(A note added later: For some related material about the flexibility of Jane's perceptions, see our extensive notes for the 653rd session in Chapter Thirteen, as well as those for the already mentioned 639th session.)

SESSION 646, MARCH 7, 1973,
10:28 P.M. WEDNESDAY

(Just yesterday Jane received a letter from a woman who described the onset, a few years ago, of extraordinary feelings of transcendent love for mankind. Her profound emotions still continued, although she had them under control. She had told no one about them, though, and wanted to know if we could ask Seth about their meaning. In addition, she had recently received a medical verdict about the certainty of her death within a year or two.

(Aside from her sympathetic response, Jane found the letter

evocative of some of her own psychic experiences, and asked me to put it in our Seth notebook for an answer—we felt that Seth's reply would be of interest to many. For the same reason, at the end of the session [in Chapter Twelve] we're including a local resident's experience with a certain set of beliefs.

(Jane was tired after supper, so I didn't ask her about having a session. Then at about 9:00 a neighbor couldn't get her door unlocked and asked us for help. By the time this episode was resolved Jane had come alert, and surprised me by saying she wanted to hold the session. She began speaking for Seth very quietly.)

Good evening.

("Good evening, Seth.")

Now: Dictation: When you allow your emotions their natural spontaneous flow they will never engulf you, and always return you refreshed to "logical" conscious-mind thought.

It is only when you dam them up that they appear to be opposed to the intellect, or overwhelming. It is of the utmost importance, however, that you understand the power and directing nature of your conscious mind, for otherwise you will believe yourself to be forever at the mercy of conditions and situations over which you feel you have no control.

Again, while the conscious mind is meant to <u>direct</u> the flow of your experience through your beliefs, and to materialize them, the actual mechanics are taken care of automatically by other portions of the self. You must indeed trust that your new beliefs will work as completely for you as your old ones.

(Long pause.) It may seem that your religious beliefs have little to do with your health or with your day-to-day experience. Those of you who have left organized religions may feel relatively free from what you consider to be the adverse connotations of original sin and the like. Yet no one is free of belief of any kind in that area. Indeed, a belief in atheism is a belief.

In the next chapter, let us consider more closely your ideas about good and evil, the morality of the self, and examine the ways in which your ideas are reflected in your lives.

262

End of chapter.
(*"All right." Pause at 10:38.*)
Now: A note to the woman whose letter you have there. Give us a moment . . .

No man or woman consciously knows for sure which day will be the last for him or her in this particular life, that each calls the present one. Mortality with its birth and death is the framework in which the soul, for now, is expressed in flesh. Birth and death contain between them the earthly experience that you perceive as happening within a given period of time, through various seasons, and involving unique perceptions within areas of space—encountered with other human beings, all to one extent or another sharing with you events caused by the intersection of the self and time and space.

Birth and death then have their function, intensifying and focusing your attention. Life seems more dear in your terms, corporeal terms, because of the existence of death. It seems, perhaps, easier to have no conscious idea of the year or time that death might occur. Unconsciously of course each man and woman knows, and yet hides the knowledge.

The knowledge is usually hidden for many reasons, but the fact of death, personal death, is never forgotten. It seems obvious, but the full enjoyment of life would be impossible in the framework, now, of earthly reality without the knowledge of death.

You have been given an opportunity to study life and to experience it more fully than you ever have before in this existence. Its intensity and brilliance, its contrasts and similarities, its joys and its sorrows, are here for you to perceive, whose eyes are opened by the fact of the doctor's pronouncement.

Now I tell you: That intensification, appreciated and understood, and the experience of life and living, accepted unconditionally, can bring you in this lifetime another birth in which the doctor's pronouncements are meaningless. Spiritually the death sentence given you is another chance at life, if you are freely able to accept life with all of its conditions and to feel its full dimensions, for that alone will rejuvenate your spiritual and physical self.

The experience that you wrote of was significant on several levels, and of course was meant to reassure you ahead of time because of the events you knew would occur. The experience was to inform you emotionally and spiritually of the great meaning of each individual, portray the lovely brilliance that is within each human being, and let you know that the integrity of the self and the soul exists beyond the possibility of annihilation, as you yourself will continue to exist regardless of which path you choose to take—dying within two years, or living physically on for many more. In other words, you will continue to exist and to be <u>fulfilled</u> within that love you sensed.

You felt before, unconsciously, that you were drifting and that life had little meaning. Beneath the surface of events you felt unfulfilled, and felt that you had great courage and abilities with never a chance to use them, and no "heroic" episodes then to rouse you to fuller understanding, and no real impetus to lift you or to bring excitement into your days. Unconsciously, therefore, you chose a situation in which a crisis was precipitated, rousing all the greatest elements of heart and soul, so that they must strain to understand, to perceive, to triumph. And so you shall, in whatever way is most important for you, and you will learn more and be more fulfilled than you would have been had those conditions not been initiated.

This does not mean that there were not other ways available that you could have chosen. You chose the set of conditions that you did because in past existences you were so terrified of death that you tried to hide its knowledge from yourself, and this time you placed it in the forefront of your attention.

In the entire fabric of your existence, this life is a brilliant, eternally unique and precious portion, but only a portion, from which you emerge with joy and understanding whether you die tomorrow or in years to come. The choice of life and death is always yours.

Life and death are but two faces of your eternal, ever-changing existence, however. Feel and appreciate the joy of your own being. Many live into their nineties without ever appreciating to that extent the beauty of their being. You have lived before, and will again, and your new life, in your terms, springs out of the old, and is growing in the old and <u>contained</u> within it as the seed is already contained within the flower.

We are all travelers, whatever our position, and as one traveler to another, I salute you. End of reply.

You may take your break.

(11:11. But this wasn't break after all. Instead Seth decided to relay a page of material for Jane and me before launching into Chapter Twelve. Break lasted then from 11:22 to 11:40.)

CHAPTER 12

Grace, Conscience,
and Your Daily Experience

Now: Give us a moment for dictation. We are beginning the next chapter and the heading is: "Grace, Conscience, and Your Daily Experience."

Thus far I have rather frequently mentioned the state of grace *(in the 636th session in Chapter Nine, for instance),* because while it has many dimensions it is, practically speaking, the cause of your sense of well-being and accomplishment. It is a condition of your existence. Each of you may put the following in your own terms, but often it may seem as if your conscience tells you that you have "fallen out of grace," and that some inner, mysterious, joyous sense of support no longer sustains you. Unfortunately, conscience as you think of it is an untrustworthy guide, speaking to you through the mouths of mothers and fathers, teachers and clergy—all perhaps from distant years, and each of whom had their own ideas of what was right and wrong for you and for humanity at large.

(11:45.) These people of course were, and are, quite fallible. When you are a child however adults seem godlike. Their words fall with great weight because you are so at the mercy of their

support. As a child it was quite necessary that you accept beliefs from others before your conscious mind could form its own.

You accepted the concepts for your own reasons. Those given beliefs represent the spiritual and mental fabric of ideas—the raw material, so to speak, with which you have to work. In adolescence certain beliefs will be easily and immediately abandoned, or altered to fit the expanding pattern of experience. Still other beliefs will remain, with perhaps certain elements being changed. The beliefs may be revised to fit your new image, for example, while the main pattern remains the same.

Let us consider the idea of original sin, all of the colorful forms it may take within your body of concepts, and the ways in which these will affect your behavior and experience.

(11:55.) The concept itself existed long before Christianity's initiation, and was told in various forms throughout the centuries and in all civilizations. On the side of consciousness, it is a tale symbolically representing the birth of the conscious mind in the species as a whole, and the emergence of self-responsibility. It also stands for the separation of the self who perceives—and therefore judges and values—from the object which is perceived and evaluated. It represents the emergence of the conscious mind and of the strongly oriented individual self from that ground of being from which all consciousness comes.

It portrays the new consciousness seeing itself unique and separate, evolving from the tree of life and therefore able to examine its fruits, to see itself for the first time as different from others, like the serpent who crawled upon the surface of the earth. Man came forth as a creature of distinctions. In so doing he quite purposefully detached himself, in your terms now, from the body of his planet in a new way. A part of him very naturally yearned for that primeval *(louder)* knowing unknowingness that had to be abandoned, in which all things were given—no judgments or distinctions were necessary, and all responsibilities were biologically foreordained.

267

He saw himself as rising above the serpent, which was a symbol of unconscious knowledge. Yet the serpent would always mystify and attract man, even though he must stand upon its head, symbolically speaking, and rise from its knowledge.

With the birth of this consciousness came conscious responsibility for the fruits of the planet. Man became the caretaker.

Now that is the end of dictation. You may or may not, as you wish, include the following as a part of the book.

(12:07. A couple of months ago, a close friend developed painful tooth and jaw symptoms—resulting in a loss of weight— for the reasons given below.)

As soon as your friend began reading his book on health foods he received, or presented himself with, an excellent example of the way in which beliefs work. If he realizes this now the experience can be invaluable.

If certain foods are good then other foods must be bad. If he had a symptom after eating specific items, then he avoided those. Before he read the book the idea would not have occurred to him in that context.

The refusal of particular foods, therefore, became a symbol for the avoidance of certain beliefs, so that for a while the beliefs were not faced while the foods were not eaten. This is done with many such methods on a consistent basis by people all the time. In your friend's case, the realization that he can eat those foods means that he understands that he can encounter those beliefs in himself, as he is now beginning to do.

His rejection of the foods for this length of time persisted as a symbol that he was still not facing his beliefs. With each "triumph," now—and there have been several with your help and Ruburt's—he shows himself that beliefs and not food are important, and reinforces his independence and freedom.

He has read a book that discusses massaging the feet in relationship with affecting reflexes in the body. Now: The natural consideration given to the body during such "therapy" is highly beneficial because the body's rights are taken into consideration, <u>without</u> the value judgment of right and wrong carried by the health foods.

In this book, I will have more to say regarding health foods. The less <u>contaminated</u> your food, for example, the better off you are, but not if you believe that the body in its wisdom cannot handle the ordinary foods with which you are provided. Natural massage is of great value, particularly when done by another with healing intent. It will not <u>solve</u> inner problems. It is not an answer in itself, but it can help in promoting relaxation momentarily.

The reflexes mentioned do exist. If the proper inner attitude is maintained, such massage can be of good value. It simply acts then to familiarize the body with those deep feelings of relaxation that the mind has denied it, and can be an excellent learning process.

Now you may end the session or take a break, as you prefer.

("I'm afraid we'll have to end it, then.")

Then I bid you a fond good evening—

("The same to you.")

—and what blessings I have, I give you.

("Thank you, Seth. Good night.")

(12:25 A.M. Seth, Jane said, was all ready to keep going if we gave the word—the rest of the chapter "was right there." Also there for the asking was more material about ourselves, but . . .)

SESSION 647, MARCH 12, 1973,
9:37 P.M. MONDAY

(I had only part of the last session typed, so I read the rest of it to Jane from my notes. Just before tonight's session began she said with unwitting humor, "I'm starting to get stuff from Seth, but it's about us. I don't want that, I want material on the book—" But Seth did come through with a couple of pages relative to a discussion we'd had today. After a pause at 9:50, he resumed dictation on Chapter Twelve.)

Now give us a moment . . . Dictation: The serpent is the symbol of the deepest knowledge within creaturehood; it also

269

contains the impetus to rise above or beyond itself in <u>certain respects</u>. Eve, rather than Adam, for example, eats of the apple first because it was the intuitive elements of the race, portrayed in the story as female, that would bring about this initiation; only afterward could the ego, symbolized by Adam, attain its new birth and its necessary alienation. The tree of knowledge, then, did indeed offer its fruits—and "good and bad"—because this was the first time there were any kinds of choices available, and free will.

There were other tales, some that have not come down to you, in which Adam and Eve were created together, and in a dream fell apart into the separate male and female. In your particular legend Adam appears first. The woman being created from his rib symbolized the necessary emergence, even from the new creature, of the intuitive forces that will always come forth—for without that development the race would not have attained self-consciousness in your terms.

Good and evil then simply represented the birth of choices, initially in terms of survival, where earlier instinct alone had provided all that was needed. In deeper terms, there is still another meaning that mirrors all of those apparent divisions that occur as All That Is seemingly separates portions of itself from itself, scattering its omnipotence into new patterns of being that, in your terms, remember their source and look back to it longingly, while still glorying in the unique individuality that is their own.

(10:06. Jane was very intent in her delivery.) The story of the fall, the rebellious angels, and the leader Satan who becomes the devil—all of this refers to the same phenomena on a different level. Satan represents—in the terms of the story—the part of All That Is, or God, <u>who stepped outside of Himself</u>, so to' speak, and became earthbound with His creatures, offering them the free will and choice that "previously" had not been available.

(Pause.) Hence you have the majestic elements given to Satan, and the power. The earthly characteristics often appear

as he is depicted in animal form, for he was also of course connected with the intuitive terrestrial attributes from which the new human consciousness would spring.

In terms of simple biological function, you now had a species no longer completely dependent upon instinct, yet still with all the natural built-in desires for survival, and the appearance within it of a mind able to make decisions and distinctions.

You may take your break.

(10:16 to 10:30.)

Now: This new kind of consciousness brought with it the open mirror of memory in which past joy and pain could be recalled, and so the realization of mortal death became more immediate than it was with the animals.

An association could trigger the clear memory of a past agony in the bewildered new mind. At first, there was a difficulty in separating the remembered image from the moment in the present. Man's mind then struggled to contain many images—past, present, and future imagined ones—and was forced to correlate these in any given moment of time. A vast acceleration took place.

It was only natural that certain experiences would seem better than others, but the species' new abilities made it necessary that sharp distinctions be made. Good and evil, the desirable and the less so, were invaluable aids then in helping form the basis for such separations.

The birth of imagination initiated the largest possibilities, and at the same time put great strain upon the biological creature whose entire corporeal structure would now react not only to present objective situations, but imaginative ones. At the same time members of the species had to cope with the natural environment as did any other animal. Imagination helped because an individual could anticipate the behavior of other creatures.

(10:41.) In another way, animals also possess an "unconscious" anticipation, but they do not have to come to terms with it on an aware basis as the new consciousness did. Again,

good and evil and the freedom of choice came to the species' aid. The evil animal was the natural predator, for example. It would help here if the reader remembers what has been said about natural guilt earlier in this book. It would aid in understanding the later myths and the variations that came from them. *(See the 634th session in Chapter Eight, among others.)*

As the mind developed, the species could hand down to its offspring the wisdom and law of the elders. This is still being done in modern society, of course, when each child inherits the beliefs of its parents about the nature of reality. Apart from all other considerations, this is also a characteristic of creature-hood. Only the means are different with the animals.

The acceleration continues, however. Ideas of right and wrong are always guidelines that are then individually inter-preted. Because of the connection with survival mentioned earlier *(in the last session)*, there is a great charge here. Initially the child had to be impressed with the fact, for example, that a predator animal was "bad" because it could kill. Today a mother might unwittingly say the same thing about a car.

The early acquiescence to beliefs has a biological importance, therefore, but as the conscious mind attains its maturity it is also natural for it to question those beliefs, and to assess them in relation to its own environment. Many of my readers may have certain ideas about good and evil that are very hampering. These may be old beliefs in new clothing. You may think that you are quite free, only to discover that you hold old ideas but have simply put new terms to them, or concentrated upon other aspects.

Your daily experience is intimately connected with your ideas of worth and personal value.

You may take your break.

("Thank you.")

Read Ruburt my earlier note.

("All right."

(10:55. Seth referred to the personal material he'd given for

us before book work, so I read it to Jane now. It concerned ways by which we could increase our feelings of freedom on a daily basis, and, I thought, was excellent. Resume at 11:23.)

Dictation: Now: You may be quite able to see through the distortions of conventional Christianity. You may have changed your ideas to such an extent that you can see little similarity between your current ones and those of the past. Now you may believe in the theories of Buddhism, for example, or of another Eastern philosophy.

The differences between any of those systems of thought and Christianity may be so apparent that the similarities escape you. You may follow one of the schools of Buddhism in which great stress is laid upon the denial of the body, discipline of the flesh, and the avoidance of desire. These elements are quite characteristic of Christianity also, of course, but they may appear more palatable, exotic, or reasonable coming from a source foreign to your childhood education. So you may leap from one to the other, shouting emancipation and feeling yourself quite free of old limiting ideas.

Philosophies that teach denial of the flesh <u>must</u> ultimately end up preaching a denial of the self and building a contempt for it, because even though the soul is couched in muscle and bone it is <u>meant</u> to experience that reality, not to refute it.

All such dogmas use artificial guilt, and natural guilt is distorted to serve those ends. In whatever terms, the devotee is told that there is something wrong with earthly experience. You are, therefore, considered evil as a self in flesh by virtue of your very existence.

This alone will cause adverse experience, making you reject the very basis of your own framework of experience. You will consider the body as a thing, a fine vehicle but not in itself the natural <u>living</u> expression of your being in material form. Many such Eastern schools also stress—as do numerous spiritualistic schools—the importance of the "unconscious levels of the self," and teach you to mistrust the conscious mind.

The concept of nirvana *(see the 637th session in Chapter*

Nine) and the idea of heaven are two versions of the same picture, the former being one in which individuality is lost in the bliss of undifferentiated consciousness, and the latter one in which still-conscious individuals perform mindless adoration. Neither theory contains an understanding of the functions of the conscious mind, or the evolution of consciousness—or, for that matter, certain aspects of greater physics. No energy is ever lost. The expanding universe theory* applies to the mind as well as to the universe.

(11:43.) However, these philosophies <u>can</u> lead you to a deep mistrust of both your body and mind. You are told that the spirit is perfect, and so you can try to live up to standards of perfection quite impossible to achieve. The failure adds to the sense of guilt.

You attempt then to further banish the characteristic enjoyment of your own creaturehood, denying the lusty spirituality of your flesh and the strong present corporeal leanings of your soul. You will try to rid yourself of very natural emotions, and so be cheated of their great spiritual and physical motion. *(Pause.)* On the other hand, some leaders may give little consideration to such issues, but still be deeply convinced of the misery of the human condition, focusing upon all the "darker" elements, seeing the world's destruction ever closer to hand without really examining the beliefs that arouse such constant feelings.

They may find it easy to cluck their tongues at obvious fanatics who cry out for God's vengeance, and speak about the world's end in brimstone and ashes. They may be as equally convinced, however, of man's basic unworthiness, and so of course of their own. In daily life such people will concentrate upon negative events, store them up, and unfortunately cause personal experience that will seem to quite reinforce the basic ideas.

---

*The "big bang" theory postulates that 10-15 billion years ago all matter—or energy—was concentrated in one great primordial "atom." This colossus exploded, and the still expanding universe we see today is the aftermath of that event. One variation of the theory considered a pulsating universe that results from the repeated collapsing and expanding of all matter-energy.

Here in different context is the same denial of the worth and integrity of earth experience. In some such cases, all of the desirable human attributes are magnified and projected outward into a god or superconsciousness, while all the less admirable characteristics are left to the race and the individual.

The individual therefore deprives himself of the use of much of his ability. He does not consider it his own, and is astounded when any others of his race display such superior qualities.

You may take a break or end the session as you prefer.

("We'll take the break."

(11:57. I told Jane that it was all right with me if she wanted to end the session. She chose to wait and see. Resume at 12:12.)

To some extent, such beliefs follow certain rhythms in both civilizations and in time.

The mind is a system of checks and balances even as the body, and so often a set of beliefs that can be seen as highly negative will often serve beneficial ends in countering other beliefs. For some time Western civilization stressed a <u>distorted</u> version of intellectual reasoning, for example, and so the current stress about other portions of the self serves a purpose.

The people alive within the world come into it with their own problems and challenges, and this will have much to do with the kind of national and worldwide beliefs that are generated and that dominate. The beliefs, of course, are frameworks in which various kinds of experience are tested. This also applies to religions, and political and social situations as well. There is always a give and take between the individual and the mass system of beliefs in which he has chosen his environment.

There is a belief in illness as being morally wrong, and a countering belief in it as being ennobling, uplifting and spiritually good. These value judgments are extremely important, for they will be reflected in your own experience with any illness or disease.

Now: That is the end of dictation and the end of our session. A hearty good evening to you both.

("Thank you, Seth. Good night." 12:22 A.M.)

SESSION 648, MARCH 14, 1973,
9:51 P.M. WEDNESDAY

(On September 25, 1972, the day of the 617th session in Chapter Three, I wrote a note describing how Jane and I had seen and heard geese flying south, in a spectacle both inscrutable and moving. Last night, we had reminders that a natural rhythmic cycle was completing itself six months later: As we retired I thought I heard the barking of geese migrating north, although Jane didn't. I woke up around four A.M., though, and heard a flight clearly in the silent hour. Then early this morning as I was painting in my studio, that same cadence came sounding down through a fine rain.

(I caught my first actual sighting of geese just before dusk this evening. I was working on this book when I heard the sound of another flight, intermixed with traffic noise. I opened a studio window. It was still raining lightly. A giant Seckel pear tree grows almost close enough to touch, and through its branches I saw the uneven V-formation, flying north just below the cloud cover and sounding off all the way . . .

(Jane had given a very long session in ESP class last night, along with Sumari. I thought she might not want to go back into trance tonight, but at 9:30 she said she was ready. We held the session in her study for a change. "I felt exhilarated earlier," she said, "but now that's gone and I'm just relaxed."

(Last night's session had presented some new information about animal dreams. We'll get a copy of it at next week's class. Those sessions are recorded; then during the week a dedicated class member goes to all the work of transcribing the tape and having the script duplicated.

(Jane's pace was easy tonight.)

Now: Good evening.

("Good evening, Seth.")

Dictation: There are too many aspects of what you think of as health and illness to discuss even in a book that is directed to personal reality, in which the body plays such an important role.

Health and illness are both evidences of the body's attempt to maintain stability. There is a difference in the overall health patterns in men and animals because of the quite diverse nature of their physical experience. More will be said about this particular subject later. Overall, however, in the animals illness and disease play a life-giving role, keeping balance both within a species and between them, therefore insuring the future existence of all involved.

In their own ways, the animals are quite aware of this fact. Some of them even bring themselves to their own destruction through what you would call suicide, and en masse. At that level the animals understand, and are always in touch with deep biological connections in which they know their own continuances within the chain of nature.

Man grants rich psychological activity to his own species but denies it in others. There are as many luxuriant and diverse kinds of psychological movement as there are species, however. The cycles of health and disease are felt as rhythms of the body by the large variety of animals, and even with them illness or disease has life-saving qualities on another level.

Instinct is fairly accurate, for example, guiding the beasts to those territories in which proper conditions can be found; and even for them the well-being of the body represents physical evidence of their "being in the proper place at the proper time." It reinforces the animals' sense of grace, in terms mentioned earlier in this book. *(See the 636th session in Chapter Nine.)*

(Intently:) They understand the beneficial teaching quality of disease, and follow their own instinctive ways of treating it. In a natural situation, this might involve a mass migration from one territory to another. In such cases the illness of only a few animals might send a whole herd to its safety, and a new food supply.

Man is so highly verbal that he finds it difficult to understand that other species work with idea-complexes (with a hyphen) of

277

a different kind, in which of course thought as you consider it is not involved. But an equivalent exists; using an analogy, it is as if ideas are built up not through sentence structure reinforced by inner visual images, but by like "mental" patterns structured through touch and scent—in other words, thinking, but within a framework entirely different and alien to you.

(10:15. Seth repeated the last two sentences to make sure I had taken them down correctly.)

Such "thinking" exists, using the analogy, within the framework of instinct, whereas your own verbalized thoughts can also intrude outside of that framework. One of the main differences between you and the animals, and one of the significant meanings in terms of free will, is involved here.

Animals, then, understand the beneficial directing elements of disease. They also comprehend the nature of stress as a necessary stimulant to physical activity. Observing even a pet, you will notice its marvelous complete relaxation, and yet its immediate total response to stimulus. So animals in captivity will fight to provide themselves with necessary health-giving stress factors.

(We had a window open because the night was quite warm. Now I tilted my head toward it, listening. Faintly, above the sound of the rain, I heard geese once more.)

Do you want to take a break and listen to your geese?

("No . . . They'll be gone in a minute anyhow.")

They are more melodious than I am.

("They're certainly fascinating. But," I added jokingly, "so are you."

(Rather seriously:) I thank you for the compliment.

Animals, then, do not think of illness in terms of good or bad. Disease in itself on that level is a part of the life-survival process, and a system of checks and balances. With the emergence of man's particular kind of consciousness, other issues become involved. Mankind feels its own mortality even more than the beasts do.

(Long pause.) With the growth of this particular variety of self-consciousness came the exteriorization, magnification and

intensification of definite elements that lie latent in other animals, the individuation of strong emotional activity to a new degree, for example. The emergence of the "pause of reflection" mentioned earlier *(in the 635th session in Chapter Eight, for instance)*, and the blossoming of memory along with the emotional intensification, led to a situation in which members of the new species recalled, in the present, the dead and the diseases that killed them. They became frightened of disease, particularly in the case of plagues.

Man forgot the teaching and <u>healing</u> elements, and concentrated instead upon the unpleasant experience itself. To some extent this was quite natural, for the new species developed in order to change the nature of its consciousness, to follow a reality in which instinct was no longer "blindly" followed, and to individualize in strong personal focus corporeal experience that had previously taken a different pattern.

You may take your break.

(10:36. At break, Jane said she felt "very relaxed and sleepy, but not tired." She had heard the geese while in trance.

(This was one of those times when she was consciously aware that several channels of information were available from Seth. We had but to decide which subject we wanted material on after break:

(1. How idea structures work in animals as opposed to mankind.

(2. The use of animals—rats, say—in experiments involving injections, before giving them to human beings. [Man's psychological reality is so sweepingly different from that of the animals, Jane added now, that he would inevitably show a wide variety of reactions.]

(3. Material on Jane herself, concerning her relaxed state.

(We chose the first category since it would continue the subject matter of this chapter. See the notes for the 616th session, in Chapter Two, for descriptions of Jane's first experience with Seth's multiple channels. Resume in the same unhurried manner at 10:58.)

Now: Man has a far greater leeway. He forms his reality according to his conscious beliefs, even while its basis lies in the deep unconscious nature of the earth in corporeal terms. Man's "I am," [seemingly] apart from nature—a characteristic necessary for the development of his kind of consciousness—led him into value judgments, and also necessitated some break with the deep inner certainties of other species.

Illness therefore was experienced as "bad." An entire tribe could be endangered by one sick member. At the same time, as the mind developed, cunning and memory became highly effective survival tools. In some societies or tribes, the old or infirm were killed lest their care take too much attention from the able-bodied and endanger the group.

In others, however, the old were honored for the wisdom that they had accumulated with age, and this became very practical in tribes where many did not survive. History was dependent upon the old with their memory of past events, and the group's sense of continuity was also in the hands of its oldest members, who passed memories on to others.

An individual who had himself survived many diseases was considered a sage. Such people often watched the animals and observed nature's own therapies and treatments.

In certain eras, the lines between the species were not completely drawn, and there were long periods where men and animals mixed and learned from each other. Man's imagination made him a great maker of myths. Myths as you know them represent bridges of psychological activity, and point quite clearly to patterns of perception and behavior through which, in your terms, the race passed as it traveled to its present state. Mythology bridges the gap between instinctive knowledge and the individualization of idea.

When an animal is sick it immediately begins to remedy the situation, and unconsciously it knows what to do. It does not bother thinking in your terms of good and evil. It does not wonder what it did to get into such a situation. It does not think of itself as inferior. It automatically begins its own therapy.

A human being, however, has another dimension to deal with, a new area of creativity, a diverse mixture of beliefs. His or her ideas about the self must be examined, for they are being materialized in flesh. Again, the situation has great complexity, for the condition is still a healthy attempt on the part of the body to maintain balance. Overall there is also the world situation to be taken into consideration—the status of the species on the planet, in which, say, overpopulation problems will bring about death to insure new growth.

(11:21.) The individuals alive at such a time will also have a hand in such decisions, however. Once more, because you are self-conscious beings your beliefs regulate your reality. An animal knows unconsciously that it is unique and has a place in the scheme of being. Its sense of grace is built-in. Your free will allows for the freedom of any belief, including one that says you are unworthy, with no right to your existence.

If you misinterpret the myths, then you may believe that man has fallen from grace and that his very creaturehood is cursed, in which case you will not trust your body or allow it its "natural" pattern of self-therapy.

In order for consciousness to develop in your terms, there must be freedom for the exploration of all ideas individually and en masse. Each of you are living entities, growing toward your own development. Each of your beliefs, therefore, has its own unique origin and feeling patterns, so you must for yourself travel back through your beliefs and your own feelings until intellectually and emotionally you realize your rightness, your completely original existence in time and space as you know it.

This knowing will give you the conscious knowledge that is a counterpart of the animal's unconscious comprehension.

Take a brief break.

(11:30. "I feel a strange combination of tiredness and exhilaration now, as though I'd had a whole lot to drink," Jane said. "I know a little alcohol helps in these sessions, but it wouldn't if I carried it very far." She had been sipping wine tonight.

(Jane said there was much more to the idea of natural therapy in animals. She began tuning in to this information on her own, rather than getting it through one of Seth's channels. Ages ago, humans not only watched the animals, but went to them for help. It had to do with shock treatment, she said wonderingly. If a human was in a catatonic state after a battle, for instance, the "animal medicine man" would purposely shock the patient into an emotional reaction to bring him out of the state.

("I think these animal doctors were a variety of apelike ancestor," Jane said. "Not apes as we think of them, but a bridge between animals and human beings. They were our size, more or less. They weren't four-footed. I saw creatures who walked upright—hairy, with brilliant compassionate eyes ..."

(Jane told me that she could delve into the available data in much★more detail, but since it would go off from the chapter at a tangent we reluctantly decided not to pursue it. I thought of racial memory and our ancient heritage of gods that were half man and half beast, bird or reptile. Resume at 11:50.)

Now: An animal has no need of conscience, in any terms.

Because of the great flexibility of your natures, however, mankind needs a framework in which the ramifications of what I have referred to as normal healthy guilt can be considered.

What you consider conscience is often an applied-from-without sense of right and wrong instilled in you in your youth. As a rule these ideas represent your parents' conceptions of natural guilt, distorted by their own beliefs. *(See the 619th session in Chapter Four, as well as the first session in this chapter.)* You accepted those ideas for a reason, individually and en masse, for mankind at any given "time" has a strong idea of the particular sort of world experience it will create.

Because you have free will you have the responsibility and the gift, the joy and the necessity, of working with your beliefs and of choosing your personal reality as you desire. I told you earlier *(in the 636th session in Chapter Nine)* that you cannot fall out of a state of grace. Each of you must intellectually and emotionally accept it, however.

While this may seem like the sheerest Pollyanna, nevertheless there is no evil in basic terms. This does not mean that you do not meet with effects that appear evil, but as you each move individually through the dimensions of your own consciousness, you will understand that all seeming opposites are other faces of the one supreme drive toward creativity.

End of dictation. A personal note before we close . . .

(Rather unexpectedly, Seth digressed here to give half a page of information about a letter and some photographs that we had received today. Then, smiling:)

Now, I could continue for some time.

("Say a little about the geese, then.")

I will indeed, and give us a moment.

(Pause.) They attract you because of their instinctive knowledge, and they represent the inner freedom that man is in the process of objectifying on a conscious level. They also remind you of the deep certainty of your creaturehood, and by their flight evoke within you the knowledge that you are leaping from creaturehood into dimensions of actuality you only barely sense.

Their migration is perfect in its simplicity and complexity, yet your journey as a species is far less predictable, opening avenues of probabilities in which your consciousness and free will allows you to become conscious creators in worlds that you initiate and then inhabit.

(Amused and louder:) Will _that_ do?

("Yes. That was nice.")

Then I bid you a fond good evening, and my heartiest regards to you both.

("Thank you very much, Seth. Good night."

(12:13 A.M. Jane still felt exhilarated, yet tired. A note: Lately she's been working on a sequel to her novel, The Education of Oversoul 7, *which she finished early in July, 1972. [See Jane's Introduction, and Chapter One.] The new book is*

called, appropriately enough, The Further Education of Oversoul 7.*)*

SESSION 649, MARCH 19, 1973,
9:37 P.M. MONDAY

Good evening.

("Good evening, Seth.")

The writer's hour.

("Yes.")

Dictation. *(Long pause.)* At any given time there will be various climates of belief pervading the world. Some will be clustered in certain areas, for example, like low-pressure systems. Some will <u>generally</u> be local, and others will sweep across the continents like great periodic storms.

Remember that ideas <u>are</u> as natural as the weather. They follow patterns, then, and obey certain laws even as more strictly physical phenomena do. Unfortunately, no one examines the nature of mental reality from such a viewpoint. You will be born in the midst of certain mass beliefs, and these may vary according to the country of your nativity. As you come into your body with all of its physical surroundings, so at birth do you emerge into a rich natural psychological environment in which beliefs and ideas are every bit as real.

As you become more proficient at using your conscious mind, then of course you examine the beliefs that surround you, even as you question and often move out of your native environment. You may migrate to a climate in which the prevailing <u>ideas</u> suit you better, as well as the weather.

Regardless, there are certain tendencies, mental stances, that you will take about yourself, your body and your life to one degree or another. Many of these will be directly or indirectly connected with old myths and beliefs of your forefathers. Your ideas of good and evil as applied to health and illness are highly important, for instance. *(Pause.)* Few can escape putting value judgments in such areas. If you consider illness as a kind of

284

moral stigma, then you will simply add an unneeded quality to any condition of ill health.

Such judgments are very simplistic, and ignore the great range of human motivation and experience. If you are bound and determined that "GOD" (in capitals and quotes) creates only "good," then any physical deficiency, illness or deformity becomes an affront to your belief, threatens it, and makes you angry and resentful. If you become ill you can hate yourself for not being what you think you should be—a perfect physical image made in the likeness of a perfect God.

If on the other hand you carry the idea too far—that illness can also be a learning process—then you can fall into the other extreme, glorifying sickness or disease as a necessary ennobling experience in which the body is purged so that the soul can be saved.

(9:55.) Following such a belief, you will confuse suffering with saintliness, desolation with purity, and the denial of the body as spirituality and a badge of holiness. Under such conditions you can even seek out illness to prove to yourself the strength of your own spirituality—and to impress it upon others. The same kind of moral value judgment can be placed in almost any area of human activity, and will of course have social repercussions. Those reactions will add to the prevailing beliefs and in turn affect the individual.

You may believe that wealth is a result of a moral virtue, and comes from "God's" direct benevolence. As a result, poverty becomes evidence of a lack of morality. "God" made so many people poor that obviously no man should dare try to change the situation—that rationale is often used. The poor, then, following these beliefs, are looked down upon as are the diseased.

What sin did the poor person or the sick person commit? That question, often asked unconsciously—if not consciously— brings you back to beliefs in punishment that have nothing to do with the concept of natural guilt, but with those distortions placed upon it. There is also a connection with misinterpretation of the Bible. Christ as you think of him was simply saying that you form your own reality. He tried to rise above the idea-systems of those times, yet even he had to use them, and so the connotations of sin and punishment distorted the message given.

Some of you will have a contradictory belief that poverty is virtuous, and that wealth is a vice and represents evidence of a spiritual lack. *(See the 614th session in Chapter Two.)* This belief in your society also harks back to the Bible and Christ's association with the poor rather than the rich.

In all such cases, however, blanket moral judgments are being applied that involve feelings of guilt in which individual experience is forgotten.

You may take your break.

(10:10 to 10:19.)

Now: Such critical evaluations are placed upon colors as well. Often white is considered pure, and black impure, white good and black evil.

This of course involves considerations of race, and you must realize that your present race is the one into which you were born, in your terms, in this place and time. Each of you have been members of different races, and so each of you have shared in both the advantages and ignominies attached, in historic terms, to such conditions of birth.

This is not the place for me to go into a long discussion concerning the significance of races, yet each one is highly meaningful, and represents a different aspect of humanity as a whole. Therefore, each race has a symbolic meaning to mankind's psyche. The outside experience and structure of any given race's experience may change, but the inner symbolism will still remain, and be creatively grappled with.

Your daily experience will be affected by your race, your beliefs about it, your beliefs about other races, and the climate of opinion in general. On a quite simple basis, if you consider God in human terms you will project him as belonging to your own race. If you belong to a minority or if you are black, then you may be caught in a conflict of beliefs.

It is impossible to separate your daily experience in any of its aspects from your beliefs and those judgments that you place upon them. The beliefs boil down to your ideas of right and wrong, and they involve all of your attitudes concerning illness and health, wealth and poverty, the relationships of the races, religious conflicts, and more important, your intimate day-by-day psychological reality.

Let us pursue this subject further as it involves you personally at those levels in which you live your lives and intermix with others.

(Heartily:) End of chapter.

CHAPTER 13

*Good and Evil, Personal and Mass Beliefs,
and Their Effect Upon Your Private
and Social Experience*

Give us a moment.

("Yes." Pause at 10:31.)

Chapter Thirteen. I want this done in a certain way—the heading, "A State of Grace," written thusly *(with horizontal gestures)*, then a line drawn down . . . and under it, "Health" . . . and under that, "Wealth" . . .

(Drawing in the air, Seth-Jane finished the list, then told me that I was to place a second one, with its own heading, opposite the first. I groped along, not having time to ask more than a couple of questions.)

A State of Grace	Out of Grace
Health	Disease
Wealth	Poverty
White	Black
Christian	Not Christian

Do you have that much clearly?

("Yes," I said, although I didn't have the opposing lists

arranged as neatly as they're shown here. I felt oddly confused, since I wasn't sure yet of what Seth was up to.)

That is not the chapter heading. It is a diagram. Now: Another one of the same kind:

A State of Grace	Out of Grace
Indian or Oriental	American
Proud Poverty	Embarrassing Riches
Brown Skin	White Skin
Great Mystic Understanding	Callousness
Cosmic Understanding	Spiritual Poverty and Disintegration

Another category:

A State of Grace	Out of Grace
Youth	Age
Intuitive Understanding	Rigidity, Mental and Spiritual Ignorance
Knowledge	Ignorance
Beauty	Ugliness
Intellectual Capacity	Disintegration of Mental Capacity
Physical Vigor	Loss of Vigor
An Unfolding Future	The Closing of All Doors to Activity

Heading for the chapter: "Good and Evil, Personal and Mass Beliefs, and Their Effect Upon Your Private and Social Experience." Do you have that?

("Yes.")

In this chapter we will deal with some current beliefs involving your most intimate behavior and social connotations.

Take your break now.

(10:54. I asked Jane if anything had bothered her, since the house wasn't exactly quiet tonight. She said no, that her trance had been deep enough. She was supposed to get

289

the diagrams just right though, and it had been difficult to do.

(She went over them with me now, checking my placement of them on the page. Note that Seth would give a complete list under one heading, then match its components item by item with their opposites—no small feat, I would say, considering the number of issues involved. Resume at 11:03.)

Now: I outlined some opposing ideas held by many people— all involving concepts of good or evil being applied in areas in which they do not belong.

The designations will make certain contrasts clear visually. I simply wanted to launch into the next chapter, and to make sure the visual aspects were clearly stated. *(Pleased:)* I will give you the rest of the evening off, therefore, as we are doing very well indeed, and will get to some beliefs not dealt with, of a social nature.

I bid you then a fond good evening. And other issues are working with Ruburt, which is another reason for the briefer session.

("Thank you, Seth. Good night.")

(11:06 P.M. Seth was gone before I finished writing, after referring to some other work that Jane and I are doing on our own. Jane said she was tired now.)

SESSION 650, MARCH 22, 1973, 9:50 P.M. THURSDAY

(The session started late because of our experimenting with a high-quality stereo recording and playing system we bought yesterday. Jane has wanted this especially for work with Sumari. Acting upon impulse while we were in the store, I bought one of those watches that gives not only the time of day but the day of the month. For some reason I find this latter feature quite amusing.)

Good evening.

("Good evening, Seth.")

I am glad that you know the day of the month automatically now.

("Me too—I guess.")

You will be using your other new gadget often, and also in ways you may not now suspect.

Dictation: The simple diagrams merely represent some general belief systems from the standpoint of "moral values." Your ideas of good and evil affect not only your behavior with others, but your activity in a community and in the world at large.

Many believe—using the first diagram—that it is "good" and morally superior to be Christian, white, wealthy and in excellent health. Now, though this does not appear in the diagram, the word "male" can also be added to the list of preferred attributes.

Reality, then, is viewed through this system of beliefs. If you hold them you will feel that those characteristics are given by God. According to the fervor with which you cherish these ideas you will find that they enclose you, for in a very limited manner they will define your concept of good. People entertaining such beliefs are often very religious in conventional terms. Countries emphasizing like beliefs send missionaries to "convert" those who are pagan, and therefore inferior.

Individuals feeling this way will be very uncomfortable when they mingle with others of a different race, creed or color, and despite themselves may be revengefully conservative in dealing, for example, with problems of a community nature. They will consider poverty as a sign of God's displeasure and so be inclined to leave the entire matter in his "hands." They may speak with seeming compassion about the plight of others, and yet all the while consider that difficulty the simple result of inferiority, of inequality.

These people may be of any age. They may come from any economic environment. Now if you happen to be Protestant, male, white, American, rich, and healthy, at least within the framework of your beliefs you can look at yourself with "clear" eyes. Your foundation is shaky indeed, but at least you fit within it for the moment. You will notice that I added

"Protestant" to our value system, as well as "American." If however you hold this group of beliefs and you fall short—that is, if in some way you do not fit in—then even within that system you are in trouble.

(10:05.) Some of the components are more charged than others. A Catholic or a Jew possessing these beliefs is obviously out of step to some extent, and will feel guilty as he measures himself against them. *(Intently:)* A black man who accepts the same system is indeed in difficulty. If he happens to be a <u>poor</u> black man he is in <u>double</u> jeopardy.

In that chart of belief, disease, poverty, femininity to some extent, non-Christian concepts, and a non-Caucasion racial heritage, are all considered wrong to one degree or another.

Now: Any intrusion of other beliefs here will be considered threatening. Both racial problems and religious dissension will be rationalized from the standpoint of these beliefs. Some of my readers may consider themselves quite enlightened, believing, for example, in reincarnation as a series of consecutive lives. However, they may then use <u>that</u> concept to justify their belief in the inferiority of other races. They may say that since an individual <u>chose</u> his or her problems in this life—deciding for instance to be born black, or poor, or both—that karma is being worked out; therefore such issues should not be adjusted through a change of law or custom. Period.

(See the 636th session in Chapter Nine for some material on karma, reincarnation, and Seth's idea of "simultaneous" time.)

On the left side, looking at the second diagram, you will find people in this case, and in this country, of a more "liberal" frame of mind. But you will not find them quite as liberal if you understand that they are as prejudiced in one direction as the first group is in another.

Here we have a system of belief in which it is wrong to be white, American, or wealthy, or even at all well-off in financial terms. All of the distortions in Christianity are apparent, where the first group is blind to them, of course. Here, though, wealth and a white skin are not only bad, but obvious symptoms of moral deterioration. If the first system of beliefs sees money and goods as a sign of God's blessing, the second group views all material possessions as evidence of spiritual decay.

Here the exotic is romanticized, the foreign held up, the picturesque seen as the real. Black skin or brown skin becomes the criteria of spiritual perfection, and poverty a badge of honor to be worn not only proudly, but often to be used as an aggressive tool. The people who follow these belief systems think that they are right. Their living style, community affiliations, and political leanings will be in direct opposition to the "white-wealthy" ethic.

Now if you happen to be black or brown, poor, and believe in this system, you will at least feel secure within it. If you are instead white and wealthy and hold such beliefs, you will think yourself quite inferior indeed, and do everything in your power to show how picturesque, and liberal and open-minded, and black or brown you can be, while still being white, fairly well-off, and perhaps secretly addicted to your Christianity.

You will doubtlessly have Buddhas tastefully displayed, and Indian beads.

We will take a break.

(10:27 to 10:45.)

Now: The third diagram can cut across the other systems of belief, of course. In the first two groups there are many leeways. You may have one, two or three preferred characteristics that correlate with your ideas, for example, but your concepts about age leave you no such freedom; for at one time or another all of you, "if you are lucky" in your terms, will approach old age.

Many believe that it is a time of spiritual and/or physical deterioration, an era in which all those hard-won attributes of maturity vanish, and the reasoning faculties disappear like grains of sand held too long by the thinking hands of the mind.

If life is seen as good in this system of belief, then youth is viewed as the crowning glory, from which summit there is no further journey except descent. The old are not granted characteristics of wisdom, but feared as evil, bad, undesirable or frightening. To these people senility seems a natural, inevitable end to life.

As mentioned earlier in this book *(in the 644th session in Chapter Eleven),* many who follow such beliefs try to hide them from themselves, desperately attempting to be young. Youth and old age both have their place, and within the framework of your race each play important roles.

You are used to thinking in terms of heredity. In physical terms, and in a different way than you imagine, this is important. Certain earth experiences however are dependent upon duration in time, and result as a consequence of the mind playing upon its experience through long earth seasons.

There are specific functions brought into operation quite naturally that are scarcely perceived by your scientists, much less understood. As the mind within the body clearly sees its earthly time coming to an end, mental and psychic accelerations take place. These are in many ways like adolescent experiences in their great bursts of creative activity, with the resulting formation of questions, and the preparation for a completely new kind of personality growth and fulfillment.

(Jane spoke very emphatically, gesturing often.) This would be quite apparent were it not for your current belief systems, through which the old are forced to interpret their experience. Many instances of expansion of consciousness, and mental and psychic growth, are interpreted by you as senility. No important correlations have been made between the subjective experiences of the old, particularly in "senile" conditions, with those of other ages involved in expansion of consciousness, whether natural or drug induced.

(11:06.) Any such sensations are immediately repressed by the old for fear that "senility" will be the diagnosis. The experiences, however, affect the right hemisphere of the brain, and in such a way that abilities are released in somewhat the same manner as an adolescent's.

The individual, when it is time then, begins to see beyond

temporal life, to open up dimensions of awareness that in your terms he or she could not afford while involved in the intense physical focus of normal adult life. Unfortunately the personality has no system of beliefs, as a rule, to support such an expansion. The natural therapies, both physical and mental, are denied. Drugs are often used as depressants, clouding the clarity of what seems to be distorted vision. This is one of the most creative, valuable aspects of your lives. Instead the old are made to feel useless in your society. Often of course they share this value judgment, and their experience within your communities has in no way prepared them to face subjective experience.

There are no teachers to guide them. Old age is a highly creative part of living. The connections between it and childhood are often made in a derogatory fashion, but the personality is in just as creative a state. I am speaking generally now, of course, for your living conditions so distort the natural situation.

Even the chemical and hormonal changes that occur <u>are</u> those that are conducive to spiritual and psychic growth at that time. The joyful affirmation possible is denied to the old because of your system of beliefs.

Take your break.

(*11:17. Jane, in a very deep and active trance, had been so focused on the material that she'd been unaware of anything else. "Boy, I felt Seth was getting into some really good stuff—a whole new system of geriatrics," she said. "I was right into those feelings. Animals already know all of this unconsciously. But it's so strange and funny to be going into things about old age," she continued, surprised. "Our society doesn't suspect any of this. I feel very excited about it."*

(*Jane and I have had some preparation for the information, at least on emotional levels. My father died in February, 1971, after spending three years in a county "home." Diagnosis: senility. For much of that time he had been under varying degrees of sedation. In light of tonight's material, I couldn't help feeling that he'd lost part of his natural heritage—whether he had decided upon that course himself, whether it had been imposed upon him, or both. Seth, I thought, would say that my father chose all the circumstances of his life, and that such a deprivation in old age was a probable result that materialized physically. But while agreeing, I could still wish it had been otherwise . . .*

(A note about the material at 11:06. The brain consists of two independent coiled hemispheres lying side by side and joined by a common base. Usually one hemisphere is dominant. Each one is made up of areas, or lobes, which have specific roles. Brain-wave patterns from each hemisphere often vary, as do those from the different lobes making up each side. No two brains are alike, however.

(Now Jane discovered that she had but one cigarette left. "Well," she said, lightening the mood, "it's going to be a short session, then." Resume at 11:35.)

Dictation. *(A one-minute pause.)* In certain terms, "psychedelic experience" cannot be explained within your limited frameworks of reference—not because such illuminations are beyond explanation but because your present systems of belief are too limiting.

So at whatever age, a revelatory episode is difficult to relate to others. In older age, however, no one is interested, and yet it is here, as in adolescence, that the greatest creativity may emerge but go unrecognized. This era could be more advantageous to the individual and to the race than any other period, were it recognized for what it is and understood.

The peculiar chemical changes that occur are often precisely those that lead to greater conceptions and experience, but these are free from what you think of as practical application. There is a trigger set off then, an impetus in which the personality tries to free itself from time-space orientation released from the usual necessity to participate in "adult" terms.

The personality, again, looks at the nature of experience in its purest terms. In some previous civilizations this was done within a natural framework *(pause),* in which the old were cared for physically while their words were listened to most carefully.

Ideas of the "wise old man," and similar legends apply here, as do the mystical concepts of the powerful old woman. In their natural progression, and left alone, the old understand their own "visions" quite well. Body and mind operate beautifully together.

Now (louder:) End of session. My heartiest regards to you both.

("Thank you. Good night, Seth." 11:49 P.M.)

SESSION 651, MARCH 26, 1973, 9:46 P.M. MONDAY

(We held the session in Jane's study so that she could sit before the double microphones of her new recording system. So far, though, we haven't succeeded in obtaining the best results from the equipment.)

Now: Good evening—

("Good evening, Seth.")

—and we will resume dictation .. Your beliefs about age, like everything else, will form your experience, and your mass beliefs will affect your civilization. With the current concepts held by your society, men and women fear old age from the time of youth. If young adulthood is considered the epitome of life, blessedness, and success, then old age is viewed as the opposite—a time of failure and decay.

Some of this has to do with distorted ideas of both the conscious and unconscious minds, using your terms now. Generally speaking, in Western society the conscious mind is seen as coming into its own in early adulthood, as the self rises from the bed of childhood unconsciousness into its critical awareness and differentiation. The appreciation of distinctions and differences is considered one of the greatest characteristics of consciousness, and so those aspects of it are valued. On the other hand the equally significant assimilating, combining, correlating characteristics of consciousness are overlooked. In scholarly circles, and many that are not scholarly at all, the intellect is equated only with the critical faculties, so that the more diagnostic you are the more intellectual you are considered.

During Western years of adulthood, consciousness is focused most intently in one specific area of activity and physical manipulation. From childhood, the mind is trained to use its argumentative, separating qualities above all others. Creativity is allowed to flow only through certain highly limited, accepted channels.

When an individual becomes older—and retired, for example— the focus for that particular kind of concentration is no longer so immediately available. The mind actually becomes more <u>itself</u>, freer to use more of its abilities, allowed to stray from restricted areas, to assimilate, acknowledge and create.

Precisely at this time however the individual is told to beware of any such straying, and to consider that kind of behavior a symptom of mental deterioration. Those following mass beliefs will find that their own image of themselves has changed. They fear that their very age, or existence in time, has betrayed them. They see themselves as leftovers, dim vestiges of better selves, and in their own system of value judgment they condemn themselves through the very fact of their continued existence in time. If they ever did, they no longer trust the integrity of their bodies. They begin to act out the drama in a script written by others—to which, however, they have acquiesced.

It may not seem that there is any connection between that situation and your beliefs involving color, and yet the two are intimately associated.

I will let you take a break and listen to your recording.

(10:05. We played the tape back, then made some adjustments in our recording setup. Resume at 10:23.)

Now: You equate the color white with brilliant consciousness, good, and youth, and the color black with the <u>un</u>conscious, old age and death.

In this value system the black races are feared, as, basically, the aged are feared. The blacks are considered the primitives. To them are assigned creative musical abilities, for example, but for a long time these were "underground" activities: They gave birth to acceptable musical productions but were not admitted themselves into the concert halls of the respectable nation.

In your society therefore the black race has represented what you think of as the chaotic, primitive, spontaneous, savage, unconscious portions of the self, the underside of the "proper American citizen."

The blacks were to be oppressed then on the one hand, and yet treated indulgently as children on the other. There was always a great fear that the blacks as a race would escape their bounds—given an inch they would take a yard—simply because the whites so greatly feared the nature of the inner self, and recognized the power that they tried so desperately to strangle within themselves.

Nations, like individuals, can have split personalities at times. So there was a give-and-take involved in which the blacks expressed certain tendencies for the country as a whole, while the whites expressed other characteristics.

Both groups acquiesced to their roles. In larger terms, of course, each has belonged to other races in other times and places; or to be more accurate, in simultaneous existences one plays out the other's role.

Applied to old age, the color black denotes a returning to those unconscious forces. Now all of this so far is from the standpoint of American and Western belief. It is simply the reality in which many of my readers are involved. In other "underground" systems of belief, however, black is seen as a symbol of great knowledge, power and strength. When this is carried to an extreme you wind up with devil cults, in which the poorly understood powers of creativity and exuberance rush out in distorted form; the undersides of consciousness are then glorified at the expense of the other, white, "conscious and objective" values.

Yet in both of these systems the old are denied their unique power, strength and wisdom, and hence the civilization is robbed as well as the individuals within it.

(Amused:) My friend Ruburt is out of his beer, so I will let you pause briefly.

(10:37 to 10:48.)

All of this is also connected with your beliefs about the waking and dreaming states, white being acquainted with the day, and black with the dreaming condition. Here again is the old connection between the God of Light and the Prince of Darkness, or Satan—all distinctions made at various levels of development, and having to do with the nature of the origin of the present consciousness.

Through the ages, again, underground philosophies have tried to combine the two concepts, usually going from one extreme to the other in combating the current ideas in historical terms. In some of these philosophies the daylight is seen as pallid, for example, in comparison with the true brilliance of knowledge that illuminates the dream state, and black is the symbol then of secret knowledge that cannot be found with normal consciousness, or be scrutinized in the light of day.

Here you find stories of black magicians; and, once more, age enters in so that the legends of the wise old man or woman rise into folklore. Death is viewed in terms of value judgments of good and evil and black and white—the annihilation of consciousness being perceived as black, and its resurrection as white.

The light of illumination is experienced as white, yet it often appears to delineate the darkness of the soul, or to shine in the black of night. So in your terms of reference the two are dependent one upon the other, changing their connotations according to your beliefs.

In many ancient civilizations, the night with its blackness was revered, and the secrets of nighttime consciousness explored. Correlations were made in which such knowledge was used consciously in the daytime. The two seemingly separate aspects of consciousness merged, and there were flowerings of art and civilization that are, in your terms now, almost impossible to conceive. And in such civilizations all races were accorded their place, joyfully, and those of all ages were respected for their particular contributions.

In such societies the limited value judgments discussed in this chapter did not apply. Individuals—or races—did not have to take certain specific roles, acting out various portions of humanity's characteristics; each person was allowed to be unique, with all that that implies.

This does not mean that humanity has fallen from that state of grace into what may seem to be a lower condition. It does mean that you have chosen to diversify functions and abilities, to isolate them, so to speak, in order to learn and understand and even to develop their peculiar natures.

There are ways of assimilating your inner knowledge, your contrasting values of light and darkness, good and bad, youth and old age, and of using such criteria to enrich your own experience in a most practical fashion. In so doing you will enhance not only yourself and your society, but the world at large. You will also recognize the state of grace in which you must exist. Let us look at some of those ways.

Now you may take a break as Ruburt checks his mechanism over there.

(11:01 to 11:19.)

An attempt must be made to correlate seemingly diverse aspects of experience, to combine ideas of light and dark, consciousness and unconsciousness, and so forth, not only in private but mass experience.

As mentioned in *Seth Speaks,* my earlier book, great distinctions are made between your waking and sleeping states. *(See the 532nd session in Chapter Eight of that book.)* They are neatly divided, with little effort really made to relate the two. Many of you will not find it practical to alter your sleeping hours because of work commitments. Some of you will be able to do so, however, and those of you who are really interested in this endeavor can at least achieve some variation, on occasion, that will allow you to connect your sleeping and waking activities with far greater effectiveness.

Those of you who are able will discover that a somewhat altered arrangement will work greatly to your advantage. I suggest a six-hour sleeping block of time at one session, and no more. If you still feel the need for a greater amount of rest, then a two-hour-at-the-most nap can be added.

(*Pause.*) Many will find that a five-hour steady sleeping period is quite sufficient, with a nap as required. A four-hour block is ideal, however, reinforced by whatever nap feels natural.

In such circumstances, there are not the great artificial divisions created between the two states of consciousness. The conscious mind is better able to remember and assimilate its dreaming experience, and in dreams the self can use its waking experience more efficiently.

Often in the aged you find such frameworks coming into being naturally, but those who awaken spontaneously after four hours consider themselves insomniacs because of their beliefs, and so cannot utilize their experience properly. Both the conscious and unconscious would operate far more effectively, however, under an abbreviated sleeping program, and for those involved in "creative" endeavors this kind of schedule would bring greater intuition and applied knowledge.

Individuals following such natural behavior would feel much greater stability in themselves. Within the general patterns I have mentioned, each will, of course, find his or her own particular rhythm, and some experimentation might be necessary until you learn the maximum balance. But the flow of vitality would be heightened.

It is true that the patterns will have their own flow at certain points in your life. Following your own rhythm, longer or shorter periods will naturally ensue. Your consciousness as you think of it will be expanded through such practices. Generally speaking, eight-hour sleep periods, or longer ones, are not beneficial, nor in larger terms are they natural for the race.

(11:37.) There is a give-and-take chemical reaction, or rather chemical rhythms of reactions, that are far more effective in the shorter sleep periods. Many of you sleep through periods that should be those of your greatest creativity and alertness, in which the conscious and unconscious are most beautifully focused and at one. The conscious mind is often drugged with sleep just when it could be deriving its greatest benefits from the unconscious, and be able to poise most meaningfully in the reality that you know. In these instances the beauty and illumination of your dream state can be clear in the conscious mind, and used to enrich your physical life. Contrasts in your experience will appear to you in their united clarity.

Now *(heartily:)* That is the end of dictation, and of our session unless you have questions.

("Well . . . none that I can think of offhand." Actually I was pretty tired.)

I bid you then a fond good evening—and I suggest that you two at least <u>try</u> some of these ideas that we are offering to others. You may be quite surprised.

("Okay.")

My heartiest good wishes to you both, and to your machine.

("Thank you, Seth. Good night.")

(End at 11:43 P.M. Jane had been very well dissociated. She'd heard the recorder turn itself off some ten minutes ago, but no other external sounds.

(We usually sleep six hours at night, then supplement this with a half-hour nap late in the afternoon. Rather often, too, Jane will break up her nighttime sleep period by spontaneously waking and getting up for an hour or so.)

SESSION 652, MARCH 28, 1973,
9:13 P.M. WEDNESDAY

Good evening.

("Good evening, Seth.")

Now: Dictation. *(Pause.)* Such a change in your waking and sleeping patterns very nicely helps cut through your habitual ways of looking at the nature of your own personal world, and so alters your conception of reality in general.

To some extent, there is a natural and spontaneous merging of what you would think of as conscious and unconscious activity. This in itself brings about a greater understanding of the give-and-take that exists between the ego and other portions of the self. The unconscious is no longer equated with darkness, or with unknown frightening elements. Its character is transformed, so that the "dark" qualities are seen as actually illuminating portions of conscious life, while also providing great sources of power and energy for normal ego-oriented experience.

On the other hand, areas of ordinary behavior that may have seemed opaque before, cloudy or dark—personal characteristic behavior that was not understood, for instance—may suddenly become quite clear as a result of this transformation, in which the shadowy aspects of the unconscious are perceived as brilliant.

Barriers are broken down, and with them certain beliefs that were based upon them. If the unconscious is no longer feared, then the races that symbolized it are no longer to be feared either.

There are many other natural and spontaneous kinds of comprehension that can also result from the waking and sleeping rhythms that I have suggested. The unconscious, the color black, and death all have strongly negative connotations in which the inner self is feared; the dream state is mistrusted and often suggests thoughts of both death and/or evil. But changed wake-sleep habits can, again, bring about a transformation in which it is obvious that dreams contain great wisdom and creativity, that the unconscious is indeed quite conscious, and that in fact the individual sense of identity can be retained in the dream state. The fear of self-annihilation, symbolically thought of as death, can then no longer apply as it did before.

As a result, other individually built-up beliefs that depended upon the existence of such opposites also spontaneously break down.

(9:30. I saw a large black winged ant crawling on the back of Jane's rocker, close to her head. The next second it was on her neck. She jumped up in mid-delivery, brushing instinctively at something she couldn't have seen. Dazed, she sank back into her chair. "A bug will do it," she finally said. After resting briefly she lit a cigarette and went back into trance.)

Do you have it?

(I read the last sentence aloud, and Seth-Jane continued.)

When you find yourself as alert, responsive, and intellectual in the dream state as you are in waking life, it becomes impossible to operate within the old framework. This does not mean that in all dreams that particular kind of awareness is achieved, but it is often accomplished <u>within</u> the suggested wake-sleep pattern.

(Quite forcefully:) A certain beneficial and natural situation is arrived at, in which the conscious and unconscious minds meet. This occurs spontaneously whatever your sleep patterns, but is very brief and seldom remembered. The optimum state is so short because of the prolonged drugging of the conscious mind.

Animals follow their own natural waking-sleeping schedules, and in their way derive far greater benefits from <u>both</u> states than you, and use them with greater effectiveness—particularly along the lines of the body's built-in system of therapy. They know exactly when to alter their patterns to longer or shorter sleep periods, therefore adjusting the adrenalin output and regulating all of the bodily hormones.

In humans, the idea of nutrition is also involved. With your habits the body is literally starved for long periods at night, then often overfed during the day. Important therapeutic information that is given in dreams, and meant to be recalled, is not remembered because your sleep habits plunge you into what you think of as unconsciousness far too long.

The body itself can be physically refreshed and rested in

much less than eight hours, and after five hours the muscles themselves yearn for activity. This need is also a signal to awaken so that unconscious material and dream information can be consciously assimilated.

Take your break.

(9:45 to 9:55.)

Many of your misconceptions about the nature of reality are directly related to the division you place between your sleeping and waking experience, your conscious and unconscious activity. Opposites seem to occur that do not exist in actuality. Myths, symbols and rationalizations all become necessary to explain the seeming divergences, the seeming contradictions between realities that appear to be so different.

Individual psychological mechanisms are activated, sometimes, in terms of neurosis or other mental problems; these bring out into the open inner challenges or dilemmas that otherwise would be worked out more easily through an open give-and-take of conscious and unconscious reality—

(10:01. Again we were interrupted—this time by the telephone. I answered it, then Jane took over when she was out of trance; for five minutes or so she talked to a woman who lived a couple of hours away and wanted to come to ESP class.)

Dictation. *(Whispering.*

("Okay.")

In the natural body-mind relationship the sleep state operates as a great connector, an interpreter, allowing the free flow of conscious and unconscious material. In the kind of sleep patterns suggested, optimum conditions are set up. Neurosis and psychosis simply would not occur under such conditions. And in the natural back-and-forth leeway of the system, exterior dilemmas or problems are worked out in the dream situation, and interior difficulty may also be solved symbolically through physical experience.

Illumination concerning the inner self may appear clearly during waking reality, and in the same way invaluable information about the conscious self may be received in the dream state. There is a spontaneous flow of psychic energy with appropriate hormonal reaction in both situations. You do not have energy dammed up through repressions, for example, and emotions and their expression are not feared.

In your present system of beliefs, and with the dubious light in which the unconscious is considered, a fear of the emotions is often generated. Not only are they often hindered in waking life, then, but censored as much as possible in dreams. Their expression becomes very difficult; great blockages of energy occur, which in your terms can result in neurotic or even stronger, psychotic, behavior.

The inhibition of such emotions also interferes with the nervous system and its therapeutic devices. These repressed emotions, and the whole charge behind such distorted concepts about the unconscious, result in a projection outward upon others. In your individual area there will be persons upon whom you will project all of those charged, frightening emotions or characteristics. At the same time you will be <u>drawn to</u> those individuals because the projections represent a part of you.

On a national basis the characteristics or qualities will be projected outward onto an enemy. Within a nation they can be directed against those of a particular race, creed or color.

(Long pause at 10:24.) You did not simply come upon your sleep patterns. They are not the result of your technology or industrial habits. Instead they are a part of those beliefs that <u>caused</u> you to develop your technological, industrial society. They emerged as you began to categorize experience more and more, to see yourselves as separate from the spring or fountainhead of your own psychological reality. In natural circumstances the animals, while sleeping at night, are still partially alert against predators and danger. There is within the innate characteristics of the mammalian brain, then, a great balance in which complete physical relaxation can occur in sleep, while consciousness is maintained in a "partially suspended, passive-yet-alert" manner. That state allows conscious participation and interpretation of "unconscious" dream

activity. The condition gives the body its refreshment, yet it does not lie inert for such long periods of time.

(*Pause.*) Mammals have also changed their habits to accommodate those conditions you have thrust upon them, so the behavior studied in laboratories is not necessarily that shown by the same animals in their natural state.

Taken alone, this statement can appear deceptive. The alterations in behavior are themselves natural, of course.

Animal consciousness is different than your own. With yours, a finer discrimination is necessary so that unconscious material can be assimilated. (*Long pause.*) All of mankind's developments however are <u>latent</u> in the animal brain, and many attributes of which you are unaware are latent in your own. The biological pathways for them already exist.

(*Very actively delivered:*) In your current beliefs, again, consciousness is equated in very limited terms with your <u>conception</u> of intellectual behavior: you consider this to be a peak of mental achievement, growing from the "undifferentiated" perceptions of childhood, and returning ignominiously to them again in old age. Such wake-sleep patterns as I have suggested would acquaint you with the great creative and energetic portions of psychological behavior—that are not undifferentiated at all, but simply distinct from your usual concepts of consciousness; and these operate throughout your life.

The natural experiences of what you think of as time distortion, for example, occurring in childhood and old age alike, represent quite normal experiences of your basic "time-environment"—much more so than the clock time with which you are so familiar.

The patterns I have suggested, therefore, will bring you far closer to an understanding of the reality of your being, and help you break down beliefs that cause personal and social division.

You may take your break.

(*10:46. "Well, it was a good trance," Jane laughed, "in spite of bugs and phones." Then, at 10:56: "He's about ready again . . ."*)

Now: The long period of continuous waking conscious activity is to some extent at variance with your natural inclinations.

It cuts you off from the spontaneous give-and-take of conscious and unconscious material mentioned earlier *(in this session)*, and of <u>itself</u> you see necessitates certain changes that then <u>make</u> your prolonged sleep period necessary *(intently)*. The body is denied the frequent rests it requires. Conscious stimuli is over-applied, making assimilation difficult and placing a strain upon the mind-body relationship.

The division between the two aspects of experience begins to take on the characteristics of completely diverse behavior. The unconscious becomes more and more unfamiliar to consciousness. Those beliefs build up about it, and the symbolisms involved are exaggerated. The unknown seems to be threatening and degenerate. The color black assumes stronger tendencies in its connection with evil—something to be avoided. Self-annihilation seems to be a threat ever-present in the dream or sleep state. At the same time all of those flamboyant, creative, spontaneous, emotional surges that <u>emerge</u> normally from the unconscious become feared and projected outward, then, upon enemies, other races and creeds.

Sexual behavior obviously will be considered depraved by those most afraid of their own sensual natures. They will ascribe it to primitive or evil or unconscious sources, and even attempt to censor their dreams in that regard. They will then project the greatest sexual license upon those groups they choose to represent their own repressed behavior. If sex is equated with evil, the other group will of course be considered evil.

If the members of such a rigid group believe that youth is innocent, then they will deny sexual experience as having any place in childhood, and alter their own memories to fit their beliefs.

If a young adult believes that sex is good but old age is bad, then he or she will find it impossible to consider exuberant sexuality as a portion of an older person's experience. In the dream state the child and the old man or woman can exist simultaneously, and the individual is made quite aware of the full range of creaturehood.

(11:12.) The wisdom of the child and of the aged are both available. Lessons from "future experience" are also at hand. There are quite natural physical mechanisms in the body that provide for such interaction. You deny yourself many of these advantages however through the artificial alienation that you have set up by your present wake-sleep patterns, to which, again, your ideas of good and evil are intimately connected.

Those of you who cannot practically make any alterations in sleeping habits can still obtain some benefits by changing your beliefs in the areas discussed, learning to recall your dreams and resting briefly when you can, and immediately afterward recording those impressions that you retain.

You must give up any ideas that you have as to the unsavory nature of unconscious activity. You must learn to believe in the goodness of your being. Otherwise you will not explore these other states of your own reality.

When you trust yourself then you will trust your own dream interpretations—and these will lead you to greater self-understanding. Your beliefs of good and evil will become much more clear to you, and you will no longer need to project repressed tendencies out upon others in exaggerated fashion.

End of dictation and of the session.

("Thank you.")

My heartiest regards to you both. And have Ruburt discuss his notes.

("All right. Good night, Seth.")

(End at 11:24 P.M. Seth referred to some writing Jane did today on her long-range theoretical project, Aspect Psychology. *See her Introduction to this book, and the notes for the 618th session in Chapter Three.)*

SESSION 653, APRIL 4, 1973,
9:23 P.M. WEDNESDAY

(We were visited over the weekend by Robert Monroe and his wife, Nancy; they live on a farm in central Virginia. Bob Monroe is the author of Journeys Out of the Body,* *the book that Jane and I regard as the premier work on the subject. Among many things, he wanted to tell Jane about the research complex, tentatively called The Mentronics Institute—or System—that he's building on his farm. It will be used "by just a bunch of guys" to study various phases of psychic activity. These "guys" then will be doctors, parapsychologists, psychiatrists, and members of other scientific disciplines.*

(Seth came through Sunday night, April 1, in a long recorded discussion with the Monroes. We were all to meet again late Monday. Beginning Monday morning, however, Jane began experiencing another strongly surging burst of creative inspiration—a clearly transcendent one that lasted for several hours. She'd had intimations of it Sunday afternoon before our guests arrived. I'm describing the phenomenon here, and including rather long excerpts from her written report of it, to show some of her other psychic activities while this book is being produced. At the same time such perceptions give insights into the book itself.

(Jane described her altered state of consciousness to me while it was in progress on Monday, of course, then the next morning she wrote as complete an account of it as she could. This took over six thousand words—and even while typing she found herself reliving portions of the experience to some moderate degree ...

("Sunday afternoon before our visitors came," she wrote, "I'd begun reading a book by Ralph Waldo Emerson [the poet and philosopher who lived from 1803-82]. I came across his essay, The Poet, *in which he talked about the 'speakers' as being*

*Garden City, N.Y., Doubleday & Company, Inc., 1971.

311

those who use their inner abilities to 'speak the inner secrets of nature.' The essay impressed me strongly, seeming to echo elements in my own writing and psychic characteristics; and of course I thought of Seth's 'Speakers' as he described them in Chapter Twenty of Seth Speaks. [According to Seth, Emerson was a Speaker too!] Then Bob Monroe and his wife arrived, and we had a busy evening. Seth came through, and so forth.

("As I sat at my desk the next morning, April 2, I was suddenly filled with the strongest, most vivid kind of inspiration I think I've ever had. I was swept along by it all day long, writing in a fever, agitated yet exultant. The result was a nine-page poem called Dialogues of the Speakers, which may or may not continue into a book. This is the way the book of poetry that I finished early in March, Dialogues of the Soul and Mortal Self in Time, began.

("As I came to the end of the long poem in mid-afternoon, I had more and more difficulty describing my feelings, and even in typing. Here are the last two verses:

Do the Speakers live?
Their massive lives straddle ours,
and through the pupils of their eyes
we look out upon a universe,
but all that we know or see
is but a detail
in a scheme so overpowering
that writing, now, I grow weak
and cry that what I sense
falls through my words
which cannot hold
such inner evidence.

I am left with gaps so huge
that what is unsaid is all—
and there
what I cannot hold
is what I am and what you are.
My thoughts are as weak
as my cupped hands

to grasp these meanings,
but our lives are like
the shadows of my fingertips.
So are we
sent out by other ones,
massive relatives
in a family so vast,
yet in which
each member basks.

("As I struggled through these, my subjective state changed to such a degree that I called Rob again. I began to sense the Speakers' 'massive lives,' and I realized that I had gone beyond the poem. The inspiration was now directing my perception so that as I looked around, the world was altered. When this happens to me, this state that we think of as subjective life turns real and objective, and is then viewed in the same way that our normal physical life is.

("This is never a complete process, but the transformation of inner data outward is a splendid—though sometimes disquieting—experience.

("From my desk in my study I faced the windows of our small kitchen. I could look through the treetops beyond them—we live on the second floor—and down to the street on the next block. Not three-dimensionally, but in another way more vividly, I . . . saw . . . sensed . . . massive figures standing around the edge of that physical view; and around the edges of the world. My eyes were open, of course. With my inner sight I felt that one of those forms, sturdy and impossibly massive, might bend down and with his gigantic face peek into my kitchen window . . . though I was also aware that all of this was my interpretation of what I was receiving.

("At the same time, in contrast, my perception of my room underwent a transformation. Everything in it, while retaining its own size to my vision, became microscopically small and dear, like a child's model of a world—but one that was real and living, with my rooms inside one of the innumerable toy houses.

313

I was exhilarated yet disquieted. I tried to go along with what was happening, yet still retain a certain 'as if' distance so that I wouldn't be completely lost in the experience.

("Rob suggested I take a nap, since the Monroes were to arrive in an hour or so. While I attempted to sleep, one idea from among many sprang out at me, literally shocking me: 'We are IN God. We were NEVER externalized!' These words do little to explain my emotional, subjective feelings of participation in this idea. For suddenly I felt being-in-God as being-in-a-house. Everything we imagine and know is inside. _There is no outside_.

("I felt claustrophobic for a bit . . . my visual perception was again altered in a strange smoother way, so that everything I saw was an inside that was inside itself, ad infinitum. I felt dwarfed. But almost immediately came the oddest feeling of fantastic security, and I realized that being inside God . . . we were literally made of God-stuff and were therefore eternal.

("Next came the feeling that this inside quality was so inconceivably vast that within it was all of the ever-expanding 'space' possible; only an _inside_ could possess those characteristics of constant expansion.

("Each of these ideas came as emotional revelations, accompanied by various bodily sensations and alterations of visual perception. In here other experiences began, and to different degrees I did get lost in them. One involved my body becoming massive—not _as if_ it was massive, but massive itself. To all intents and purposes I was massive, lying there. I expanded in some way, rising higher . . . "

(Jane then experienced a whole series of events involving various facets of the concept of massiveness. While these were perfectly "real" to her physically, she also knew that they were symbolic interpretations of inner realities. We think the cellular memory that Seth describes was also involved, as witness these excerpts from her account:

("... the next thing I knew I was back in bed, but massive again, and for a moment frightened: My left hand, above me on the pillow, had turned into an eagle's claw. My eyes were closed, but as far as physical sensation was concerned that's what it was. I felt this fantastic power in my hand; it tried to grip as an eagle's claw would. I felt... the weirdest kind of... armor, the alien yet tough and resilient claw instead of flesh in our terms. Then my shoulders and the whole top area of my back began to turn into a great eagle, wings flapping; the surging power and alien sensations were astounding...

("In a process impossible to describe, another change took place. This time I was a dinosaur. I mean, I WAS one. I stood on two legs, making loud, hoarse and guttural noises of... exultation as I stood upon a great plain. There was a similarity between the eagle and the dinosaur in that body armor or whatever, that strange toughness... these were all stages that I had been through—or at least that some of the cells in my body remembered—but the immediacy was very vivid on my part...

("Rob called me, then left to pick up the Monroes at the hotel. I felt exhilarated to a high degree, yet exhausted. I began to dress, still aware of the inside-God feeling. The birds began to sing outside and I stopped, transfixed. The birds were the gods singing! This wasn't a symbolic or artistic sensation—this was sudden known fact!

("The incredible sweetness of their songs followed me even while I found myself laughing... For now I was touching up my nails—I'd worn off all the new polish on their edges from typing my Speaker poetry all day. And inside God or not, here I was, quite capable of thinking in such mundane terms. As I went into the living room to prepare it for guests, that room was also an inside that was an inside..."

(Echoes of Jane's transcendent experience persisted for days. She also recalled details she had omitted from her written record—usually the memory of these was triggered by ordinary events in our daily lives.

(Those who are interested can check out the references in the next two paragraphs.

315

(1. Seth deals with cellular memory to some extent in the 638th session in Chapter Ten; also see the 632nd and 637th sessions. Among other material covering altered states of consciousness on Jane's part, refer to her Introduction, as well as the notes for the 639th session in Chapter Ten, and the 645th session in Chapter Eleven. By the looks of things, she'll have more such episodes that we can add to later chapters. She plans to study all of her experiences with various stages of consciousness in her book, Aspect Psychology.

(2. There are clear connections between the "massive" portions of Jane's latest psychic adventure and her first encounters with Seth Two in April, 1968; she goes into those experiences in some detail in Chapter Seventeen of The Seth Material. There is more on Seth Two in Chapter Twenty-two of Seth Speaks. In Chapter One of The Seth Material, she describes her first "trip" through an altered state of consciousness—and how it resulted in the production of her manuscript, The Physical Universe as Idea Construction. See the notes preceding the 633rd session in Chapter Eight.

(No session was held Monday evening. Instead Jane used her "own" abilities to tune in on the diagram of a machine that Bob Monroe drew; he had seen this on one of his out-of-body journeys. Questions involving physics arose—the Fermi gap [having to do with the movement of certain electrons], and so forth—and Jane ended up drawing diagrams of her own. She enjoys using her abilities this way.

(She gave her notes and drawings to Bob. On Tuesday, then, beside writing about her transcendent episode, she wrote an account of Monday evening's discussion, and reconstructed her notes and sketches for her own records.

("Well, I feel Seth around," Jane said tonight at 9:22. "I'll be ready in a minute. It's funny, but as I sit here waiting I feel a great sense of color and expectation. I often do—it's almost the same high-flying feeling I get when I do some good poetry, like on Monday . . ." Off came her glasses.)

Good evening.

("*Good evening, Seth.*")

Dictation. *(Quietly:)* Your attitudes toward sleep, dreams, or any alterations of consciousness are all colored to some extent then by beliefs concerning good and evil in your Western society. These emerge from the old Puritan work ethic: "The devil finds evil work for idle hands."

This kind of thinking by itself brings about an overall attitude in which rest is frowned upon, and dreams are considered suspect. Daydreaming and even mild alterations of consciousness take on moral connotations. Such ideas are mirrored in your society in innumerable fashions, and in areas in which values of good and evil are not apparent. Active sports are considered good, however, but often contrasted to passive intuitive activities which are then seen as bad.

You insist upon a material product of some physically demonstrative kind. In that context, dreams or daydreams are not viewed as constructive or productive.

Young people are urged to tackle life aggressively, but in the usage of the term this means competitively. It also implies, and of course, promotes, the direction of individual consciousness in an exterior fashion only. Not only is consciousness to be focused to the external reality, but <u>within</u> those limits it is still further harnessed toward certain specific goals. Other inclinations are frowned upon.

Such individuals are trained to consider any alterations of consciousness, any seemingly "passive" endeavor as dangerous to one degree or another. An artist will be tolerated—only if his work sells well, for example, in which case it will be thought that the artist is simply <u>trickier</u> than most in discovering a way of making money.

The writer is put up with if books result in either fame or fortune. The poet is scarcely tolerated, for usually his or her gifts bring neither.

The dreamer, whatever his age, job or family background, is considered most suspect, for it seems that he doesn't even have a craft to excuse his moral laziness. People with such beliefs will find it most difficult to understand the creativity of their own being. The work done in dreams, the multitudinous experience encountered there, will be invisible to them. They will have little regard or respect for the dreamers or visionaries of the world, and will be the first to leap upon those in their own generation who display such tendencies.

For all of this, however, inner portions of each individual's being are not touched by those beliefs. The ideas will be reflected in their daily experience, certainly, and seem to be justified. Yet beneath, the inner self is quite aware of the great thrusting creativity that occurs in dreams, and realizes that the source of individual energy has nothing to do with such superficial concepts as the nature of good and evil.

Take your break, for that is the end of the chapter.

(*"All right."*)

CHAPTER **14**

Which You?
Which World?
Your Daily Reality as the Expression
of Specific Probable Events

(9:43. Jane had no idea of what Chapter Fourteen would be about: "I'm just waiting . . . ." At 9:51 she said, "In fact, I haven't the slightest idea in my head about Seth or anything else." We continued to wait. It had begun to rain gently; traffic seemed to hiss upon the pavement. We heard a television set sounding off in one of the downstairs apartments, though not loudly. Resume, finally, at 10:01.)

Dictation: Chapter Fourteen: "Which You?" Beneath that *(gesturing horizontally:)* "Which World?"

(In trance, her eyes closed, Jane sat quite still for well over a minute.)

Continuing with the heading: "Your Daily Reality as the Expression of Specific Probable Events." That is all the heading.

(A long pause at 10:06.) The brain can be called simply the physical counterpart of the mind. By means of the brain the functions of the soul and intellect are connected with the body. Through the characteristics of the brain, events that are of nonphysical origin become physically valid. There is a definite filtering and focusing effect at work, then. Practically speaking,

319

you do indeed form the appearance that reality takes through your conscious beliefs. Those beliefs are used as screening and directing agents, separating certain nonphysical probable events from others, and bringing them into three-dimensional actuality,

Other probable events could just as well become physically experienced ones. Those beliefs about yourself form your own self-image, and define your concepts of what is possible or not possible for you. You will choose from those nonphysical probable events, therefore, only those you feel you are in accord with.

Because of your psychological and psychic structure, there is within the rich makeup of your being a literally endless variety of what you may call probable selves. In one reality or another these will all be experienced. In your present existence however you will utilize only those psychological characteristics that you believe you possess. So, you see, the personality cannot be defined as being thus-and-so.

The physical constitution of the body follows your beliefs, and so all of its sense data will faithfully mirror the beliefs that direct its activity. In certain terms hypnosis is simply an exercise in the alteration of beliefs, and only too clearly shows that sense experience follows expectations.

The "you" that you presently conceive yourself to be represents the emergence into physical experience of but one probable state of your being, who then directs corporeal life and "frames" and defines all sense data. When your ideas about yourself change, so does your experience.

Even the intimate body experience alters. You may say that you are you, but which you are you? In the most personal terms each individual creates his own world. The biological equipment of your creaturehood directs your mass experience enough so that agreement is reached, but only along certain general lines.

(*Pause at 10:27.*) The overall private experience that you perceive forms your world, period. But which world do you

320

inhabit? For if you altered your beliefs and therefore your private sensations of reality, then that world, seemingly the only one, would also change. You do go through transformations of beliefs all the time, and your perception of the world is different. You seem to be, no longer, the person that you were. You are quite correct—you are <u>not</u> the person that you were, and your world <u>has</u> changed, and not just symbolically.

Often you fall into lapses in which you actually pull in your consciousness, so to speak, and experience life in a lesser fashion. In such a state you do not seem to experience yourself directly, and indeed in the midst of what you think of as the waking state you act in the most mechanical of fashions, following habit and being less aware of sensual stimuli.

On such occasions your beliefs usually lose their edge, the directions you give to your body are not clear, and the world seems fuzzy. This is often a time of deep unconscious activity, when new latent probable characteristics are biding their time, so to speak, waiting for emergence.

You may take your break.

(10:37 to 10:55.)

In your terms probable events are brought into actuality by utilizing the body's nerve structure through certain intensities of will or conscious belief.

These beliefs obviously have another reality beside the one with which you are familiar. They attract and bring into being certain events instead of others. Therefore, they determine the <u>entry</u> of experienced events from an endless variety of probable ones. You seem to be at the center of your world, because for you your world begins with that point of intersection where soul and physical consciousness meet.

(Long pause at 11:04.) Give us time . . .

In surface terms the sense of "I" that you possess is the result of constantly emerging probable identities, given continuity in time through the physical apparatus of the body with its built-in intervals of nerve reaction. You only <u>remember</u> the portion of your identity that is physically realized—those portions that are drawn into corporeal pattern. *(With gestures, and forcefully:)* This is the result of the focusing and yet limiting behavior of the physical brain, for effective survival behavior in your reality depends upon time reactions. The nerve patterns' activity therefore causes the illusion of a present, in which your consciousness appears focused and alert.

In certain terms "future" events exist now, but they are too fast. They jump over the nerve endings too quickly, and physically you cannot perceive or experience them as yet.

Impulses possess a far different reality than physicists or biologists suppose. As you think now, "past" is still occurring. The "drag" still leaps the synapses, but, again, is not physically recorded. Past events continue. Consciously you only experience portions of events with your corporeal structure, yet the structure itself records them.

In such a way the cells retain their memory, though you do not perceive it, and the body is aware of so-called future occurrences, though as a rule you do not consciously sense this. *(Suddenly very intense and fast:)* At other levels of psychic activity however such knowledge is also available to you, but only when you disconnect your experience from the time-activated neuronal structure—and this you can do through various alterations of consciousness, often quite spontaneously adopted.

Many such states can give you a far greater direct experience with the nature of your noncorporeal reality than any normally conscious questioning. Which you? Which world? You can to some extent discover for yourself the other probable you's that are a portion of your being.

Take your break.

(11:20. Jane said that while in trance she hadn't been aware that her delivery had been slow at times—yet she seemed to recall these fluctuations when I asked her about them. She thought Seth was "trying to couch the stuff in terms that would make sense to someone who didn't know much about such

things, while keeping it of interest to a physicist, say—which wasn't easy to do. There was a lot more about synapses and neurons, and things like that, that he didn't put in . . ."

(The junction between two nerve cells, or neurons, is called the synapse. [See the 637th session in Chapter Nine.] Jane is receiving more letters from scientists these days, many of whom ask intriguing questions about the type of material covered in this session. Resume in a faster manner at 11:45.)

Now: Future events are also your selection of probable ones, however, and many occurrences in which you are involved speed past you too quickly for your neuronal structure. These are not served up to you as your present.

They represent your experience on other than physical levels. My dear friend Ruburt *(briefly louder)* has to some extent given an analogy of this in the first Oversoul 7 book, a novel. You perceive a certain event as present. Your beliefs give it entry through the nerve synapses, and attract it. It then seems to become the past. You have only tuned into a portion of it physically, though; that past event continues to exist with its own "future," which you may or may not perceive, according to which probable action you pull into your next experiences of actuality.

The past does have its own past, present and future, therefore. From a given past event you will only materialize a particular future, but the event itself continues, and possesses a dimensionality of its own—or rather a multidimensionality that you also possess.

You can dip into cellular memory, for example. Using memory, you follow but one recognized sequence of remembered events backward. There are elements in your past that are as unpredictable, however, as the elements in your future now appear to be *(emphatically)*. There is creativity in your past waiting for you even as there is in your future, but to utilize such experiences you must learn to alter your beliefs, and to some degree escape from the particular kind of limited conscious focus that you habitually use.

Now: We can continue the session—
("Go ahead.")
—or end it as you prefer. If you continue, take a brief break . . . Some of these sessions can go on for longer periods of time.

(11:55. "Didn't I just get a break?" Jane asked, puzzled. I explained the situation to her. These sessions don't often work this way. Resume at 12:05.)

Now give us a moment. The physical structure itself contains within it the necessary prerequisites for what you would call evolutions of consciousness—and even for, within certain limits, the organization of experience in ways that might seem quite alien to you now.

Sense data <u>can</u> be organized in different fashions. Mechanisms and pathways exist, making it quite possible for you to <u>see</u> sound, or hear color, although that is not your primary habit at this time.

(Pause.) In certain terms time intervals are jumped, as when a "past" smell or sight is suddenly perceived with present vividness, though you would say it has already occurred in the past. Under particular conditions a memory may suddenly become more real than the event of the present moment, and so rush again into your current experience as validly as when it was first lived, and even seem to blot out the occurrences of the moment.

This could not happen if your physical structure did not have built-in mechanisms allowing it to, and if under certain conditions the normal intervals between the synapses of the nerve cells could not be leaped in a different fashion. In the same way, a future experience may also be physically perceived in your present. Now beneath your usual consciousness, your physical organism can react to future events without your knowledge, as it can to past ones. In such cases the intensity of the initially nonphysical event is enough to break through normal neuronal patterns.

If you are aware of such a future episode, you will be forced

324

to react to it as a conscious being. In any case your temporal structure will respond whether or not you are aware of the reasons for such behavior. The future incident may then occur in its time sequence, and you recognize it through memory, in which case your reactions in that future present will be altered because of the seemingly past memory.

In your terms that event may never come to pass, however, because it may be arising from a probable past that was once your present, but from which you have diverged. This is one of the reasons why psychics' predictions often do not seem to bear out, for at every point you do indeed have the free will, through your beliefs, to alter your experience.

Your beliefs form the pivot of your present experience.

Now: End of dictation. A few remarks . . .

(12:20. Seth now delivered two pages of material for Jane and me, and the session ended at 12:37 A.M.

(Those who are interested in probabilities can also see chapters Fifteen, Sixteen, and Seventeen in Seth Speaks.*)*

SESSION 654, APRIL 9, 1973,
9:45 P.M. MONDAY

Now: Good evening and dictation.

("Good evening, Seth.")

In your terms, practically speaking, probable events seem to make more sense when you think of them as latent future ones.

The fact remains that there are probable past events that "can still happen" within your personal previous experience. A new event can literally be born in the past—"now."

On a grand scale this rarely occurs in such a way that you perceive it—and you had better underline that whole last part.

A new belief in the present, however, can cause changes in the past on a neuronal level. You must understand that basically time is simultaneous. Present beliefs can indeed alter the past. In some cases of healing, in the spontaneous disappearance of cancer, for instance, or of any other disease, certain alterations are made that affect cellular memory, genetic codes, or neuronal patterns in the past.

In such instances there is, as easily as I can explain it, a reaching into deep biological structures as they existed at one time; at that point the probabilities are altered, and the condition erased in your present—but also in your past.

(*Pause at 10:01.*) A sudden or intense belief in health can indeed "reverse" a disease, but in a very practical way it is a reversal in terms of time. New memories are inserted in place of the old ones, as far as cells are concerned under such conditions. This kind of therapy happens quite frequently on a spontaneous basis when people rid themselves of diseases they do not even know they possess.

Learning is not simply passed on from living tissue to living tissue—this your biologists have discovered—but it is also passed on through the body's present corporeal reality, sometimes entirely changing the messages to past cells, that in your terms no longer exist.

In somewhat the same way, a strong belief in a particular ability generated in the present will reach into the past and effect whatever changes would have had to occur there (*with gestures*) in order to now make the ability apparent.

This is the reason for the results of some experiments being conducted abroad, in which accelerated learning takes place, when under hypnosis or otherwise a present individual is convinced that he or she is, for example, a great painter, or a linguist. The present belief activates "latent" abilities within each person.*

(*Pause.*) The biological structure as it existed in the past is therefore affected. Experience is built into the organism that it did not have before, in your terms. It is a sort of reprogramming. It is impossible, of course, for you to examine cellular structure now as it exists in the present and

---

*Seth seems to refer to "Artificial Reincarnation" as practiced by the Soviets. See Sheila Ostrander and Lynn Schroeder's *Psychic Discoveries Behind the Iron Curtain,* (Bantam Books).

simultaneously as it existed in the past *(very positively)*. Scientifically, you can only probe those effects that appear within your present. When you alter your beliefs today you also reprogram your past. As far as you are concerned the present is your point of action, focus, and power, and from that point of volition you form both your future and past. Realizing this, you will understand that you are not at the mercy of a past over which you have no control.

Take your break.

(10:20. "Seth was doing it slow so that I got it right," Jane said. "The biologists won't accept that, though ... Pretty tricky." Resume in the same manner at 10:35.)

While your present conscious beliefs dictate your current experience, and while your physical body wears its solidity only in present time to your senses, beneath this both the ever-changing elements of your body and your consciousness are relatively free in time. They exist in a multidimensionality with which rational consciousness is not yet equipped to deal.

This is not meant to dilute the function or natural abilities of reasoning awareness, for its powers allow you to focus experience in a highly specific manner, and to direct energy with great purposeful attention. *(Pause.)* In your terms, this action is in the process of automatically changing the nature of rational consciousness—which is, as you think of it, in a state of evolution.

Your consciousness is not a thing that you possess. Your individuality is not a thing with limits. If you ask, "What is my individuality in all of this?" or, "Which 'I' am I?" then you are automatically thinking of yourself as a psychological entity with definite boundaries that must be protected at all costs. You may say, "I was born in a house on a certain street in a certain town, and no present belief to the contrary will change that fact." If, in the present, one past event can be altered within your neuronal structure, however, then basically no event is safe from such change.

In your practical experience, tables remain tables, although physicists well know that physical appearance is in some ways a mirage. At your level of experience many effects are accepted and used quite practically, as are your solid tables. You do not perceive the atoms or molecules that compose them; so in the same way, but in a different manner of speaking, events seem "solid" as tables do.

Yet at other levels this seeming solidity of events also breaks down. Which you? Which world? A sudden contemporary belief in illness will actually reach back into the past, affecting the organism at that level, and inserting into the past experience of the cells the initiation of those biological events that will then seem to give birth to a present disease.

In the current pivoting of its experience, therefore, your conscious mind directs not only the present, but future and past experience of deep neurological events.

(Long pause at 10:59.) Give us time . .

Cellular memory can be changed at any point. Present beliefs can insert into the past new memory, both psychologically and physically. The future is in no way predetermined on <u>basic</u> levels. This does not mean that the future cannot be predicted sometimes, for in practical terms you will often continue with certain lines of probability which can be seen "ahead of time."

Such predictions can affect the probabilities, of course, and reinforce a present line of belief. Physicians often wonder whether they should tell terminal patients of their impending deaths. There is great controversy. In some cases such a prediction can make death a fact—while its opposite <u>can</u> regenerate the patient's belief in his or her own ability to live.

No man will die simply because a physician tells him he is going to, however. No one is so at the mercy of another's beliefs. Each individual, generally speaking, knows his challenges and <u>overall</u> programs, and the time of his death. But even such decisions can be altered at any time in your "now"—the entire body can be regenerated in a way that would be impossible to predict in usual medical terms. *(See the 624th session in Chapter Five.)*

328

You rule your experiences from the focal point of your present, where your beliefs directly intercept with the body and the physical world on the one hand, and the invisible world from which you draw your energy and strength on the other. This applies to individuals, societies, races and nations, and to sociological, biological and psychic activities.

In daily practical experience, try to concentrate for a while upon seemingly subordinate abilities, ones that you think of as latent. If you do so consistently, using your imagination and will, then those abilities will become prominent in your present. The current beliefs will reprogram and alter past experience. It is not simply that past, forgotten, unconsciously perceived events will be put together in a new way and organized under a new heading, but that in that past (now not perceivable), the entire bodily response to seemingly past events will change.

(Very forcefully, if with many pauses:) Your desire or belief will literally be reaching back into time, teaching the nerves new tricks. Definite reorganizations in that past will occur in your present, allowing you to behave in entirely new fashions.

(A one-minute pause at 11:21.) Learned behavior therefore alters not only present and future but also past conduct. Your power as a rational consciousness focused in the present provides you with opportunities for creativity that you are but vaguely learning to understand. As you do learn, you will automatically begin to appreciate the multidimensional nature of not only your own species but of others as well. The moment as you think of it, then, is the creative framework through which you, the nonphysical self, constantly form corporeal reality; and through that window into earthly existence you form both its future and its past.

You may take a break.

(11:30. "Boy," Jane said after she was out of an excellent trance, "I had the feeling we were getting some new stuff. I remember thinking, 'It's great, Seth, but I hope people can read it and follow it . . .'" Resume at 11:47.)

Now: In purely physical terms, what you think of as consciousness of the self arises from a certain peak of intensity reached by the gestalt consciousness of the atoms and molecules, and cells and organs, that compose the body.

(*Pause.*) The peculiarly physically oriented self that you know has its reality in that context, but even in physical terms its reality is more than any analysis of its entirety would show. It then directs the activity of the body, and is to that extent dependent upon neurological activity.

The psychic structure of consciousness that organizes that bodily gestalt is, however, not dependent upon it, and so the you that you experience is only a portion of this greater identity.

During certain stages in sleep states you short-circuit the neurological structures, and perceive experiences of a multidimensional nature that you then attempt to translate, as best you can, into stimuli that can be physically assimilated—hence you often convert these into symbolic images that can be understood, and to some extent reacted to, by your bodily structure.

Many times such constructions are used as inner visual patterns, for example. Visually they often bear a similarity to the inner architecture of the cells, and to planets. Your dream images are biologically structured, then. The experiences behind them bring you in contact with the deepest portions of your nonphysical reality, and it is the unconscious who translates these for you into recognizable images and forms.

In the same way your unconscious also transforms for you, from an otherwise undifferentiated maze of reality, fields of activation into recognizable objects and events in your daily life.

You are now rooted in your creaturehood, graced to perceive through your body a unique living experience. So when I mention techniques that will allow you to perceive other fields of reality beside your own, I want you to realize that these should be used to enhance your enjoyment of that creaturehood, and to enrich your sensual as well as spiritual expression.

In the brilliance of your physical being, both are entwined.

End of dictation.

(12:05. But not quite of the session: Seth continued with a page of material for Jane and me about our work, so things actually wound up at 12:15 A.M.)

SESSION 655, APRIL 11, 1973, 9:36 P.M. WEDNESDAY

(Today Jane wrote two poems—one of them several pages long—that, she said, fit into the scheme of her potential book of poetry, Dialogues of the Speakers. *See the notes prefacing the 653rd session for April 4, in Chapter Thirteen, describing how she gave birth to the original long Speaker poem while in an altered state of consciousness. Her inspired working environment today contained elements similar to that experience.)*

Good evening.

("Good evening, Seth.")

Dictation: Your neuronal activity structures your conscious experience, then. The overall rhythms of your creaturehood automatically bring you into periods of rest and intense focus.

The night and day constitute a framework within which your experience is couched, providing the conscious mind with needed stimuli and relaxation, and allowing for proper assimilation of events. As mentioned *(in sessions 651-52 in Chapter Thirteen)*, even then the body construction has built-in mechanisms to alter such an arrangement when further data can be handled.

As a rule you have enough difficulty dealing with the day's occurrences, much less next week's, and so in the sequence of events the reality of probable actions is usually hidden from your view. *(Pause.)* This more complex reality is an ever-existing property of your personal creaturehood. Beside this, in your terms you exist as a creature more than once. In each of your "reincarnational" existences you are faced with the same relationship with probabilities. In each case, also, the nature of the conscious mind sets up its own territory-of-identity (with hyphens) that it regards as its own. This provides a clear focus in which "present" action can be considered. These incarnations are all simultaneous.

(Long pause at 9:50.) A death is but one night to the soul. The vaster entity of which you are part follows your progress as easily as you follow your own through the days. As a rule most of you wake up in the same bed in the same house or town, but certainly you wake up as the same person in the same century. In those terms the entity wakes up as a different person each day, in a different century, each life seeming like a day in its level of experience. It carries the memory and simultaneous experience of each of those selves.

(A one-minute pause at 9:55.) Give us time . . .

A form is basically nonphysical. What you see of form is only that part that can be effectively active or materialized within your system of reality. So the entity in its own way possesses what you can think of as future neuronal structures. Underline that whole last sentence.

Within that vast form is your own, which is briefer, yet is not lost, not limited and not predetermined. You form your corner of the universe, which is itself a part of another one. Within this the actions and beliefs of one affect all.

(Slowly at 10:03:) Each part is vital, and in one way or another there is instant communication between the smallest and the largest, the cobweb and the spider, the man, the entity, and the star—and each spins its own web of probabilities from which other universes continually spring.

You may take your break.

(10:05 to 10:18.)

Which you? Which world?

All of this may seem to have little to do with your daily personal experience, and yet it is intimately connected, for personally and en masse you can indeed create "the best" of all possible worlds.

The performance of a great athlete gives evidence of abilities inherent in the human form that are little used. Great artists by their very works demonstrate other attributes latent in the race as a whole. They still represent one-line delineations, however. Within the experience of your race as you know it lie all the patterns that would point to some fully developed human being, in which all inherent tendencies were given full play and came to fruition.

You would have an individual who displayed within himself [or herself] all of those great abilities known to the race, fulfilled according to his own unique temper—the artist, mathematician, athlete, the inventor—all the extraordinary qualities of creaturedom; the emotional realities would be used to their capacity, and any of the racial qualities or characteristics of the species would be given their complete freedom.

Wisdom and foolishness would be seen as aspects, one of the other. Religion and science would each be unhampered by dogma in such an individual. In the same way, following your own "trace" experiences and characteristics, you can discover those "probable" abilities that are yours, and uncover to some degree the nature of probable actions open to you for physical materialization.

There are traces in your present experience of your probable selves, even as there are signs in each individual of all the great talents shown and developed so flamboyantly by a few. These traces can be brought into your experience to enrich it. They do so in any case on unconscious levels, where they form the basis from which you choose your current experience.

The next brief chapter will be devoted to methods that will allow you to take advantage of greater options, to bring into your daily experience events and experiences that have so far remained "latent." In each individual case the options will be different, of course, yet you can draw into your present life some knowledge and intimate connection with your own probable realities.

On a conscious basis, then, you can learn to deepen the dimensions of your life by pulling into it the rich fabric of probabilities. Period. End of chapter, and break.

CHAPTER **15**

Which You?
Which World?
Only You Can Answer.
How to Free Yourself From Limitations.

(10:41 to 10:47.)

Now: I will begin the next chapter, or you can have an early session if you prefer.

("No, go ahead. I feel all right," I said, although I was a little tired.)

Chapter Fifteen: "Which You? Which World? Only You Can Answer. How to Free Yourself From Limitations."

Give us a moment. *(Pause.)* Since your conscious beliefs determine those unconscious functions that bring about your personal experience, your first step is to enlarge those beliefs.

The concepts given in this book should have already helped you do that to some extent. Within your own subjective reality are traces of all those roads not taken, those abilities not used. You may think of yourself as primarily a parent, or mainly in terms of your job or profession. As much as possible, for now, forget the normal familiar light in which you see yourself, and consider your identity.

Write down or enumerate all of your known physical and mental abilities, whether they have been developed or not, and

334

all of those inclinations toward particular activities—even those only remotely considered—as well as those that have come at all vividly to mind.

These represent the varied probable characteristics from which you have chosen to activate your particular main interest. Out of these attributes, therefore, you chose what you now consider to be your hard-bed reality.

(10:59.) Any of those directions, followed, can enrich the existence that you know, and in turn open up other probabilities that now escape you. The main image of yourself that you have held has, to a large extent, also closed your mind to these other probable interests and identifications. If you think in terms of a multidimensional self, then you will realize that you have many more avenues open to expression and fulfillment than you have been using. These probable achievements will lie latent unless you consciously decide to bring them into being.

Whatever talents you sense you have can be developed only if you determine to do so. The simple act of decision will then activate the unconscious mechanisms. You, as a personality, regardless of your health, wealth or circumstances, have a rich variety of probable experience from which to choose. Consciously you must realize this and seize the direction for your own life. Even if you say, "I will go along with all life offers," you are making a conscious decision. If you say, "I am powerless to direct my life," you are also making a deliberate choice—and in that case a limiting one.

(Pause.) The path of experience is nowhere settled. There is no one road that does not have avenues to another. There are deep veins of probable actions ever available to you at any given time. Your imagination can be of great value, allowing you to open yourself to such courses; you can then use it to help you bring these into being.

If you are poor, you chose that reality from many probable ones that did not involve poverty—and that are still open. If you chose illness, again there is a probable reality ready for initiation in which you choose health. If you are lonely there are probable friends you refused to meet in the past, but who are readily available.

(11:14.) In your mind, therefore, see those probable abilities or events taking place. As you do, the intensity of your desire brings them into your experience. There are no boundaries, again, set about the self. There are literally many other probable you's. You can draw upon their abilities, as in their own way they call upon your own, for you are all intimately connected.

You must realize that you are indeed a probable you. Your experience is the result of beliefs. Your neuronal structure necessitates a certain focus so that other experiences counter to your conscious assumptions remain probable or latent. Alter the beliefs and <u>any</u> probable self can, within certain limitations, be actualized.

Now—that is the end of dictation, and the end for the evening. *(Louder, smiling:)* My heartiest good wishes to you both, and a fond good evening.

("Good night, Seth. Thank you very much.")
(The abrupt end of the session came then at 11:22 P.M.)

SESSION 656, APRIL 16, 1973,
9:14 P.M. MONDAY

Good evening.

("Good evening, Seth.")

(With a smile:) <u>Probable</u> dictation: What you must understand is this: Each of the events in each of your lives was "once" <u>probable</u>. From a given field of action, then, you choose those happenings that will be physically materialized.

This operates in individual and mass terms. Suppose that today your home was robbed. Yesterday, the theft was one of innumerable probable events. I chose such an example because more than one person would have to be involved—the victim and the robber. *(Pause.)* Why was your home ransacked, and not your neighbor's? In one way or another, through your conscious thought you attracted such an event, and drew it from probability into actuality. The occurrence would be an accumulation of energy—turned into action—and be brought about by corollary beliefs.

You may be convinced that human nature is evil, or that no one is safe from another's aggression, or that people are motivated mainly by greed. Such beliefs attract their own reality. If you have anything worth losing, you are then automatically convinced that someone else will take it from you, or try their hardest to do so. In your own way you send out messages to just such a person. On basic levels your convictions will be quite similar, but one will see himself as the victim and one as the aggressor—that is, each of you will react differently to the same set of beliefs. However the two of you are necessary if a crime of that nature is, or is to be, committed.

(9:25.) The beliefs of both of you find justification in physical life, and only reinforce themselves. The fear of robbers attracts robbers. If you think that men are evil, however, you are often not able to examine that as a belief, but take it as a condition of reality.

All of your present experience was drawn from probable reality. During your life, any event must come through your creaturehood, with the built-in time recognition that is so largely a part of your neurological structure; so usually there is a lag, a lapse in time, during which your beliefs cause material actualization. When you try to change your convictions in order to change your experience, you also have to first stop the momentum that you have already built up, so to speak. You are changing the messages while the body is used to reacting smoothly, unquestioningly, to a certain set of beliefs.

There is a steady even flow in which conscious activity through the neurological structure brings about events, and a familiar pattern of reaction is established. When you alter these conscious beliefs through effort, then a period of time is necessary while the structure learns to adjust to the new preferred situation. If beliefs are changed overnight, comparatively less time is required.

337

In a manner of speaking, each belief can be seen as a powerful station, pulling to it from fields of probabilities only those signals to which it is attuned, and blocking out all others. When you set up a new station there may be some static or bleed-through from an old one for a while.

Any ability you have, then, can be "brought in more clearly," amplified, and become practical rather than probable. But in such a case you must concentrate upon the attribute—not, for example, upon the fact that you have not used it well thus far.

You may take your break.

(9:44 to 10:01.)

Now: An artist produces a body of work in his lifetime. Each painting is but one materialization, one focused presentation, of an endless variety of _probable_ paintings. The actual work involved in the selection of data is still made according to the beliefs in the artist's conscious mind as to who he is, how good an artist he is, what _kind_ of artist he is, what "school" of artistic beliefs he subscribes to, his ideas of society and his place in it, and esthetic and economic values, to name but a few.

(Long pause.) The same sort of thing operates in the actualization of any event in which you are involved. You create your life, then. Inner images are of great importance to the artist. He tries to project them upon his canvas or board. Again, you are each your own artist, and your inner visualizations become models for other situations and events. The artist utilizes training and mixes his colors in order to give artistic flesh to his painting. The images in your mind draw to themselves all the proper emotional energy and power needed to fill _them_ out as physical events.

You can change the picture of your life at any time if only you realize that it is simply the one portrait of yourself that you have created from an unlimited amount of probable ones. The peculiar aspect of your own probable portraits will still be characteristic of you, and no other.

The abilities, strengths and variants that you may want to

actualize are already latent, in your terms, and at your disposal. Suppose that you are unhealthy and desire health. If you understand the nature of probabilities, you will not need to pretend to ignore your present situation. You will recognize it instead as a probable reality that you have physically materialized. Taking that for granted, you will then begin the process necessary to bring a different probability into physical experience.

(10:19.) You will do this by concentrating upon what you want, but feeling no conflict between that and what you have, because one will not contradict the other; each will be seen as a reflection of belief in daily life. As it took some time to build up your present image with its unhealthy aspects, so it may take time to change that picture. But concentration upon the present unhealthy situation will only prolong it. Period.

Each condition is as real or unreal as the other. Which you? Which world? You have your choice, broadly, within certain frameworks that you have chosen as a part of your creaturehood. The past as you think of it, and the subconscious, again as you think of it, have little to do with your present experience outside of your beliefs about them. The past contains for each of you some moments of joy, strength, creativity and splendor, as well as episodes of unhappiness, despair perhaps, turmoil and cruelty. Your present convictions will act like a magnet, activating all such past issues, happy or sad. You will choose from your previous experience all of those events that reinforce your conscious beliefs, and so ignore those that do not; the latter may even seem to be nonexistent.

As mentioned in this book *(in Chapter Four, for instance),* the emerging memories will then turn on the body mechanisms, merging past and present in some kind of harmonious picture. This means that the pieces will fit together whether they are joyful or not.

This joining of the past and present, in that context, predisposes you to similar future events, for you have geared yourself for them. Change now quite practically alters both the past and the future. For you, because of your neurological organization, the present is obviously the only point from which past and future can be changed, or when action becomes effected.

I am not speaking symbolically. In the most intimate of terms, your past and future are modified by your present reactions. Alterations occur within the body. Circuits within the nervous system are changed, and energies that you do not understand seek out new connections on much deeper levels far beyond consciousness.

Your present beliefs govern the actualization of events. Creativity and experience are being formed moment by moment by each individual. Period, and break.

(10:35 to 10:59.)

Now: You must understand that your present is the point at which flesh and matter meet with the spirit. Therefore the present is your point of power in your current lifetime, as you think of it. If you assign greater force to the past, then you will feel ineffective and deny yourself your own energy.

For an exercise, sit with your eyes wide open, looking about you, and realize that this moment represents the point of your power, through which you can affect both past and future events.

The present seen before you, with its intimate physical experience, is the result of action in other such presents. Do not be intimidated therefore by the past or the future. There is no need at all for undesirable aspects of your contemporary reality to be projected into the future, unless you use the power of the present to do so.

If you learn to get hold of this feeling of power now, you can use it most effectively to alter your life situation in whatever way you choose—again, within those limitations set by your creature-hood. If you were born without a limb, for example, your power in the present cannot automatically regenerate it in this life, although in other systems of reality you do possess that limb. *(See Seth's Preface, as well as the 615th session in Chapter Two.)*

Exterior conditions can always be changed if you understand the principles of which I am speaking. Diseases can be eliminated, even those that seem fatal—but only if the beliefs behind them are erased or altered enough so that their specific focusing effect upon the body is sufficiently released. The present as you think of it, and in practical working terms, is that point at which you select your physical experience from all those events that <u>could</u> be materialized. Your physical circumstances change automatically as your beliefs do. As your knowledge grows, so your experience becomes more fulfilling. This does not <u>necessarily</u> mean that it evens out in any way, or that there are not peaks and valleys. Each aspiration presupposes the admission of a lack, each challenge presupposes a barrier to be overcome. The more adventurous will often choose greater challenges, and so in their minds the contrasts between what they want to achieve and their present status can seem to be impossible.

In each case, however, the <u>point of power</u> is the present, and from that moment you choose which you, and which world. The experience of a country is the cumulative result of the choice of each individual in it, so as you choose your own circumstances you affect each other person within your country and your world.

(Pause at 11:15.) In many "native" cultures an individual is not considered in terms of his age at all, and the numbering of years is regarded as insignificant. In fact, a man may not know his age as you think of it. It would do you all good—young, middle-aged and old alike—to forget the number of your years, because in your culture so many beliefs are limiting in those ways. Youth is denied its wisdom and old age is denied its joy.

To <u>pretend</u> to ignore your age, to act young because you fear your age, is no answer. *(See the 644th session in Chapter Eleven.)* In your terms your point of reality and power is, once more, in your current experience. A realization of this would allow you at any age to draw upon qualities and knowledge that "existed" in your past or "will exist" in your future. Your ages are probable [simultaneous].

Although time does not basically exist as you "know" it, you are neurologically forced to perceive your life as a series of passing moments. As creatures you are born young and grow older. Yet the animals, as creatures, are not as limited in their experience in that regard. They have no beliefs in old age that automatically shut down their abilities; so left alone, while they do physically die as all creatures must in <u>those</u> terms, they do not deteriorate in the same way.

You do not understand the communications between yourselves and pets, for example, where in their own <u>way</u> they interpret and react to your beliefs.* They mirror your ideas, then, and so become vulnerable as they would not be in their natural circumstances. In greater terms their relationship with you <u>is</u> natural, of course, but their innate realization that the creature's point of power is in the present is to some degree undermined by their own receptivity and translation of your beliefs. A young kitten is treated differently than an older one. The cat responds to such conditioning. In the same way your own conclusions about age become fact in your experience. In line with them, if you could convince yourself that you were ten years younger, or ten years older, then it would be faithfully reflected in your personal environment.

<u>If you were twenty, you would be able to draw upon the wisdom you imagine you would have at thirty.</u>

If you were sixty, you would be able to use the physical strength you imagined was denied you now, but available then. All of this would be physically and biologically expressed within your body as well.

Which you? Which world? If you are lonely it is because you believe in your loneliness in this present point that you acknowledge as time. From what seems to be the past you draw only those memories that reinforce your condition, and you project those into the future. Physically, you are overwhelming your body as it responds to a state of loneliness through

*See the 639th session in Chapter Ten for material on the life and death of our cat, Rooney. Seth mentioned probabilities in connection with Rooney, too.

chemical and hormonal reactions. You are also denying your own point of action within the present.

Vitamins, better food, medical attention, may temporarily rejuvenate the body, but unless you change your beliefs it will quickly become swamped again by your feelings of depression. In such a case you must realize that you make your own loneliness, and resolve to change through both thought and action. Action is thought in physical motion, outwardly perceived.

Now: That is the end of dictation, and give us a moment. I have a few words for you . . .

(11:37. Seth rather suddenly launched into a page of data for me. It was about some limiting attitudes I had concerning painting and age; it was very perceptive, and I was somewhat surprised to realize that the ideas had been right there before me all along. The session ended at 11:45 P.M.

("I don't remember anything since last break," Jane said. Her delivery and manner had grown increasingly forceful and driving as the session progressed. Both of us felt relaxed but active now. I talked about going out for a beer, then speculated that it was too late. In a moment Jane went back into trance for Seth's amused comment:)

I told you to go to your establishments *(last week)*, but no one listened.

("I heard that," Jane said, laughing.

(Jane was much taken with the phrase, "point of power." She found it very evocative. After the session she remarked several times that she wished Seth had used it in the heading for this chapter. She even discussed adding it to the heading, without really intending to do so . . .)

SESSION 657, APRIL 18, 1973,
9:05 P.M. WEDNESDAY

(During recent nights Jane has been aware of receiving book material from Seth, and of dictating it to me. "I'll wake up confused," she said. "It's usually advanced stuff that we haven't

come to yet, and I'll say, 'Hey, what's happening?' Sometimes it's just information for me—but anyhow, I know dictation's been going on and that you've been taking notes. Then I'll realize that can't be, because we're still in bed . . ." She's had experiences like this before. See the notes following the 619th session in Chapter Four, for example.)

Good evening.

("Good evening, Seth.")

Dictation: I would like the sentence that I am going to give you placed separately on the page, in larger type so it is set off, and underlined.

("Okay.")

THE PRESENT IS THE POINT OF POWER.

The above is one of the most important sentences in this book in practical terms, and working within the framework of time as you understand it. As mentioned earlier *(in the 653rd session in Chapter Fourteen),* you actualize events from the present intersection of spirit and flesh, choosing them from probabilities according to your beliefs.

All of your physical, mental and spiritual abilities are focused together, then, in the brilliant concentration of "present" experience. You are not at the mercy of the past, or of previous convictions, unless you <u>believe</u> that you are. If you fully comprehend your <u>power</u> in the present, you will realize that action at that point also alters the past, its beliefs and your reactions.

In other words I am telling you that your present beliefs, in a manner of speaking, are like the directions given to the entire personality, simultaneously organizing and reorganizing past experience according to your current concepts of reality.

The future—the probable future—is being altered in the same way, of course. To look backward for the source of current problems can lead you into the habit of seeking only negative episodes from your past, and prevent you from experiencing it as a source of pleasure, accomplishment, or success *(very intently)*.

You are structuring your earlier life through the dissatisfactions of the present, and therefore reinforcing your problems.

It is as if you were reading a history book that was devoted only to the failures, cruelties and errors of the race, ignoring all of its accomplishments. Such practices can lead you to use your own "history" so that it gives a very distorted picture of who and what you are—a picture that then paints your present circumstances.

(Pause at 9:21.) Those given to such practices—constant examination of the past in order to discover what is wrong in the present—too often miss the point. Instead, they constantly reinforce the negative experience from which they are trying to escape. Their initial problems were caused precisely as a result of the same kind of thinking. A great many unsatisfactory conditions result because individuals become frightened at various periods in their lives, doubt themselves, and begin to concentrate upon "negative" aspects.

The situation may be quite different in some ways. Large areas of life may not be touched by certain attitudes, while others are. One person may be completely free physically and in excellent health, and yet, because of certain experiences, begin to doubt his ability to get along with others. So he may begin to look into his past—with that belief in mind, that he cannot relate—and then find within previous conduct all kinds of reasons to support the idea.

If he journeyed through his memories trying to find a different kind of proof instead, then in that same past he would discover instances when he did relate well with others. Your present beliefs structure the memories which will parade before you now—and what you remember will then seem to justify the beliefs.

When you are trying to alter your beliefs, look through your past with the new conceptions in mind. If you are ill, remember

345

when you were not. Search your life for proofs of your health. Your very life itself is hard evidence that health is within you!

In almost all cases of present limitation, there is one main theme in that particular area: The individual has schooled himself or herself to stress "negative" aspects, for whatever reasons.

(Pause at 9:40. Jane's delivery throughout this material was as forceful as it could be without increasing the volume of her Seth voice a great deal.)

I have frequently said that beliefs cause reality, and that no symptom will simply fade away unless the "reason" is ascertained—but such reasons go far beneath your current ideas of cause and effect. They involve intimate philosophical value judgments on the part of each individual. Beneath them, the apparent causes of limitations in personal life, there are other far-reaching beliefs, and each individual will use those elements in his private experience to back these up. This applies to any kind of lack or hindrance severe enough to be a problem.

You have been taught that you are at the mercy of previous events, so your idea of looking for the source of personal difficulty is to examine the past, but—to find what you did wrong there, or what mistakes occurred there, or what inadequate interpretations were made there! Again, regardless of what you have been taught, the point of power is in the present; and again, your present beliefs will be used to structure your recollections.

Those memories will be used to reach any conclusion, as statistics can be used, for example. Along the way you may settle for a given remembered event or two, and assign to them the reasons for your present behavior. If so, you are already prepared to change your current beliefs and mode of action, and simply use the occurrences or habits of the past as a stimulus or motivation. *(See the 616th session in Chapter Two.)*

The question, "What is wrong with me?" will only lead you to create further limitations, and to reinforce those that you do have, through exaggerating such activities in the present and projecting them into the future.

Which you? Which world? These questions are to be answered in the "now," as you understand it, through the realization that your power of action is in the present and not in the past. Your only effective point of changing any aspect of your world lies in that miraculous instant connection of spirit and self through neurological impact.

Do you want a break?

("No." Pause at 9:56. Then, intensely:) To rid yourself of annoying restrictions then, my dear friend, <u>you repattern your past from the present</u>. Whatever your circumstances, you use the past as a rich source, looking through it for your successes, restructuring it. When you search it looking for what is wrong, then you become blind to what was right, in those terms, so that the past only mirrors the shortcomings that now face you.

Other events literally become invisible to you. Since basically past and future exist at once, you are at the same time dangerously constructing your future along the same lines.

Individuals can go from psychologist to psychologist, from self-therapy to self-therapy, always with the same question: "What is wrong?" The question itself becomes a format through which experience is seen, and itself represents one of the main reasons for all limitations, physical, psychic or spiritual. *(See the 624th session in Chapter Five.)*

At one point or another the individual ceased concentrating upon what was <u>right</u> in certain personal areas, and began to focus upon and <u>magnify</u> specific "lacks." With all good intentions, then, various solutions are looked for, but all based upon the premise that something is <u>wrong</u>.

If such a practice is continued, the concentration upon negatives can gradually bleed out into other previously unblemished areas of experience.

Take your break—and mark this session well.

("Yes."

(10:05. Jane's trance had been profound. I told her there was

347

little I could add to my belief that the material was excellent indeed. Resume in the same fast manner at 10:16.)

You are not at the mercy of past beliefs, therefore. On the other hand, the sooner you begin to act upon new ones the better. Otherwise you are not trusting them in the present. If you are poor and want to have more money, and try to maintain a belief in abundance—while still faced with the fact of present poverty—you must in your reality make some symbolic move that shows you are willing to accept a change.

As foolish as it may sound, you should give some money away, or in whatever manner that suits you act <u>as if</u> you did have more money than you physically have. You must respond to your new beliefs, so that neurologically the new message gets across.

You perform habitually in certain manners as a result of your beliefs. Now if you willfully change some of those habits then you are also getting the message across. The initiative must come from you, and in the present. In a very real manner of speaking, this means <u>changing</u> your viewpoint, that particular perspective with which you view your past and present and imagine your future.

You must look within yourself for evidences of what you want in terms of positive experience. Examine your past with that in mind. Imagine your future from the power point of the present. In such a way at least you are not using the past to reinforce your limitations, or projecting them into the future. It is only natural to contrast what you want with what you <u>have</u>, and it is very easy to become discouraged in so doing, but looking for errors in the past will not help you. A correctly utilized five-minute period of time can be of great benefit, however. In this period concentrate upon the fact that the point of power <u>is</u> now. Feel and dwell upon the certainty that your emotional, spiritual and psychic abilities are focused through the flesh, and for five minutes only direct all of your attention toward what you want. Use visualization or verbal thought—whatever comes most naturally to you; but for that period do no⁺ concentrate upon any lacks, just upon your desire.

(10:30.) Use all of your energy and attention. <u>Then</u> forget about it. Do not check to see how well it is working. Simply make sure that in that period your intentions are clear. Then in one way or another, according to your own individual situation, make one physical gesture or act that is in line with your belief or desire. Behave physically, then, at least once a day in a way that shows that you have faith in what you are doing. The act can be a very simple one. If you are lonely and feel unwanted, it can merely involve your smiling at someone else. If you are poor, it can involve such a simple thing as buying an item you want that costs two cents more than the one you would usually buy—acting on the faith, even that feebly, that the two cents will somehow be given you or come into your experience; but acting <u>as if</u> you had more than you do.

In health terms, it involves conducting yourself once a day as though you were not sick in whatever way given you. But the belief in the present, reinforced for five minutes, plus such a physical action, will sometimes bring literally awesome results.

Such effects will occur however only if you cease looking into the past "for what is wrong," and stop reinforcing your negative experience. These same principles can be used in any area of your life, and in each you are choosing from a variety of probable events.

Those of you who believe in reincarnation in more or less conventional terms, can make the error of using or blaming "past" lives, organizing them through your current beliefs. It is bad enough to believe that you are at the mercy of <u>one</u> past, but to consider yourself helpless before innumerable previous errors from other lives puts you in an impossible situation; the conscious will is robbed of its power to act. Such lives exist simultaneously. They are other expressions of yourself, inter-acting, but with <u>each</u> conscious self possessing the point of power in its own present.

(10:45.) It is for this reason that "past-life information" is so

often used to reinforce current personal social situations—because, like the past in this life, such memories are constructed through present belief.

If such information is given to you by another, by a psychic, for example, that individual is also very apt to pick up those "lives" that make sense to you now, and—unconsciously of course—to structure them precisely along the lines of your beliefs. This may not seem obvious. (Emphatically:) If an individual believes that he is basically unworthy he will recall, or be given, those lives that justify that idea. If he thinks he must pay for his sins now, then that belief will attract memory of those lives that will reinforce it; this will be highly organized recall, leaving out everything that does not apply.

If an individual believes that he is being taken advantage of, and is caught in a mundane existence, unappreciated, then he may receive from himself or others information showing that in other lives he was greatly honored—thereby reinforcing his belief that now he is taken for granted, or worse.

These statements of mine are general, for each individual will have his or her own way of reinforcing beliefs. If you think you are ill, most likely past-life information will show that you committed crimes for which you are now doing penance. In whatever framework you choose, you will always find proper reinforcement for your belief.

The truth as far as it can be stated is this: YOU FORM YOUR REALITY NOW, in capital letters, through the intersection of soul in flesh, and in your terms the present is your point of power.

Do you want a break?

("Yes."

(10:55. Jane's trance had been excellent, her delivery steady and often very emphatic. "Boy, I've got the whole thing right there," she said enthusiastically. "I like it when the material comes like that. I know just where it's going afterward, too—into reincarnational selves and this power thing. Then over here"—she pointed off to her right, indicating there was more *than one channel available from Seth now—"there's information on how this stuff can be applied to us, if we ask for it.*

("Hmmm," she added, "I just remembered: Seth gave material something like this in [ESP] class last night . . ." I'd forgotten too; Jane had talked about it while I helped her straighten up the living room at about 1:15 A.M. But we won't see a transcript of the class tapes until next Tuesday night.

(Seth returned at 11:07.)

Now: Each of your reincarnational selves is born as a creature in flesh, like you. Each one has its own "points of power," or successive moments in which it also materializes daily existence in a linear manner from all the probabilities available to it.

In a way that will be explained in another book for those interested in such matters, there is a kind of coincidence with all of these present points of power that exist between you and your "reincarnational" selves. There are even biological connections in terms of cellular "memory." *(See the 653rd session in Chapter Thirteen.)* So through your current beliefs you can, in your own space and time, attract tendencies toward certain experiences shared by these others. There is a constant interaction in this multidimensional point of power, therefore, so that in your terms one incarnated self draws from all of the others what abilities it wants, according to its own specific, localized beliefs.

(Pause.) These selves are different counterparts of yourself in creaturehood, experiencing bodily reality; but at the same time your organism itself shuts out the simultaneous nature of experience. This does not mean that at other levels you cannot perceive it, but that generally speaking events must seem to appear in a series.

In quite real personal and racial terms, the past is still happening. You create it from your present according to your beliefs. A removed appendix will not reappear physically. There are certain frameworks that are accepted, built into your creaturehood. There is far greater freedom, however, even on the cellular level.

351

End of dictation.

(11:21. *Now, Seth did give a page or so of material on how Jane and I can put the material in this session to use—at last break, Jane had said that a channel for personal material was open. We plan to talk about this session at our Friday night gathering also. End at 11:38 P.M.*

(*A note: My own hunch is that there's a good connection between Seth's reincarnational points of power, cellular memory, and the coordinate points he discusses in Chapter Five of* Seth Speaks: *"These coordinate points act as channels through which energy flows, and as warps or invisible paths from one reality to another. They also act as transformers, and provide much of the generating energy that makes creation continuous in your terms . . . These points impinge upon what you call time, as well as space . . ." Also see the 593rd session in the Appendix of* Seth Speaks.)

SESSION 658, APRIL 23, 1973,
9:43 P.M. MONDAY

(*Yesterday Jane began writing a rather long poem, in Sumari, that she calls* The Song of the Silver Brothers. *She started it in a "normal" state of consciousness and ended up in an altered one—"immersed in a high state of inner concentration," she said. As the work progressed she found herself actually writing two poems together, for after each verse of Sumari she did its English counterpart. Usually she doesn't attempt to translate a work in Sumari until some time later. Days, weeks, even months can pass before this comes about.*

(*When Jane went back to the poem this afternoon, her heightened sensations returned in a considerably intensified form. [They began to approach those described in the 639th session in Chapter Ten, and the 653rd session in Chapter Thirteen, to name but two such instances mentioned in this book.] Finally she called me at 3:30 P.M. as I was painting in my studio, and read* Silver Brothers *to me. It still wasn't finished. "But now I don't know what to do," she said several times, looking quite bewildered. "I'm getting it so fast mentally, in Sumari, that I don't have time to write it down—let alone do it in English—before I go into the next concept . . .*

("At the same time, I'm <u>living</u> these ideas. They aren't just words any more . . . Wow . . ." Her head nodded. She was growing more and more relaxed. "Sometimes what I get down—even when it's good poetry—can't come close to what I <u>feel</u>—it's too weak. I'm even making new words out of old ones, like 'fossiling' out of 'fossil,' for instance . . . I was going to do more, but I'm too high and exhausted to go on . . ." Finally, she wanted nothing more than to sleep.

(Last night, incidentally, Jane was again busily at work on Seth's book in her sleep, dictating material that we haven't actually gotten to yet.

(A note: Today she received a copy of her novel, The Education of Oversoul 7, *from her publisher, Prentice-Hall, Inc. It's just off the press. The "official" publication date isn't until September 10, however. See Jane's Introduction.)*

Now: Good evening.

("Good evening, Seth.")

Dictation: Any good demonstration of hypnosis will clearly show that the point of power is in the present, and that beliefs dictate your experience.

There is no magic in hypnosis. Each of you utilize it constantly. *(See the 620th session in Chapter Four.)* Only when particular procedures are assigned to it, and when it is set aside from normal life, does hypnotic suggestion seem so esoteric. Structured hypnosis merely allows the subject to utilize full powers of concentration, thereby activating unconscious mechanisms.

With the distortions present in organized procedures, however, and the misunderstandings of the practitioners, the phenomenon seems to show a different face indeed. The subject agrees to accept the beliefs of the hypnotist. Since telepathy exists *(as described in Chapter Three)*, the subject will react not only to verbal commands but to the unspoken beliefs of the practitioner, thereby "proving," of course, the hypnotist's theory of what his profession is.

Hypnosis clearly shows in concentrated form the way in which your beliefs affect your behavior in normal life. The various methods simply focus all of your concentration upon a specific area, shutting out any distractions.

(Long pause at 9:54.) Your beliefs act like a hypnotist, then. As long as the particular directions are given, so will your "automatic" experience conform. The one suggestion that can break through is this: "I create my reality, and the present is my point of power." If you do not like the effects of a belief you must alter it, for no manipulation of the exterior conditions themselves will release you. If you truly understand your power of action and decision in the present, then you will not be hypnotized by past events.

Think of the present as a pool of experience drawn from many sources, fed, in your terms, by tributaries from both the past and the future. There are an infinite number of such tributaries (probabilities), and through your beliefs you choose from these, adjusting their currents. For example: If you constantly focus on the belief that your early background was damaging and negative, then only such experiences will flow into your present life from the past. It does no good to say, "But my life was traumatic," therefore reinforcing the belief. You must in one way or another modify that conviction, or preferably change it entirely—or you will never escape from its effects. This does not mean "lying" to yourself; but if it seems to you that your background held no joys, accomplishments or pleasures, then you are lying to yourself now. You have concentrated upon the negative to such a degree that anything else seems invisible. *(See the 644th session in Chapter Eleven.)* From the present you have hypnotized yourself, viewing the past not as it was to your experience, but as it appears now in the light of your current beliefs.

You have reconstructed it. So when I tell you to restructure your past, I am not telling you to do something that you have not already done. Hypnosis, again, is merely a state of concentrated attention, in which you focus upon beliefs. Popular demonstrations lead the public to believe that the subject must fall asleep or be completely relaxed, yet this is not the case. The one prerequisite is an intense concentration upon specific incoming data to the exclusion of everything else. Therefore the orders given are clear-cut, to the point. No conflicting information is received, no cross messages.

(10:12.) The shutting out of superfluous data and the narrowing of focus are the two most important ingredients. Relaxation can help simply because the body messages are also quieted, and the mind not concerned with them.

Many beliefs were originally accepted as a result of such a situation, without any formal induction, but when the circumstances were right. A period of panic induces immediate accelerated concentration. All the forces of energy are mobilized at once, while little relaxation is usually involved.

(Pause.) On the other hand, such beliefs can be accepted when it appears that the conscious mind is asleep, or dulled as in periods of shock, or during operations. The focus of attention is narrowed then, and intensified. One of the troubles is that too specific distinctions are made between the conscious and unconscious minds. They interlap. Hypnosis, used properly without the mumbo jumbo usually assigned to it, is an excellent method of inserting new beliefs and getting rid of old ones. This is only true, however, if you realize the power of your conscious mind in that moment, and understand the ability of your consciousness to mobilize unconscious reactions.

You may take your break.

(10:20 to 10:29.)

It is of greatest importance that you realize several points before you try the method I suggest.

First of all, the unconscious is not a sponge, indiscriminately accepting material regardless of the considerations of your conscious self. All beliefs or suggestions are first sifted through your conscious mind, and only those that you accept are then permitted their penetration into the other areas of the self.

No negative beliefs were thrust upon you, therefore, despite your will. Period. None can be inflicted upon you that you do not consciously accept. In formal hypnosis, the hypnotist and the subject play a game. If the hypnotist orders the subject to forget what happened, that individual will pretend to do so. In that context both hold the belief in the resulting forgetfulness, and it is the power of belief that is being demonstrated. But instead this is taken as an indication that the conscious mind is helpless under such conditions, generally speaking, and this is not the case.

Quite without any inductions, you have "hypnotized" yourself into all the beliefs that you have. This simply means that you have consciously accepted them, focused upon them, excluded data to the contrary, narrowed your interests to those specific points, and accordingly activated the unconscious mechanisms that then materialize those convictions through physical experience.

(Pause.) Formal hypnosis merely brings about an accelerated version of what goes on all the time. It is a perfect example of the instantaneous results possible ideally—but not usually seen practically—as present beliefs negate past ones.

(Pause at 10:42.) We are going to deal with practical methods that will allow you to alter beliefs and change your experience. Later in the book we'll show how your individual beliefs attract you to joys or disasters. We will also discuss the ways in which mass beliefs will bring many of you together both in great periods of celebration, or as victims or survivors of disasters that seem to exist apart from yourselves.

Let us first of all discuss the nature of hypnosis, quite natural hypnosis, and the ways in which you use it now. Then you will see how you can utilize it quite easily and deliberately in your present point of power.

End of chapter. I said that would be a short one.

("Yes.")

356

CHAPTER **16**

Natural Hypnosis:
A Trance Is a Trance Is a Trance

And give us a moment.

(Pause at 10:46.) Chapter . . .

("Sixteen," I said, when Seth-Jane hesitated.

(Smiling, and progressively louder and deeper:) Sixteen, entitled: "Natural Hypnosis: A Trance Is a Trance Is a Trance." End of heading.

What is the reality behind reality? Is physical life a hallucination? Is there some definable concrete reality, of which your own is a mere shadow?

Your reality is the result of a hallucination, if by this you mean that it is only the picture shown by your senses. Physically, of course, your existence is perceived through the senses. In that context corporeal life is an entranced one, with the focus of attention largely concentrated through the senses' belief in the reality of their sensations. Yet that experience is the image that reality takes for you now, and so in other terms earthly life is one version of reality—not reality in its entirety, but a part of it. It is in itself an avenue through which you perceive what reality is. In order to explore that experience, you direct your attention to it and use all of your other (nonphysical) abilities as corollaries, adjuncts, additions. You hypnotize your very nerves, and the cells within your body, for they will react as you expect them to react, and the beliefs of your conscious mind are followed in degree by all portions of the self down to the smallest atom and molecule. The large events of your life, your interactions with others, including the habitual workings of the most minute physical events within your body—all of this follows your conscious belief.

(11:04.) Again, if you are ill you may say, "I did not want to be sick," or if you are poor, "I did not want to be poor," or if you are unloved, "I did not want to be lonely." Yet for your own reasons you began to believe in illness more than health, in poverty more than abundance, in loneliness rather than affection.

You may have accepted some of these ideas from your parents. Their effects may have surrounded you, or you may have switched beliefs in one particular area of your life; but each can be changed if you utilize the power of action in the present. I am not saying that every one of you must or should be healthy, wealthy and wise. I am only addressing those here now who have effects in their lives with which they are dissatisfied. In one manner of speaking, then, the suggestions you give yourselves constantly operate overall as beliefs that are reflected in your experience.

Some of you are simply mentally lazy. You do not consciously examine the data that you receive. Many who make a practice of "denying" negative suggestions from others, asserting positive affirmations instead, actually do so because they are so fully convinced that the power of negative beliefs is stronger than that of beneficial ones.

Each of you will find habitual thought patterns in your own life backed up by resulting action—conditioned behavior as it were—by which you continually reinforce negative aspects, concentrate upon them to the exclusion of conflicting data, and so bring them into experience through natural hypnosis.

Take your break.
(11:14 to 11:29.)
Many people assign great power to a hypnotist, yet whenever you have the undivided attention of another, you act as a hypnotist to a large degree.

Whenever you have your <u>own</u> undivided attention you act as hypnotist and subject simultaneously. You give yourselves post-hypnotic suggestions all the time, particularly when you project present conditions into the future. I want to impress upon you the fact that all of this simply follows the natural function of the mind, and to dispel any ideas that you have about the "magical" aspects of hypnosis.

For five or ten minutes a day at the most, then, use natural hypnosis as a method of accepting desired new beliefs. During that period concentrate your attention as vividly as possible upon one simple statement. Repeat it over and over while focusing upon it <u>for this time.</u> Try to feel the statement in whatever way is possible—that is, do not allow distractions, but if your mind insists upon running about then channel its images in line with your declaration.

The repetition, verbally or mentally, is important because it activates biological patterns and reflects them. Do not strain. This exercise should not be done along with the point of power exercise given earlier. *(See the 657th session in Chapter Fifteen.)* One should not run into the other, but should be carried out on separate occasions during the day.

(11:40.) During the period, however, do remember that you are using the present as a moment of power to insert new beliefs, and that these will indeed be materialized. When the exercise is finished do not dwell upon it. Put it from your mind. You will have utilized natural hypnosis in a concentrated form.

You may have to experiment some for the proper wording of your message, but three days at the very least are necessary before you can tell, through results, how effective it has been. A change of wording may be in order. When you feel right about the statement, then continue it. Your attention should be completely relaxed otherwise, for time is needed. You may experience spectacular results at once. But continue the exercise even if this happens.

Inner channels must become repatterned. There will be a feel to this that will serve as your own individual guideline. There is no need to continue the practice over ten minutes. In fact, many will find that difficult to do. Spending a longer period of time simply reinforces the idea of problems involved.

That is the end of the session.

("All right.")

My heartiest regards to both of you.

("Thank you. The same to you. Good night." End at 11:50 P.M.)

SESSION 659, APRIL 25, 1973,
9:18 P.M. WEDNESDAY

Good evening.

("Good evening, Seth.")

Dictation: Natural hypnosis is the acquiescence of the unconscious to conscious belief. In periods of concentrated focus, with all distractions cut out, the desired ideas are then implanted (in formal hypnosis). The same processes occur in normal life, however; areas of primary concentration then regulate your experience both biologically and mentally, and generate similar conditions.

Let us give a simple example, using a positive belief instilled in childhood. An individual is told that he is comely, well-proportioned, and possesses a likeable personality. The idea takes. hold. The person acts in line with this belief in all ways; but also a variety of subsidiary beliefs grow up about the main one.

The belief in personal worth draws about it the belief in the personal value of others, for they show their best faces to our fortunate friend. His life constantly reinforces this concept, and while he is peripherally aware that some people are "nicer" than others, his main intimate experience allows him to see the best in others <u>and</u> in himself. This becomes one of the strong frameworks through which he views existence.

Data or stimuli that does not <u>agree</u> is a side issue, not personally applicable but present, he realizes, as fact for others. He will not need to prove himself, so it will be easier for him to accept contemporaries with fairness.

There may be areas in which he realizes he is not adequate, yet because of his belief in his basic worth he will be able to accept these lacks as a part of himself without feeling threatened by them. He will be able to try to improve his condition without knocking himself down at the same time.

Now: In those terms he may or may not be as attractive, feature by feature, as some other individuals who believe, in fact, that they are <u>un</u>attractive. The <u>belief</u> in his own comeliness is so important that others will react to him in the same fashion. An individual can have great native beauty, for example, but this beauty is <u>not</u> apparent to others, or to the individual. The person does not believe that he or she possesses it, and mars the actual physical features so that the comeliness becomes literally invisible.

Your beliefs, then, are like hypnotic focuses. You reinforce them constantly through the normal inner talking in which you all indulge.

(9:38.) This inner communication acts like the constant repetition of a hypnotist. In this case, however, you are your own hypnotist. Few people will have simply one main area of concentration. Usually several are involved, but these represent the ways in which you are using your energy. The individual who takes it for granted that he is worthwhile does not need to belabor the point. His ensuing experiences come naturally to him. In many areas of your own life, those in which you are satisfied, you need make no effort. Your conscious thoughts and concentrations bring about results with which you are pleased. It is only in those compartments of your life that confound you that you suddenly begin to wonder what is happening—but here also, natural hypnosis is at work just as

361

easily and naturally, and your conscious ideas are automatically coming to physical fruition. So it is in these areas that you must realize that you are the hypnotist.

Take a brief break.

(9:43 to 9:50.)

Now: The unconscious accepts those orders given to it by the conscious mind.

In each person's experience, there are areas with which he or she is pleased. When you find yourself dissatisfied, however, question the orders you are giving in that particular arena of experience. The results do not seem, now, to follow your conscious desires. But you will find that they do follow your conscious beliefs, which may be quite different.

You may desire health, but believe implicitly in your state of poor health. You may desire spiritual understanding, while thinking that you are spiritually unworthy and opaque. *(Pause.)* When you set your longing against a present belief there is always conflict. Your belief will generate the proper feelings and imaginative endeavors characteristic of it. If you want to be healthy and continually contrast what you want with the present conviction in your poor health, then the belief itself, set up against the desire, will cause added difficulties. In such a case you seem to want the impossible. Desire and belief are not united but apart.

In formal hypnosis you make an agreement with the hypnotist: For a while you will accept his ideas about reality instead of your own. If he tells you that there is a pink elephant in front of you, then you will see it and believe it is there, and act according to the suggestions given. If you are a good subject and your hypnotist a good practitioner, then blisters can arise on your skin if he tells you that you have been burned.

(Long pause at 10:03.) You can perform physical feats that you would consider impossible otherwise—all of this because you willingly suspend certain beliefs and allow yourself to accept others for the moment. Unfortunately, because of the patter considered necessary, it is thought that the conscious

mind is lulled and its activity suspended. Quite the contrary. It is focused, intensified, narrowed to a specific area, and all other stimuli are cut out.

This intensity of conscious concentration cuts down barriers and allows the messages to go directly to the unconscious, where they are acted upon. The hypnotist, however, is important in that he acts as a direct representative of authority.

In your terms, beliefs are accepted initially from the parents—this, as mentioned earlier, having to do with mammalian experience. *(See the 619th session in Chapter Four.)* The hypnotist then acts as a parent substitute. In cases of therapy, an individual is already frightened, and because of the beliefs in your civilization he looks not to himself but to an authority figure for help.

(10:10.) Even in primitive societies, witch doctors and other natural therapists have understood that the point of power is in the present, and they have utilized natural hypnosis as a method of helping other individuals to concentrate their own energy. All of the gestures, dances, and other procedures are shock treatments, startling the subject out of habitual reactions so that he or she is forced to focus upon the present moment. The resulting disorientation simply shakes current beliefs and dislodges set frameworks. The hypnotist, or witch doctor, or therapist, then immediately inserts the beliefs he thinks the subject needs.

Within this context, subsidiary groupings will be included that involve the therapist's own ideas. In your society regression is often involved; the patient will remember and relive a traumatic experience from the past. This will then appear to be the cause of the present difficulty. If hypnotist and subject both accept this, then at that level there will be progress.

If the cultural concepts include voodoo or witchcraft, then the therapeutic situation will be seen in that context, and a curse uncovered; which, using the power point of the present, the doctor will then reverse.

Quite without the context of formal hypnosis, however, the

same issues apply. With the greatest understanding and compassion, let me mention that Western medicine is in its way one of the most uncivilized hypnotic devices. The most educated Western doctors will look with utter dismay and horror at the thought of a chicken being sacrificed in a primitive witch doctor's hut, and yet will consider it quite scientific and inevitable that a woman sacrifice two breasts to cancer. The doctors will simply see no other way out, and unfortunately neither will the patient.

(*Pause.*) A modern Western physician—granted, with the greatest discomfiture—will inform his patient that he is about to die, impressing upon him that his situation is hopeless, and yet will react with scorn and loathing when he reads that a voodoo practitioner has put a curse upon some innocent victim.

In your time, medical men, again with great superiority, look at primitive cultures and harshly judge the villagers they think are held in the sway of witch doctors or voodooism; and yet through advertisement and organization, your doctors impress upon each individual in your culture that you must have a physical examination every six months or you will get cancer; that you must have medical insurance because you will become ill.

In many instances, therefore, modern physicians are inadequate witch doctors who have forgotten their craft—hypnotists who no longer believe in the power of healing, and whose suggestions bring about other diseases which are diagnosed in advance.

You are told what to look for; you are as cursed—far more—as any native in a tiny village, only you lose breasts, appendixes, and other portions of your anatomy. The doctors follow their own ideas, of course, and in that system they see themselves as completely justified—as humane.

In the medical field, as in no other, you are faced directly with the full impact of your beliefs, for doctors are not the healthiest, but the least healthy. They fall prey to the beliefs to which they so heartily subscribe. Their concentration is upon disease, not health.

364

You may take your break.

("Thank you.")

(Humorously:) Our next book will be on the A.M.A. preferred reading list.

("I'll bet." Here Seth referred to the American Medical Association.)

Include that.

(10:34. Jane's state of dissociation had been excellent, her delivery fast and steady. "Boy, was he going strong," she said, meaning Seth. "He's going to get into some more real good material after this, too." In connection with Seth's delivery since 10:10, we'd like the reader to refer to these sessions: the 616th in Chapter Two; the 624th in Chapter Five; and the 654th in Chapter Fourteen. Resume at 10:48.)

Now: Your doctors are also the victims of their own belief system, in other words.

They constantly surround themselves with negative suggestions. When disease is seen as an invader, forced upon the integrity of the self for no reason, then the individual seems powerless and the conscious mind an adjunct. The patient is sometimes compelled to sacrifice one organ after another to his beliefs, and to the doctor's.

(Pause.) Luckily you have other "underground" beliefs, in chiropractic, health foods, and even quacks. These all provide some other framework in which problems can be solved in matters of health. At least in these cases damaging drugs are not given, and the integrity of the body is not further maligned.

Chiropractors, again, are hypnotists. Unfortunately they are trying to gain respectability in medical terms, and are therefore emphasizing the "scientific" aspects of their work, and playing down the intuitive elements and natural healing. The "quacks" end up with those who are hopeless, who realize the ineffectiveness of other belief systems, find them wanting, and have no place to go. Some of the "quacks" may be unscrupulous and dishonest, yet many of them possess an intuitive understanding, and can work "cures" through the instant alteration of belief.

The medical profession is fond of saying that such individuals prevent patients from seeking proper treatment. The fact is that such patients no longer believe in the doctors' system of belief, and so could not be helped by them.

To a medical man all of this will seem like the sheerest heresy, because disease will always be seen as an objective thing in the body, to be objectively treated and removed. But a man who feels "that he has no heart" will not be saved by the most sophisticated heart transplant, unless first that belief is changed.

In other areas, an individual who thinks that he is poor will lose or misuse, or badly invest, any amount of money, whether he works hard for it or is given it. A person who has hypnotized himself into a state of loneliness will be desolate although surrounded by a hundred friends and admirers.

(11:02.) What does all of this mean to you in your daily life, and how can you utilize natural hypnosis to better your experience?

In those areas in which you are dissatisfied, you feel that you are powerless, or that your will is paralyzed, or that conditions continue despite what you think of as your intent. Yet if you pay attention to your own quite conscious thoughts, you will find that you are concentrating upon precisely those negative aspects that so appall you. You are hypnotizing yourself quite effectively and so reinforcing the situation. You may say, horrified, "What can I do? I am hypnotizing myself into my overweight condition (or my loneliness, or my poor health)." Yet in other facets of your life you may be hypnotizing yourself into wealth, accomplishment, satisfaction—and here you do not complain. The same issues are involved. The same principles are operating. In those positive life situations you are certain of your initiative. There is no doubt. Your beliefs become reality.

Now: In the unsatisfactory aspects, you must understand this: there is also no doubt. You are utterly convinced that you are sick, or poor, or lonely, or spiritually opaque, or unhappy.

The results, then, as easily and effortlessly follow. Natural hypnosis, in the terms given here, operates as well in one case as in the other.

What should you do, then? First of all, you must realize that you are the hypnotist. You must seize the initiative here as you have in other positive aspects of your life. Whatever the superficial reasons for your beliefs, you must say:

> For a certain amount of time I will momentarily suspend what I believe in this area, and willfully accept the belief I want. I will pretend that I am under hypnosis, with myself as hypnotist and subject. For that time desire and belief will be one. There will be no conflict because I do this willingly. For this period I will completely alter my old beliefs. Even though I sit quietly, in my mind I will act as if the belief I want were mine completely.

At this point do not think of the future, but only of the present. If you are overweight, insert the weight that you think is ideal for you while you are following this exercise. Imagine that you are healthy if you have the belief that you are not. If you are lonely, believe that you are filled with the feeling of companionship instead. Realize that you are exerting your initiative to imagine such situations. Here there can be no comparison with your normal situation. Use visual data, or words—whatever is most natural to you. And again, no more than ten minutes is required.

If you do this faithfully, within a month you will find the new conditions materializing in your experience. Your neurological structure will respond automatically. The unconscious will be aroused, bringing its great powers to bear, bringing you the new results. Do not try to overdo this, to go through the entire day worrying about beliefs, for example. This can only cause you to contrast what you have with what you want. Forget the exercise when it is completed. You will find yourself with impulses that arrive in line with these newly inserted beliefs, and then it is up to you to act on these and not ignore them.

(Pause.) The initiative must be yours. You will never know unless you try the exercise. Now if you are in poor health, and have a physician, you had better continue going to him, because you still rely on that system of belief—but use these exercises as supplements to build up your own sense of inner health, and to protect you against any negative suggestions given by your doctor. Utilize the belief in physicians since you have it.

You may take your break.

(11:26 P.M. Jane's trance had been very good, her pace fast and definite. She began to feel sleepy during break, though, so this proved to be the end of the session.)

SESSION 660, MAY 2, 1973,
9:27 P.M. WEDNESDAY

(A group of notes and references . . .

(No session was held Monday night. Jane and I had taken a few days off to travel.

("Honestly," Jane said the morning after last Wednesday's session, "I think I was doing book work in my sleep the whole night—only I kept hearing my own voice instead of Seth's. I even thought of getting up and trying to write down the material, except that I didn't think it would really work that way. I just hope we'll get all that great stuff when we do have sessions . . ." These sleep-state effects were surprisingly persistent; although they were somewhat reduced when she encountered them again on Thursday night, they didn't taper off altogether until the weekend. One of Jane's previous experiences in obtaining book material in advance—that on bridge beliefs—is described in the 644th session in Chapter Eleven. Her next nighttime involvement with Seth's book is reported at the end of this session.

(I reminded her of a couple of subjects I hoped Seth would discuss, as he'd promised to do some time ago: 1. The great flood of June, 1972, in this area, and our roles in it; see the notes for the 613th session in Chapter One. 2. Birth

defects, as occasionally referred to by Seth in the course of this book.

(Jane was very active in ESP class last night, and especially so while speaking and singing in Sumari. A new, more complex dimension has been showing itself in the songs lately—now, often, the "words" and notes are short and rapid as they flit agilely up and down the scale. They remind me of a verbal shorthand. At the same time it seems that Jane is trying to convey several sounds or ideas at once, with but one set of vocal chords.

(During class, Seth commented that this latest Sumari development would help her decipher the very ancient—and largely oral—Speaker "manuscripts" that she mentions in her Introduction. He didn't say just how this translation was to be accomplished, though. For more notes on the Speakers, and Sumari, see the 623rd session in Chapter Five.)

Good evening.

("Good evening, Seth.")

Dictation: There is a definite correlation between what is called conditioning, and compulsive action.

Here posthypnotic suggestion operates as well as constant daily "conditioning." Now: For an example, take a woman who feels compelled to wash her hands twenty or thirty times a day. It is easy to recognize the fact that such repeated behavior is compulsive. But when a man's ulcers bother him every time he eats certain foods, it is more difficult to perceive the fact that this behavior is also <u>compulsive</u> and repetitive.

This is an excellent example of the way in which natural hypnotism can act to affect your system adversely. In a manner of speaking, repetitive actions intimately involve beliefs at the "magical" level. The behavior usually represents efforts to ward off "evil" that the individual feels is imminent. While it is easy then to understand the nature of exterior actions of repetitive quality, it is far more difficult to see many physical symptoms in the same light—but here also whole groups of recurring reactions to certain stimuli are involved. Behind them there is often the same kind of compulsion. In their own way symptoms frequently operate, actually, as repetitive neurological ritual, meant to protect the sufferer from something else that he fears even more.

(Pause at 9:42.) That is why belief systems are so important in dealing with health and illness. Each of the systems uses paraphernalia—gestures, medicine, treatment—that are the exterior manifestations of beliefs shared by healer and patient alike.

The same sort of situation operates in hay fever, for instance, and for that matter in most other dis-eases (with the hyphen).

Natural hypnosis and conscious beliefs give their proper instructions to the <u>un</u>conscious, which then dutifully affects the body mechanism so that it responds in a manner harmonious with the beliefs. So you <u>condition</u> your body to react in certain fashions. Dealing with this is not a simple problem, of course, for the original suggestion of dis-ease was in itself given because of another belief. Using formal hypnosis, and in the West, you may regress and discover where the suggestion was first given you. If you and your hypnotist believe in reincarnation, the source may be discovered in another life.

In either case, if the therapy is effective you <u>may</u> give up your symptoms, if both you and the hypnotist implicitly believe in the situation and framework of those convictions.

But behind that there is far more; for if you do not believe in your own worth as a human being, then you will simply get other symptoms that have to be removed in the same manner, using other "past" events as the excuse for the condition—if you are lucky. If you are not so lucky and your illness happens to involve your inner organs, then you may end up sacrificing one after another.

<u>All</u> of this can be avoided through the realization that your point of power is in the present, as stated earlier *(in the 657th session in Chapter Fifteen).* Not only do you operate within

your own personal beliefs, of course, but within a mass system to which you subscribe to one degree or another. Within that organization medical insurance becomes a necessity for most of you, so I am not suggesting that you drop it. Nevertheless, let us look more closely at the situation.

You are paying in advance for illness that you are certain will come your way. You are making all preparations in the present for a future of illness. You are betting upon disease and not health. This is the worst kind of natural hypnosis, and yet within your system insurance is indeed a necessity, because the belief in illness so pervades your mental atmosphere.

Many become ill only <u>after</u> taking out such "insurance"—and for those, the act itself symbolically represents an acceptance of disease. Even more unfortunate are the special policies for the elderly that detail in advance all of the most stereotyped and distorted concepts about health and age. There is a great correlation between the kind of policies that people take out, and the illnesses that they then fall prey to.

(*10:02. All through this material Jane's delivery for Seth was most emphatic and fast, and accompanied by many gestures.*)

Even more disadvantageous are the suggestions given, with the best of purposes in mind, concerning specific health areas dealing with prevention. There are two in particular that I would like to mention here.

One is the cancer drive literature, and television "public service" announcements, in which the seven danger signals of cancer are given. Unfortunately, again, within the <u>framework</u> of your beliefs this also becomes almost a necessity for many—especially for those who, because of previous experience of one kind or another with the disease, are almost irrational in their fear of it. The literature and announcements act as strong negative suggestions, following the nature of natural hypnosis—as a conditioning process, you see, where you are <u>looking for</u> specific symptoms, and examining your body under the impetus of <u>fear</u>.

To those already conditioned in such a manner, such

procedures can cause cancers that would not otherwise occur. This does not mean that those individuals might not come down with another disease instead, but it <u>does</u> mean that the belief in disease is patterned and focused to particular symptoms by such methods. <u>No wonder</u> you need health insurance! Illness is not a foreign agency thrust upon you, but as long as you believe that it is, then you will accept it as such. You will also feel powerless to combat it.

The second health area I want to touch upon concerns the elderly. Ideas of retirement fall generally into the same pattern, for hidden within them is the belief that at one time or another, at a specific age, your powers will begin to fail. These ideas are usually accepted by young and old alike. In believing them, the young automatically begin the gradual conditioning of their own bodies and minds. The results will be reaped.

In your society particularly, given over so thoroughly to the pursuit of money, such beliefs bring about the most humiliating situations, especially for the male, who has often been told to equate his virility with his earning power. It is easy then to understand that when his capacity to earn is taken away he feels castrated. Period, break.

(10:15. "I have the feeling that we've been going to town," *Jane laughed. Indeed—but she was out of trance almost at once.* *Her pace had been good throughout. Resume in the same* *manner at 10:29.)*

Now: <u>Generally speaking</u>, those who advocate health foods or natural foods subscribe to some of the same overall beliefs held by your physicians.

They believe that diseases are the result of exterior conditions. Quite simply, their policy can be read: "You are what you eat." Some in this group also subscribe to philosophical ideas that somewhat moderate those concepts, recognizing the importance of the mind. Often though, some strong suggestions of a very negative character are given, so that all foods except certain accepted ones are seen as bad for the body, and the cause of diseases. People become afraid of the food they eat, and the field of eating then becomes the arena.

Moral values become attached to food, with some seen as good and some as bad. Symptoms appear, and are quite directly considered to be the natural result of ingesting foods on the forbidden list. In this system, at least, the body is not insulted with a bewildering assortment of drugs for therapy. It may, however, be starved of very needed nourishment. Beyond that the whole problem of health and illness becomes simplistically applied, and here food is scrutinized. You are what you think, not what you eat—and to a large extent what you think about what you eat is far more important.

What you think about your body, health, and illness will determine how your food is used, and how your chemistry handles fats, for instance, or carbohydrates. Your attitudes in preparing meals are highly important.

Physically, it is true, but again generally speaking, that your body needs certain nourishments. But within that pattern there is great leeway, and the organism itself has the amazing capacity to make use of substitutes and alternates. The best diet in the world, by anyone's standards, will not keep you healthy if you have a belief in illness.

A belief in health can help you utilize a "poor" diet to an amazing degree. If you are convinced that a specific food will give you a particular disease, it will indeed do so. It appears that certain vitamins will prevent certain diseases. The belief itself works while you are operating within that framework, of course. A Western doctor may give vitamin shots or pills to a native child in another culture. The child need not know what particular vitamin is being given, or the name for his disease, but if he believes in the physician and Western medicine he will indeed improve, and he will need the vitamins from then on. So will all the other children.

Again, I am not saying, "Do not give vitamins to children," for within your framework this becomes nearly mandatory. You will find more vitamins to treat more diseases. As long as the system

373

works it will be accepted—but the trouble is that it is not working very well.

If you are feeling poorly and happen to read an advertisement for vitamins, or a book about them, and are impressed, you will indeed benefit—at least for a while. Your belief will make them work for you, but if your insistence upon poor health persists, then the counter suggestion represented by the vitamins will not be effective for long.

(10:53.) The same applies to the "public service announcements" dealing with tobacco and drugs alike. The suggestion that smoking will give you cancer is far more dangerous than the physical effects of smoking, <u>and can give cancer to people who</u> might otherwise <u>not be so affected</u> *(very intently)*.

The well-meaning announcements pertaining to heroin, marijuana, and acid (LSD) can also be damaging, in that they structure in advance any experience that people who take drugs might have. On the one hand, you have a culture that publicly points out as common the often exaggerated dangers that <u>can</u> occur with drugs, and on the other holds out drugs as a method of therapy. Here the dangers become something like initiation rites, in which loss of life must be faced before full acceptance into the community can be established. But those involved with <u>native</u> initiation rituals knew far more what they were doing, and understood a framework of beliefs in which the outcome—success—was fairly well assured.

All of this involves natural hypnosis.

Let us return to the example of a gentleman who has ulcers. He believes implicitly that certain foods cause his stomach to behave in a particular manner. There is a medicine, however, that will stop his pain. As long as it is effective, the medicine further convinces him that his stomach difficulty can only be relieved in this fashion.

It becomes a counter suggestion, yet it is all a part of the same hypnotic process, based upon his belief in his original illness. While it gives temporary results, the fact that he needs it reinforces his dependency upon it. If his belief in his poor health continues unchecked, the medicine will no longer serve as an adequate counter measure. It would seem only good sense to refrain from the foods that bring on the condition. Yet each time this is done, the individual acquiesces more and more to the hypnotic suggestion.

He fully believes he will become ill if he eats the forbidden foods, and so he does. It never occurs to him to dispense with the belief—to realize that it alone sets up the conditioning process through the operation of self-hypnotism.

The point of power is in the present. You must thoroughly understand that, and then you can take hold of your life and begin to use natural hypnosis for your benefit in all areas. It works advantageously for each of you now in those portions of your lives with which you are pleased.

Take your break.

(11:13 to 11:25.)

In all such situations, it is highly important that you do not concentrate your main attention in that area of experience with which you are least satisfied. This acts as a deepening of hypnotic suggestion. Just reminding yourself of your other accomplishments will by itself operate in a constructive fashion, even if nothing else is done. Such focus of attention on positive aspects automatically pulls your energy away from the problem. It also builds up your own sense of worth and power as you are reminded of adequate performance at other levels of experience.

Whenever you are trying to rid yourself of a dilemma, make sure that you do not concentrate your attention upon it instead. This acts to cut out other data, and to further intensify your focus upon your difficulty. When you break that focus the problem is solved.

(Pause, in another fast delivery.) Let us take another example, a very simple one. You are overweight. It is a physical fact. It grieves you, but you believe it completely. You begin a round of diets, all based on the idea that you are overweight because you eat too much. Instead, you eat too much because

375

you believe that you are overweight. The physical picture always fits because your belief in being overweight conditions your body to behave in just such a manner.

In the oddest fashion, then, your diets simply reinforce the condition—since you diet because you believe so deeply in your overweight condition.

Until you change your belief, you will continue to utilize your food in the same fashion—and to overeat. Momentary gains will not last. Your entire behavior pattern operates according to the strong hypnotic suggestions given, and then of course your appearance and experience always reinforce your belief.

(11:39.) You must, therefore, willingly suspend that belief. Using the exercises given in this chapter, you must make a conscious effort to insert a different belief; employ natural hypnosis in this new way. If you realize your own worth after reading this book, then that realization in the present can negate any past ideas of unworthiness that may have attracted you to the condition.

The same applies if you are underweight, of course. You can eat a great deal for a while and only gain a few pounds, or find all kinds of excuses for not eating. You can be served the richest diet, yet gain no weight. You are not underweight because you do not eat enough food, or utilize it properly. Instead, you do not eat enough because you believe that you are underweight.

No amount of food will be sufficient until you alter your belief.

The same procedures as just given for those who are overweight should be used. In each case body conditioning is set up through natural hypnosis. Daily behavior and chemical functioning smoothly follow according to the belief.

Ideas of worth are involved here also, and the point of power as mentioned earlier. *(See the 657th session in Chapter Fifteen.)* In any area, great clues can be received simply through paying more attention to the conscious thoughts that you have during the day, for each of them serve as minute suggestions, modifying your behavioral patterns and affecting bodily mechanisms.

Give us a moment.

(Long pause at 11:47.) Next chapter.

CHAPTER 17

Natural Hypnosis, Healing,
and the Transference of Physical Symptoms
Into Other Levels of Activity

(Another long pause at 11:49. Jane's pace had abruptly slowed drastically. Mysteriously, she now took over six minutes to deliver the title for Chapter Seventeen.)

"Natural Hypnosis, Healing, and the Transference of Physical Symptoms Into Other Levels of Activity." That is the heading.

(11:55. Now her pace began to pick up.) Some people who have been ill for years suddenly recover, and then throw themselves into some great beneficial social endeavor in which their own problems are lost, and a new stability is maintained. Often this represents a symbolic transference of symptoms from the body outward into the social structure.

I will end. I simply wanted to give the heading and the direction.

(11:57. "Yes.")

I have one small but important personal note for Ruburt . . .

(This took half a page or so, and the session ended at 12:03 A.M. Jane was very surprised at the time involved in delivering the title for Chapter Seventeen. She had no explanations to offer; in trance she'd experienced only "a brief sense of waiting.")

(*Apropos of the notes preceding this session, concerning Jane's nighttime work on Seth's book last week: the same kind of effects returned when she went to sleep after this session—but this time she decided to try an experiment.* "When I woke up I felt I 'had' the whole of four or five chapters 'all there' if I could somehow instantly transcribe them," *she wrote the next morning.* "I got up at 3:15 A.M., intending to write everything down—and found that the bulk of it had just vanished.*

(*"By the time I got to my desk, all of those fine points and the smooth polished prose had gone. I had only a few ideas left. Apparently this material* has *to go through the session format—which automatically translates it . . . ?"*

(*Jane was left with a page or so of fragmented notes and a couple of possible chapter headings. This is still evocative material, even though she doesn't know whether Seth will use any of it in his book:* "For a 'Power Chapter': Each person has his or her own 'psychic territory of power' which is not to be relinquished," *she wrote.* ". . . no illness or other condition is allowed to impinge upon this . . . It's far better to think in terms of power than of lacks—the power* of *life,* of *motion,* of *speech, etc. People confuse this with power* over *their environment, or others, then wonder why* power over *doesn't work . . .*

(*"Yet each individual must eventually realize that you can't give up power in one area without . . . ultimately threatening the inner core or psychic territory of power to some extent . . . A belief in powerlessness in any area sets up its possibility in others—it operates as negative suggestion."*

(*And:* "A chapter on a person's 'Effective Personal Reality'—about the private purposes in one's life, and the bounds of creaturehood as set by your body; what you choose to be born with as far as health, disease, poverty or wealth, ability, etc., are concerned."*

(*And:* "Faith and belief can move mountains, as they say—but it can also cause natural catastrophies."*

(Jane and I discussed the above data at breakfast the morning after the session. This led me to read her my notes on Seth's delivery from 11:25 to 11:47, concerning beliefs in relation to body weight. Then after lunch Jane spontaneously wrote the material beginning in the next paragraph; she regards this data as supplementing Seth's own information on weight. "I didn't hear any voice while I was doing this," she said later. "I felt these ideas being inserted, but I did the writing." The work is close to the way Seth would present it; it probably stems from her efforts last night, we think, to see what she could do with "book work" on her own:

("Thursday afternoon at desk, May 3/73, on Seth's book:

("Diets do serve momentarily as outer signs that you are in control, and can seize the initiative; and as such they can be important. Usually, however, a pattern of unsuccessful diets occurs, operating then as a series of negative suggestions. The resistance is the result of conflicts in beliefs. You think you are overweight and accept this as reality. Steps to lose weight do not make sense in the face of that belief. They are 'unrealistic' or even impossible.

("The same applies to underweight conditions. In each case frequent attention to the scales serves as another negative stimulus, reinforcing the condition. The effort to eat more will be as resisted by the chronically underweight, as the effort to refrain from eating will be by the obese. Not only will these reactions occur, but opposing tendencies will be brought to bear. The concentration upon not eating, and the resulting tension, may instead cause increased consumption. And the underweight person may actually eat less the harder he or she tries to eat more—the latter being interpreted as an impossibility by the overriding belief in the underweight condition.

("The best thing to do is to stop all such efforts, but instantly begin altering your beliefs as instructed in this chapter.

("The reason why some lose-weight groups succeed in their therapy, at least momentarily, is that belief in the worth of the self is stressed. Unfortunately, weight is attacked as 'bad' or

380

'evil'; symbolic moral judgments enter the act. The therapy seldom has long-reaching effects because from then on any gained weight is even more negatively charged.

("Last night I also felt that Seth's Appendix—if there is one—could deal with notes on particular chapters; methods of using natural hypnosis in certain cases; work on beliefs, etc.")

SESSION 661, MAY 7, 1973,
9:40 P.M. MONDAY

(Tomorrow is Jane's birthday . . .)

Good evening.

("Good evening, Seth.")

Dictation: I am not implying that all social workers are driven by personal problems. On the other hand, it is quite true to say that many such questions turn into challenges with a change of mind, and are then used as impetuses to affect social alterations.

In such cases the dilemma is projected outside of the self and seen as an exterior condition which can be manipulated. Indeed, a "magical" transformation is involved. This is not to be construed, however, as a statement that all creative acts result from individual problems or neuroses. Quite the contrary, in fact. Such problems projected outward can never really be solved as far as the individual is concerned, of course, since their source is not understood.

(9:45. The telephone rang. Jane, as Seth, gestured toward it.)

You may do as you wish.

(But there was only the one ring. We waited a moment, then resumed the session.)

Since the source is not understood, no exterior manipulation in the social structure will be effective enough, and the person involved will see the problem personified in every issue. Hence, even improvements in the social framework will be "invisible" to the individual's perception—not noticed. They will seem so minute in comparison with the problem.

The same <u>sort</u> of reaction occurs if you concentrate upon a personal illness, and then find any improvements insignificant because of the great focus of your attention upon the negative aspects.

A sudden conversion .may completely rid an individual of physical symptoms—any kind of conversion. Under that general term I include a strong emotional arousal and fresh emotional involvement, affiliation, or sense of belonging. This may involve religion, politics, art, or simply falling in love.

(Pause.) In all of these areas the problem, whatever its nature or cause, is in one way or another "magically" transferred to another facet of activity, projected away from the self. Huge energy blocks are moved. The man who has believed that he was evil may now see the world, or persons of another faith or political affiliation, as evil instead. He then feels rid of the problem itself but is quite ready to attack it in others, and with great self-righteousness and justification.

(9:55.) I am making a distinction here between such conversion experience and genuine mystic understanding,* which may also come in a flash of time. Mystic enlightenment does not see an enemy, however, and there is no need for arrogance, attack, or self-justification.

(Pause.) Love, as it is often experienced, allows an individual to take his sense of self-worth from another for a time, and to at least momentarily let the other's belief in his goodness supersede his own beliefs in lack of worth. Again, I make a distinction between this and a greater love in which two individuals, knowing their own worth, are able to give and to receive.

(10:01.) You may take a break, or get Ruburt some beer while I leave him in trance. It is up to you.

("I'll get the beer," I said, since Jane was doing well and I felt like continuing. As Seth, Jane sat waiting quietly until I came back from the kitchen.)

Again, you make your own reality. When you view the world,

---

*An obvious example here is the conversion of the Apostle Paul (Saul of Tarsus) on the road to Damascus around A.D. 36, a few years after the "death" of Jesus.

social groups, political groups, your friends, your private experience—these are all attracted into your realm of activity by your beliefs. Natural hypnosis, as explained in the last chapter, leads you to seek out those situations that will confirm your beliefs, and to avoid those that threaten them.

You will often try to project a problem outward to free yourself. If this is done the question at issue will seem forever outside of you, beyond solution, and of mass proportion. Let us look into a situation involving a woman I will call Dineen, who telephoned Ruburt today from a Western state, and see one of the predicaments that can arise.

(*Pause.*) Dineen is a well-educated woman of middle age with several grown children, financially at ease, possessing all of the things that money can buy. She called Ruburt, nearly in a frenzy—desperate, she said, for help. Since she has written Ruburt several times, he was aware of the situation. Dineen was convinced that she was being cursed, hypnotized, and had fallen under the domination of another.

She had been going from psychic to psychic, dabbling in automatic writing and seeing little of her husband, who was involved in his own business affairs. She had been told by different "psychics" that she would be a psychic teacher, and various words and techniques had been given her to ward off the "evil" influence.

(*10:13.*) Ruburt correctly perceived the great need for a zest and excitement in this woman's life, for initiative. It was apparent that Dineen sat alone all day in her lovely home with nothing to do; that she was making no effort to face her situation truly, but looking to others to do it for her, and therefore reinforcing her sense of powerlessness. She felt she had no power in the moment.

This is an abdication of the severest kind, involving both your spirituality and your biological nature; you feel trapped far more than an animal in a dire situation, and you deny yourself the ability to act. The withheld power is itself transferred, then. In Dineen's case it was put onto another. If she could not make decisions this other person could, through long-distance hypnosis, _force_ her to act whether she wanted to or not.

Now the other individual has no power that Dineen does not possess. (_Pause._) Dineen heartily believes in good and evil; so, being convinced that she was at the mercy of demoniacal forces, she began to pray. As Ruburt pointed out, however, the prayers themselves were merely a weak surrender to the idea that evil is so powerful. They were not based on any real belief in the power of good, but only upon a superstitious hope that if bad forces exist, good ones must also.

Ruburt explained, after hearing about the automatic communications, that these were simply repressed elements of the subconscious finding needed outlet. He suggested that Dineen find herself a job, stop seeing psychics, and assert her own individuality and her own responsibility for action. Dineen believed that other people acted oddly toward her because they had all been hypnotized into doing so. If someone frowned at her, this was the result of hypnotic suggestion. All of this may sound exotic to some of you, and be only too real to others, but _any_ time that you assign elements of your experience to exterior sources, you are really doing the same thing that Dineen did.

She felt that certain rituals or foods warded off this evil hypnotic suggestion. Yet many of you take vitamins, convinced that they will save you from various diseases. Within Dineen's belief system she was acting quite rationally—and in your belief system you are doing the same.

You are convinced of the _reality_ of illness. It may not be "out to get you" as viciously as Dineen believes that evil is bent on threatening her, but the issues are the same.

(_10:29._) If you believe that you come down with a cold every time you are in a draft, you are using natural hypnosis. If you think that you must come and go at everyone else's beck and call, then you are like Dineen, who believes that she must do what this "hypnotist" tells her to do. In her case Dineen gave up the responsibility for action and initiative, yet because one must act the reasons were assigned to another. Ruburt also pointed this out. Dineen asked for advice from me and again Ruburt said, quite correctly, "You must learn to stop depending upon others, to use your own common sense. You must stop trying to use one symbol against another, and look at your own life and your beliefs."

You can project your dilemmas or your abilities outward into other avenues of activity, then, but until you realize that you form your reality and that your power resides in the moment, you will not be able to solve your problems nor utilize your strengths properly.

You may take your break.

(10:36 to 10:49.)

Now: Dineen carefully chose the territory in which these adventures would take place. For some time, with her children grown, she had felt alone, unnecessary, denied the structure of vital action in which she had to care for her family earlier. And so the great energy of her being, before taken up by her children, had no outlet.

Now her life, while difficult, has its own excitement. She is a heroine, battling cosmic forces of good and evil, important enough so that another person even wants to control her. Even the animals seek stimuli and feel a zest for existence; so in this way Dineen, in a misguided manner, is still giving expression to a definite need of her being.

Ruburt also suggested a counselor, but until Dineen is ready to exchange the beliefs she has for others that will allow her to fulfill her own abilities, she will still be in difficulty.

Dineen is in excellent physical health, however, and is an extremely attractive woman. She did not choose a situation in which either her health or beauty would be imperiled. She also stayed clear of any sexual involvement outside of marriage. She chose the psychic arena because she felt it to be out of the ordinary to begin with, and invested with all kinds of mystery. Any difficulties encountered there would automatically have a kind of glamour and distinction. The more she was reassured by others with the same beliefs, the deeper her involvement grew.

(10:59. Now notice how Seth begins to develop some of the material that Jane had received in the sleep state after the last session. See her notes there.)

Each individual has what I will call a psychic territory of power. This represents an inviolate area in which the person insists upon remaining supreme, aware of his or her uniqueness and abilities. This psychic region will be protected at all costs, and here there is indeed immunity from all disease or lack. Other portions of the psyche may be battlegrounds for problems, but the individual will not really feel threatened in a critical way as long as this primary territory is intact.

For all her talk of desperation, then, Dineen has chosen her field of conflict. She will avoid any kind of disfiguration or severe health problem, which to her would be a far greater danger. Because of different personal characteristics, another individual will hold qualities of the mind, say, inviolate, and work out challenges through bodily illness. Another may choose the severest poverty, projecting into that situation his or her own resolved conflicts. Another may choose alcoholism.

In these cases there can be some feeling of panic if an analyst, or friend, tries to switch the areas of conflict. For instance, the alcoholic is well acquainted with the battleground he or she has picked. An ill person, suddenly well, has to face dilemmas that were ignored before, or personified in disease.

Dineen, denied the support of the framework she had chosen, would have to face the questions that she had projected there. But all of the inner difficulties can be resolved by understanding that you form your own reality, and that your point of power is in the present *(with emphasis).*

(11:09.) The habit of not facing problems, which indeed are challenges, can be addictive. A feeling of powerlessness in one field can be transferred to others. When this happens through natural hypnosis, then even the psychic territory of power can be assailed. Here the individual becomes thoroughly aroused,

threatened, and realizes for the first time perhaps the nature of belief and his or her predicament. Here you have life and death struggles in creative terms. Some miraculous cures or change-abouts in midlife occur as a result.

All of this is intimately connected with your biological structure, which is meant to follow the conscious mind's interpretation of reality. Give us a moment . . .

(Beginning at 11:14, Jane sat quite still and silent for well over a minute.)

As I have said before, your thoughts are reality. They directly affect your body. It seems that you are highly civilized people because you put your ill into hospitals where they can be cared for. What you do, of course, is to isolate a group of people who are filled with negative beliefs about illness. The contagion of beliefs spreads. Patients are obviously in hospitals because they are ill. The sick and their doctors both work on that principle.

(See the 659th session in the last chapter; it contains other references to this kind of material also.

(Very intently all through here:) Women delivering children are placed in the same environment. This may seem very humane to you, and yet the entire system is structured so that childbirth does not seem to be the result of health but of illness.

Stimuli pertaining to health is effectively blocked in such organizations. The ill are gathered together and denied all of their normal and natural conditions, including the compensating motivations that alone would sometimes be enough to restore health if given time.

This isolation would be unfortunate enough without the application of drugs meant to help, but often given without understanding. Loved ones are permitted to visit the sick on but certain occasions, so those who wish them well in the strongest terms, who are closest to them and who love them, are efficiently prevented from exerting any natural constructive behavior.

(11:23.) For all practical purposes the ill are put into prison. They are forced to concentrate upon their condition. All of this

387

applies quite apart from any other dehumanizing effects, such as overcrowded conditions, the denial of human privacy, and often the negation of dignity.

The individual is made to feel powerless, at the mercy of doctors or nurses who often do not have the time or energy to be personable, or to explain his [or her] condition in terms that he can understand. The patient is therefore forced to transfer his own sense of power to others, which further deepens his misery; this in turn reinforces the sense of powerlessness that initiated his condition.

Furthermore, the natural elements of sun, air, and earth are refused him. The stability of familiarity is withdrawn. Now with your set of beliefs you are indeed more or less obligated to go to hospitals in severe conditions. I am not saying here that many doctors and nurses do not try their best to promote healing, and certainly healings occur—but they do so despite the system and not because of it. In many cases the belief of a doctor in a person who is ill revives him and rearouses his own belief in himself. The patient's confidence in the doctor will then reinforce the entire medical procedure, and he may then be filled with faith in his recovery. But as there are natural healing processes within animals, so there are in your race.

(11:32.) Illnesses usually represent unfaced problems, in your terms, and these dilemmas embody challenges meant to lead you to greater achievement and fulfillment. Because body and mind operate so well together, one will attempt to cure the other, and will often succeed if left alone. The organism has its own beliefs in health that are unconscious on your part.

You are a part of your environment. You form it. Yet the energy that forms you and the environment springs alive in each of you through your intersection with the physical world. The sun makes you smile. The smiling of itself activates pleasant memories, neurological connections, hormonal workings. It reminds you of your creaturehood.

The old witch doctors operated within the surroundings of

nature, utilizing its great healing ability, directing its practical and symbolic qualities in a creative fashion.

(Pause.) In your hospitals however you take your patients out of their natural environment, and often deny them the comforts of creaturehood. There is little emotional involvement. *(Long pause.)* The senile, in their efforts to run away from their closeted rooms in sanitariums, often show far greater sanity in their way than the relative or society who imprisoned them. For they intuitively recognize the need to be free, and they sense the lack of the mystic communion with the earth that has been denied them. *(See the 650th session in Chapter Thirteen.)*

Small hospitals on spacious grounds, with freedom for all but the bedridden to use their bodies, would far surpass what you have. But in your system as it is set up, such an environment is impossible except for the most wealthy.

Do you want a break?

("Yes, I guess so."

(11:44. Break came only so that I could rest. Jane had realized during the delivery that Seth was elaborating upon some of her "own" data, which is described at the end of the last session. This had been one of those times when, in the context of an excellent dissociated state, both her energy and the material had seemed to be inexhaustible. For the most part her delivery had been faster than usual, very intent, and animated.

(I read some of the information to her. We had many questions but decided not to interrupt the session's flow. Resume at 11:55.)

In many animal groups the sick animal isolates itself for a period of rest, in which it is also free to seek out those natural conditions most conducive to its health. It travels to find certain herbs, or it lies in the mud or clay by certain rivers. Often it is helped by others of its kind, but it is free.

When and if it is killed by its brothers, this is not an act of cruelty but an innate understanding that the creature can no longer operate physically without agony; a quite natural euthanasia is involved, in which the "patient" also acquieces.

In your society such a natural death is most difficult, and because of the power structures can hardly be promoted. No one who decides upon death is saved from it by the medical profession, however. On deeper levels the quite normal desire for survival requires that the individual leave his or her body, in your terms, at one time or another. When that period arrives the person knows it, and the great vitality of the spirit no longer wants to be encased by a suffering physical body.

Yet here the medical profession often takes care to see that every technological advance is brought to bear to force the self to remain within its flesh, when naturally soul and flesh would part. There are normal interlocking mechanisms that prepare the self for death, even chemical interactions that make this easier physically—bursts of acceleration, in your terms, to propel the individual easily out of the body. Drugs can only hamper this.

Certain kinds of medications can indeed help, but those given in your hospitals simply drug the consciousness out of its own understanding, and inhibit the body mechanisms that make for an easy transition. In your prisons you do the same thing, of course, isolating groups of people with like beliefs—denying them all natural stimuli so that a greater contagion of similar beliefs ensues. You separate such people from the normal contact of their loved ones, and all usual conditions for growth or development.

Now: That is the end of our session. Tell Ruburt to continue working with this book in his class as he has been doing. And my heartiest regards to you both, and a fond good evening.

(*"Thank you very much, Seth. Good night." 12:07 A.M.*)

SESSION 662, MAY 9, 1973,
9:40 P.M. WEDNESDAY

Good evening.

(*"Good evening, Seth."*)

Now: Dictation: Most criminals, in or out of prison, share a sense of powerlessness and a feeling of resentment because of it. Therefore they seek to assure themselves that they are indeed powerful through antisocial acts, often of violence.

They desire to be strong, then, while believing in a lack of personal strength. They have been conditioned, and furthermore have conditioned themselves, to believe that they must fight for any benefits. Aggression becomes a method of survival. Since they believe so strongly in the power of others, and in their own relative powerlessness, they feel forced into aggressive actions almost as <u>preventative</u> measures against greater violence that will be done against them.

They feel isolated and alone, unappreciated, filled with rage which is being constantly expressed—in many cases, though not all—through a steady series of minor social crimes. This applies whether or not major crimes are committed; so the simple expression of aggression without understanding does not help.

In the case of criminals and their belief systems, aggression has a positive value. It becomes a condition for survival. Many other characteristics that might mitigate such behavior are minimized, and <u>can</u> be seen as dangerous by them. They believe—

(9:52. The telephone began to ring.)

Do as you wish.

(I took the call while Jane came out of trance. It was for her, from a woman friend who lives in New York City. Professional matters were also involved, so their conversation lasted until 10:47 P.M. We didn't go back to the session. This made it one of the shortest on record, although [without checking] I remember an even briefer, spontaneous one on a Christmas Day several years ago . . .

(This is a good place to describe Jane's latest "psychedelic thing," as she put it, or experience with an altered state of consciousness. Time: about 12:30 A.M., Friday, May 11. Place: outside one of our favorite dancing establishments, a few blocks down Water Street from our apartment house.

(As soon as we stepped out of the door, Jane began to talk

about the supernal beauty of the warm night. We walked toward our car. A gentle rain had recently stopped and everything looked washed and renewed, so it took me a few minutes to realize that her perceptions did indeed go beyond that fresh appearance. She began to stop at intervals, exclaiming over all of those surroundings that were, of course, very familiar to us: the swooping automobiles, the street lights and neon signs, the buildings themselves, the Chemung River rolling quietly behind its dike in back of the emporium we'd just left.

("I was suddenly caught up by swift joy," Jane wrote the next morning. "The night colors damned near transfixed me—they were so brilliant, glowing, and spectacular. This was the first time I'd had such an experience outside, walking; I found my body moving faster, easier, freer. It was an instant thing. It was so joyful I couldn't sleep for a while. Later, I wished I'd asked Rob to drive around so I could prolong it, but neither of us thought of doing that at the time . . ."

(For notes on a couple of Jane's other experiences with altered states of consciousness, see the 645th session in Chapter Eleven, and the 653rd session in Chapter Thirteen.)

SESSION 663, MAY 14, 1973,
9:09 P.M. MONDAY

Good evening.

("Good evening, Seth.")

Now: Dictation. *(Pause.)* I put back Ruburt's curls . . .

(As Seth, Jane pushed her hair back over each ear. It had been falling forward each time she lowered her head.)

You isolate the criminal element, therefore, in an environment in which any compensations are refused. The entire framework of a prison—with its bars—is a constant reminder to the convict of his situation, and reinforces his original difficulty.

Any normal home life is denied him; and along with the overall concentration upon the problem at hand, all other stimuli is purposely held to a minimum. In their ways, the

392

warden and guards subscribe to the same set of beliefs as that held by their prisoners—the idea of force and power is accentuated on both sides, and each believes the other its enemy.

The guards are certain that the incarcerated are the dregs of the earth and must be held down at all costs. Both sides accept the concept of human aggression and violence as a method of survival. The prisoners' energies are usually used in boring, innocuous tasks, even though some attempt is made to provide vocational training in many institutions.

Both prisoners and officials, however, take it for granted that most of those now behind bars will return time and time again. The confined project their personal problems out upon the society. Society returns the "favor." In the same way individuals often think of certain characteristics as criminal or evil, and attempt to isolate those portions from other areas of their own activity. Power or the lack of it, and the attitudes surrounding either mode, are often involved.

Remember Augustus, in the case mentioned earlier in this book. *(See Chapter Six, and the 633rd session in Chapter Eight.)* Augustus felt power<u>less</u>, considering power in terms of aggression and violence, so he isolated that portion of himself from himself and projected it into a "second self." Only when this second self became operative could he display any power. Because his basic concept held aggressiveness and power as one, however, then the strength to act automatically meant the strength to be aggressive. And here aggression was equated with violence.

(9:24.) Now in its way that was a transference of a problem in a unique manner. The need to act and be in control of action is paramount in conscious beings. Augustus therefore actually created from himself a position of power from which he <u>could</u>, at least for a while, operate. He had to pretend amnesia so as to hide this mechanism from himself. As long as power is equated with violence, then you will feel it necessary to regulate normal aggression in your behavior; and considering power as violent,

you will be afraid to act to some extent. You will then consider goodness and powerlessness to be somewhat synonymous, and equate power with evil. Not wanting to face such "evil" in yourself, you may then direct it outward and transfer it to another area.

As a society you may project it upon the criminal, as a nation upon a foreign country. As an individual you may place this power upon an employer, a labor union, or any other segment of society. In whatever area you choose, though, you will feel relatively weak in comparison with the strength that you have projected outward. You meet your own denied power, you see, whenever you find yourself in a situation where you feel weak in comparison to another person or situation that frightens you.

(9:33. Once again, Seth started enlarging upon the material Jane had written during the early morning hours of May 3, after receiving it in the sleep state. See her notes at the end of the 660th session in this chapter.)

Power does not basically imply superiority *over*. There is the power *of* love, for example, and the power *to* love. Both imply great action and vitality, and an aggressive thrust that has nothing to do with violence. Yet many people have physical symptoms or suffer unpleasant situations because they are afraid to utilize their own power of action, and equate power with aggression—meaning violence. *(See the 634th session in Chapter Eight.)*

Such feelings arouse artificial guilts. *(Gesturing:)* The individual who speaks out most loudly for the death penalty feels that he himself should really be condemned to death, to pay for the great aggression (violence) within him that he dares not express.

The criminal or murderer being executed dies for the "evil" within each member of his society, then, and a magical transference takes place.

(Pause.) Love is propelled by all of the elements of natural aggression, and it *is* powerful; yet because you have made such divisions between good and evil, love appears to be weak and

394

violence strong. This is reflected in many levels of your activities. The "devil" becomes a powerful evil figure, for example. *(Emphatically:)* Hate is seen as far more <u>efficient</u> than love. The male in your society is taught to personify aggressiveness with all of those antisocial attitudes that he cannot normally demonstrate. The criminal mind expresses these for him, hence the ambiguous attitudes on the part of society, in which renegades are often romanticized.

The detective and his criminal wear versions of the same mask. Following such ideas, you end up with segregations in which the ill, being powerless, are isolated; the criminals are kept together; and the old are held in institutions or in cultural ghettos with their own kind. Transferences of personal problems are all involved here, and clusters of beliefs.

(Long pause at 9:46.) The criminal element represents the individual's own feared and unfaced aggressions. These fears are closeted on an individual basis, and those people who express them socially are imprisoned. The enforced incarceration of violent men often leads to a riot, and the private closeting of normal aggression often brings psychological rioting and outbursts of physical symptoms.

In all cases, little effort is made to understand the basic problems beneath, and the social segregations merely build up the pressure, so to speak, so that those with like beliefs are kept in situations that only perpetuate the basic causes.

Unknowingly, the sick often give up their power to act in a healthy manner to the physicians. The doctors accept this mandate since they share the same framework of belief, so the medical profession obviously needs patients as badly as the ill need the hospitals. Society as you know it, not understanding the nature of normal aggression, considers it violent. The prisons and law enforcement agencies need criminals in the same way that criminals need them, for they operate within the same system of belief. Each accepts violence as a method of behavior and survival. *(Pause.)* If you do not understand that you create your own reality, then you may assign all good results to a personified god, and need the existence of a devil to explain the undesirable reality. So churches as they now exist in Western society need a devil as well as a god.

Natural aggression is simply the power to act.

You may take your break.

(10:00 to 10:21.)

Your own attitude about these issues will tell you much about yourself and influence your own personal reality.

If you equate power with youth then you will isolate the elderly, transferring upon them your own rejected power-lessness, and they will seem to be a threat to your well-being. If you agree that violence is power then you will punish the criminal with great vindictiveness, for you will see life as a power struggle, and will concentrate upon the acts of violence about which you read. This may bring such aspects into your personal life, so that you yourself meet with violence—hence deepening your conviction. *(Pause.)* If you accept the basic idea that evil is more powerful than good, then your beneficial acts will bear little fruit because of your own framework; you assign such small power of action to them.

There are many subsidiary beliefs connected to these convictions. They can all work in such a way that you deny yourself the use of your abilities—and this in turn causes you to project them outward upon others.

If you accept the idea that knowledge is "bad," for instance, then in line with that belief all of your efforts to learn will be futile, or bring you great discomfort. You will not trust any knowledge that comes easily for you will feel that you have to pay, do penance for the attainment of any wisdom. Fundamental interpretations of the Bible often lead to such conclusions, so that the pursuit of knowledge itself, which has a built-in biological impetus, becomes a taboo activity.

You must then project wisdom onto others and reject it in yourself, or be faced with a dilemma in personal values.

(Long pause at 10:36.) Throughout the ages monks, priests, and religious organizations have become segregated from the

rest of humanity. They have been alternately honored and feared, loved and hated. Their knowledge has been envied and yet held in superstitious awe.

The voodoo and the healer, the witch doctor and the priest, are all held in honor, yet are also looked upon with a certain terror because of the power and knowledge involved. The man who heals or the man who curses both imply a power of knowledge to many individuals. To those who are caught up with fundamental ideas in pious terms, religious power is a frightening thing. Normal aggression, seen as evil, is therefore segregated within the self—and also seen everywhere <u>outside</u>. Period.

(Pause.) Some individuals will make artificial divisions within their own lives, in which it is safe to act in certain areas but dangerous in others. If you believe that wealth is evil, as an example, you automatically rob yourself of any ability that might bring you riches. Talents that are accepted as good in themselves may be inhibited simply because their fulfillment might lead to success in financial terms.

(10:46.) Your beliefs then are highly important in the way in which you handle the power of personal action.

The use of your private energy brings you into intimate relationship with your own source of power. Healing involves great natural aggressive thrusts of energy, growth, and the focus of vitality. The more power<u>less</u> you feel, the less <u>able</u> you are to utilize your own healing abilities. You are then forced to project these outward upon a physician, a healer, or any outside agency. If your own <u>belief</u> in the physician "works" and you are cured of symptoms, you are physically relieved, and yet your own belief in yourself may be further infringed upon. If you are making no effective efforts to handle your own problems, then the symptoms will simply reappear in a new fashion, and the same process will be reinitiated. You may lose faith in your doctor while still retaining confidence in doctors as a whole, and run from one to another.

But the body has its own integrity, and illness is often simply a natural sign of imbalance, a physical message to which you are to listen and make inner adjustments accordingly.

When these realignments are always made from the outside, the body's innate coherence becomes jeopardized, and its intimate relationship with mind confused. More, its natural healing powers are <u>dulled</u>. The built-in initiating triggers of reactions that are meant to follow inner stimuli are activated instead by "exterior" means.

The individual's faith is transferred more and more to an outside agency. This usually means that no time is allowed for necessary inner dialogues of self-questioning, and the self-healing that might otherwise occur is brought about through <u>belief</u> in another. This can only go on for so long, however.

(10:59.) I am dealing here mainly with Western culture. In some other civilizations, and particularly in the past as you think of it, witch doctors operated within a context of nature accepted by all. The witch doctor, while initiating natural forces on <u>behalf of</u> his patient, who seemed momentarily unable to do so, was then returning the patient to the source of himself and reviving his own buried sense of power. <u>That</u> is the source of physical life, the sense of power and action. When a man or a woman feels powerless, as you think of it, he or she will die.

The point of power, again, is in the present, when your nonphysical self merges with corporeal reality. The recognition of that fact alone can revitalize your life.

You may take your break or end the session as you prefer.

("We'll take the break, then."

(11:05 to 11:19.)

In your terms, you are in a state of evolution as a species. Part of this experience includes a natural fascination with exterior events. You are developing properties of consciousness that are in their own way uniquely your own, as your environment is. A strong focus is a necessary counterpart, since you are involved in a learning process in which all elements inherent in the situation will be explored.

Throughout this venture however you are, in the dream state, always kept in touch with the realities from which your physical experience springs. As you understand time, you will eventually be able to merge your inner comprehension with your physical self, and form your world on a conscious basis. Such manuscripts as mine are meant to help you do precisely that.

The more involved you become with complicated physical organisms, the more energy you project outward and the more entranced you become with "exterior" manifestations. In itself this was—and is—a natural learning method. Your inner life is being translated into corporeal reality. As you perceive it and relate to it, you begin to question first its origin and then its meaning.

(*Pause.*) This leads you back into yourself and to a recognition of your own abilities. What you now create unconsciously your species will create consciously. The infinite abilities of consciousness become individualized, focused into a particular reality which then becomes expanded. Your own temporal creations add to the abilities with which you made them. You learn through your creations. Mind, as physically directed, utilizes the greatest sources of power and energy along with unlimited aspects of creativity, so that each physical day is indeed absolutely unique. You cannot expect any portion of your environment to remain static, therefore, and the condition of your body is constantly in a state of flux and change.

(*11:35.*) Your social structure, from the largest metropolis to the smallest farm, from the wealthiest areas to the poorest ghettos, from the monasteries to the prisons, reflects the inner situation of the individual self and the personal beliefs that each of you hold.

If you utilize the point of power properly (*as described in the 657th session in Chapter Fifteen*), you will feel the nonphysical energy translated into effective personal power through your intersection with flesh. You will be able to use that power consciously, with purpose, to change your personal experience, and so to change the social framework at least partially. Such exercises aid in the evolution of your consciousness, and will also serve you in fashions you may not suspect. The acquiescence to your own power will automatically flow through your experience, activating your dream life as well and providing additional helpful impetus to your waking reality. You will no longer need to transfer your sense of power to others. All of the exercises given earlier in this book are prerequisites, however; they are necessary so that you <u>understand</u> how the point of power is to be used. The recognition of personal feelings and the working through of beliefs—all of this will expand your understanding of yourself.

(11:44.) If you hate a parent, for example, you cannot use the point of power to tell yourself that you love the parent instead. The earlier exercises will have helped you understand the reasons for the hate.

You cannot use the point of power to gain control over another, for your own beliefs will automatically trap you. In any case you must be <u>aware</u> of your own power and believe that you are worthy of it. Many of the previous chapters in this book have been written precisely to convince you of your own worth. You have been told to experience your feelings and not to deny them, so you are not to use the point of power as an attempt to refute the reality of your emotions at any given time.

As you understand the nature of natural hypnosis, you will no longer feel the need to generate <u>new</u> negative feelings. Your load of inhibitions will recede. As you trust yourself more you will naturally express your feelings, and their suppression will not bring about explosive reactions any more. They will come and go. The channel to power will be opened more clearly. Attention to your own stream of consciousness is highly important. <u>This alone</u> will help you see in what areas you are denying impulses or giving yourself directions that lead to powerlessness.

The point of power exercise is meant to familiarize you with your own energy and your ability to direct it. The natural hypnosis exercises *(given in the last chapter)* allows you greater effectiveness in directing and focusing that power.

Each of you must work from the point of your own reality. There is no other way. Period. If you feel filled with rage, then do not say, "I am filled with peace," and expect results. You will only be blanketing your feelings and <u>inhibiting</u> your energy and power. If you are furious, then beat a pillow and experience the rage, but without violence to another. Work it through until you are physically exhausted. If you do this honestly the reasons for the fury will come to you, and they will often be quite obvious. You simply did not want to face them.

In almost all cases [of this kind], your feelings will represent a sense of powerless<u>ness</u> on your part, where you delegated strength to a situation or an individual and felt your effort futile in contrast. <u>Then</u> use the point of power and feel the energy of your own being surge through your experience. The knowledge of your own power releases you from all fears, and hence of all rage.

(Louder:) End of session.

("All right—"

(Heartily:) A fond good evening to you both, then—in your point of power, and ours.

("Thank you, Seth. Good night."

(11:59 P.M. Jane's trances had been uniformly deep throughout the session, <u>her</u> deliveries strong, steady and businesslike.

(She told me that Seth would soon be going into the effects of our beliefs upon our environment, explaining how our racial mental climate is responsible for our exteriorized "weather." He plans to use local aspects of the great flood of June, 1972, as the focal point for his material because we'd had personal experience with that disaster here in Elmira. [See the notes for the 613th session in Chapter One.] Seth, Jane added, would say that as a species we've grown used to thinking of ourselves as being outside of nature—so much so that we've forgotten we're really part of it.

(No session was held last Wednesday so that Jane could rest. Seth devoted the first delivery this evening to material for her, then began working on his book when break ended at 10:07.)

Now: Dictation: There is a constant give and take between each individual and his or her society; the divisions and characteristics of any particular civilization will be a perfect exterior representation of the overall attributes of the people within it, as they relate to one another and as they see themselves.

The exterior dimensions are replicas of interior personal ones. The accomplishments, wars, difficulties and institutions are all "after the event"—that is, they are outward actions of an inward existence. Under certain conditions water turns into ice. In the same way, interior events can appear in physical reality in a quite different <u>form</u> than the original.

As creatures you are a part of nature. The change of thoughts, feelings and beliefs into physical, objectively perceived phenomena is as natural as water changing into ice, for example, or a caterpillar turning into a butterfly. You not only form the structure of your civilizations and social institutions through the transference of beliefs, thoughts and feelings; but in this natural exchange you also help on quite intimate levels in the "psychic manufacture" of the physical environment itself, with all of its great sweeping variety, and yet seasonal stability.

Medicine men may do a rain dance. They understand the innate relationship that exists within all portions of nature. You are taught to believe that faith can move mountains, yet many of you will find it extremely difficult to accept your own relationship with the environment. Your beliefs (often as opposed to your desires) cause wars. Your feelings represent the inner reality behind what you think of as purely natural phenomena, such as weather.

(10:25. Jane had touched upon this material in her notes of

*May 3, which are attached to the 660th session; and again after
the last session.)*

Catastrophies, such as earthquakes or floods, are not
perpetuated by certain elements of nature against other portions of itself. Your feelings have as much natural validity as the
tides, and they have their own kind of attraction—mind does
move matter. A ring manipulated at a seance under controlled
conditions is but the most simple kind of demonstration of the
great ability of mind to interact with matter. You each
participate in the creation of each thunderstorm, each new
spring, each flood, earthquake, and summer rain.

A war is one kind of natural event brought about as feelings
and beliefs interact on one level. A natural catastrophe represents the same kind of phenomenon at a different level. Your
part in these feelings and beliefs will place you in your own
"natural" position within such events.

End of chapter.

CHAPTER 18

Inner Storms and Outer Storms.
Creative "Destruction."
The Length of the Day and the Natural Reach
of a Biologically Based Consciousness

(Pause at 10:32.) Next chapter [Eighteen] : "Inner Storms and Outer Storms. Creative 'Destruction.' The Length of the Day and the Natural Reach of a Biologically Based Consciousness."

("That's all in the heading?")

First sentence: Your reality exists independently of your physically oriented consciousness, but while you are a creature your awareness must be interpreted through your neurological structure and your corporeal aliveness. There are indeed various kinds of memory, so that the right information can be at your fingertips when you need it. Other data will seldom be required consciously, yet it must always be available to unconscious portions of the self. Biologically the reach and capacity of your physically oriented consciousness is directly connected with the length of your days and nights, and of course with the seasons. Physically speaking, there are chemical interactions when thought occurs, and memories <u>ride</u> on the chemicals' smooth flow. With the precise night and day schedule that it possesses, your planet would, in those terms, give birth to a creature consciousness uniquely suited to fit it. In other terms, the night and day represent the innate rhythms of your consciousness physically materialized through natural phenomena, for you are not yet equipped to perceive longer-duration days. Your nervous system would find great difficulty in a rhythm in which a day was stretched out to be three or four times as long, for instance.

(10:44.) The rhythms of your body and of your consciousness follow the patterns of your planet. The planet itself is composed of atoms and molecules, each with their own kind of consciousness, however; and in the gestalt and cumulative cooperative organization of their nature the physical structure is formed—out of consciousness.

As this formation took place there was constant give-and-take between interior and exterior realities, in your terms. The growth of feelings, sensations, I am-ness, concepts and beliefs was paralleled by the resulting exterior manifestations of animal species, and mineral and vegetable emergences; with these came the growth of complementary neurological structures, and the precise physical formations, such as mountains, valleys, seas, and so forth needed to sustain them.

In greater terms all of these events occur simultaneously. To make this easier to understand, however, I am talking in terms of your time.

Your feelings are as natural a part of the environment as trees are. They have a great effect upon the weather. There are even connections that can be made, for instance, between epilepsy and earthquakes, where great energy and instability come together, affecting the physical properties of the earth.

Take your break.

(10:55. As far back as the 613th session in Chapter One, Seth was making statements like this: "Your feelings have electromagnetic realities that rise outward, affecting the atmosphere itself," but at the time we paid little attention to the implications behind such ideas. Resume at 11:06.)

Beliefs are the formations of self-conscious minds, even as buildings are at another level.

Beliefs direct, generate, focus, and harness feelings. In this context then feelings are being compared to mountains, lakes, and rivers. Ideas and beliefs bring about those obviously man-made structures that imply self-conscious minds and the ocean of interrelated social events.

(*Slowly:*) Feelings are still dependent upon your neurological structure and its impact with physical reality. An animal <u>feels</u> but it does not <u>believe</u>. Your feelings with their chemical interactions have, beside their subjective reality to you, electromagnetic properties, as indeed your thoughts have. But your bodies must rid themselves of chemical excesses in the same way that land must clear itself of excess water. There are what I am going to call here "ghost" chemicals—aspects of normal chemicals that you have not perceived so far, where certain thresholds are approached in which chemicals are changed into purely electromagnetic properties, and energy released that directly affects the physical atmosphere.

(*11:20.*) As your body is in a state of constant flux and chemical interaction, so is the atmosphere, which reflects on another level all of the psychic, chemical, and electromagnetic properties that exist within the body.

There is little difference between the currents of blood that flow through your veins, and the wind current, except that the one seems to be within you and the other without. Both are manifestations of the same interrelationship and motion, however. Your planet has a body as much as you have. Your blood follows certain prescribed patterns and so does the wind. You are <u>inside</u> the body of the earth in those terms. As cells within your body influence it, so does your <u>body</u> affect the larger body of the earth. The weather faithfully reflects the feelings of the individuals in any given local territory. Overall weather patterns follow deeper inner rhythms of emotion.

(*11:28.*) Those in earthquake regions are <u>attracted</u> to such spots because of their innate understanding of the astonishing relationship between exterior circumstances and their own quite private mental and emotional patterns.

Here you can find individuals of great energy; of unstable, "excessively" temperamental natures, and with intense capacities for creativity and innovation. They need a strong stimulus or impact with reality against which to pit themselves, however. There is often a great impatience with social situations, and unusual vitality. Such individuals operate at a high pitch, and en masse emit inordinate excesses of what I have called ghost chemicals.

Such emotional nonphysical qualities are unstable, and affect the deep electromagnetic integrity of the earth's structure. Obviously there have been earthquakes where there are no people, but in all cases the origins are to be found in mental properties rather than exterior ones. (Pause.) Earthquakes are very often associated with periods of great social change or unrest, and from such locations the fault lines originate and are projected outward. They may then affect a generally unpopulated area on another continent, or an island, or cause a tidal wave on the other side of the world, even as a stroke might affect a portion of the body far from the original damage.

(Pause at 11:38.) You do not need a self-conscious mind to feel, and in the "past," earthquakes represented the feeling-patterns of species in the same way—unstable conditions of consciousness that in themselves initiated natural phenomena, further altering the state of consciousness and the conditions of species as well.

In your terms consciousness is wedded with matter, and any of its experiences are physically materialized through that interaction. There are great correlations between thunderstorms and psychic storms, for example, and between unstable electromagnetic properties of both feeling and thought, the brain's ability to handle these, and its need to rid itself of excesses. You do not simply react to the weather. You help form it, even as you breathe the air and then send it outward again. The brain is a nest of electromagnetic relationships that you do not understand. In certain terms it is a controlled storm.

(11:45.) From it spring ideas that are quite as natural as

lightning. When lightning strikes the earth, it changes it. There are also changes that come about through the impact of your thoughts upon the atmosphere. The great overall inner <u>trust</u> with which you were born forms the basis for the encompassing <u>reliability</u> of the physical earth. Your body dwells in the earth as you dwell in your body. You were born with a faith in your existence that automatically directed the proper functioning of your personal corporeal self. This provided the necessary stabilizing properties <u>upon which</u> your consciousness could play, and through which it could effectively and creatively operate. The smallest atom has its own kind of built-in integrity, upon which all of its organizations and alterations are based, so generally there is a gestalt kind of permanence within the body of the earth.

(*Long pause at 11:54.*) Yet with all of this there is always change, as with the experience of time in a linear fashion any event must "knock out" another one. In terms of your <u>focus</u> a given occurrence "takes time." You know that many events occur that you do not consciously perceive, but take on the word of others. In your terms, therefore, change is apparent. The body is altered.

I told you that a dis-ease (with the hyphen) can have a creative basis (*in the 620th session in Chapter Four*). And so can an earthquake or a natural disaster.

Now you may take a break or end the session as you prefer. (*"We'll take the break then."*

(*12:01. During break we speculated about what might be learned from a computerized global study—one extending back to the beginning of our recorded history, say—to see what correlations could be discovered between earthquakes and periods of great emotional and social upheaval throughout the world . . . Resume at 12:10.*)

Now: On other than conscious levels, simply as creatures, you are well aware of impending storms, floods, tornadoes, earthquakes, and so forth.

There are many hints and signs picked up by the body

itself—alterations in air pressure, magnetic orientation in terms of balance, minute electrical differentiations of which the skin itself is aware. On that level the body is often prepared for natural calamities before they occur. Defenses are set up.

Many additional issues operate, however, that have to do with any given personal reaction. Here other psychological conditions enter in. People live in regions threatened by earthquakes with clear conscious knowledge of them. Regardless of what they might say, they need and enjoy the constant stimuli and excitement; the very unpredictable nature of the circumstances arouses them to action. There are many different attitudes and characteristics that apply, so that it is difficult to make generalizations, but there are always reasons why any individual is involved in a disastrous natural catastrophe.

(Pause.) In many cases a near-conscious realization of the circumstances occurs beforehand. In other cases the body's foreknowledge is reflected in dreams, and so alters daily life that an escape takes place. Some people change their plans and leave town a day before a disaster comes about. Others stay.

None of this is accidental. Unconscious material is admitted into consciousness according to those beliefs an individual holds about himself, his reality, and his place in it. No one dies in a disaster who has not chosen to do so. There is always some conscious recognition, however, though the individual may play tricks with himself and pretend it is not there. Even animals sense their dying ahead of time, and on that level man is no different.

(12:23.) Those who want to use their unconscious precognition of such an event will take advantage of it—save themselves, and choose not to be involved. If they do not believe in such advance warnings and deny themselves conscious knowledge, yet still believe in their overall security, they will unconsciously act without knowledge of their reasons. There will be others who are a part of the calamity for their own reasons.

Psychically, mentally and physically, they will be as much a

409

part of such an event as, say, the water that sweeps through a town in a flood. They will utilize the physical catastrophe as an individual might use a symptom for purposes of challenge, growth, or understanding—but they will <u>choose</u> their disaster just as they will choose their symptoms. They will be aware of the framework, therefore. It will not be thrust upon them.

They may not consciously accept such information, but if they knew how to examine themselves, they would discover that their beliefs added up to precisely the given kind of situation. (*Pause.*) An illness of a severe nature may be used by an individual to put him or her into the most intimate contact with the powers of life and death, to initiate a crisis in order to mobilize buried survival instincts, to vividly portray great points of contrast and summon all of his or her strength.

So can a catastrophe be used consciously or unconsciously, according to the individual.

(*Heartily:*) End of session.

(*"Thank you."*)

My heartiest regards to you both; and we will come to your flood.

(*"Fine. Good night, Seth."*)

(*12:36 A.M. Each of Jane's trances and deliveries tonight had been deep and very steady. "Seth just stopped for us," she said as she put her glasses on. "I can feel more material right there. I'll bet I could sleep for an hour, then start another session—we won't bother, I know," she laughed as I thought about trying it, "but when I feel the information coming I hate to stop . . ."*

(*Concerning Seth's reference to "your flood," see Jane's comments at the end of the last session.*)

SESSION 665, MAY 23, 1973,
9:41 P.M. WEDNESDAY

Good evening.

(*"Good evening, Seth."*)

Now: Dictation: Again, there are no accidents. No one dies under any circumstances who is not prepared to die. This applies to death through natural catastrophe as well as to any other situation.

Your own choice will dictate the way you die, as well as the time. We are dealing now with your beliefs as you know them in this life, and leaving for a later chapter any bleed-throughs of beliefs that may occur from other existences. But whatever beliefs you accept, for whatever reasons, your point of power is in the present.

It is far more important that you understand this than that you become overly concerned with labyrinthian "past reasons," for you can get so lost in a negative approach that you forget that these beliefs can be changed in the present. For various reasons, you hold beliefs that you can alter at any time. Many individuals die young, for example, because they believe so strongly that old age represents a degradation of the spirit and an insult to the body. They do not want to live under the conditions as they believe them to be. Some quite frankly prefer to die in what others would consider to be the most dire circumstances—swept away by the raging waves of an ocean, or crushed in an earthquake, or battered by the winds of a hurricane.

Slow death in a hospital, or an experience with an illness, would be unthinkable to these same people. Some of this has to do with temperament, and with quite normal individual differences and preferences. Many more human beings are aware of their own impending deaths than is generally known. They know and yet pretend they do not know, but those who die in catastrophes choose the experience—the drama, even the terror when that occurs. They prefer to leave physical life in a blaze of perception, battling for their lives, at a point of challenge, "fighting" and not acquiescent.

(9:54.) Natural disasters possess the great rousing energy of powers unleashed, of nature escaping man's discipline, and by their very characteristics also remind man of his own psyche; for in their way such profound events always involve creativity being born, rising even from the bowels of the earth, reshaping the land and the lives of men.

Individual reactions follow this innate knowledge, for while man fears the unleashed power of nature and tries to protect himself from it, he revels in it and identifies with it at the same time. *(Pause.)* The more "civilized" man becomes, the more his social structures and practices separate him from intimate relationship with nature—and the more natural catastrophes there will be, because underneath he senses his great need for identification with nature; he will himself conjure it into earthquakes, tornadoes, and floods, so that he can once again feel not only their energy but his own.

(Pause.) As nothing else can, a great encounter with the full energy of the elements puts man face to face with the incredible potency from which he springs.

For many people, a natural calamity provides their first personal experience with the realities of creaturehood's connection with the planet. Under such conditions men who feel a part of nothing, of no structure or family or country, can understand in a flash their comradeship with the earth, their place upon it and its energy; through suddenly recognizing that relationship they feel their own power for action.

(10:09.) On quite a different level, riots often serve the same purpose, where the release of energy, for whatever reasons, introduces a group of individuals to the intimate recognition that highly concentrated vitality exists. They may not have found it earlier in their lives.

This recognition can lead them—and often does—to seize their own energy and use it in a strong creative manner. A natural catastrophe or a riot are both energy baths, potent and highly positive in their ways despite their obvious connotations. In your terms this in no way absolves those who start riots, for example, for they will be working within a system of conscious beliefs in which violence begets violence. Yet even here individual differences apply. The inciters of riots are often seaching for the manifestation of energy which they do not believe they possess on their own. They light and start psychological fires, and are as transfixed by the results as any

412

arsonist. If they understood and could experience power and energy in themselves they would not need such tactics.

(Pause at 10:19.) As racial problems may be worked out on many levels, through a riot or a natural disaster, or a combination of both, according to the intensity of the situation on a psychological level; and as physical symptoms can be pleas for help and recognition, so can natural misfortunes be utilized by members of one portion of the country, or one part of the world, to obtain aid from other portions.

Obviously, many riots are quite consciously instigated. Certainly thousands of individuals, or millions of them, do not consciously decide to bring about a hurricane, or a flood or an earthquake, in the same manner. In the first place, on that level they do not believe such a thing possible. While conscious beliefs have a part to play in such cases, on an individual basis the "inner work" is done just as unconsciously as the body produces physical symptoms. The symptoms often seem to be inflicted upon the body, just as a natural disaster seems to be visited upon the body of the earth. Sudden illnesses are thought of as frightening and unpredictable, with the sufferer a victim, perhaps, of a virus. Sudden tornadoes or earthquakes are seen in the same light, as the result of air currents and temperature, or fault lines instead of viruses. The basic causes of both, however, are the same.

(10:27.) There are as many reasons then for "earth illnesses" as there are for body illnesses. To some extent the same can be said of wars, if you consider a war as a small infection; in the case of a world war, it would be a massive disease. War will finally teach you to revere life. Natural catastrophes will remind you that you cannot ignore your planet or your creaturehood. At the same time such experiences themselves provide contact with the deepest energies of your being—even when they are being used "destructively."

Take your break.

(10:31. Jane came right out of an excellent trance. Her delivery had marched along at a brisk pace. The house was

exceptionally quiet this evening; we could hear a light rain. Resume at a bit slower rate at 10:56.)

Now: Natural disasters are brought about more at an emotional level than at a belief level, though beliefs have an important part to play, for they generate the emotions to begin with.

The overall emotional tone or feeling-level of masses of people, through their body connections with the environment, brings about the exterior physical conditions that initiate such an onslaught of natural energy. *(Seth describes feeling-tones in the 613th session in Chapter One.)* According to the mass emotional conditions, various excesses are built up physically; these are then thrown off into the atmosphere in different form. The ghost chemicals mentioned earlier *(in the last session)* play a part here, and the electromagnetic properties of emotions. A rock in a stream will divide the water so that it must flow around the impediment. Your emotions are quite as real as rocks. Your collective feelings affect the flow of energy and their force—in terms of natural phenomena—can be seen quite clearly in a thunderstorm, which is the <u>exteriorized</u> local materialization of the inner emotional state of the people experiencing the storm.

As your conscious beliefs determine your bodily condition, and as your body is maintained at an unconscious level (though in line with your beliefs), so natural catastrophies are the result of the beliefs that give rise to emotional states which are then automatically transformed into exterior atmospheric conditions.

(11:09.) Then, according to your beliefs, you deal with the physical dilemma as it is presented in those terms. You will react individually with your own purposes in mind. Your own unique and highly private beliefs help bring about the overall emotional condition. The pool of emotional energy into which your emotions flow is still composed of <u>unalike</u> charges, but generally speaking, the individual contribution of all those participating will fall into a coherent pattern that gives impetus

and direction to the storm, providing the charge and the power behind it.

(Pause.) As mentioned earlier in this book, Ruburt and Joseph were both involved in a flood situation *(in June, 1972)*, and so I will use that as a case in point and this specific area in particular, although the flood itself was much more far-reaching.

Locally, there were some general beliefs held: The Elmira region was economically depressed and considered to be in a backwash area of the state of New York, yet the condition was not bad enough for crisis aid. Industry had been moving away. People were out of work; the old routines of livelihood had been uprooted. There was no inspiring local leadership, and a variety of different kinds of individuals felt ill at ease, depressed and forced to the wall.

Urban renewal projects ripped up the homes of the poor and destroyed older established neighborhoods. This often involved social divisions, for the impoverished were a mixture of blacks and "lower-class" whites. The better off sat at city councils, however, and the displaced poor were not able to afford the new structures. Through various manipulations, all underground, they were kept out of the "better" neighborhoods.

The rich and well-to-do felt threatened, for they had changed the status quo by their insistence upon modernity and progress, thus releasing the energy of the needy. There was movement of the middle class from the city proper into the suburbs, with a change in the tax balance, and the city merchants began to suffer. The locality had no great sense of unity as a region, or overall pride in itself as a cultural or natural identity.

(11:29.) There was some racial tension, hints of impending riots that did not occur. A very capable mayor who had been in office for some time was defeated. Politics entered in, for many reasons not necessary to this discussion. Politically oriented people felt that they had no really strong hold, so that effective communication with the federal government could not be expected. In that area a sense of powerlessness grew.

415

Culturally the region did not have its own identity, though it has always striven for some kind of characteristic expression. It saw government funds go past it to other sectors more economically depressed. The people had individual dreams and hopes, and *en masse* these represented a regional vision of improvement at many levels. At the same time feelings of discouragement grew. The young and the old, the conventional and the unconventional, had small skirmishes, where some of the city fathers objected to the long-haired youths in a city park—quite trivial incidents, and yet indicative of splits of values and misunderstandings between the generations.

You may take your break.

(11:40 to 11:47.)

To one extent or another, these same problems existed in all areas (of the East Coast) that were directly involved with that particular flood.

Locally you had a depressed region not yet in the kind of crisis situation that would draw great federal funds, and highly unstable social and economic conditions coupled with a sense of hopelessness.

(Pause.) Instead of a flood, disastrous social upheavals could have erupted. Because of the peculiar, unique and characteristic feeling-tones involved, however, the resulting emotional tensions were released, automatically transformed, into the atmosphere. A natural catastrophe provided many answers. The [Chemung] river was close by, directly in the heart of the business section [of Elmira], for example.

Again, all of this involved other areas affected by the flood. As certain primitives do rain dances and consciously bring about rain, deliberately directing unconscious forces, so the people in these different places did the same thing quite automatically, without awareness of the processes involved.

They seeded the clouds therefore through unconscious intent, and through the spontaneous release of emotional states operating biologically, so that excess hormonal and chemical reactions directly affected the atmosphere.

416

Some time earlier, local religious organizations had made plans for a mass revival. Followers of a popular religious group were signed up and some considerable publicity given for the event. Again, this was not accidental. It was an attempt on the part of fundamental denominations to solve the problems at another level, through an influx of religious identification, conversion, and enthusiasm.

The beliefs upon which these plans were based did not correlate, however, with the mass beliefs of the populace, and so the attempt failed. The program was based on precognitive knowledge of the flood event. The crusade never took place for the revivalist organization was frightened away by the flood.

(12:02.) Many in the religious community said that the flood was the will of God at that level, or that people were being punished for their transgressions. In its own way the flood was a religious event, for it united diverse groups of people—who did not always have the most humanistic of intents—with the community. In a strange way it also served to isolate certain portions of the people, and to highlight their predicament in a way that no riot could.

It also humbled some, denying them the comfort of social position and belongings at least momentarily, and brought them face to face with others of varying backgrounds with whom they would not have become acquainted otherwise.

Crises such as this provide spotlighted views of reality, in which what has been hidden is suddenly only too apparent. In many cases the poor were saved, for most of the old homes and apartment houses survived while the newer ranch-style homes could not stand the onslaught of the water. Yet the college [Elmira College] still found itself with many of the dispossessed needy at its doorstep. Women who had no stronger purpose than playing bridge ended up struggling for survival beside their more destitute sisters. Many of the poor who lost their living quarters discovered qualities of leadership in themselves that astonished them.

417

(12:11.) The downtown area saw its inner, always known but hidden predicament, physically materialized. It was in a state of near ruin and needed drastic help. City government was suddenly confronted with a reality that had little to do with conference rooms. The crisis united the people. The feeling of hopelessness was out in the open for all to see, and therefore action could be taken.

There were old people, laden with negative beliefs about age, who discovered great vitality and further purpose under the stimuli of survival. There were people blinded and lost by a belief in the supreme importance of things, who found themselves with nothing left. They realized the relative unimportance of belongings, and felt within themselves the stirring of a freedom they had not experienced since youth.

Do you want a break?

(12:17. "No." The pace was good, though.

(Pause.) The hidden "illness" of the area was plain for everyone to see. People came from all around to help. For once comradeship ignored social structure. Taken-for-granted patterns of existence had been ripped away quite effectively in a day's time. To one extent or another each individual involved saw himself in clear personal relationship with the nature of his life thus far, and sensed his kinship with the community. More than this, however, each human being felt the enduring energy of nature and was reminded, even in the seeming unpredictability of the flood, of the great permanent stability upon which normal life is based.

The power of the water put each individual in touch with intimate recognition of his dependence upon nature, and made him question values taken for granted too long. Such a crisis automatically forces each person to examine values, to make instant choices that will provide him with recognitions to which he had been blind earlier.

Take your break.

(12:26 to 12:40.)

The flood therefore physically materialized the inner

problems of the region, and at the same time released energies that had been trapped in hopelessness.

The area became a psychic and physical focus point of attention, thereby attracting other energy to it. Each individual involved had his or her own reasons for participating, and through the mass-created framework, worked out private purposes and dilemmas.

Many past beliefs were automatically shattered in the reality of the moment. Powers of initiation and action, long buried, were released in numberless individuals. Federal funds were directed instantly to this region. The spotlight was turned on to the section. *(Pause.)* Many lonely people were forced, or rather forced themselves, into a situation where it was imperative that they relate with others. Since this is not the main topic of this book, I cannot go deeply into the ways and means involved.

As a case in point, however, we will deal with Ruburt's and Joseph's experience with the flood situation, for their participation will have application to many others.

Now *(smiling and louder:)* End of session. My heartiest regards to you both, and a fond good evening.

("Thank you, Seth. Very good—we're looking forward to that information." End at 12:48 A.M.

(Before I typed this material from my notes, Jane and I discussed whether we should supplement Seth's rather generalized local data with specific names, dates, and events involving Elmira and Chemung County; this information would cover periods of at least several months before and after the flood of June 23, 1972. We decided it wasn't necessary—Seth has already made his points sufficiently for this book.

(However, we think a thorough search for relationships between emotional states and the weather in our county would be most interesting. Questions of geographical limits, time, and money enter in, of course; but if the study was at all illuminating, it could be expanded to include the state of New York, for instance, then Pennsylvania—and finally the entire eastern seaboard of the United States. For Tropical

Storm Agnes, which had led to the flooding, had been mammoth indeed.

(In connection with the flood material in this session and the next one, we refer the reader once again to the notes for the 613th session in Chapter One.)

SESSION 666, MAY 28, 1973,
9:31 P.M. MONDAY

Good evening.

("Good evening, Seth."

(Smiling:) Now do you want to know why you stayed *(in our living quarters)* during the flood?

("Yes, very much so.")

—And none of it should be mysterious to you. The reasons and the habits were all quite consciously available.

Now: Dictation: Ruburt and Joseph *(as Seth calls Jane and me)* have always seen themselves in a one-to-one relationship with nature and with the universe. They are individually motivated, in a sense loners. They shy away from large groups.

Nevertheless it was surprising to many that these two stayed here during the flood. To some it seemed quite foolhardy. In one manner of speaking, however, Ruburt and Joseph were quite prepared. Since the Bay of Pigs, they had kept a small pantry of stocked food, pure water in old wine jugs, candles, and a transistor radio. But they were not "looking for" a disaster.*

Before Ruburt became involved in psychic work he wrote a [short] novel, *Bundu*** in which nuclear destruction had taken place. For reference he read up on requirements for survival. Later, at the time of the Bay of Pigs, the necessary supplies

---

*Seth didn't say that we also had a small-bore rifle (which has yet to be fired, even now), and a few medical supplies in our stock ... In April, 1961, a group of Cuban exiles landed at Cuba's Bahia de Cochinos (Bay of Pigs) in a disastrous attempt to overthrow the regime of Fidel Castro. The confrontation between the United States and Russia over the latter's missiles in Cuba followed in October, 1962, so once again it had seemed like a good idea to have supplies on hand.

**Published in *The Magazine of Fantasy and Science Fiction, March, 1958.*

were purchased. Quite as a matter of course, household habits were such that those procedures were maintained almost automatically. There was always a stock of candles and food and water. No stress was laid on these provisions. When the flood came, however, Ruburt and Joseph found themselves, in that way at least, prepared to go without help from the outside world if necessary.

All of this had to do with past conscious decisions and responses to situations that, in your terms, no longer existed at the time of the flood. Yet the pattern of reaction was clear. They had decided to face any great crisis together in their own territory.

(Pause at 9:43.) The beliefs that led to their decision to stay had not changed in that regard. The one-to-one feeling of involvement with nature operated strongly here; they would take their chances then on individual bases. Now they were also used to working alone, even while together. In their artistic endeavors and psychic work they were acclimated to trusting themselves. Their past involved camping out, and, at least once, in very primitive surroundings *(in Baja California).*

This, again, deepened their intimate sense of relationship with nature, and encouraged their tendency to go along with it, to survive within its context rather than combat it. With this set of beliefs, attitudes and background, their decision to stay was highly predictable.

They knew there was a third story to the house they lived in. Therefore they planned to move our manuscripts, Ruburt's writings, and Joseph's paintings upstairs if the need arose. Other elements were also involved. For one thing, of course, they lived *(and still do)* on the second floor. The crisis brought many of their attitudes into critical awareness. The situation did become so serious that for a while they <u>did</u> fear for their survival.

(9:51.) In those few moments they saw their life situation clearly and brilliantly in symbolic focus; for they were isolated, with nearly ten feet of water rapidly ascending, and carrying with it the odor of fumes that could be combustible. They had

told no one in authority of their decision to remain, and had instead closed all the curtains so that others would not be aware of their presence. At the moment of their fear, help from outside was impossible.

Helicopters could not land. They found themselves alone with the Seth material, their paintings, and other manuscripts of Ruburt's. They had been using a mild version of self-hypnosis to produce a calmness and reduce any panic. But it was Joseph who suggested that Ruburt "tune in" to discover what could be learned about their situation personally.

Now because of their knowledge and temperaments, they had already begun to play cards—to distract their conscious attention—and to drink wine to help reduce tension. Ruburt then went into an altered state of consciousness, and quite correctly foresaw their situation. The bridge a mere half a block away would collapse, but they would be safe as long as they did not panic and try to leave.

The crisis would be over by five o'clock, even though the news media would not realize it. As soon as the information was received both of them felt more at ease, and the panic that had at least threatened, vanished.

(10:00.) They were left to observe the physical phenomenon, still watching the water's rise but with the inner knowledge of safety. Ruburt needed the experience in order to gain added faith in his own abilities. Both of them needed the assurance that those abilities are natural, and can be used in private dealings with nature. Ruburt also found that he had put himself in a position in which he had underrated the importance of physical manipulation. Both Ruburt and Joseph are very mental people, however, and so they sought out this physical meeting with material phenomena and solved the problem according to their beliefs.

Now those who have a great faith in groups, who work primarily with others, left their homes immediately for the comfort they found with the companionship of their neighbors. Ruburt and Joseph discovered their own attitudes in a crisis situation, clearly delineating their psychic position. They were led to question why they chose to face the flood alone.

In other terms the flood waters became the waters of time, and of the passage of the phenomenal world.

Despite all natural personal problems, they had taken their stand. The waters receded as Ruburt had predicted. They were forced to face the aftermath. Joseph helped physically as the other tenants returned to their apartments. He worked at the quite physical labor involved. Both Ruburt and Joseph threw open their two apartments. A couple was given shelter in one apartment while Ruburt and Joseph confined themselves to the other. Here they found themselves in daily intimate contact with others in a way not usual for them. This particular situation made clear to them important insights that were invaluable. It also showed them that through their own relationship, they still did interact with others. Period, and take your break.

(10:17. "I was getting a lot of other stuff, too, but it doesn't belong in the book so Seth didn't say it," Jane told me, "about different people we met during the flood thing." Since she had spoken quite steadily throughout her delivery, I began to speculate about some interesting questions: Was it possible for her to experience two channels "at once" from Seth? If so, what were the mechanics involved? Or even if her awareness had alternated between the two, why hadn't this interfered with her spoken material?

("I don't know how I got it," she said. "In between, I guess, but that doesn't say much." Actually, how many channels were involved? For Jane added that she'd also had information about herself available—again, "in between . . ." She was unable to be more specific. Resume at 10:40.)

For a short period of time after the water receded, there were excited radio recommendations: Clinics were set up and the populace was told that tetanus injections were imperative.

Again Ruburt "tuned in," altered his state of consciousness, and was told not to take them. Joseph was not to have them either. The unconscious knowledge was given *(pause),* and statements of each body's condition. Both were safe as long as shots were <u>not</u> taken. In this case Ruburt and Joseph acted in direct contradiction to authoritative radio statements, and held their own despite the fact that others in the immediate environment rushed off to the medical centers. They placed their lives on the line. Only an hour later the radio announcements completely changed; people were told that they did not need shots, and that indeed the inoculations could cause severe reactions.

Again, Ruburt and Joseph gained necessary confidence that would be used in other areas. In ways too numerous and personal to enumerate, the conditions of their lives became clear to them. They did not enjoy living in a cold, sodden environment for several weeks. They did not look forward to all of the inconveniences involved, and yet for their own reasons they chose to be part of the flood.

Only a few days before it took place, Ruburt was offered a television engagement in Baltimore, and refused it.* Their car was submerged. Income from Ruburt's classes was lost, yet these side effects were chosen quite in line with Ruburt's and Joseph's conscious beliefs, habits, and practices.

(10:50.) The same applied to everyone else involved. On symbolic levels a flood represents a washing away of the old, of course, the sweeping power and energy of unconscious forces and the resulting emergence of new birth. The fact is that your society often involves you in petty annoyances and problems that do not bring out your full strengths; disasters often serve as encounters with nature, in which you can experience the great power and range of your own identities in a situation in which you are pushed to the utmost.

In a highly materialistic society, the loss of an expensive home and other material possessions is a matter of great

*Jane said to the program director who called her: "I'm sorry, but I can't be on your show. I feel very strongly that I should be right here in Elmira these days." And when she heard herself say this, she was quite mystified . . .

practical and symbolic nature. Many individuals therefore sought out that experience. *(Long pause.)* Many also found themselves reacting with a heroism they did not realize they possessed. A sense of community unity was born, a deep feeling of companionship that had not existed earlier.

War has often served as an emotional stimulus, as an escape in terms of drama, excitement and belonging for those who have felt alone, powerless and isolated.

In its own way, a neighborhood fire serves the same purpose, among others, and so does a local or regional disaster. The nature of your conscious mind demands change and dramatic meaning, a sense of power, and aspirations against which to judge individual direction. A "perfect" society, idealistically speaking, would provide these qualities by encouraging each individual to use his potentials to the fullest, to revel in his challenges, and to be led on by his great natural excitement as he tries to extend powers of creative potency in his own unique way.

(Slowly at 11:06:) When such opportunities are denied then there are riots, wars, and natural catastrophes. A sense of power is any creature's right. I speak here again of power as the ability to act creatively and with some effectiveness. A dog chained too long often becomes vicious. A man who believes his actions have no value seeks out situations in which he uses his power to act, yet often without worrying about whether the action will have a constructive or negative effect.

You cannot act positively if you cannot act.

(Pause.) You do not understand the nature, then, of your own energy or your ability to direct it. Storms, say, or tornadoes, are brought about by angry men precisely as wars are. They are simply versions of the same phenomena.

The flood represented a mass psychic symptom projected upon the earth. In a quite natural manner, all of those involved not only chose the situation but helped in the "healing" process that still continues *(over eleven months later).* But you can no more separate yourselves from the body of the earth and its condition than you can from your own bodies.

Though it may <u>not seem so</u> to you, these are all creative procedures, and <u>corrective</u> ones. *(Long pause.)* You intuitively feel a great connection between your individual subjective moods and the weather, yet you attribute this to mean that you are reacting <u>to</u> exterior physical events that exist quite independently of yourselves. This is hardly the case.

When you move from one area of the country to another, it is because <u>you</u> have changed, and so you are drawn to others with the same kind of beliefs and needs, attracted therefore by entirely different natural situations. You will then help perpetuate the "characteristic" climate to which you travel.

(Forcefully, and with a smile:) Period, and take your break. *(11:23.)*

CHAPTER 19

The Concentration of Energy, Beliefs, and the Present Point of Power

(11:36.) Next chapter [Nineteen]: "The Concentration of Energy, Beliefs, and the Present Point of Power."

The concentration of energy follows your beliefs. Many beliefs, not negative in themselves but overemphasized, lead to what certainly <u>appear</u> to be negative results.

This material is highly important to many of you who find yourselves in situations with which you are not pleased. I am using Ruburt as an example for several reasons. Many of you have a tendency to believe that anyone with such abilities as Ruburt has, has no problems or challenges. Ruburt has often said, "Some of my correspondents expect me to be completely healthy, wealthy and wise, and indeed beyond any human feelings," and he is quite correct.

Numbers of you are looking for a state of "peace" in which there is a static sort of bliss, with all questions forever answered and all problems solved. Some of you think that this will somehow be miraculously accomplished <u>for</u> you. If you recognized the power of your own being, you would know that it ever seeks <u>greater realms</u> of creativity and experience, in which new challenges are inherent—for all problems are challenges.

In Ruburt's case, he began with a group of ideas and beliefs that only became restrictive when carried to extremes. *(See the 645th session in Chapter Eleven.)* In your own experiences, many of you may find yourselves concentrating upon certain areas of activity with such energy that you ignore others, considering them restrictions.

(Slowly at 11:46:) Ruburt's condition involved a situation in this life. Some of you may find yourselves concentrating upon the physical aspects of existence, which are themselves quite legitimate, but to the exclusion of other important elements. In larger terms, such focusing in particular areas can involve an entire life situation, reincarnationally speaking, where you choose ahead of time, so to speak, to concentrate your attention in certain areas rather than others; you may pick for yourself a body that does not perform normally, or a mind that is not up to par in usual terms.

Your given situation at birth, therefore, is one in which you cannot manipulate adequately in whatever way you have chosen. If you have decided upon a situation in which a critical organic lack or disability is involved, and are born with a severe disease, for example, then that is the context in which you will experience this particular focus in corporeal reality. There will be a reason for it, and that reason will lie in those abilities that you have left free and open for yourself to pursue.

All existences are simultaneous. Within the bounds of creaturehood certain things are possible and certain things are not. You cannot regenerate a limb, or grow a new one. You can cure yourself of an "incurable" disease if you realize that your point of power is in the present.

(Pause.) Whatever your situation, you have chosen it for a reason. If it involves a circumstance that cannot be altered in physical terms, then you have settled upon it as a framework in order to enhance and use other abilities in concentrated form. The main point is not to concentrate upon the liabilities but to

pursue those abilities that you have, for the great energies of your personality will be directed in those avenues.

Now: That is the end of dictation. One personal note . . .

(Seth added a few lines for Jane, then described a method by which I could help her work with her own beliefs.)

Do you follow me?

("Yes—if I can do it.")

(Louder, with humor:) You can. My heartiest wishes to you both, then, and a fond good evening.

("Good night, Seth." End at 12:05 A.M.)

SESSION 667, MAY 30, 1973, 9:26 P.M. WEDNESDAY

(In the early hours of May 29, following the last session, Jane had her most vivid experience yet involving book work during the sleep state. While this one contained elements similar to those described in earlier encounters, new ideas and questions were generated also. [See the notes for the 619th session in Chapter Four, for instance, or for the 660th session, which bridges chapters Sixteen and Seventeen.]

("Already the thing is starting to slip away," Jane wrote the next morning. "I was speaking for Seth on an Introduction or an early chapter for a book. It was so real and awake-seeming that I was shocked when I finally began to realize 'I' had been asleep. I could hardly believe it. My thrashing around in bed woke Rob up.

("Then I thought: I didn't want to give real book sessions while I was asleep—who would take them down? Unless Rob could while he was asleep too. I knew we were on Chapter Nineteen of Seth's book, and this confused me. How come I was doing an early chapter—or was this work for a different book?")

(While she was waking up, Jane asked me several times if she had really been asleep. It was easy for me to say yes, since I had come awake first. Before the session tonight Jane said she hoped Seth would explain the occurrence, but surprisingly—

429

even though a considerable amount of personal material <u>was</u> received—the matter wasn't covered.

(I read Jane the last page of the 666th session from my notes, since I hadn't finished typing it yet.)

Good evening.

("Good evening, Seth.")

Dictation: Ruburt was working with alterations of consciousness this afternoon. At the same time he had the radio playing softly. The rock-music program was interrupted by an announcement having to do with the Indianapolis speed-car racing exhibition *(the 57th Indianapolis 500-mile race)*. One driver had already been severely injured *(on Monday)*; and the race, put off on that account, and because of inclement weather *(on Tuesday)*, finally began today.

As it progressed, the radio announcements continued also, and Ruburt learned that another very severe accident had occurred. Beside this, a man—not a driver—was killed by an emergency vehicle speeding to the scene. The victim was connected with the race, however.

(As a crewman. A subsequent note: The driver involved in this accident died a little over a month later.

(9:32.) As he resumed "normal" consciousness Ruburt found himself wondering about the great violence involved, and the entire situation in which such people placed themselves. (He often has the radio on when he is working with alternate states of consciousness, by the way, using it as a <u>point of reference</u>.)

Some of the material in the last chapter should help to explain the reasons for frameworks in which violence is built-in, so to speak, and indeed becomes a challenging context through which reality is perceived. The situation <u>is</u> one of danger, yet is chosen by those involved, and is not inflicted upon them. In somewhat the same way, entire life contexts are selected that might appear to be incomprehensible, foolhardy, or even insane to an observer.

(9:38.) These lifetime organizations may involve very drastic physical disabilities from birth. From the outside it seems

430

impossible that anyone would <u>choose</u> such a background, such a highly restricted or even painful situation in which to live. From that viewpoint birth defects, or lifetime diseases of any kind, make no sense.

No one begins a race with a handicap, you may say, but that is obviously not the case. Individuals have often chosen such situations precisely as incentives, and many great men have done so. This does not mean that such disabilities are necessary. At any point that an individual realizes his point of power in the present, he will not need a barrier to test himself against, or to focus him in what he thinks of as the proper direction.

You live many lives simultaneously. You often think of these as reincarnational existences, one before the other. If you are severely ill and believe that the reasons for your symptoms exist in a past life, that you must "put up with it," then you will not realize that your point of power is in the present, and you will not believe in the possibility of recovery.

Again, even so-called incurable diseases can be healed as long as this does not involve regenerations <u>not possible</u> within the context of creaturehood.

In your terms, birth defects of whatever kind are chosen before this life. This is done for many different reasons (just as people choose to be ill <u>in</u> this life, regardless of the duration involved). That is, a certain psychic framework is set up through which an individual decides "ahead of time" to experience an entire life situation. Some information on this has been given in my other writings.*

A person with several existences stressing intellectual achievement might purposely then decide upon a life in which mental abilities are beyond him, and the emotions allowed a full play that he had denied them "earlier."

(9:54.) Since all existences are simultaneous, this simply means his stressing certain aspects in this life—at the expense of others, <u>you</u> would say—and setting up a frame of reference that

*See both *The Seth Material* and *Seth Speaks.* We've also accumulated considerable unpublished material on the subject.

may <u>seem</u> to be limiting. On the other hand the personality involved may see this as a most rewarding and expansive experience, in which the emotions are allowed freedoms ordinarily denied. Characteristically, some personalities prefer lifetime experiences in which accomplishment and development follows an even course. Others demand great contrast. One of the latter may be miserably poor in one life, luxuriously rich in another, an intellectual giant in still another, a great athlete, and then a complete invalid. Individual differences operate then in the kinds of life situations chosen.

In many cases it is the family, rather than the incapacitated member, who questions and does not understand—as in cases of severely mentally retarded children, for example. Yet in all instances not only do children choose their parents ahead of time, but parents choose their children, of course.

In such a situation, there are fulfillments to be gained from the parents' standpoints. There are always opportunities of growth and unusual creativity possible under those conditions for all involved. That is why the framework was <u>chosen</u>. The same applies to seeming tragedies such as accidents, or severe illnesses that come at any time.

(*Very emphatically at 10:03:*) On an individual basis a grave illness, for instance, will represent the adoption of a particular highly intense focus in which a given aspect of usual experience is deliberately cut out or denied; the context of life itself must then be magnified along other lines. In somewhat the same manner, this also applies to those born in extreme poverty or in the most seemingly unfortunate of family situations. The life challenge is <u>inherent</u> within the problem itself and springs from it. Usually, though not always, a peculiar personal achievement results precisely because of the given difficulty (*intently*).

Now this accomplishment need not involve some great artwork or invention, or political leadership, for example, though it may. Often the successful activity represents a challenge on the part of the personality who set it in terms of psychological creativity, and the overall enrichment of experience. Those involved, such as family, will have acquiesced to the situation "earlier." Often, particularly in the case of mental or physical birth defects, the incapacitated person will be accepting that role not only because of personal reasons; he or she will also be choosing that part for the family as a whole.

Highly intelligent parents, therefore, may find themselves with a retarded child. If they place a great value upon intellect at the expense of the emotions, then the child may be acting out for them the emotional spontaneity of which they are so afraid themselves.

You may take your break.

(10:15. Peculiarly, in spite of her deep trance and the mass of material she'd delivered, Jane remembered one line—Seth's remark about her using the radio as a point of reference while she worked with states of consciousness. See the session at 9:32. This was an obvious thing that neither of us had realized before.

(Jane plays the radio often while writing, too. She joked now that she must use it as "a lifeline between realities." Resume in the same intent manner at 10:47.)

A birth defect is obvious, and sets up certain conditions that cannot be ignored.

Many ordinary illnesses also involve the family group to some degree. The predominating beliefs of the sick person will always be paramount, however. The group situation will encompass an acquiescence on the part of other family members.

Now understand that the same thing applies in the case of unusual achievements. In those instances the achiever's beliefs predominate, and yet apart from this he may also be acting out the unrealized aspirations of his family members, or of the group in which he is intimately involved. There will always be reasons for such interrelationships.

(Pause.) Many great contrasts of a social nature have the same kind of inner meaning; here whole groups of individuals chose particular life situations in which, for example, poverty and illness predominate, while other areas of the world (or of any

given nation) enjoy the highest technological advances, wealth and prosperity. Separately each personality has a <u>private</u> reason for such an affiliation. But on other levels, through the contrasting focuses of poverty and wealth, scientific accomplishments or the lack of them, opposites are brilliantly apparent. Technological progress, followed as a main focus, automatically portrays its benefits and its disadvantages.

A nation which pursues this course is like one individual who primarily follows a strictly "objective, male," externally oriented path in terms of your Western understanding. Certain values have been stressed in your country, particularly in the recent present. These attributes were pursued at the expense of others for individual reasons and those *en masse*. The rest of the world agreed to such actions, however, and various portions of it took entirely different courses, so that in your experience global society would show a kaleidoscope of varying focuses and their results.

(Pause at 11:05.) On a much smaller scale and to different degrees, any tribe, town, family or group will show the same tendencies, and from the shared experience each individual will learn and grow.

A person may choose a great talent instead, through which he or she will perceive reality and concentrate all experience. This will serve as a formidable focus, yet by its nature it may often preclude <u>other</u> experiences that many individuals find quite normal. Some artists with great ability may shut out intellectual maturity, utilizing native emotional qualities to such an extent and with such intensity that the mental reasoning faculties are largely shunted aside. *(Pause.)* Without rational illumination, the emotional elements may be so unwieldy that the artist, for all of his spontaneous expression, cannot relate in any kind of permanent situation of an intimate nature. For reason and emotion are natural counterparts.

Someone else may choose to focus upon intellectual achievement to such a degree that he shuts out all true closeness, and though he can accept a permanent relationship, he will not experience the emotional richness that others may derive from a much briefer encounter. Therefore each of you choose—ahead of time, in your terms—the kind of framework through which you will contend with this life situation. This applies personally and collectively.

Those who believe in reincarnation will ask, "What about past-life beliefs? And even if I forget the idea of guilt, am I bound to follow the rules of karma?" *(See the 614th session in Chapter Two.)*

Since all is simultaneous, your present beliefs can alter your past ones, whether from this life or a "previous" one. Existences are open-ended. Now with your ideas of progressive time and the resulting beliefs in cause and effect, I realize this is difficult for you to understand. Yet within the abilities of your creaturehood, your current beliefs can change your experience; you can restructure your "reincarnational past" in the same way that you can restructure the past in this present life *(as explained in sessions 657-58 in Chapter Fifteen.)*

(With gestures:) In the center of the page:

The Point of Power Is in the Present.

This experienced present also represents your psychic touchstone to all of your other existences. You are consciously aware of certain events, and unconsciously aware of much more that in one way or another you are learning to bring into conscious focus.

The same applies to all of your other "reincarnational selves." They are unconsciously aware of your conscious experience, as you are unconsciously aware of theirs.

The interaction is constant, however, and in all of your presents, creative. You draw on their knowledge as they draw on yours, and this of course applies to personalities that you would consider future. You have a gigantic pool of information and experience to draw upon, but this will be utilized according to your present conscious beliefs. If you understand that the point of power is in the present, then you have an inexhaustible realm of ability and energy at your command.

You may take a break.

(11:27. Jane went back into trance at 11:41, and delivered several pages of material for ourselves and others. Our night's work ended at 12:17 A.M.

(I might add that Seth has briefly discussed reincarnation in connection with probabilities in the 631st session in Chapter Seven; in connection with the moment of reflection in the 636th session in Chapter Nine; and in connection with present beliefs in the 657th session in Chapter Fifteen.)

SESSION 668, JUNE 6, 1973, 9:12 P.M. WEDNESDAY

(No book dictation was involved in Monday's session for June 4, which was held for a scientist visiting Jane from the West Coast. Some of his questions dealt with earthquake prediction, which he is studying with the aid of computers. It's interesting to note that Seth completed Chapter Eighteen, concerning our psychic creation of the environment [including earthquakes, of course] a week before our guest's arrival. The visit had been scheduled since May 9, however.)

Good evening.

("Good evening, Seth.")

Dictation. *(Slowly:)* You must remember that beginnings and endings are realities only within your own system of three-dimensional life.

The energy of your being exists <u>outside</u> of your system, however, and impinges upon it in your terms, becoming "alive" physically at certain points of time and space. Your own greater energy dips in and out of the space-time continuum as you understand it. As it does, its experience becomes physical. Within that system then it leaves a life-trace. When you think in terms of reincarnation it seems that one tracing exists before the other, but the entire "chart" exists at once, with all the individual life-tracings.

(*Long pause.*) Since these offshoots or life-tracings each come from your entity, they are connected psychologically and in terms of electromagnetic energy patterns. Consider this analogy: Taking it for granted that you are indeed multi-dimensional, you can perceive only so much of your own experience <u>at a time</u> because of the characteristics of physical creaturehood; the three-dimensional system automatically specializes in before-and-after effects.

You exist, say, in seven different centuries at once. However, the normal experience-patterns of your temporal being prevent any comprehensive view of all of those lives in <u>creature terms</u>.

(*9:26.*) Again, what actually happens is that the energy of your being impinges, say, at seven [moment] points* into the three-dimensional system. At each of these points, what seems to be an isolated life is experienced. Just beyond those intersections, however, there is a more or less unitary and overall recognition of wholeness that "rides" above them. This represents the multidimensional entity that is both apart from and yet part <u>of</u> the separate life-traces. You may have an existence in the seventeenth century, for example. To you it would appear that the life was a past one, finished. You may believe that your current existence, with all of its abilities and challenges, is the result of that past life, yet both exist at once. The seventeenth century is not dead. You follow a one-line pattern of history, pursuing certain actions as reality and identifying with these so completely that they are all you perceive. Other probable actions are always occurring, however, and are quite as valid as the ones which you happen to choose and thus experience.

Your reincarnational selves have as many probable lives as

---

*Seth first discussed his theory of "moment points" in a set of four sessions in April and May, 1965, in connection with reincarnation and the dream universe. In the 152nd session he stated: "The whole self of which Ruburt is a part is an extremely elastic one. The various portions of this whole self reach outward and inward with much more resilience than most. [It] surrounds many more moment points simultaneously . . ." Through one of these, Seth added in a very simplified explanation, he could enter within the limits of Jane's "psychic comprehension."

you do. Your beliefs and actions in your present alter "their" experiences, as each of them, in their presents, change yours. If you see these reincarnational selves as one entity, then this becomes quite natural. The whole self is changed by all of its comprehensions.

Now take your break.

(9:49 to 9:55.)

Each portion of the entity is unique and independent, and through its own beliefs determines what it will accept in terms of influences within its immediate life situation. The great miracle, in fact, is that each consciousness, whatever its degree, is itself and no other, even while in the unending fields of interaction it may be a portion of another—as a city is part of a state, or an individual is part of a family.

In terms of personality as you understand it, the individual chooses the abilities he or she will have, and the life challenges. In the present then each person has unlimited opportunity to draw upon the entity's energy, and the understanding and powers of all of its parts. *(Long pause.)* It goes without saying that any human being possesses the latent ability shown by a great artist or athlete, or statesman or philosopher. Within creaturehood there are wide ranges of abilities; these may be seldom used, but they are there as practical ideals that can be expressed within that system. In the same way, every individual possesses the abilities of its entity in latent form. These too serve as practical ideals, but in a different kind of context, for you have other centuries to play with and many existences instead of one.

You often excel in situations that utterly escape you at a physical level. These accomplishments still operate through the focus of your present, since you are physically aware of but one line of probable events, so the meaning of many dream events escapes you. But in dreams you often do work quite as valid as any performed in the day, and in the dream state you meet and interact with your own reincarnational selves.

(10:11.) Actually, I prefer that you think of them as

438

simultaneous selves. In the dreaming condition there is a great interchange of information with these other portions of your selves. Your physical brain automatically converts such data into temporal terms so that many of your significant, remembered dream experiences are already translations by the time you recall them. Otherwise they would make no sense to you at all.

In many instances you travel outside of three-dimensional reality while dreaming, but your experiences must then be recalled in physical terms or you would have no memory of them. Even your dreams, you see, must come through that point in the present—of spirit's intersection with flesh. Dreaming <u>does</u> represent an open channel through which the material environment is transcended. There are as yet undiscovered, bizarre changes in the brain during <u>certain</u> dream states, an acceleration that quite literally <u>propels</u> the consciousness out of its usual space-time continuum into those other realities from which it comes.

These serve as points of unity, wherein all the various simultaneous selves meet; and certain seasonal rhythms are involved here in physical terms.

(10:20.) Do you want a break now?

("No, I guess not." I wasn't too sharp this evening, though.)

As your spaceships to the moon must wait for the most effective overall conditions before taking off, so in other terms are there rhythms having to do with energy. Practically speaking, this means that certain times are more effective than others for these communications in the dream state. Privately, they often involve illuminations and sudden advantageous decisions. En masse they imply great historical changes.

Take your break.

(10:24 to 10:35.)

These interchanges represent periods in which the soul and flesh meet under the most optimum conditions. There are individual variations and yet mass patterns. The energy of the personal self constantly comes from the entity. There is not just one intersection of soul with the flesh, therefore, but at the least a constant series as you would think of it. Because of the characteristics of energy as it impinges upon the three-dimensional system, there are fluctuations—always involving your present.

These cycles merge at several points, so that you do have major changes in all areas in any span of two thousand years. For other reasons and in a smaller context, the month of August is highly significant in a twenty-five year sequence. Within this, a seven-year period is important individually. These are simply rhythms depicting the greatest impact of spirit as it intersects with flesh and time.

In physical terms the tides and geographical aspects are involved, but these are "effects" having to do with curves of energy of which consciousness is composed. These rhythms are minutely but perfectly reflected in other ways. The seventh dream of any given night is the most important—not (louder, smiling) that anyone is counting, and say I said it humorously.

The greatest abilities of a personality may often be brought into physical expression, however, because of certain rhythms that are not understood. In a manner of speaking you can say that the energy of an entity is dispersed, striking the space-time continuum at certain angles and always bouncing back. But the energy is always in contact with itself even while it impinges into physical existence.

(10:47.) In your terms, the energy springs back in the dream state, but it must always pass through what you think of as the window of the present.

(Pause.) This bouncing back of energy into itself is the meaning of the dream state, in which experience that is basically nonphysical is embarked upon, and is then interpreted as a dream through the brain. Your deepest dreams involve nonmaterial comprehensions, however. Your dream, though clearly remembered, is already a translation of the physical brain. The information then enters your present, where it biologically and mentally colors your life.

440

It is also automatically transformed according to your beliefs, so that it makes sense to you at least to some degree. In energy terms, think of your selves as particles, and of your experiences as the waves that flow through the particles and gives each of them its sensations. When you are physical you are a particle. The form of the particle defines your experience as the waves permeate it, but your greater reality cannot be expressed in such limited terms.

Take your break.

(10:55. Once again Jane's delivery for Seth had been steady and forceful. "I don't really remember what I said," she told me, "yet I do feel that in this material we've gone beyond what we've gotten before. It'll revolutionize science if physicists can understand it. Even as limited as we are as human beings, I think we've latched onto some ideas, through Seth, that are vitally important . . ."

(It had just stopped raining and the humidity was high. Seeking some relief, Jane left the house for a short walk during break. Resume at 11:24.)

Now: As there are better times than others in your sphere of activity for sending rockets or spaceships to the moon, so there are peak periods when the self and the soul (or entity) coincide—when communication is at its best.

All of this happens through the window of your present. In terms of energy, again, the vitality of your entity impinging into three-dimensional reality forms a particle that is your present being. But this particle is also deflected away from the earth in a rhythmic pattern. The same happens to other portions of your self at other points in the space-time continuum, but at certain intervals you meet, so to speak. Each of your "presents" becomes charged, filled with potentiality; and your entity, itself conscious energy, is also enriched by your various experiences, by the combined and magnified power of its own "past."

Apexes are therefore formed within each self. These apexes serve as attractions, now opened, through which the magnified potency of the entity can flow. This may appear as erratic

441

energy, however, an analogy being sunspots. Psychologically, great ferment occurs, and often the individual personalities involved organize themselves along new lines.

Privately this is when human beings find themselves aware of greater illumination, when they make sudden decisions and experience new strengths. Now such a time is in the offing socially. This may be reflected in periods of seeming unrest in which, however, new creativity is looming. There will then be great planetary changes in terms of your organizations, but these will reflect private interior illuminations that become physically materialized. (More powerfully:) You do not trust your inner selves enough, or realize the creative ferment brewing. If you did you could save yourselves much trouble.

I am speaking to you both individually and for the book here: Any point in your present is a potential point of great creative change, but because of the rhythms spoken of, it is easier for changes to occur in certain cycles.

(Abruptly:) End of dictation, and the session. My heartiest regards to you both.

("Good night, Seth. Thank you very much." 11:40 P.M.)

SESSION 669, JUNE 11, 1973, 9:40 P.M. MONDAY

(The night was very hot and uncomfortably humid, but Jane didn't want to miss the session. We held it in her study for a change, with all the doors and windows open.

(Before the session, we voiced the hope once more that Seth would at least comment on Jane's latest experience involving book work in the sleep state. This had taken place during the early hours of May 29, and had been very vivid; see the notes leading off the 667th session in this chapter. Once again, though, for whatever reasons, Seth didn't mention it. I also forgot to remind him to do so. It's easy to miss out on asking specific questions during a session—I've done this even when I had a list of them prepared beforehand.

(And yet, as if to puzzle us further, Seth did talk about

442

dream material that Jane had obtained just last night. This turned out to be in connection with Chapter Twenty . . .

(Jane's pace tonight was rather slow, her voice quiet.)

Now good evening.

("Good evening, Seth.")

Dictation: Because the point of power and action <u>is</u> in your present as you understand it, so each day is like the kind of window that can provide many views through its different panes.

The window of each day can be opened or closed, but it is framed by your current psychological experience. Even when it is shut light shines through it, illuminating your daily life. In miniature form each day contains, in its own way, clues to all of your own simultaneous existences. The present self does not exist in isolation.

Within any given twenty-four hour period, then, traces and aspects of all of your other experiences appear in their own way. You each contain aspects of your other identities within your current selves—some very obvious perhaps and others barely noticeable. Abilities focused upon in one life may be recognized as your own now, for example, but not strongly utilized.

Vague yearnings toward certain accomplishments may be clues that the necessary characteristics are inherent but untrained in the self that you know. In its own way, the twenty-four period represents both an entire lifetime and many lives in one. In it, symbolically, you have "death" as your physically attuned consciousness comes to the end of the amount of stimuli it can comfortably handle without rest. So, at your normal physical death, you come to the point where your earth-attuned consciousness can no longer handle further data without a "longer rest," and organize it into a creative meaningful whole—<u>in terms of time</u>.

(9:56.) Each day therefore is an incarnation, so to speak, but not only symbolically—for through soul's intersection with the flesh, each self mirrors daily its "reincarnational" or simultaneous selves.

The same applies on what you may think of as a more practical level, in that each day also holds within it the answers to current problems. If you are aware of a particular problem (challenge), therefore, you can be assured that its solution is as much there and with you as the problem is. (*Intently:*) The solution is simply the problem's other side, upon which you may not be focusing. There will even be clear clues as to the proper direction for you to take—these will already be within your experience, but unrecognized because you are concentrating so upon the problem.

This applies to any kind of dilemma.

(*Pause.*) Although you are an individual and with free will, you are also part of another you. You simply do not identify with your greater self now. You have your own unique characteristics. Your greater being also possesses its own originality, yet there will be what you may think of as a family resemblance, and so overall you and your other self often choose the same kinds of challenges, if in dissimilar ways.

In their own ways, other portions of your multidimensional being are involved in experiences, then, somewhat similar to your own, though on the outside the situation may be completely different. Their progress lies latent within the window of the moment point—the moment point simply being your current intersection with the reality that you know.

The adventures of your simultaneous selves, again, appear as traces in your own consciousness, as ideas or daydreams or disconnected images, or sometimes even in sudden intuitions. They can be drawn upon, drawn out, to help you understand current problems.

You may take your break.

(*10:10. "That was one of the few times in all of these sessions," Jane said, "when I was hot even in trance." She had squirmed about on her chair constantly, but her delivery had picked up to its usual steady pace. For more data on moment points, see the material at 9:26 in the last session. Resume at 10:28.*)

Now: This does not mean that you will necessarily have a flood of reincarnational information, instant intuitive recognition of "past" lives, or experience any such intrusive data. It does mean that in your own life such information automatically appears in intimate ways, but couched within the framework of your own comprehensions, even passing unobstrusively through your conscious thoughts.

Many artists unknowingly paint portraits of their simultaneous selves.* Many mothers find themselves feeling younger than their offspring at times, or about to call some of their children by different names. Impulses to try activities you have not tried before may indeed be messages from other portions of your own being.

There simply is no time as you think of it, only a present in which all things occur. There are miracles of condensed information within the cells themselves that scientists cannot perceive, for they exist outside of the scope of physical instruments. In its own way, cellular comprehension includes a vast recognition of probabilities in your terms, and works with flashing manipulations in which these probabilities are contended with and responded to—and therefore altered.

(10:42.) The physically attuned conscious mind in your now cannot handle those staggering probabilities while maintaining a sense of identity, yet there are conscious traces within your daily thoughts that are the psychological representations of such knowledge.

Often you do not trust your imagination, considering that it deals with phenomena that cannot be called fact. Therefore you artificially form a situation in which overall traces must be

*I feel that I am such an artist. For some related material see my notes for the 582nd session in Chapter Twenty of *Seth Speaks.* It's enough to say here that it wasn't until after these sessions began, in 1963, that I realized my inner models were quite as valid as those who physically sat before me. Indeed, I often saw the former was a clearer vision, but my early training and work as a commercial artist, beginning in New York City in 1939, conditioned me to believe that the artist was supposed to deal only with what he could "see" objectively.

For many years I ignored the fact that in grade school I'd very happily and freely covered my yellow tablets with drawings of "imaginary" people and places . . .

made. If you are too imaginative, for example, you may not be able to adequately deal with physical life. This applies only in the cultural media in which you presently operate, however. Originally, and in your terms of time, it was precisely the imagination that in its own way set you apart from other creatures, enabling you to form realities in your mind that you could "later" exteriorize.

Because you now distrust the imagination so, you do not understand the great clues it gives you, both in terms of problem solving and of creative expression. Many quite valid reincarnational memories come as imaginings, but you do not trust them. A good percentage of your problems can be worked out rather easily through the use of your imagination.

(Pause at 10:50.) Often you inadvertently use it to prolong "negative" circumstances, as you think of all the things that you could do wrong. Yet you can employ it very constructively, altering past, present and future. To do so in your present, freely imagine a situation in which you are happy. To begin with your imaginings may seem foolish. If you are elderly, poor and lonely, it may seem highly ludicrous to think of yourself as twenty, wealthy, and surrounded by friends and admirers.

Indeed, if after such an enjoyable exercise you look about you and compare what you have envisioned with what you have, then you may feel worse than you did before. You are to realize that this imaginative world does exist—but not in the world of facts that you know. To some extent, however, according to your freedom within it, such an exercise will automatically rejuvenate your body, mind and spirit, and begin to draw to you whatever equivalent is possible for you within the world of facts that you know (emphatically).

Using age as an example now, it may seem to you that you are a given age, that within your subjective experience it must be paramount, that regardless of your age you are to some extent closed off from the experience of being any other age. In some simultaneous existences you are very young, however, and in others very old. Some of your physical cells are brand new,

446

so to speak—the regeneration of fresh life is physically within you; in your terms this is true not only until your death but even after it, when your hair and nails can still grow. Identify then with the constantly new energy alive within you in this now of your being (*very intently*) and realize that on all levels you are biologically and psychologically connected with that greater identity that is your own.

You may take a break.

(*11:04 to 11:24.*)

Now: No matter what your current situation, the answers lie within your own aspirations and abilities. Often you will hold down or inhibit certain aspects of your experience in order to use others—using those available will automatically free you from inhibitions in other areas.

There may be physical circumstances involving birth defects that are beyond alteration, where experience must be focused along other than usual pathways, yet even here those talents and characteristics that are available will open up vistas of experience and achievement.

When you are utilizing your imagination in the way I have suggested, purposefully do so in a playful manner, knowing that in so-called realistic terms there may be great discrepancies between imagination and fact. In your reality take that for granted. Yet often your freewheeling, "silly," seemingly unrealistic imagination will bring you quite practical solutions to your problems, for if the exercise is done properly you will be automatically releasing yourself from restrictions that you have taken for granted.

Even if a direct solution does not appear, rejuvenation will of itself begin to point you in the proper direction. If you are a woman in an unhappy marriage, for example, you may begin by imagining yourself with a fine suitor. Now: no Sir Galahad may appear, but if the exercise is pursued properly you will automatically begin to feel loved, and therefore worthy of love, and lovable, where before you felt rejected, unworthy and inferior. This feeling of being loved will alter your reality,

447

drawing love to you. You will act loved. Your spouse may then find you exhibiting characteristics of a most pleasant nature, and he himself may change.

On the other hand you may draw another man to you, and end the marriage that has served its purposes in all ways, finding now the impetus and the reasons for change. Because your imagination transcends time, it is one of your greatest touchstones to your own identity.

You must, of course, be able to distinguish between the world of imagination and the physical world of fact in order to be able to manipulate effectively. But physical reality springs from the imagination, which follows the path of your beliefs.

In the exercise just given, you use the belief in effective change in any given area, and then allow your imagination freedom along those directed lines. Such an exercise automatically does even more, opening up the window of perception and letting in the knowledge and experience of other portions of the self. As this light and energy flows through, it will be tinted or colored by your own psychological reality, as the rays of the sun are through colored glass. This simply means that the other-dimensional information will often appear in ordinary guise, through an intuitive hunch, a sudden idea, or some solution that has already occurred to you but has not been acted upon.

Do you want a break?

(11:45. "No." Though I did get Jane a drink when, still in trance, she held up her empty glass.)

Your cells' multidimensional knowledge is usually not consciously available, nor can they put it into psychological terms for you. Such work with the imagination acts as a trigger, however, drawing information to you from other levels of your greater reality, and concentrating it on the specific problem at hand. It will then appear in terms understandable to your own experience.

In itself, such an exercise creatively alters probabilities, for you no longer live with the problem as an unchanging concrete reality. This is a psychological and psychic impetus, altering the messages that you habitually send to your body and to its cellular construction. You are then creatively manipulating in several layers of experience.

Take for example the two instances just given: The older person imagining youth will, during such an exercise, reactivate certain hormonal and chemical changes, becoming younger; and the woman who feels rejected does the same thing when imagining herself loved.

Such practice also activates within the self all of its unconscious but quite valid experiences, drawing out similar episodes on the part of other simultaneous lives. In one existence the old person is young. The unloved woman is indeed beloved. These unconscious realities become turned on through the use of the imagination. Each day is a window into each life.

You may take your break or end the session as you prefer.

("We'll take the break, then."

(11:59. The evening had cooled off somewhat by now and Jane felt better, although she said noise in the house had bothered her while she'd been under. This seldom happens.

(At break I reminded Jane that we wanted Seth to discuss her May 29 dream experience with book work, but no sooner had I done so than she began describing her dreams of last night. I'd forgotten about those for the moment.

(Last evening had also been very warm, and Jane had slept poorly: She kept waking up with data about dream landscapes being "right there" before her, and wondered if she could travel among them "like crossing fences from one backyard to the next." At the same time she knew that all of these localities were part of a mass dream landscape. As far as she knew the material hadn't come from Seth, Jane said, but in retrospect it seems obvious that it had been in preparation for Chapter Twenty.

(Seth was all ready to go, Jane added now as we discussed her dream material, so the session resumed at 12:03.)

CHAPTER **20**

*The Dream Landscape, the Physical World,
Probabilities, and Your Daily Experience*

Now: Give us a moment . . .

(Whispering:) Chapter Twenty: "The Dream Landscape, the Physical World, Probabilities, and Your Daily Experience."

(Long pause at 12:06.) Because you are physical creatures even your dreams must be translated through the reality of your flesh. En masse and through the methods I have described, you help form a physical reality in which, however, each experience is unique, period.

In the same way each of you form an overall dream world in which there is some general agreement, comma, but in which each experience is original. The dream world has its reaches as the physical one does. In waking reality, beliefs take time before their materialization is apparent. From infinite probable acts, comma, only one can be physically experienced as a rule, period.

The dream world operates as a creative situation in which probable acts are instantly materialized, laid out in actual or symbolic form. From these you then choose the most appropriate for physical expression. There are other important reasons for dreaming, but here we will confine ourselves to this particular issue and to the dream landscape itself, period.

(Louder and humorously:) I hope you enjoy the punctuation. *(12:15. "It's beautiful.")*

It is only because you seem to expect dream experience to be like daily life that you find so many dreams chaotic. Normally a tree does not change into a peacock, for example. If you remember such a dream event, comma, it seems meaningless in the morning.

Now that is enough. We will end our session.

("All right. Good night, Seth." End at 12:23 A.M.

(Since break Seth had taken to calling out more periods, commas, and other such indicia than he usually does, so I included a few examples. He's indicated this kind of punctuation throughout the book, but is usually more concerned about words to be underlined, or put in quotes or parentheses. See the notes following the 610th session in Chapter One.

(For some of Seth's earlier material on dreams, dream symbols and healing, nightmare therapy, etc., see sessions 639-41 in Chapter Ten.)

SESSION 670, JUNE 13, 1973,
9:25 P.M. WEDNESDAY

(Both of us were looking forward to some private material we'd asked for earlier today; Jane already "knew" that Seth would give it tonight, but first she wanted some dictation on Chapter Twenty. Her delivery was quiet and steady.)

Good evening.

("Good evening, Seth.")

To begin with dictation: Your moods and emotions have greater mobility in the dream state. You may feel rooted like a tree at one moment and in the next experience yourself as a beautiful peacock, in which case you will perceive the tree change into the bird.

Disconnected from their usual daily attraction to physical

451

events, your emotions will often form their own landscapes, utilizing dreams as their creative medium. I have explained the great correlation that exists between your feelings and beliefs and physical conditions such as weather. (*See Chapter Eighteen.*) In somewhat the same way, you have a part to play individually in the creation of the dream landscape. It is also the result of your feelings and beliefs on a different level, and while it is not perceivable in physical terms—laid out with its mountains and continents as your planet is, to be examined by your instruments—it exists in terms quite as valid.

(*Pause.*) This does <u>not</u> mean that dreams can be deciphered by the use of any given [general] symbols. As you create and experience your daily life through your personal feelings and beliefs, so the same applies to dream reality.

There, however, your thoughts and feelings become "instantly" alive, springing up one upon another, coming full blown as it were. The dream world exists in terms of energy also, of course, but simply at ranges that are not physically obvious. Much of your interior creative work and planning is done at this level. There must be some differentiation between dream and waking experience just so that you can manipulate in the more narrowly focused daily life.

(*9:35.*) However, there is no great reason for the vast separation that now exists between your waking and sleeping lives. As I mentioned earlier (*in the 652nd session in Chapter Thirteen, for instance*), the division is largely the result of your mass and private beliefs in the nature of reality, and in the habits the race has acquired of separating "objective" data from subjective.

When you are determined to <u>manipulate</u> your environment, then you separate yourself from it. Since you are part of it, this also leads you to try to place yourself apart from your own subjective reality. It is quite possible to take your normally conscious "I" into the dream state, to your advantage. When you do this you will see that the dreaming "I" and the waking

"I" are one, but <u>operating</u> in entirely different environments. Therefore, you become familiar with depths of experience and knowledge unknown to you before. You acquire a true flexibility and expanded awareness of your own being, and open channels of communication between your waking and dreaming realities. This means that you are far better able to utilize unconscious knowledge, and also to acquaint the unconscious with your present physical situation.

Such a procedure can bring you in contact with wisdom you have been denying yourself, help unify your entire life situation, and release your energy for practical everyday purposes. Even the decision to <u>try</u> such a venture is beneficial, since it automatically presupposes a flexibility of attitude on the part of the conscious self.

<u>If you are afraid of your dreams, you are afraid of yourself.</u>

As your present situation with all of its challenges, joys and problems is contained in condensed form within each of your days, so the same applies to your life. Each night's dreams then provide you with a rich bed of creativity. Spread out before you in great profusion, you will find not only any problems but their solutions.

Now, in physical terms it may take some time before your conscious mind accepts or recognizes a diagnosis given in a dream. It may come to you later in altered form as a hunch or sudden intuition, or an urge for action. If you do not <u>trust</u> yourself you may ignore such impetuses and not take advantage of the answers.

The enlightened conscious mind is always alert for such messages. You can also go steps beyond this into the dream condition itself, requesting certain dreams, certain solutions, and therefore shortening the time, so to speak, that may be involved otherwise.

Take your break.

(9:53. The rest of the session was given over to the material that Jane and I had requested, and ended then at 11:35 P.M.)

*(Since we'd missed both regular sessions this week, Jane
decided to make up one of them tonight; she wanted to
maintain her usual momentum on the book as much as possible.
It was another hot night, and her delivery was leisurely.)*

Now: Good evening.

("Good evening, Seth.")

A note: I can finish the book at any number of consecutive
sessions, if you wish.

*("Yes." Seth meant that we could hold sessions on a daily
basis. Jane and I had talked about this earlier tonight, without
being too serious about it. Actually, though, we won't have any
extra time; the finished manuscript of this book is due at
Prentice-Hall in October, and will require much work in order
to get it done by then.)*

Dictation: Generally speaking, if you do not believe that you
can become conscious in the dream state, then that feat will
be relatively impossible. It will go against your idea of
reality, thereby preventing the opening and acceptance that is
necessary.

New paragraph: While your beliefs do structure much of your
dream activity, other issues are also involved simply because the
focus of your awareness is not acutely directed toward physical
reality, but is only opaquely concerned with it.

(9:04.) Once again, thoughts and ideas have their own
electromagnetic validity also. In waking life you test your ideas
in the world of facts. Facts are only accepted fiction, of course,
but the ideas must make sense and fit into the accepted
"story."

*("Fiction" is the word Seth wanted here, he said when I
interrupted the session to ask him.)*

In the dream state you allow yourself greater freedom, trying
out certain ideas and beliefs in this more plastic framework.
You may therefore accept new beliefs initially in the dream

454

state, and the intellectual or emotional realization may only come "later." In dreaming, the conscious mind itself is far more lenient and playful. It can afford this greater permissiveness because it well knows that it need not immediately test out theory in the daily context. It very willingly looks inward toward those areas of the inner self's experience to see what it can find for its own use, quite like an explorer searching for resources in virgin territory.

(9:15.) The earth-tuned consciousness must deal within the space-time context, for only inside this framework can it clearly perceive events. In the dream state consciousness ignores space-time relationships to a large degree, and yet it is still firmly based upon the body's corporeal mechanism. Dreams then are physically experienced. You perceive yourself running, talking, eating, in quite physical activities—except that they are not performed by the body that lies on the bed.

The orientation is that of sense data lived most vividly, and yet, again, at an opaque angle. In other words, in most dreams data is still being received and interpreted in the light of corporeal life. These are the dreams most remembered also.

Beyond this there are experiences but seldom recalled, in which the usual identification of your consciousness with physical-life orientation is gone. (Pause.) Images as you think of them are based upon your own neurological structure, and your interpretations of these. When you consider survival after death, for instance, you imagine all the senses fully operating, though perhaps in a nonphysical body. Perception without images seems impossible in that context. Yet in some dream situations you enter a state of awareness quite divorced from that kind of sense data. Images as such are not involved, though later they may be manufactured unconsciously for the sake of translation. In those conditions you come close to an understanding of what your consciousness is when it is not physically oriented at all.

(9:27.) In your daily life you may suddenly know something without knowing how you know, without being aware of any

455

particular image or sense impression. The knowledge is simply "there." This kind of activity approaches the sort of knowing of your own consciousness when it is uninvolved with any kind of ordinary sense stimuli. It simply knows. In those certain dream states, then, you know in the same fashion. You experience your being unallied with flesh.

That kind of dream awareness can literally regenerate your life, though the original impact will be forgotten, and the entire event will usually be translated into images before awakening. Such dream events may be called experiences of basic being. During them, the self or consciousness literally travels to the source of its own energy. On another level atoms possess this same kind of knowing.

(*Slowly:*) It may seem that such comprehensions have little to do with your daily life, particularly since they are so seldom recalled, and then only in translation; yet they provide you with additional energy—and when you need it most.

In periods of stress, the physically attuned consciousness will often momentarily forsake its usual orientation and let itself fall back, as it were, into the source of its own being, where it knows it will be regenerated and indeed reborn.

You may take your break.

(*9:40. Jane said she'd used the phrase given by Seth at 9:04, "Facts are only accepted fiction . . ." just this afternoon in her own theoretical work,* Aspect Psychology; *she had also written about ideas very much like those Seth presented at 9:15.*

(*Resume at 9:56.*)

While you are physically connected you must interpret experience in sense terms, even that in dreams. At times your consciousness can range into other areas, but then the events must be physically translated in some way.

In waking life you perceive only certain portions of events that fall within your space-time continuum. In dreams you may have a greater glimpse. You may for example see in the past, present and future, objects that in your time will take up any given space. Often such a dream will be considered meaningless because at your "fact level," past, present and future objects cannot appear at once in the same space.

(Very intently:) <u>The space is not the same, or identical, in any case</u>. It only appears to be so to you.

Space itself accelerates in ways that you do not understand. You are not tuned into those frequencies. Any point in space <u>is</u> also a point in what you think of as time, a doorway that you have not learned to open.*

New paragraph: In somewhat the same manner, your physical brain is a doorway that triggers activity in your mind. Your beliefs then are largely responsible for the areas of the <u>brain</u> that you activate, and for the resulting nonphysical action of the mind.

Physical focus provides you with a magnificent reality, intent and specialized. Were it not for dream activity however you would be, relatively speaking, enclosed within it, afraid to try out new concepts and intuitive realizations in the face of what seems to be such rockbed reality.

(10:10.) The dream state provides you with a preliminary stage in which working hypotheses can be creatively formed and tried out in a context of playfulness. Still, the dreams that you have and recall, and the resulting solution of many problems, represent only the surface layer of dream activity. To follow yourself into your own dreams is a fascinating endeavor, and there in the dream context you can become aware of the working of your own consciousness. To do so you must believe in the integrity of your own being. If you do not trust your waking self you will not trust your dreaming self, and the landscape of your dreams will <u>appear</u> threatening. Your <u>belief</u> that dreams are unpleasant can make them so, or at best you will only remember frightening dream events.

---

*Seth has some material analogous to this in the 582nd session in Chapter Twenty of *Seth Speaks:* "What you perceive of time is a portion of other events intruding into your own system, often interpreted as movement in space . . ." That session, as well as the 581st, also contains some applicable data on Seth's electromagnetic energy (EE) units, their various speeds, and our interpretations of them as events, dream events, movement-through-time, and so forth.

(Long pause at 10:20.) If you believe that you do not dream, however, you will inhibit memory of them—but you will still dream. Those rich experiences will not form a part of your conscious life because of your belief.

Your dreams are private, as your waking life is, and yet there is a mass waking experience and a mass dreaming experience in which each individual finds his or her own place, and accepts or rejects events. In your terms, the race at any given "time" simultaneously works out problems in the dream state, and those solutions are then physically materialized. Because there is more freedom from time and space in the dream state, there is greater overall perspective; many solutions that may appear poor in the short range—as they are physically activated—will in the longer range be seen as highly creative.

Both privately and en masse, then, mankind utilizes the dream world as a preliminary working ground. From these "fantasized" realities and probable dream events come all the physically accepted "facts" in your world of true and false.

(Pause at 10:29. See Chapter Fourteen for some of Seth's material on probabilities.)

Probable events, experienced dream-wise, and quite valid in other areas of reality, become, say, false in your world, while the same kind of event, physically actualized, becomes true.

New paragraph: Your wars are fought, lost or won in the dream world first of all, and your physical rendition of history follows the thin line of only one series of probabilities. To you a given war was either lost or won by a particular side. In your skimpy *(whispering humorously)* comprehension of events there can be only one definite outcome of a battle, for instance. There will be certain hard facts; a fight with so many people involved, occurring on a particular day at a given place, culminating in a definite victory. Historically there will be treaties signed, yet in far greater terms you are perceiving but one small dimension, or one corner, of a much larger happening that quite transcends your ideas of the times or places involved.

(10:35.) The initial battle, so to speak, took place on a dream

level, then privately and en masse the race decided <u>which</u> <u>portions</u> of the event to actualize in physical terms. Even in those recognized terms, however, it is quite apparent that the victor is often the loser.

The <u>entire</u> event transcends any true or false judgments. An entire event, with all of its probabilities included, obviously cannot fit within your current frame of reference.

Again, in your dreams you work with probabilities and decide which ones will become your physical "true facts." Here you have great freedom both individually and as a race. Here each man works out his own destiny, and with the use of this dream information quite consciously chooses which episodes he will physically materialize and experience.

You will accept from your dreams that information that largely agrees with your waking conscious beliefs. There <u>is</u> interaction, as mentioned previously, in which new beliefs are tried out, so to speak. In that regard, you are not at the mercy of your dreams in any meaning of the word.

You have not understood the great give-and-take that exists between waking and dream experience. You have been taught to believe in the existence of an artificial barrier between the two that does not in fact exist. By suggesting before sleep that solutions to problems be given you, you automatically begin to utilize your dream knowledge to a greater extent, and to open the doors to your own greater creativity.

You may take your break.

(10:47 to 11:05.)

Now: I have a note for you. Or I can continue dictation.

("The note's okay . . .")

(Seth caught me. I wanted book work to continue, yet I was sure that his unexpected digression would also be interesting. It was—very much so: In material covering several pages, he discussed my mother and her recent experiences with probabilities in her advanced old age. The complicated family situation involving Mother Butts isn't gone into here, but Jane and I decided to include the more generalized parts of Seth's

information; we think it will help others in their relationships with old people.

(See the 650th session in Chapter Thirteen for data related to the psychic accelerations discussed below. Seth also comments on the hemispheres of the brain in that session.)

. . . your mother is experiencing a mental and intuitive acceleration, a barrage of stimuli hereto withheld. She is perceiving probabilities quite clearly, but confusing them with the physical world of facts. This is only being done when her physical work is finished; not, for example, when disorientation could disrupt any <u>necessary</u> important physical purposes of her own.

There are definite material changes. The portions of the brain not used during highly focused physical life are turned on, as they also are in infancy and in certain stages of adolescence. The changes are triggered in each person individually.

I said probabilities were realized *(in the 653rd session in Chapter Fourteen)* . . . and she is suddenly open to her (imagined) events <u>as</u> actualities. Because you are space-time oriented, her realizations, accepted momentarily as physical reality, cause gaps in what you think of as normal experience.

She must experience such events in your time series, where to others they do not fit. I am giving you this material not only because of your personal concern but for its general application. The grappling with probabilities enables your mother to judge the circumstances of her physical life, and to program herself ahead of time, so to speak, for her next adventure.

Her very actions are serving as learning patterns for the entire family. Despite appearances there is not a dulling of sense impressions on her part, but an infusion. The difficulty in concentrating <u>does</u> result from this, but <u>then</u> she is concentrating elsewhere.

(Long pause at 11:25.) Her feelings of independence are reincited, and will at last lead her to want to leave the family in general—not to cling to her "boys" *(my two*

460

brothers and myself)—and they will also serve as an impetus to growth on her part not realized earlier.

She will finally want to be independent of her body, but she is not cowering; she is struggling to free herself. There is much more . . . In one way the family's treatment of her like a child is accepted, for it provides the thrust for independence in the same way that a child wants to grow up and leave the house. So your mother's independence is aroused. In a way she wants to be free of the house of life that she has literally formed, to find a new endeavor . . . to begin anew. In a teenager her remarks would seem legitimate. She also wants to begin a new life.

(Briskly:) Now that is the end of that. I hope that your mind is set somewhat at rest. You may end the session or take a break as you prefer.

("I guess we'll end it, then.")

My heartiest regards to you both, and a fond good evening.

("Thank you, Seth. Good night." 11:33 P.M.)

SESSION 672, JUNE 25, 1973,
9:27 P.M. MONDAY

(Saturday, June 23, 1973, was the first anniversary of the flood caused by Tropical Storm Agnes—or, as the local newspaper put it in a flood supplement, the occasion was Agnes Plus One.

(Our area is still recovering. Jane and I, of course, are very conscious of how our involvement in the flood interrupted the production of this book in the middle of Chapter One. See the notes for the 613th session. [In them, incidentally, I mentioned the destruction of Elmira's Walnut Street Bridge; the old steel span had crossed the Chemung River half a block from our apartment house. Work—very noisy work, which is to continue for a year—is now underway to replace it.] In Chapter Eighteen, Seth explains the emotional origins of Agnes as a whole, and our personal behavior within it.

(Jane's delivery was rather slow, and her eyes were closed for much of the session.)

Good evening.

(*"Good evening, Seth."*)

Dictation: Currently, mankind has little knowledge of the interior dream world, his place in it, or its effects upon his daily conscious life.

Many of the most powerful aspects of consciousness are at work precisely when it seems to you that you are relatively unconscious and asleep to physical reality. It would be impossible for you to handle the vast amount of material available, in the context of time as you presently experience it. To operate adequately in your highly specific field *(pause)*, an almost infinite amount of information must be instantly assimilated, probabilities calculated, and certain balances maintained of which you are not even aware.

Latently, your consciousness is capable of performing these feats, but the work cannot be done with the part of your consciousness that is strongly attached to the space-time relationship. What you think of as your conscious mind is given the task of assessing the "facts" of daily living. It then forms beliefs about reality, and these are used in the dream state as one of the main yardsticks, so to speak, that activate the emergence of certain probable events rather than others.

(9:37.) You use your beliefs like searchlights in the dream state, looking for other events that fit in with your ideas about reality. Your convictions help you sift out probable actions— appearing as dreams, of course—from others that do not concern you.

(Slowly:) Since you are not only a physically focused creature, however, other issues also operate. You have within yourself the condensed knowledge of your entire being. This information cannot appear in any complete fashion within a consciousness connected with a physical brain. The multidimensional reality simply cannot be expressed. In the dreaming state, when consciousness relates opaquely to physical concerns, glimpses of the multidimensional self can appear in dream imagery and fantasies that will symbolically express your greater existence.

If your conscious beliefs are causing you great distress, countering beneficial beliefs may be received from this source. Your being, the greater consciousness that is yourself, intersects with space and time; it is born in flesh simultaneously at many [moment] "points." *(See the 668th session in Chapter Nineteen.)* You would call each of these immersions into three-dimensional existence a life, with its own self. And you are one of these.

(Slowly at 9:53:) Each self must experience itself in temporal terms. But every self is also a part of its own greater being, a part of the energy from which it continually comes. In dreams your energy pulsates back toward the being that you are.

(9:56.) In a manner of speaking, you travel back and forth each night through atmospheres and entry points of which you are not aware. In your sleep you do indeed travel, again, those vast distances between birth and death. Your consciousness as you think of it transcends these leaps and holds its own sense of continuity. All of this has to do with pulsations of energy and consciousness, and in one way what you think of as your life is the apparent "length" of a light ray seen from another perspective.

(10:00.) Beneath the dreams that you recall are experiences of consciousness that appear only now and then, and in distorted form. These express in nonphysical terms your relationship with your own being. Here you are regenerated, and you are quite free of any conscious beliefs. From this level individual and mass ideals are formed.

(10:05.) This activity often goes on beneath ordinary dreaming. To a far lesser extent it goes on all the time, for it represents the basis upon which your present consciousness rides.

You may take a break.

(10:09. Resume in the same slow manner at 10:28.)

The physical reality into which you are born is not nearly as solid or predetermined or definite as it appears to be. Instead there is a field of rich interaction. Your consciousness must be focused at one particular range of frequencies before it can even perceive matter, much less solidity. In sleep your consciousness fluctuates between ranges of intensities, literally flowing into and out of the physical-matter grouping, and forming from more plastic "pre-matter" (with a hyphen) stages, the final shape that matter will take in your world. The same applies to events, where some will be crystallized in physical terms and others will not. The deep portions of your own being are aware of those purposes and intents that are uniquely yours. Unconsciously, then, you have within you what you might think of as a set of blueprints for the particular kind of physical reality you want to materialize. You are the architect.

A system of checks and balances exists, however, so that in certain dreams you are made aware of these blueprints. They may appear throughout your lifetime as recurring dreams of a certain nature—dreams of illumination; and even if you do not remember them you will awaken with your purposes strengthened or suddenly clear.

(*Deliberately at 10:42:*) When you are working with your beliefs, find out what you really think about the dream condition, for if you trust it it can become an even more important ally because of your conscious cooperation.

If you want to clear up an argument, tell yourself that you will do so in the dream state. There you can speak freely to those who may avoid you otherwise. Many reconciliations take place at that level. Request the answer to any problem and it will be given, but you must trust yourself and learn to interpret your own dreams. There is no other way to do this except by beginning yourself and working with your own dreams, for this will awaken your intuitive abilities and give you the knowledge that you need.

Your belief in the value of dreams can, therefore, increase their practical effectiveness.

End of chapter.

(*A note: Those who are interested in material on the fluctuations of consciousness can refer to the following sessions in* Seth Speaks: *the 567th session in Chapter Sixteen, on the phasing of atoms in and out of our system; the 576th session in Chapter Nineteen, on alternate presents; and the ESP class session for June, 23, 1970, in the Appendix, on organization in our present reality. Seth states therein: "But the fact is that physical matter is not solid except when you believe that it is . . .")*

*Affirmation, Love,
Acceptance, and Denial*

Now give us a good long moment.

(10:45. Jane, as Seth, took but a moderate pause. She lit a cigarette and sipped at a beer. Eyes closed, she sat rocking back and forth with one foot on the edge of the coffee table between us.)

Chapter Twenty-one: "Affirmation, Love, Acceptance, and Denial." That is the heading.

Now: Affirmation means saying "yes" to yourself and to the life you lead, and to accepting your own unique personhood.

(Pause.) That affirmation means that you declare your individuality. Affirmation means that you embrace the life that is yours and flows through you. Your affirmation of yourself is one of your greatest strengths. You can at times quite properly deny certain portions of experience, while still confirming your own vitality. You do not have to say "yes" to people, issues, or to events with which you are deeply disturbed. Affirmation does not mean a bland wishy-washy acceptance of anything that comes your way, regardless of your feelings about it. Biologically, affirmation means health. You go along with your life,

understanding that you <u>form</u> your experience, emphasizing your ability to do so.

(11:00.) Affirmation does not mean sitting back and saying, "I can do nothing. It is all in Fate's hands, therefore whatever happens, happens." Affirmation is based upon the realization that no other consciousness is the same as your own, that your abilities are uniquely yours and like no other's. It is the acceptance of your individuality in flesh. Basically it is a spiritual, psychic, and biological necessity, and represents your appreciation of your singular integrity.

(Amused:) An atom can take care of itself, but atoms themselves are somewhat like domesticated animals; joining in the biological family of the body, to some extent they become like friendly cats or dogs under your domain.

Animals pick up the characteristics of their owners. Cells are highly influenced by your behavior and beliefs. If you affirm the rightness of your physical being, then you <u>help</u> the cells and organs in your body, and without knowing it treat them kindly. If you do not trust your physical nature you radiate this feeling also, regardless of what health procedures you may take. The cells and organs know that you do not trust them, even as animals do. In a way you set up antibodies against yourself, simply because you do not confirm the rightness of your physical being as it exists in space and time.

Now: You may take a break or end the session as you prefer.

("Let's have the break, then."

(11:10 to 11:29.)

You can affirm your uniqueness quite properly at times by saying "no."

Individuality grants you the right of making decisions. <u>In your terms</u> this means saying "yes" or "no." By implication, to always acquiesce may very well mean that you are denying your own personhood.

"I hate." A person who says "I hate" is at least stating that he <u>has</u> an "I" capable of hating. The one who says, "I have no right to hate," is not facing his own individuality.

A man or woman who knows hate also understands the difference between that emotion and love. The ambiguities, the contrasts, the similarities, the affirmation of the creature self, allows for the free flow of emotion. *(Pause.)* Many disavow the experience of feelings they consider negative. They try to "affirm" what they think of as positive emotions. They do not permit themselves the dimensions of their creaturehood, and by pretending not to feel what they feel, they deny the integrity of their own experience.

(11:37.) The emotions follow beliefs. They are natural ever-changing states of feeling, each leading into another in a free flow of energy and activity—colorful, rich, glowing tints that bring variety to the quality of consciousness. Such states of personality can be compared to colors alone, bright and dark, the strong patterns of energy that always represent motion, life and variety.

To refuse them is futile. They are one of the means by which physically attuned consciousness knows itself. They are not destructive. One emotion is not good and another one evil.

Emotions simply are. They are elements of the power of consciousness, filled with energy. They merge into a powerful sea of being when left alone. You cannot affirm one emotion and deny another without setting up barriers. You try to hide what you think of as negative feelings in the closet of your mind, as in the past they closeted insane relatives. All of this because you do not trust the aspects of your individuality in flesh.

Affirmation means accepting your soul as it appears in your creaturehood. I said this earlier *(in chapters Seven, Nine, etc.),* but you cannot deny your creaturehood without denying your soul, and you cannot deny your soul without denying your creaturehood.

That is the end of our session.

(11:43. "Thank you very much." Seth proceeded to add half a page of material about some beliefs of Jane's that we'd discussed this afternoon. We hadn't thought of asking him to comment on them. End at 11:56 P.M.)

SESSION 673, JUNE 27, 1973,
9:38 P.M. WEDNESDAY

Now: Dictation. *(Slowly, to begin:)* Left alone, hate does not last.

Often it is akin to love, for the hater is attracted to the object of his hatred by deep bonds. It can also be a method of communication, but it is never a steady constant state, and will automatically change if not tampered with.

If you believe that hate is wrong and evil, and then find yourself hating someone, you may try to inhibit the emotion or turn it against yourself—raging against yourself rather than another. On the other hand you may try to pretend the feeling out of existence, in which case you dam up that massive energy and cannot use it for other purposes.

In its natural state, hatred has a powerful rousing characteristic that initiates change and action. Regardless of what you have been told, hatred does not initiate strong violence. As covered earlier in this book, the outbreak of violence is often the result of a built-in sense of powerlessness. Period. *(See sessions 662-63 in Chapter Seventeen.)*

Many who unexpectedly commit great crimes, sudden murders, even bringing about mass death, have a history of docility and conventional attitudes, and were considered models, in fact, of deportment. All natural aggressive elements were denied in their natures, and any evidence of momentary hatred was considered evil and wrong. As a result such individuals find it difficult, finally, to express the most normal denial, or to go against their given code of conventionality and respect. They cannot communicate as, say, even animals can, with their fellow men as far as the expression of a disagreement is concerned.

(9:50.) Psychologically, only a massive explosion can free them. They feel so powerless that this adds to their difficulties—so they try to liberate themselves by showing great power in terms of violence. Some such individuals, model sons,

for example, who seldom even spoke back to their parents, were suddenly sent to war and given carte blanche to release all such feelings in combat; and I am referring particularly to the last two wars *(the war in Korea, 1950-53, and the war in Vietnam, 1964-73)*, not the Second World War.

In these wars aggressions could be released and codes still followed. The individuals were faced, however, with the horror of their violently released, pent-up hatreds and aggressions. Seeing these bloody results, they became even more frightened, more awed by what they thought of as this terrible energy that sometimes seemed to drive them to kill.

On their return home the code of behavior changed back to one suited to civilian life, and they clamped down upon themselves again as hard as they could. Many would appear as superconventional. The "luxury" of expressing emotion even in exaggerated form was suddenly denied them, and the sense of powerlessness grew by contrast.

(Pause at 9:59.) Give us a moment... This is not to be a chapter devoted to war. However, there are a few points that I do want to make. It is a sense of powerlessness that also causes nations to initiate wars. This has little to do with their "actual" world situation or with the power that others might assign to them, but to an overall sense of powerlessness—even, sometimes, regardless of world dominance.

In a way I am sorry that this is not the place to discuss the Second World War *(1939-45)*, for it was also the result of a sense of powerlessness which then erupted into a mass blood bath on a grand scale. The same course was followed privately in the cases of such individuals as just mentioned.

Give us a moment . . . Without going into any detail, I simply want to point out that in the United States strong national efforts were made after World War II to divert the servicemen's energies into other areas on their return home. Many who entered that war feeling powerless were given advantages after it was over—incentives, education, benefits they did not have before it. They were given the means to power in their own eyes. They were also accepted home as <u>heroes</u>, and while many certainly were disillusioned, in the whole framework of the country's mood the veterans were welcomed.

(Pause at 10:11.) I am speaking generally now about the war under discussion, for there were certainly exceptions, yet most of the men involved in it learned something from their experiences. They turned against the idea of violence, and each in his own way recognized the <u>personal</u> psychological ambiguities of their feelings during combat.

They were told by politicians that it was to be the last war, and the irony is that most of those in uniform believed it. *(I, Robert Butts, was one of the believers.)* The lie did not become truth but it became more nearly so, for despite their failures the ex-servicemen managed to bring up children who would not go to war willingly, who would question its premise.

In an odd way this made it even more difficult for those who <u>did</u> go into the next two, less extensive wars, for the country was not behind either one. Any sense of powerlessness on the part of individual fighting men was given expression as before, this time in a more local blood bath, but the code itself had become shaky. This release was not as accepted as it had been before, even within the ranks. By the last war *(in Vietnam)*, the country was as much against it as for it, and the men's feelings of powerlessness were reinforced after it was over. This is the reason for the incidents of violence on the part of returning servicemen.*

Hate, left alone then, does not erupt into violence. Hatred

---

*According to Seth, then, feelings of powerlessness would have much to do with the especially high rate of violence—even to the death—among American servicemen who had once been prisoners of war. A government study of those who had been held captive in the Far East during World War II and the Korean War, for instance, shows that 40% of all the deaths that took place in the group between 1945 and 1954 resulted from murder, suicide or accident.

As for the war in Vietnam: over 500 American military prisoners were released by North Vietnam following the January, 1973, cease-fire. Officials now fear that a good number of these men will come to believe that their suffering was futile because of the war's unpopularity in the United States. There have been suicides among them (as of July), and many have undergone at least temporary stress reactions since their release from prison.

brings a sense of power, and initiates communication and action. In your terms it is the build-up of natural anger; in animals, say, it would lead to a face-to-face encounter, of battle stances in which each creature's body language, motion, and ritual would serve to communicate a dangerous position. One animal or the other would simply back down. Growling or roaring might be involved.

(10:25.) Power would be effectively shown, but symbolically. This type of animal encounter occurs infrequently, for the animals involved would have had to ignore or short-circuit many lesser preliminary anger or initiation encounters, each meant to make positions clear and to ward off violence.

Another small point here: Christ's dictum to turn the other cheek (*Matthew 5:39, for instance*) was a psychologically crafty method of warding off violence—not of accepting it. Symbolically it represented an animal showing its belly to an adversary. (*Jane, as Seth, patted her midriff.*) The remark was meant symbolically. On certain levels, it was the gesture of defeat that brought triumph and survival. It was not meant to be the cringing act of a martyr who said, "Hit me again," but represented a biologically pertinent statement, a communication of body language. Give us a moment . . . (*Softly:*) It would cleverly remind the attacker of the "old" communicative postures of the sane animals.

Now: Love is also a great inciter to action, and utilizes dynamos of energy.

You may take your break.

(*10:35. Jane's trance had been deep on a very humid night. She now told me that while delivering the World War II data for the book, she had been quite aware of another, unspoken, channel from Seth.*

(*That one had been concerned exclusively with the Second World War, Jane said with some surprise, and had contained amazingly complete information on the war's origins and the individual, racial, and reincarnational aspects of it as experienced by the peoples of various nations, whether or not said nations had been directly involved in it. The information had even considered the consequences flowing from the intensified use of technology by the societies of the world after the war. "All of that was coming from* that *way." Jane pointed to her lower left. She spent perhaps ten minutes describing some of the categories inherent in the material, and repeatedly said that she wished we had a record of it. At the same time, although the data was available, we didn't want to lay this book aside to get it.*

(Her awareness of this "probable" channel reminded me that she'd experienced a similar phenomenon in the 666th session in Chapter Eighteen. But now, [as then] when I asked how she could perceive a subjective stream of information from Seth while giving book dictation for him, she couldn't really say. See the 616th session in Chapter Two for her first encounter with multiple channels.)

(Resume at 11:01.)

Now: Love and hate are both based upon self-identification in your experience. You do not bother to love or hate persons you cannot identify with at all. They leave you relatively untouched. They do not elicit deep emotion.

Hatred always involves a painful sense of separation from love, which may be idealized. A person you feel strongly against at any given time upsets you because he or she does not live up to your expectations. The higher your expectations the greater any divergence from them seems. If you hate a parent it is precisely because you expect <u>such love</u>. A person from whom you expect nothing will never earn your bitterness.

In a strange manner, then, hatred is a means of returning to love; and left alone and expressed it is meant to communicate a separation that exists <u>in relation to</u> what is expected.

Love, therefore, can contain hate very nicely. Hatred <u>can</u> contain love and be driven by it, particularly by an idealized love. *(Pause.)* You "hate" something that separates you from a loved object. It is precisely because the object is loved that it is so disliked if expectations are not met. You may love a parent, and if the parent does not seem to return the love and denies your expectations, then you may "hate" the same parent because of the love that leads you to expect more. The hatred is meant to get you your love back. It is supposed to lead to a communication from you, stating your feelings—clearing the air, so to speak, and bringing you closer to the love object. Hatred is not the denial of love, then, but an attempt to regain it, and a painful recognition of circumstances that separate you from it.

If you understood the nature of love you would be able to accept feelings of hatred. Affirmation can include the expression of such strong emotions. Give us a moment . . .

(Pause. I yawned, and Seth caught me at it.

(Amused:) I thought it was more interesting than that.

("It is. Really.")

Dogmas or systems of thought that tell you to rise above your emotions <u>can</u> be misleading—even, in your terms, somewhat dangerous. Such theories are based upon the concept that there is something innately disruptive, base, or wrong in man's emotional nature, while the soul is always depicted as being calm, "perfect," passive and unfeeling. Only the most lofty, blissful awareness is allowed. Yet the soul is above all a fountain of energy, creativity, and action that <u>shows</u> its characteristics in life precisely through the ever-changing emotions.

(11:22.) Trusted, your feelings will lead you to psychological and spiritual states of mystic understanding, calm, and peacefulness. Followed, your emotions will lead you to deep understandings, but you cannot have a physical self without emotions any more than you can have a day without weather.

In personal contact, you can be quite aware of an enduring love for another person, and still recognize moments of hatred when separations of a kind exist that you resent <u>because</u> of the love you know involved.

(As I looked up, Seth said in anticipation of my question:) You can add the word "is" to that sentence *(before "involved")* if you want to. But it is fine without it.

(Slowly:) In the same way, it is possible to love your fellow

human beings on a grand scale, while at times hating them precisely because they so often seem to fall short of that love. When you rage against humanity it is because you love it. To deny the existence of hate then is to deny love. It is not that those emotions are opposites. It is that they are different aspects, and experienced differently. To some extent you want to identify with those you feel deeply about. You do not love someone simply because you associate portions of yourself with another. You often do love another individual because such a person evokes within you glimpses of your own "idealized" self.

(Pause at 11:34.) The loved one draws your best from you. In his or her eyes you see what you can be. In the other's love you sense your potential. This does not mean that in a beloved person you react only to your own idealized self, for you are also able to see in the other, the beloved's potential idealized self. This is a peculiar kind of vision shared by those involved—whether it be wife and husband, or parent and child. This vision is quite able to perceive the difference between the practical and the ideal, so that in ascendant periods of love the discrepancies in, say, actual behavior are overlooked and considered relatively unimportant.

Love is of course always changing. There is no one [permanent] state of deep mutual attraction in which two people are forever involved. As an emotion love is mobile, and can change quite easily to anger or hatred, and back again.

Yet, in the fabric of experience, love can be predominant even while it is not static; and if so then there is always a vision toward the ideal, and some annoyance because of the differences that naturally occur between the actualized and the vision. There are adults who quail when one of their children says, "I hate you." Often children quickly learn not to be so honest. What the child is really saying is, "I love you so. Why are you so mean to me?" Or, "What stands between us and the love for you that I feel?"

The child's antagonism is based upon a firm understanding of its love. Parents, taught to believe that hatred is wrong, do not know how to handle such a situation. Punishment simply adds to the child's problem. If a parent shows fear, then the child is effectively taught to be afraid of this anger and hatred before which the powerful parent shrinks. The young one is conditioned then to forget such instinctive understanding, and to ignore the connections between hatred and love.

You may take a break.

(11:49 to 12:06.)

Now: Often you are taught not only to repress verbal expression of hate, but also told that hateful thoughts are as bad as hateful actions.

You become conditioned so that you feel guilty when you even contemplate hating another. You try to hide such thoughts from yourself. You may succeed so well that you literally do not know what you are feeling on a conscious level. The emotions are there, but they are invisible to you because you are afraid to look. To that extent you are divorced from your own reality and disconnected from your own feelings of love. These denied emotional states may be projected outward upon others—an enemy in a war, a neighbor. Even if you find yourself hating the symbolic enemy, you will also be aware of a deep attraction.

A bond of hate will unite you, but the bond was originally based upon love. In this case however you aggravate and exaggerate all those differences from the ideal, and focus upon them predominantly. In any given case all of this is consciously available to you. It requires only an honest and determined attempt to become aware of your own feelings and beliefs. Even your hateful fantasies, left alone, will return you to a reconciliation and release love.

A fantasy of beating a parent or a child, even to death, will if followed through lead to tears of love and understanding.

Now: I will end our session. My fondest wishes to you both, and good evening.

("Thank you, Seth. Good night." 12:17 A.M.

(A note added later: After comparing the information in this

session with some of Seth's material of previous years, Jane wrote a statement for insertion here:

("In these passages on hate, and elsewhere in this book, Seth goes more deeply into the nature of our emotional life than he has before. His earlier comments on hate, for example, were made when he had to consider the level of understanding of those who were witnessing the session. One such instance is mentioned on page 248 of The Seth Material, *when, in response to a declaration by a student in my ESP class, Seth took the conventional idea of hate for granted on the part of the student. Then he answered accordingly: 'There is no justification for hatred . . . When you curse another, you curse yourselves, and the curse returns to you.' The answer must be considered in the light of the previous conversation, in which the student was trying to justify violence as a means of attaining peace. Seth's main concern was to refute that concept.*

("In this book, Seth leads the reader beyond conventional ideas of good and evil to a new framework of understanding. But even at these deeper levels, hate is not justified, since an honest confrontation with it will lead the individual back to the love upon which it is really based.

("In using the word 'curse,' Seth is not referring to swearing, but to directing hatred against another. Until the individual comes to terms with himself and his emotions, the hatred will return, because it belongs to the one who hates and not to anyone else. The earlier instructions on handling emotions, in Chapter Eleven, provide a framework in which hate can be faced and understood. Also important in this context is Seth's frequent reminder that the expression of normal aggression prevents the buildup of anger into hatred.")

SESSION 674, JULY 2, 1973,
9:23 P.M. MONDAY

Good evening.

("Good evening, Seth."

(With broad humor, eyes wide and dark:) Your friendly cosmic author will now begin dictation.

("Good.")

Affirmation means acceptance of your own miraculous complexity. It means saying "yes" to your own being. It means acquiescing to your reality as a spirit in flesh. Within the framework of your own complexity, you have the right to say "no" to certain situations, to express your desires, to communicate your feelings.

If you do so, then in the great flow and sweep of your eternal reality there will be an overall current of love and creativity that carries you. Affirmation is the acceptance of yourself in your present as the person that you are. Within that acceptance you may find qualities that you wish you did not have, or habits that annoy you. You must not expect to be "perfect." As mentioned earlier, your ideas of perfection mean a state of fulfillment beyond which there is no future growth, and no such state exists. *(See the 626th session in Chapter Five, for instance.)*

"Love your neighbor as yourself." Turn this around and say, "Love yourself as you love your neighbor," for often you will recognize the goodness in another and ignore it in yourself. Some people believe there is a great merit and holy virtue in what they think of as humility. Therefore to be proud of oneself seems a sin, and in that frame of reference true affirmation of the self is impossible. Genuine self-pride is the loving recognition of your own integrity and value. True humility is based upon this affectionate regard for yourself, plus the recognition that you live in a universe in which all other beings also possess this undeniable individuality and self-worth.

False humility tells you that you are nothing. It often hides a distorted, puffed-up, denied self-pride, because no man or woman can really accept a theory that denies personal self-worth.

Fake humility can cause you to tear down the value of others, because if you accept no worth in yourself you cannot see it in anyone else either. True self-pride allows you to perceive the integrity of your fellow human beings and permits you to help them use their strengths. Many people make a great show out of helping others, for example, encouraging them to lean upon them. They believe this to be a quite holy, virtuous enterprise. Instead they are keeping other people from recognizing and using their own strengths and abilities.

(9:40.) Regardless of what you have been told, there is no merit in self-sacrifice. For one thing it is impossible. The self grows and develops. It cannot be annihilated. Usually, self-sacrifice means throwing the "burden" of yourself upon someone else and making it their responsibility.

A mother who says to her child, "I gave up my life for you," is speaking nonsense. In basic terms such a mother believes, no matter _what_ she says, that she did not have that much to give up, and the "giving up" gave her a life that she wanted.

A child who says, "I gave up my life for my parents and devoted myself to their care," means, "I was afraid to live my own life, and afraid to let them live theirs. And so in 'giving up' my life I gained the life I wanted."

Love does not demand sacrifice. Those who fear to affirm their own being also fear to let others live for themselves. You do not help your children by keeping them chained to you, but you do not help your aged parents either by encouraging their sense of helplessness. The ordinary sense of communication given you through your creaturehood, _if_ spontaneously and honestly followed, would solve many of your problems. Only repressed communication leads to violence. The natural force of love is everywhere within you, and the normal methods of communication are always meant to bring you in greater contact with your fellow creatures.

(Pause.) Love yourselves and do yourselves just honor, and you will deal fairly with others. When you say "no," or deny, you always do so because in your mind and feelings, a present situation, or a proposed one, falls far short of some ideal. The refusal is always in response to something that is considered, at least, to be a greater good. If you do not have too-rigid ideas of perfection, then ordinary denial serves a quite practical purpose. But never negate the present reality of yourself because you compare it to some idealized perfection.

Perfection is not being, for all being is in a state of becoming. This does not mean that all being is in a state of becoming perfect, but in a state of becoming more itself. All other emotions are based on love, and in one way or another they all relate to it, and all are methods of returning to it and expanding its capacities.

Now throughout this book I have purposely stayed away from the word "love," because of various interpretations often placed upon it, and because of the errors frequently committed in its name.

Do you want a break?

(9:59. "I guess not.")

You must first love yourself before you love another.

By accepting yourself and joyfully being what you are, you fulfill your own abilities, and your simple presence can make others happy. You cannot hate yourself and love anyone else. It is impossible. You will instead project all the qualities you do not think you possess upon someone else, do them lip service, and hate the other individual for possessing them. Though you profess to love the other, you will try to undermine the very foundations of his or her being.

When you love others, you grant them their innate freedom and do not cravenly insist that they always attend you. There are no divisions to love. There is no basic difference between the love of a child for a parent, a parent for a child, a wife for a husband, a brother for a sister. There are only various expressions and characteristics of love, and all love affirms. It can accept deviations from the ideal vision without condemning them. It does not compare the practical state of the beloved's being with the idealized perceived one that is potential.

In this vision, the potential is seen as present, and the distance between the practical and the ideal forms no contradiction, since they coexist.

480

Now: Sometimes you may think that you hate mankind. You may consider people insane, the individual creatures with whom you share the planet. You may rail against what you think of as their stupid behavior, their bloodthirsty ways, and the inadequate and shortsighted methods that they use to solve their problems. All of this is based upon your idealized concept of what the race should be—your love for your fellow man, in other words. But your love can get lost if you concentrate upon those variations that are less than idyllic.

When you think you hate the race most, you are actually caught in a dilemma of love. You are comparing the race to your loving idealized conception of it. In this case however you are losing sight of the actual people involved.

You are putting love on <u>such</u> a plane that you divorce yourself from your real feelings, and do not recognize the loving emotions that are the basis for your discontent. Your affection has fallen short of itself in your experience because you have denied the <u>impact</u> of this emotion, for fear that the beloved—in this case the race as a whole—will not measure up to it. Therefore you concentrate upon the digressions from the ideal. If, instead, you allowed yourself to free the feeling of love that is actually behind your dissatisfaction, then it alone would allow you to see the loving characteristics in the race that now escape your observation to a large degree.

You may take your break.

(10:24. Jane's hour-long delivery had been steady, forceful, and immune to the very hot and damp evening. She started to become uncomfortable as soon as she left trance, though. Resume at 10:39.)

Now: There is nothing more pompous than false humility.

Many people who consider themselves <u>truth seekers</u> and spiritual are filled with it. They often use religious terms to express themselves. They will say, "I am nothing, but the spirit of God moves through me, and if I do any good it is because of God's spirit and not my own," or, "I have no ability of my own. Only the power of God has any ability."

(Intently:) Now: In those terms you <u>are</u> the power of God manifested. You are not power<u>less</u>. To the contrary. Through your being the power of God is strengthened, for <u>you</u> are a portion of what He is. You are not simply an insignificant, innocuous clump of clay through which He decides to show Himself.

<u>You are He manifesting as you.</u> You are as legitimate as He is.

If you are a part of God then He is also a part of you, and in denying your own worth you end up denying His as well. *(Pause.)* I do not like to use the term "He," meaning God, since All That Is is the origin of not only all sexes but of all realities, in some of which sex as you think of it does not exist.

Affirmation is in the spontaneous motion of the body as it dances. Many churchgoers who consider themselves quite religious do not understand the nature of love or affirmation as much as some bar patrons, who celebrate the nature of their bodies and enjoy the spontaneous transcendence as they let themselves go with the motion of their beings.

(10:48.) True religion is not repressive, as life itself is not. When Christ spoke he did so in the context of his times, using the symbolism and vocabulary that made sense to a particular people in a particular period of history, in your terms.

(It's estimated that Jesus Christ was born between 8 and 5 B.C., and died in A.D. 29 or 30.)

He began with <u>their</u> beliefs, and using their references tried to lead them into freer realms of understanding.

With every translation the Bible has changed its meaning, being interpreted in the language of the times. Christ spoke in terms of good and bad spirits because these represented the people's beliefs. *(See the 647th session in Chapter Twelve for related material.)* In their terms he showed them that "bad" spirits could be vanquished; but these were, then, symbols accepted as realities by the people—sometimes for quite "normal" diseases and human conditions.

(Long pause, eyes closed, at 10:55.) The very term, "Love your neighbor as yourself" *(Matthew 19:19, Mark 12:31)*, was

482

an ironic statement, for in that society <u>no man loved his neighbor</u>, but distrusted him heartily. Much of Christ's humor has been lost, therefore.

In the Sermon on the Mount, the phrase *(to the effect that)* ". . . the meek shall inherit the earth" *(Matthew 5:5)*, has been grossly misinterpreted.

Christ meant, "You form your own reality. Those who think thoughts of peace will find themselves safe from war and dissension. They will be <u>untouched</u> by it. They will escape, and indeed inherit the earth."

Thoughts of peace, particularly in the middle of chaos, take great energy. People who can ignore the physical evidence of wars and purposely think thoughts of peace <u>will</u> triumph—but in your terminology the word "meek" has come to mean spineless, inadequate, lacking energy. In Christ's time, the phrase about the meek inheriting the earth implied the energetic use of affirmation, of love and peace.

(Pause at 11:02. Still in trance, Jane took up a fresh cigarette. Discovering that she'd used her last book match, she pointed to our living room table.)

Will you get Ruburt's lighter?

("Yes . . .")

As I mentioned in *Seth Speaks,* the Christ entity was too great to be contained in any one man, or for that matter in any one time, so the <u>man</u> you think of as Christ was not crucified. *(See chapters Twenty-one and Twenty-two of* Seth Speaks.*)*

Nor was the idea of <u>self-sacrifice</u> then involved. The myth became more "real" than the physical event, which of course is the case in many so-called important historical events. But even the myth was distorted. God did not sacrifice his dearly beloved son by allowing that son to be physical. The Christ entity desired to be born in space and time, to <u>straddle</u> creaturehood in order to serve as a leader, and to translate certain truths in physical terms.

Each of you survive death. The man who was crucified <u>knew</u> this beyond all doubt, and he sacrificed nothing.

("In Seth Speaks *you said that Judas arranged for a substitute to be crucified in place of Christ himself—")*

The "substitute" was a personality <u>seemingly</u> deluded, but in his <u>delusion</u> he knew that each person is resurrected. He took it upon himself to become the symbol of this knowledge.

The man <u>called</u> Christ was not crucified. In the overall drama however it made little difference what was <u>fact</u>, in your terms, and what was not—for the greater reality transcends facts and creates them. You have free will. You could interpret the drama as you wished. It was given to you. Its great creative power still exists and you use it in your own way, even changing your own symbolism as your beliefs change. But the main idea is the affirmation that the physical being, the self that you know, is not annihilated with death. This comes through even in the distortions. The whole concept of God the Father, <u>as</u> given by Christ, was indeed a "new testament." The male image of God was used because of the sex orientation of the times, but beyond this the Christ personality said, ". . . the kingdom of God is <u>within</u> *(among)* you" *(Luke 17:21).*

In a certain way the Christ personality was a <u>manifestation of the evolution of consciousness</u>, leading the race beyond the violent concepts of the times, and altering behavior that had prevailed to that time.

Period. Take your break.

(11:18. Jane remembered only that Seth had talked about Christ and given some Biblical quotations. She knows little about either—or about the Bible itself. As an example, she didn't think ". . . the kingdom of God is within you" was from the Bible, but I located several versions of this saying by Jesus easily enough later: "For lo, the kingdom . . ."; ". . . for in fact . . ."; "For behold . . ."

(Many people have written or called us to ask about Seth's unpublished data on Christ, Biblical events and times, but practically all such material has either been published verbatim or referred to. See Chapter Eighteen of The Seth Material *besides* Seth Speaks *and this book.)*

(A note added later: More information is available, however, in return for the investment in time necessary to receive it. Seth finished his part of the work on this book in mid-July. Not long afterward I came across an illustrated article about Jerusalem in a travel magazine. We saved it for possible reference. One of the photographs accompanying the piece was a double-page, full-color aerial view of the entire city in its desert setting; Jane and I found this so evocative that I mounted it for easy study. Jerusalem's arid environment, coupled with its incredibly complex and active history, led us to speculate anew about the mysterious forces of religious creativity that seemingly had always emanated from there, and were still doing so.

(In a private session on September 3, Seth discussed some of the reasons behind Jerusalem's unceasing fascination for certain segments of mankind. These included probabilities, geography, and unusual interactions involving the past, present and future. Some aspects of the Christ phenomenon were also explained. Then in the next session—which concerned other subjects—Seth unexpectedly added this aside: "You can have more material on Jerusalem or Christ now, or when you want it. You can have the Christ Book *when you want it . . ." But we weren't ready to embark upon such an endeavor at this time.*

(Resume in the same forceful manner at 11:33.)

In terms of time—evolution as you think of it—emerging consciousness had come to the point where it delighted so in distinctions and differences, that even in small geographical areas multitudinous groups, cults and nationalities were assembled, each proudly asserting its own individuality and worth over the others. In the beginning in those terms, man's emerging consciousness needed the freedom to disperse itself, to become different, to originate bases for various characteristics, and assert individuations. By Christ's time, however, some principle of unity was necessary by which this diversification would also experience a sense of unity and feel its oneness.

Christ was the symbol of man's emerging consciousness, holding within himself the knowledge of man's potential. His

485

message was meant to be carried beyond the times, but this interpretation is often not made.

Christ used parables that were applicable then (*as described in all four of the Gospels*). He used priests as symbols of authority (*Matthew 21:23-27*). He turned water into wine (*John 2:1-11*), yet many who consider themselves quite holy ignore Christ at the wedding feast and think any alcoholic beverage degrading.

He "consorted" with prostitutes (*Luke 7:33-50*) and the poor, and his disciples were hardly men that would be called the city fathers. Yet, many who consider themselves religious people hold on to respectability most of all. Christ used the vernacular of the times and in his own way spoke out against dogmatic ideas, as well as temples that pretended to be repositories of holy knowledge but were instead concerned with money and prestige. (*Mark 11:15-18*). Yet many who consider themselves followers of Christ now turn against the outcasts that he himself considered brothers and sisters.

He affirmed the reality of the individual over any organization, while still realizing that some system was necessary. His whole message was that the exterior world is the manifestation of the interior one, that the "kingdom of God" is made flesh.

There are indeed lost gospels, written by men in other countries in that time, relating to Christ's unknown life, to episodes not given in the Bible. These formed a quite separate framework of knowledge that could be accepted by people who had different beliefs than the Jews at that time. The messages were given in other terms, but again they reflected the affirmation of the self and its continued existence after physical death. Love was always stressed.

(*11:52.*) One of the Gospels is counterfeit—that is, it was written after the others, and the events twisted to make it appear that some of them happened in a completely different context than they did. Regardless, Christ's message was one of affirmation.

(*Jane, in trance, paused as I looked up questioningly. "I was*

486

going to ask which Gospel is counterfeit, because we're sure to get letters about that.")

It was not Mark's or John's. There are particular reasons why I do not want to specify now.

("Okay," I said, although somewhat reluctantly.

(Pause.) At the time, Christ united man's consciousness in ways that reached out into history. The Christ consciousness was not isolated. I am speaking in your terms now. The same consciousness gave birth to all of your religions, therefore; the various frameworks through which the peoples of different times could express themselves and grow. In all cases the religions began with the beliefs prevailing, spoke through the dictums of the times, and then expanded. Now this represents the spiritual side of man's evolution. The idea-frameworks of psychic and mental life were far more important than the physical aspects as the species grew and changed.

(Abruptly stronger:) That is the end of the session. My heartiest good wishes to you both, and a fond good evening.

("Thank you very much, Seth. It's been most interesting. Good night." End at 12:02 A.M.

(After the session Jane tried a brief experiment. I explained the little I knew about the Gospels to her, and suggested that she attempt to psychically determine whether the "counterfeit" Gospel was that according to Matthew or Luke. In a moment, without trying too hard, Jane said it was Matthew's. She didn't know why she came up with that answer and she didn't try to find out more—nor, she said, did her statement necessarily constitute a reply from or through Seth. It's generally thought that the Gospel according to Mark was written first.

(All dates given are approximate: Many Biblical scholars think the Gospels were composed between A.D. 60 to 100, well after the death of Christ in A.D. 29 or 30. Various recent claims and assorted kinds of evidence have tended to push the writing of Mark's Gospel [which Seth asserts is genuine] back to as early as A.D. 35—much closer, of course, to the time when Christ lived.)

487

SESSION 675, JULY 4, 1973,
10:20 P.M. WEDNESDAY

(*Jane and I had driven through the hilly, very lush countryside around Elmira this afternoon; the sunny day had been just about perfect. Our living room was very warm, though, as we sat for the session at 9:25. All of the windows were open. We could hear the very evocative popping of firecrackers a block or so away in the night.*

(*As we waited for the session Jane began to enter a transcendent, or enhanced, state of consciousness. I started noting down her experiences, but missed out on some of her descriptions because of the speed with which she talked. Her hands acquired a velvety, luxurious "inner smoothness." Then she had the feeling of those familiar "giant faces" peering down into our universe—and rather nostalgically, too, she laughed. [See the extensive notes for the 653rd session in Chapter Thirteen, describing her various states of altered perception last April 2. In one of those intervals she'd sensed giants standing about the rim of our world.] Now, Jane said, from their massive viewpoint these observers could see "everything happening at once in our world, from California to Russia—like astronauts looking back at us . . .*

(*"I'd better get back to the session; but I'm up to something," she continued, pleased. She sat upright in her rocker, listening, making connections. "I'm getting that thrilling sound through my stomach as I hear the cars turn the corner. And those firecrackers sound like 'wrinkles' in the air, going out in all directions . . . Oh, that traffic's fascinating—it does things to my head and ears, inside. And when I poured my beer now, just for a second I got that feeling of being giant-sized myself.*

(*"When I tune into Seth Two,* I become bigger—my*

---

*Jane speaks for the Seth Two personality occasionally; and that concept is related to the giant-size phenomena.

Chapter Twenty-two of *Seth Speaks* contains additional material on Seth Two. In the 589th session Seth tells us in part: " . . . there is the same kind of connection between that personality and myself as the one that exists between Ruburt and *perceptive abilities enlarge to take that experience in . . . Right now I feel that when I close my eyes the earth, the whole globe, is inside my head. You don't understand it until you close your eyes. I wish I could put this into words; but you've got to realize that events* outside *the body are the* same *events as those* inside *the body—the behavior of its neurons and all of its chemical activities . . . and because inside and outside are so beautifully synchronized, everything will always agree.*

(*"Oh, of course!" she exclaimed. "If something dies in your head, a cell maybe, something also dies in the outside world: an insect, a person. There's an instant correlation that I can't explain. New births are the same way. The sounds of the firecrackers are the* same sounds *that events inside the body make. That's why Seth is right: An outside event* is *an inside one. But I've got to get back to the session . . .*

(*"There's a fantastic richness out there." Jane nodded toward the open windows. "There's a fantastic correlation between seasonal variations and the* length *of thoughts that nobody's suspected. Thoughts make traces on an interior level. You could make graphs of your thoughts and they'd match up with seasonal changes, with the tides and the phases of the moon. But all of those things that seem to be outside are just the manifestations of our bodily rhythms."*

(*10:05. "I do want to have a session, only this is so much fun—it makes you feel so great! But I'll have a cigarette and turn into Seth." With something of an effort Jane gradually quieted her mood. At the same time, she maintained that tonight's revelations had taken place for a reason. So they had, as we soon learned.*

(*"Right now I feel a BIG SETH around," she smiled, "and I'm trying to get him down to session size. If he came through like he is now, his voice would be so strong it would drown out everything else in the world. I know that's an analogy, of*

myself. But in your terms, Seth Two is far further divorced from my reality than I am from Ruburt's. You can imagine Seth Two as a future portion of me if you prefer, and yet far more is involved."

course . . . And now I feel, strongly enough to mention it, that my legs are growing down through the floor and my head's growing up toward the ceiling . . ."

(She flopped back in her rocker, her eyes closed. As if on signal a brisk wind swept the window curtains in; papers rustled and shifted in the room; the small explosions of the firecrackers became suddenly louder. The living room cooled off nicely—and Jane finally did bring Seth down to manageable size. She took off her glasses.)

Good evening.

("Good evening, Seth.")

Dictation: Affirmation then means the loving acceptance of your own unique individuality. It may involve denial, where you refuse to accept the visions or dogmas of others in order to more clearly perceive and form your own.

Such affirmation will lead you to your own inner discoveries, and attract from the deepest portions of your being the particular kind of information, experience, or perception that you need. The loving acceptance of yourself will allow you to ride through beliefs as you would through the changing characteristics of a countryside. The more a belief encourages you to use your abilities and vitality, then the more affirmative it is.

Ruburt's perception is highly altered this evening, and this is an example of certain kinds of both affirmation and denial. He has always emphasized his own unique creative and intuitive processes. In so doing, he denied many of the concepts believed in by others. He accepted the belief that any consciousness could be in some kind of direct intimate contact with experiences and realities usually not perceived, but ignored.

He knew there were many different ways of experiencing even the physical world, and so he rejected all concepts that told him otherwise. The very belief allowed him to use those abilities, and as muscles become more resilient with use, so do psychic and intuitive powers.

490

(Pause at 10:32. Intermittently, the breeze still whipped into the room . . .)

The legs run, and leap over areas of ground. They cannot themselves interpret the reality beneath them. The feet are not aware of the ants they crush. They may feel the grass or sidewalk or the road, but the peculiar individual sensate life of the grass itself, or of the ant, escapes the feet, which are involved in their own reality and concerned with these other things only in their <u>relationship</u> to feethood.

The mind can interpret the experiences that the legs and the feet have, however, and by imaginatively using that sensual data can perceive the ant's reality to some extent. Now when the <u>mind</u> races and runs, it sometimes has great difficulty interpreting its activities to the brain, which is usually concerned with other realities only to the extent that they impinge upon it.

Now: Ruburt's mind is far more aware of other realities than his brain is, but he consciously believes in the greater reality of himself and his perceptions. The brain also possesses this belief, and so it opens itself as much as possible to the mind's activities. <u>Because</u> it does, certain intuitive psychic and "intellectually spacious" experiences can be physically <u>felt</u> to some extent. The knowledge is interpreted through alterations in body sensation, which give it an important corporeal validity. In such cases high mental and psychic activity is reflected in the body's experience, providing a beneficial unity.

Here I have used the term "spacious" for workings of the mind and intuitions that exist in what you might call an accelerated range of action. The normal intellect, oriented so precisely <u>by beliefs</u> to the inevitability of a one-focused kind of perception, is limited.

(10:45.) A certain kind of affirmation of self allows the brain to tune into these more spacious methods of perception that are the natural characteristics of the mind. There are very good reasons why this type of assertion must first occur. The brain (and the entire physical system) is meant to insure your bodily

survival and to follow your conscious beliefs about reality. There is always a harmonious unifying connection between your beliefs and activities. Some people feel utterly confident in certain areas and are timorous in others. Some aspects of life may be ignored or even refuted for a time while others are focused upon. The individual will very cleverly and shrewdly go ahead in those areas in which he or she feels safe, often when in the process of altering beliefs. You will not use your spacious mind until you affirm its reality within yourself, and until you are ready to handle the additional data which will then become consciously available to one extent or another. But the spacious mind operates through your creaturehood; in your terms it represents latent abilities of consciousness that can be more or less normal functions.

There are built-in biological structures that are activated for the reception of such messages, and they have always been a part of your physical nature as a species. They will not be triggered on a personal basis until your own beliefs allow you to perceive the multidimensional layers of your own experience— or at least to accept the possibilities.

(*Pause.*) As Ruburt's episode tonight shows, even normal sense data then achieves a kind of multidimensionality, a richness rather impossible to describe. This automatically provides a biological learning process in which the senses can be used in a freer, deeper fashion. While such occurrences are not constant, they are frequent enough so that ordinary experience is changed. The richness overlaps.

(*11:00.*) You do not have to know anything about so-called psychic matters necessarily. Many individuals use the spacious mind and its perceptions, taking it for granted without realizing how different their own perception is from that of others.

Ruburt wondered about this next matter, which is related: Physiologically you carry within yourselves remnants of your evolution, in your terms—physical vestiges of organs and other attributes long discarded. You follow me here.

(*"Yes."*)

In the same way you also carry within you structures <u>not yet</u> fully used; those organizations point—in your terms now— toward future evolution. Use of the spacious mind involves these. Individuals through all the ages have experienced this other kind of awareness, though never to its fullest form.

(Long pause at 11:05, eyes closed.) Experience with the spacious mind dissolves any seeming conflicts that occur between the intellect and the intuitions at other levels. To whatever extent possible, the physical organism interprets that unity through a new mixture of sense data, so that materially the information makes sense.

An individual can tune into spacious-mind operation two or three times in a lifetime without realizing it, and have experiences that he finds difficult to interpret later. The affirmation involved is one of transcendence, in which for a time a person affirms his reality in flesh and at the same time states his independence from it *(smile)*—and realizes that both of these conditions exist simultaneously. A dual perception takes place in which the spacious mind is activated. By "activated" I mean that the physical organism is <u>suddenly aware</u> of [the spacious mind's] existence.

You may take your break.

(11:14. Jane's delivery had moved right along for the most part. "But I had a hell of a time getting into the session," she said, "because I was having such a ball with those sounds. I'm glad I did, though . . ." Her state of altered consciousness lingered. "Right now, even, my voice sounds just great to me, and my hands feel real liquidy, almost like water . . ."

(The wind had quieted. We didn't hear firecrackers any longer, just the smoothly rushing traffic sounds. I made Jane a peanut butter sandwich, using whole wheat bread. When she picked it up she said, staring, "It's almost as if you've got to choose between biting into the sandwich, your hand that holds it, or your knee beneath the hand—not because you're disoriented but because everything's all one. When you grow aware of that, then you're confronted with making conscious choices."

(She became really absorbed in the texture of the bread, the feel of it in her mouth. "When I break this bread apart," she said, "I know it makes sounds I don't hear, so I substitute the sound of that car turning the corner just now. I feel a strong correlation between the bread going down my throat and the traffic . . ."

(Resume very quietly at 11:51.)

Now: When utilized properly and fully in your terms of time, the spacious mind will vastly enrich the dimensions of the species, bringing the body into a greater harmony than now possible.

On a neurological basis there are unreleased, latent triggers that <u>can</u> be set off, and when they are, your practical experience with time as you know it will be altered. From your viewpoint the species will then be so different that it will seem to be another one entirely. As Ruburt once suggested, your [modern] system of communications has already expanded the data available to a private conscious mind in a given amount of time, and this on a purely physical level.

You have to handle and assimilate information now available as to happenings in other places that, in previous centuries, no ordinary individual would have been aware of. Events in distant places then become present knowledge. Time intervals between an episode and your knowledge of it are shortened, though the event may occur on the other side of the world.

Jet travel scrambles your idea and experience of time, and in so doing alters your concepts of it. But within the mechanisms of the body there are unused and unrecognized triggers that will allow you, as a species, to consciously handle greater perceptions of time just as you now handle greater perceptions of space.

(12:02.) In a very limited and fumbling manner this is hinted at through the use of computers, where you try to assess "future probabilities" and act accordingly in your present. The mind can do this far better than any computer. If it believed this, then certain portions of the brain would be activated. The

brain would become aware of more of the mind's knowledge, and the probabilities of future events would be made consciously available.

Now the brain would have to sort out this information so that the physically attuned mechanism was clearly able to maintain its temporal present. When man first developed the pause of reflection, as mentioned earlier in this book *(see sessions 635-36 in Chapter Nine)*, he did undergo initial disorientation before he learned to distinguish a vividly remembered event of the past from a presently experienced one. The growing consciousness had to make such distinctions for practical behavior. To utilize future probable events, the physical brain would be forced to enlarge its function while keeping the individual in clear relationship with the present moment of power, or corporeal effectiveness. Affirmation always involves the acknowledgement of your power in the present. In greater terms, denial is the surrendering of that power. Affirmation then is the acquiescence to your ability, as a spirit within flesh, to form the physical reality of your creaturehood.

Now you can alter your present through altering your past, or you can change your present from the future. *(See sessions 653-54 in Chapter Fourteen.)* Even these manipulations must take place in your practical-experienced present, however. Many people have at one time or another changed their present behavior in response to the advice of a "future" probable self, without ever knowing they have done so.

Suppose you have a particular goal in mind as a youngster, toward which you work. Your intent, images, desires and determination form a psychic force that is projected out ahead of you, so to speak. You send the reality of yourself from your present into what you think of as the future.

Now: Say that at a certain stage you have some decisions to make and do not know which way to turn. You may sense that you are in danger of swerving from your purpose, yet for other reasons feel strongly inclined to do so. In a dream or in daydreaming, you may suddenly hear a voice, mentally, that tells you in no uncertain terms to go ahead with your initial intent. Or in some other way you may receive the same information—through an urge, or a vision, or simply by suddenly knowing what to do. This happens in your present.

(12:21.) In other terms, the self that you have projected into the future is sending you back encouragement from a probable reality that you still can create. That focused self operates from its present, however, and some day in your own future you may find yourself thinking nostalgically of a moment back in your own past, when you were indecisive and irresolute, but took the proper course.

You may think, "I am glad I did that," or, "Knowing what I know now, how lucky I am that I made that decision." And in that moment you are the future self that "once" spoke encouragingly to the person of the past. The probable future has caught up with the practical present.

New paragraph: The early affirmation of yourself projected into the future made such an incident possible. In the same way your acceptance of yourself and your own integrity can, at any moment in your present, alter your past and future.

(Forcefully:) End of chapter.

CHAPTER **22**

*Affirmation, the Practical Betterment
of Your Life, and the New Structuring
of Beliefs*

(At once at 12:25:) New chapter heading [Twenty-two:]
"Affirmation, the Practical Betterment of Your Life, and the
New Structuring of Beliefs."

End of session.

("All right.")

(Amused:) I try to give you the heading for the next chapter
even at the end of a session, so that Ruburt knows what I am
doing. It gives him confidence. A hearty good evening to both
of you.

*("Thank you very much, Seth. Good night." End at 12:28
A.M. Jane's altered perceptions continued.)*

SESSION 676, JULY 9, 1973,
9:32 P.M. MONDAY

*(We were ready for the session at 9:15. Once again the evening
was very warm. We had our fan going, but at low speed so that it
wasn't too noisy; actually we seldom use it. I read Jane the title of
Chapter Twenty-two, thinking that its indicated subject matter
meant Seth was close to finishing his book . . .)*

Good evening.

("Good evening, Seth.")

Dictation: If you have a loving regard for yourself, then you will trust in your own direction.

You will accept your present position, whatever it is, as being a part of that direction, and realize that from it can come all the creative elements that you need. Being yourself and trusting in your own integrity, you will automatically help others. It does little good to repeat a suggestion such as, "I am a worthy person. I trust myself and my integrity," if at the same time you are afraid of your own emotions and become upset whenever you catch yourself in what you think of as a negative frame of mind.

As lovers can see the "ideal" in their beloved, and yet be well aware of certain inadequacies, certain deviations from the ideal, so can you, loving yourself, realize that what you think of as imperfections are instead gropings toward more complete becoming. You cannot love yourself and hate the emotions that flow through you at the same time; because while you are not your emotions, you identify with them so often that in hating them you hate yourself.

Use your conscious mind and its logic. If you discover that you feel unworthy, then do not simply try to apply a more positive belief over that one. Instead discover the reasons for your first belief. If you have not already done so, write down your feelings about yourself. Be perfectly honest. What would you say if someone else came to you with the same reasons?

Examine what you have written. Realize that a set of beliefs is involved. There is a difference between believing that you are unworthy and being unworthy in fact.

(9:46.) Then write a list of your abilities and accomplishments. These should include such issues as getting along well with others, being attractive, being good with plants or animals, being a good carpenter or cook. Any talent or achievement should be noted as honestly as you recorded the most minute "defects" earlier.

There is no human being alive who does not have creative abilities in his or her own way, achievements and excellent characteristics, so if you follow these instructions you will find out that you are indeed a worthy individual.

When you catch yourself falling into a mood in which you feel inferior, look at your second list, of abilities and accomplishments. Then use the positive suggestion in your own worth, backed up by your own personal self-examination. You may say, "But I know I have great abilities that I am not using. When I compare myself to others, then I fall far short. What difference does it make if I have a few mundane achievements that are shared by many others, that are in no way unique? Surely my destiny involves more than that. I have yearnings that I cannot express."

In the first place you must understand that in your own uniqueness it is futile to compare yourself to others, for in so doing you try to emulate qualities that are theirs, and to that extent deny your own miraculous being and vision. Once you begin comparing yourself to others there is no end to it. You will always find someone more talented than you are in some way, and so will continue to be dissatisfied. Instead, through working with your own beliefs, take it for granted that your life is important; begin with it and where you are. Do not deride yourself because you have not reached some great ideal, but start to use those talents that you have to the best of your ability, knowing that in them lies your own individual fulfillment.

(10:01.) Any help that you give to others will come through the creative utilization of your own characteristics and no one else's. Do not get upset with yourself when you find yourself dwelling on negative issues in your life. Instead, constructively ask yourself why you are doing so. The answer will come to you.

Use the knowledge as a bridge. Let whatever emotions are involved happen. If you do this honestly, feelings of self-worthlessness or despondency will go through and vanish, changing of their own accord. You may even find yourself impatient with the feelings themselves, or even bored, and hence dismiss them. Do not tell yourself automatically that they are wrong, however, and then try to apply a "positive" belief like a bandaid.

Have a sense of humor about yourself—not a malicious one but a kindly humorous regard for yourself. High seriousness is fine when it comes naturally and is not forced. But it can become pompous if it is prolonged.

If you allow yourself to be more and more aware of your own beliefs, you can work with them. It is silly to try to fight what you think of as negative beliefs, or to be frightened of them. They are not mysterious. You may find that many served good purposes at one time, and that they have simply been overemphasized. They may need to be restructured rather than denied.

Take your break.

(10:11 to 10:28.)

Some beliefs may work very positively for you for certain periods of your life. Because you have not examined them, however, you may carry them long after they have served their purpose, and now they may work against you.

New sentence: For example, many of the young believe at one time or another that their parents are omnipotent—a very handy belief that gives children a sense of security. Grown into adolescent years, the same offspring are then shocked to discover their parents to be quite human and fallible, and another conviction often takes over: a belief in the inadequacy and inferiority of the older generations, and in the rigidity and callousness of those who run the world.

Many embarking upon young adulthood think that the older generations have done everything wrong. However, this belief frees them from childish concepts in which older persons were always not only right but infallible, and it gives them the challenge to tackle personal and world problems.

For a while the new adults often feel themselves to be

invincible, beyond the boundaries of creaturehood, even; this belief, again, endows them with the strength and energy they need to begin a life for themselves and to form their own mass world. Yet in material terms they must all realize, sooner or later, not only the challenges but the other peculiar characteristics of creaturehood, in which basically no such generalized beliefs make sense.

(10:39.) If at the age of forty you still believe in the infallibility of your parents, then you hold that idea way beyond its advantageous state for you. Using the methods in this book, you should discover the reasons for this belief, for it will prevent you from exerting your own independence and making your own world. If you are fifty and are still convinced that the older generations are rigid, fast in the way of growing senile, mentally incompetent and physically deteriorating, then you are holding an old belief in the ineffectiveness of the older generations and setting up negative suggestions for yourself. Conversely, if you are fifty and still believe that youth is the one glorious and effective part of a lifetime, you are of course doing the same thing.

A young adult gifted in a particular area may hold a belief that this ability makes him or her superior to all others. This may be quite beneficial for the person involved at a given time, to provide the needed impetus for development and the necessary independence in which the ability can grow. The same person, years older, may find that the identical belief has been held too long, so that it denies very important emotional give-and-take with contemporaries, or becomes restrictive in other ways.

(Pause at 10:48.) A young mother may believe that her child is even more important than her husband, and according to the circumstances this belief may help her pay the necessary attention to the child—but if the concept is held as the child grows older, then this can also become highly restrictive. A woman's entire adult life can be structured according to such an idea if she does not learn to examine the contents of her mind.

A belief that has positive results for a woman of twenty will not necessarily have the same effect for a woman of forty, who, for example, may still pay far more attention to her children than her husband.

Many of your beliefs are of course cultural, but you have still accepted those that served your own purposes. As a rule, men in your society believe themselves logical while women are considered intuitive. Women, now trying to assert their rights, often fall into the same trap, but backwards—trying to deny what they think of as inferior intuitive elements for what they think of as superior logical ones.

Certain beliefs then will structure your lives, often for given periods. You will grow out of many of them. When you do, the inner structuring will change, but you must not cravenly acquiesce to "leftover" beliefs once you recognize them.

"I feel inferior because my mother hated me," or, "I feel unworthy because I was scrawny and small as a child." You may find as you work with your beliefs that a feeling of inferiority seems to stem from such episodes. It is up to you as an adult to get on top of your beliefs, to realize that a mother who hates her child is already in difficulties, and that such a hate says far more about the mother than it does about her offspring. It is up to you to understand that you are now a grown person, and not a child to be bullied.

(11:01.) Set aside:

The Point of Power Is in the Present.

That point is not in the past unless you abjectly decide to acquiesce to worn-out beliefs that no longer serve you.

If you believed you were unworthy because you were scrawny and bullied, then in some way you undoubtedly used that belief for your own purposes. Admit it. Discover what the purposes were. Perhaps you compensated—became athletic later, or used the impetus to go ahead in your own way. If your mother hated you, you may have used that to assert independence, to give you an excuse or a pathway; but in all cases you form your own reality, and so you agreed to it.

(*Pause.*) Many people who write to me feel that they have unusual psychic or writing abilities, or sense an outstanding need to help others. They constantly compare what they do with what they think they are capable of, but often without making a start toward the development of their own abilities.

They want to write great philosophical theories, for example, perhaps never putting the pen to the paper, or trusting themselves enough to begin. Some want to HELP THE WORLD AT LARGE—in capital letters—but all they do is think about this desire without trying to implement it at all in practical terms. The ideal in their minds becomes so great that they are always dissatisfied with their own performance; yet they are afraid to make a start.

The loving acknowledgement of their own uniqueness would in itself show them how to begin to use their own abilities in their own way, and to trust their present situation. The ideal is not yet materialized. It is just the essence of a direction. But that direction can only be found by using what you have in the now that you know, and be acquiescing to your own opportunities and abilities, and using those through the power of the present.

You may take your break.

(*11:13 P.M. Jane's delivery had been steady and on the quiet side, usually, except for the underlined words and phrases that Seth had called for.*

(*The night had cooled off comfortably. "But you know what?" Jane asked. "Right now I feel really tired . . ." Break proved to be the end of the session. After debating about whether or not to go back into trance, she finally decided against it.*)

SESSION 677, JULY 11, 1973,
9:36 P.M. WEDNESDAY

Good evening.

(*"Good evening, Seth."*)

Dictation: There is certainly nothing wrong in asking for help from others when you think that you need it, and sometimes much to be gained.

There are those who make a practice of seeking aid from others, however, using this as a means of avoiding responsibility. In specific physical problems, help should be sought in areas in which you have little knowledge. But many people look to those outside themselves—psychics, doctors, psychiatrists, priests, ministers, friends—for the answers to overall life situations, and in so doing they deny their own abilities of self-understanding and growth.

Because of your educational framework, the individual is taught to be wary of the inner self, as mentioned earlier *(in the 614th session in Chapter Two, for instance)*, so unfortunately the ordinary man or woman looks for the solutions of personal problems outside of the self, where they can least be found. If you use the methods given in this book, you should know yourself far more intimately than you did before, and be better equipped to handle your personal reality. Simply knowing that you form your reality can free you from some limiting concepts that have held you back in the past. You can then examine your beliefs creatively, finding the correlations between them and your experience. The conscious knowledge alone will trigger intuitional responses within the inner self so that you will receive helpful information through dreams, impulses, and ordinary thought patterns.

(Pause at 9:47.) If you affirm the basic grace of your being, then this will automatically weaken the beliefs you have that are contrary to that principle. You will be able to hold equally within your experience the vision of an "ideal self" and all those natural deviations from it.

(Quite slowly:) You will begin with where you are and joyfully start to expand those attributes that you have now, without expecting them to appear full-blown. You will love yourself and have no difficulty in loving your neighbor. That does not mean that you must be unaware of divergences from your ideal concept of the beloved. And again, it does not mean

that you must smile constantly, but that you affirm your validity and grace within the dimensions of your creaturehood.

As soon as you begin to compare what you are with some idealized concept of yourself, you automatically feel guilty. Until you work with your beliefs, this guilt can be initiated by the most harmless episodes and characteristics. It is a good idea to write down a list of specific acts or incidents that fill you with a sense of guilt. Often you will be able to trace them to early childhood beliefs quite easily—some instilled by a well-meaning parent to protect you, or out of an adult's ignorance. Brought into the open, however, many of these will dissolve before your comprehension.

When you affirm your own rightness in the universe, then you cooperate with others easily and automatically as a part of your own nature. You, being yourself, help others be themselves. You are not jealous of talents you do not possess, and so you can openheartedly encourage them in others. Because you recognize your own uniqueness you will not need to dominate others, nor cringe before them.

(10:01.) You must begin to trust yourself sometime. I suggest you do it now. If you do not then you will forever be looking to others to prove your own merit to you, and you will never be satisfied. You will always be asking others what to do, and at the same time resenting those from whom you seek such aid. It will seem to you that their experience is legitimate and yours counterfeit. You will feel shortchanged.

(Pause at 10:06. Our cat, Willy, had been sick so we'd kept him with us during the session. Waking up now, he strolled over to Jane as she sat in her rocker speaking for Seth. He crouched, preparing to spring up into her lap. I called him; whereupon he chose to curl up beside me on the couch instead.

(Jane remained in trance. Later, she told me, Seth waited with "affectionate amusement" for the episode to resolve itself.)

You will find yourself exaggerating the negative aspects of your life, and the positive sides of other people's experiences.

You are a <u>multidimensional</u> personality. Trust the miracle of your own being. Make no divisions between the physical and the spiritual in your lifetimes, for the spiritual speaks with a physical voice and the corporeal body is the creation of the spirit.

Do not place the <u>words</u> of gurus, ministers, priests, scientists, psychologists, friends—or <u>my</u> words—higher than the feelings of your own being. You can learn much from others, but the deepest knowledge must come from within yourself. Your own consciousness is embarked upon a reality that basically can be experienced by no other, that is unique and untranslatable, with its own meaning, following its own paths of becoming.

You share an existence with others who are experiencing their own journeys <u>in their own ways</u>, and you have journeying in common, then. Be kind to yourself and to your companions.

I am also journeying. What information and knowledge I have I try to give to you through Ruburt and Joseph *(pause)*, who are parts of me in your space and time. But they are <u>themselves</u> as I am myself.

You may take your break.

(10:17. Jane's trance had been good, her delivery even and rather quiet. "You know," she said, "I thought this book was going to go longer, but I've got the funny nostalgic feeling that Seth's going to end it real soon. I've got the shivers. I don't know about you," she laughed, "but I'd like to see it last another five chapters... I felt the same way about Seth Speaks; *the end always shocks me." I told her that I thought Seth would close out the book tonight. I joked that we could ask for the title of his next one. "Oh, he's got them stacked up to here," and Jane patted the top of her head.*

(A note pertaining to the material given just before break: In Chapter Nineteen Seth deals with reincarnation in a general sense, but he's said little in this book about his psychic "connections" with Jane and me. There are references to such ties scattered through The Seth Material *and* Seth Speaks *[see the 595th session in the Appendix of the latter], and we have a*

modest amount of unpublished information. But to explore the ramifications of reincarnation just as it involves the three of us, for example, would take a book in itself . . .

(Resume at 10:37.)

Now: Dictation: Ruburt's own beliefs in the nature of his consciousness helped bring about these sessions.

Ruburt and Joseph have both worked with the nature of creativity, and from an early age each of them sought for answers—but most of all they trusted the destiny and grace of their beings.

They might have felt that they had lost direction at times. For certain periods they might have had problems in which they forgot their aims momentarily, and yet their beliefs in themselves individually and together were strong enough to give them their present reality.

Many who write want to develop and use the same abilities, yet it is obvious from their letters that their beliefs prevent them from trusting the inner self enough. You cannot fear your own being and expect to travel through it, to explore its dimensions. First you must take the simple step of affirming your identity. That affirmation will release those attributes that you have and open up new avenues of experience. They will and must be your own. When you ask others to interpret your dreams, for example, you are automatically putting the fulfillment of your own potentials a step away. When you ask another to tell you the direction of your life, then to some extent you keep from yourself the realization that you yourself possess it. Without that awareness no methods will help you.

(10:49.) Now: In ordinary terms, this book has included no esoteric instructions to help you achieve what you may think of as spiritual development or psychic expertise. Yet it is a preliminary for all of those who want to use creaturehood as a framework through which to perceive and experience other realities.

As I mentioned earlier, you will not become more spiritual by denying your flesh. *(See Chapter Seven.)* This is the life you are living! Trust the living that flows through you. By doing so, other realities will make themselves known. They will add dimension and depth to your present reality.

Set apart:

> You Make Your Own Reality—Wherever You Travel,
> and in Whichever Dimension You Find Yourself.

Before you embark upon other journeys of consciousness, understand that your beliefs will follow you and form your experience there as they do here. If you believe in demons you will meet them—in this life as enemies, and in other realms of consciousness as devils or "evil spirits."

If you are frightened of your emotions and believe them wrong, then when you try "psychic" experiments you may believe that you are possessed. Your feelings, the repressed ones, will seem demonic. You will be afraid to assign them to yourself, and so will think that they belong to a disembodied spirit. It is very important then that you understand the true innocence of all feelings, for each of them, if left alone and followed, will lead you back to the reality of love.

(Pause at 11:00.) Trust no person who tells you that you are evil or guilty by reason of your nature or your physical existence, or any such dogma. Trust no one who leads you away from the reality of yourself. *(Long pause, eyes closed.)* Do not follow those who tell you that you must do penance, in whatever form. Trust instead the spontaneity of your own being and the life that is your own. If you do not like where you are, then examine those beliefs that you have. Bring them out into the open. There is nothing within yourself to fear.

Separately:

> My Life Is Mine, and I Form It.

Tell yourself this often. Create your own life now, using your beliefs as an artist uses color. There is no condition that you

508

cannot change, except one indisputably physically accepted at birth within the realms of creaturehood, such as a liability in terms of a missing organ, or a functional lack.

If you have been filled with self-pity because of a disease or a life situation, then seize the initiative. Face your beliefs honestly and find out the reason for the difficulty.

(*More intently:*) I speak with the inner vitality that is inherent within each of my readers, with the inner knowledge that also belongs to them.

I close by saying, as I have said before: You are given the gift of the gods; you create your reality according to your beliefs; yours is the creative energy that makes your world; there are no limitations to the self except those you believe in.

I am Seth. I speak my name joyfully, though names are not important. Then each of you speak your names with affirmation every morning.

You create your life through the inner power of your being (*pause*), whose source is within you and yet beyond the selves that you know. Use those creative abilities with understanding abandon. Honor yourselves and move through the godliness of your being.

End of book.

(*11:14. "Thank you. I think it's very good," I said. Seth-Jane stared at me quite soberly.*)

You both have journeys of your own to take—rhythms of your own being that ebb and flow. Ruburt has connections to make, and there will be other books of mine—and of his and yours—and centuries before we really begin what seems to have begun.

End of session.

(*"Thank you very much, Seth. Good night."*

(*11:16 P.M. Jane's final book delivery had been quiet most of the time, and steady as usual. She was both surprised—as she remarked several times—and a bit disconsolate now that Seth's part of the long project was through. Just a week ago she'd finished the first draft of her Introduction, so that too is underway. She had no feeling any more that Seth would do an Appendix, as we'd speculated about occasionally.*

("—but I can't believe it's over!" she said once again. "As far as I'm concerned the whole thing was effortless. It just came out of me, it seemed, while I was busy doing other things . . ." Which, while true, hardly considers her deep emotional and intellectual involvement with the book for the last ten months—or since Seth took up steady dictation on September 11, 1972, following the extensive delay caused by Tropical Storm Agnes.

(Jane and the members of her ESP class have worked with Seth's book practically every week during its production, and she's also read it while alone; still, she announced, "I want to go through the entire thing now so that I can see it as a whole." I told her I thought she'd produced a fine work.

(A subsequent note, with some references: Seth's closing remark about other books of Jane's proved to be quite accurate. Even as we prepared this manuscript for the printer, two more of her works, Dialogues of the Soul and Mortal Self in Time, *and* Aspect Psychology, *were contracted for publication by Prentice-Hall. Portions of each one are dealt with in these chapters, and Jane also discusses them in her Introduction. I am to illustrate both.*

(Dialogues, a book of poetry, is described in the 639th session in Chapter Ten. Aspect Psychology, *Jane's own theoretical work on psychic matters, is referred to in the 618th session in Chapter Three, among others. It was born out of her writings on* Adventures in Consciousness, *as mentioned in Chapter Twenty-one of* Seth Speaks, *and incorporates that material.)*